THE JUDICIARY AND GOVERNMENT: THE ONGOING POWER STRUGGLE

THE JUDICIARY AND GOVERNMENT: THE ONGOING POWER STRUGGLE

Dr. Anne Wade

SOCIETY Publishing

www.societypublishing.com

The Judiciary and Government: The Ongoing Power Struggle

Dr. Anne Wade

Society Publishing
224 Shoreacres Road
Burlington, ON L7L 2H2
Canada
www.societypublishing.com
Email: orders@arclereducation.com

ISBN: 978-1-77469-828-0 (Hardcover)

ABOUT THE AUTHOR

Dr. Anne Wad has been a researcher and a professor in the Criminal Justice field for over 30 years. She currently holds a position as a Provost/CAO in a University, and Director of Research at another university. She holds an Ed.D. in Educational Leadership and a Ph.D. in Public Safety Leadership/Criminal Justice. Her research interests are in Criminology, Victimology, and the Human Services. She is married to Wesley Wade. She is an artist, writer, researcher, professor, and university administrator.

TABLE OF CONTENTS

List of Figures .... *xi*

Preface .... *xv*

Chapter 1 Foundations of Judiciary and Government 1

1.1. The Origins of Judiciary 3

1.2. Evolution of Government Structures 11

1.3. The Concept of Separation of Powers 18

1.4. The Role of Judiciary in Early Societies 25

1.5. The Emergence of Democratic Governance 31

Chapter 1 Summary 39

Chapter 2 The Role and Function of the Judiciary 41

2.1. Guardian of the Constitution: Judicial Review 43

2.2. Jurisdiction and Decision-Making Process 48

2.3. Criminal Justice and Due Process 54

2.4. Civil Cases and Dispute Resolution 59

2.5. Judiciary's Role in Safeguarding Individual Rights 65

Chapter 2 Summary 69

Chapter 3 Judicial Independence and Accountability 73

3.1. Ensuring Judicial Independence 75

3.2. Mechanisms of Judicial Accountability 80

3.3. Challenges to Judicial Independence 87

3.4. The Ethics of Judicial Conduct 91

3.5. Balancing Independence and Public Interest 97

Chapter 3 Summary 102

Chapter 4 **Judiciary and Government in Policy-Making** **105**
4.1. Judicial Interpretation of Statutes 107
4.2. The Impact of Precedent in Policy Decisions 113
4.3. Judicial Activism Vs. Restraint in Policy Matters 120
4.4. Role of the Judiciary in Public Policy 125
4.5. Evaluating Policy Implications of Judicial Decisions 137
Chapter 4 Summary 153

Chapter 5 **The Judiciary and Government in Conflict Resolution** **155**
5.1. Judicial Review of Government Actions 156
5.2. Adjudication of Disputes Between Government Branches 162
5.3. The Role of International Courts in Cross-Border Conflicts 170
5.4. Mediation and Alternative Dispute Resolution 180
5.5. The Judiciary's Role In Mitigating Political Conflicts 188
Chapter 5 Summary 195

Chapter 6 **Challenges to Judicial Independence** **197**
6.1. Political Interference in the Judiciary 198
6.2. Threats to Judicial Security and Safety 206
6.3. Populism and its Impact on Judicial Independence 211
6.4. Media Influence and Public Perception of the Judiciary 219
6.5. Striking a Balance: Judicial Independence and Accountability 225
Chapter 6 Summary 231

Chapter 7 **The Role of Judiciary in a Globalized World** **233**
7.1. The Impact of Globalization on Legal Systems 235
7.2. International Cooperation and Treaty Interpretation 239
7.3. Resolving Transnational Disputes Through Judicial Means 244
7.4. Jurisdictional Challenges in a Borderless World 252
7.5. Judiciary's Role in Harmonizing International Law 259
Chapter 7 Summary 266

Chapter 8 **Future Perspectives and Emerging Challenges** **269**
8.1. Technological Advancements and the Judiciary 271
8.2. Ensuring Diversity and Inclusivity in the Judiciary 278
8.3. Adapting to Rapid Societal Changes 290

8.4. Enhancing Public Trust in the Judiciary 298
8.5. Addressing Future Power Struggles Between Judiciary and Government 304
Chapter 8 Summary 309

Concluding Remarks 311

Bibliography 315

Index 345

LIST OF FIGURES

Figure 1.1. Hammurabi and Shamash.

Figure 1.2. Law Code of King Ur-Nammu.

Figure 1.3. Administration in Upper Mesopotamia in the Neolithic period (7th–6th millennia BC).

Figure 1.4. Administrative organization of the Roman Republic.

Figure 1.5. Separation of powers in the US government today.

Figure 1.6. Conceptualizing the doctrine of separation of powers.

Figure 1.7. The Court System in Ancient Homeric Greece.

Figure 1.8. Influencing mechanisms of village committees on the withdrawal from rural homesteads (WRH) in China.

Figure 1.9. Twelve principles of good democratic governance.

Figure 1.10. Illustration of direct democracy in Switzerland.

Figure 2.1. Key elements of the administrative state.

Figure 2.2. Conceptualizing checks and balances in government.

Figure 2.3. Institutional change across all levels of the judiciary.

Figure 2.4. Example of a court hierarchy in Australia and jurisdiction.

Figure 2.5. Conceptualization of the rule of law.

Figure 2.6. Patterns of police misconduct in the USA.

Figure 2.7. Continuum of alternative dispute resolution.

Figure 2.8. Rationalization of alternative dispute resolution in Australia.

Figure 2.9. The judiciary protecting individual rights in India.

Figure 2.10. The conceptualization and elevation of rights.

Figure 3.1. Principles of the rule of law.

Figure 3.2. Statistical demonstration of democratic backsliding in the USA.

Figure 3.3. The intersection of country and regional accountabilities.

Figure 3.4. Example of a judicial review procedure.

Figure 3.5. Stakeholders in the judicial reform process.

Figure 3.6. Examples of distortions of the judicial system.

Figure 3.7. Three major sources of judicial ethics.

Figure 3.8. The falling public trust in the judicial profession within the USA.

Figure 3.9. Overview of key aspects of judicial independence and accountability.

Figure 3.10. Timeline in legal rulings on abortion in the USA 1973–2022.

Figure 4.1. Timeline of Lawsuits Challenging FFM Premium Subsidies.

Figure 4.2. Comparing textualism to contextualism in judicial interpretation.

Figure 4.3. The courts and gender equality in the USA.

Figure 4.4. Key dates in the evolution of common law.

Figure 4.5. Protests in the "Savita Halappanavar" case.

Figure 4.6. Labels attached to cases in terms of judicial activism and passivity.

Figure 4.7. Incendiary media headline following the role of judiciary in Brexit.

Figure 4.8. Example of a systems model of policy-making.

Figure 4.9. The merits of applying judicial precedents.

Figure 4.10. The checks and balances in the US government.

Figure 5.1. Example of the constitutional role and configuration of judicial review.

Figure 5.2. The scope of judicial review in USA.

Figure 5.3. Key constitutional provisions in India.

Figure 5.4. The complex and interwoven judicial system of India.

Figure 5.5. Existing forums for international environmental dispute settlement.

Figure 5.6. Structure of the Extraordinary Chambers in the Courts of Cambodia (ECCC).

Figure 5.7. Naivasha Grid that informs the development of the tactical plan of the negotiation.

Figure 5.8. Example of an alternative dispute resolution framework and processes.

Figure 5.9. Checks and balances in government.

Figure 5.10. The Shadow Effect of Courts versus Related Types of Radiating Effects.

Figure 6.1. Collage of political attacks on the judiciary in India as represented by media.

Figure 6.2. Cascade of indicators of democratic backsliding.

Figure 6.3. The effectiveness of court security in Ukraine.

Figure 6.4. Distinguishing formal from perceived judicial independence.

Figure 6.5. The rise of populism in the 20th century and early 21st century.

Figure 6.6. The leftwing and rightwing patterns of populism across the globe.

Figure 6.7. Relative consistency in the perception of the Australian justice system 2009 and 2018.

Figure 6.8. Media construction of crises of confidence in court responses to high-profile miscarriages of justice.

Figure 6.9. Example of a framework of judicial independence and accountability.

Figure 6.10. The background to Marbury v. Madison (1803).

Figure 7.1. The globalization of crime.

Figure 7.2. The globalization of transport systems.

Figure 7.3. Example of quantitative analysis of the differential impact of global treaties.

Figure 7.4. Contribution of the Montreal Protocol to the Sustainable Development Goals.

Figure 7.5. Conceptualization of foreign direct investment FDI.

Figure 7.6. The Law of the Sea.

Figure 7.7. Characterization of borders as systems of oppression.

Figure 7.8. Payment card fraud funding terrorism and other transnational crimes.

Figure 7.9. Anticipated rise in cybercrime 2018 through 2027.

Figure 7.10. The use of the European Arrest Warrant 2005–2013.

Figure 8.1. Hard technology applications in courts.

Figure 8.2. Collaboration between parties for processing criminal case.

Figure 8.3. The value and possibility of inclusiveness in the administration of justice.

Figure 8.4. Lawyers against Apartheid held its first meeting in April 1987.

Figure 8.5. The major culture war cities of the world.

Figure 8.6. Key agenda items for judicial reform in India.

Figure 8.7. Determinants of public trust and confidence in the judiciary.

Figure 8.8. Example of a research framework for understanding public perceptions of judicial technologies.

Figure 8.9. The traditional organization of government.

Figure 8.10. Press snapshot of the "Hirak Protests" of Algeria.

PREFACE

In the ever-evolving tapestry of governance and societal order, few relationships have been as enduring, intricate, and consequential as that between the judiciary and government. This book, titled "The Judiciary and Government: The Ongoing Power Struggle," seeks to illuminate the complex interplay of these foundational institutions, tracing their origins, functions, and the enduring struggle for influence and authority that defines their interaction. As we embark on this intellectual journey, let us recognize the interconnected themes that weave throughout the fabric of this narrative, creating a multidimensional understanding of the symbiotic and often adversarial relationship between the judiciary and government. In traversing the pages ahead, we engage with the multifaceted dimensions that shape this power dynamic, appreciating its historical roots, contemporary challenges, and future trajectories.

The themes explored within these chapters resonate across a diverse spectrum of readers, each finding in this discourse a wealth of insights that pertain to their specific vantage points. For undergraduate students venturing into the realm of law, political science, and governance studies, this book offers a foundational understanding of the intricate web of relationships between the judiciary and government. By tracing the evolution of judicial systems and governmental structures, these students gain a comprehensive backdrop against which to contextualize their academic pursuits. Practitioners entrenched within the spheres of law, governance, and policy-making will discover a rich tapestry of insights that resonate with their daily professional challenges. The nuanced analysis of the judiciary's role in shaping policy decisions, the ethical considerations governing judicial conduct, and the delicate balance between independence and accountability all have profound implications for those who navigate the complex terrain of legal and governmental landscapes.

Policymakers at the helm of crafting legislation and executive decisions will find themselves immersed in a contemplative exploration of the judiciary's influence on policy formulation and implementation. The chapters dedicated to examining the intersection of judicial review, precedent, and public policy offer crucial perspectives for those who bear the responsibility of creating frameworks that define societies. The wider public, often distanced from the intricacies of legal and governmental mechanisms, gains a window into the workings of these institutions that underpin modern societies. In an age where headlines are often dominated by legal battles and governmental decisions, this book serves as an avenue for fostering civic awareness and informed engagement. By illuminating the intricate dance of power between the judiciary and government, readers from all walks of life are empowered to participate in conversations that shape their collective future.

As we express gratitude for your commitment to engage with these ideas, we acknowledge that the exploration of the judiciary-government relationship transcends geographic boundaries and jurisdictional confines. The struggle for power, the pursuit of justice, and the delicate balance between independence and accountability are universal themes that resonate across cultures and societies. This book endeavors to equip you, the reader, with a nuanced understanding that enriches your perspective, elevates your discourse, and encourages your participation in the ongoing dialogue surrounding governance and the rule of law. Your journey through these pages is a testament to your dedication to unraveling the intricate threads of the judiciary-government interplay. The historical foundations, the mechanisms of conflict resolution, and the nuances of policy-making and accountability—all contribute to the holistic tapestry of this narrative. Each page turned will mark a step deeper into the intricate dance of influence, a dance that has shaped societies for centuries and will continue to do so in the ever-evolving future.

In closing, we extend our sincerest gratitude for embarking on this intellectual voyage. Your engagement with these ideas reflects a shared commitment to fostering enlightened citizenship, effective governance, and just societies. The power struggle between the judiciary and government is not confined to history; it is an ongoing narrative that requires ongoing reflection, exploration, and engagement. May the insights garnered from these pages empower you to appreciate, question, and contribute to the symphony of governance that shapes the world we inhabit.

Dr. Anne Wade

Provost/CAO Kenner University;

Dean of Education & Centre for Research and Innovation Charisma University

CHAPTER 1

Foundations of Judiciary and Government

Contents

1.1. The Origins of Judiciary 3
1.2. Evolution of Government Structures 11
1.3. The Concept of Separation of Powers 18
1.4. The Role of Judiciary in Early Societies 25
1.5. The Emergence of Democratic Governance 31
Chapter 1 Summary 39

In the intricate tapestry of governance and societal organization, the foundational underpinnings of both the judiciary and government emerge as critical keystones. This first chapter, titled "Foundations of Judiciary and Government," serves as an exploratory voyage into the origins, evolution, and interplay of these fundamental institutions. As we embark on this intellectual journey, we delve into the historical roots and philosophical concepts that have shaped the dynamics of power, justice, and authority.

1. A Historical Odyssey: Origins of Judiciary

Section 1.1, "The Origins of Judiciary," delves deep into the annals of human history to unearth the origins of judicial systems. Through the passage of time, the need to resolve disputes and administer justice evolved into formalized structures of adjudication. This section traces the gradual transformation from primitive methods of conflict resolution to the emergence of organized judiciary systems, revealing the societal forces and imperatives that compelled their development.

2. The Unfolding Complexity: Evolution of Government Structures

Section 1.2, "Evolution of Government Structures," embarks on an intellectual expedition through the corridors of governance evolution. With roots tracing back to antiquity, governmental structures have experienced multifarious shifts, influenced by cultural, economic, and political factors. This section unpacks the intricate journey from early tribal councils to sophisticated systems of governance, emphasizing the intricate relationship between governance forms and the societal contexts that shaped them.

3. The Doctrine of Division: The Concept of Separation of Powers

Section 1.3, "The Concept of Separation of Powers," delves into the philosophical underpinnings that have shaped the governance landscape. The foundational principle of the separation of powers, articulated by luminaries like Montesquieu, emerges as a cornerstone of modern governance systems. This section dissects the principles and rationales behind this doctrine, which aims to prevent concentration of power and ensure checks and balances in the exercise of authority.

4. Ancient Guardians: The Role of Judiciary in Early Societies

Section 1.4, "The Role of Judiciary in Early Societies," directs our focus to the pivotal function of the judiciary in ancient civilizations. From Hammurabi's Code to the Roman Twelve Tables, judicial institutions assumed a role as keepers of societal order, administering justice and upholding norms. This section unveils the societal significance of early judicial systems, casting light on their responsibilities and influence in shaping the moral and legal fabric of their times.

5. Democratic Dawn: The Emergence of Democratic Governance

Section 1.5, "The Emergence of Democratic Governance," brings us to the crux of political evolution—the advent of democratic ideals. The emergence of democratic governance marked a paradigm shift in the relationship between citizens, rulers, and the judiciary. This section illuminates the philosophical tenets that underpin democratic ideals, tracing their progression from the ancient Greek polis to modern representative democracies, and highlighting the profound implications for the judiciary-government dynamics.

As this chapter unfolds, each section delves into a distinct facet of the intricate relationship between the judiciary and government, tracing their origins, evolution, and mutual influences. The pages that follow beckon readers to engage with the intellectual exploration of the intricate dance that has shaped human societies and continues to shape the governance structures that underpin them. The foundational themes introduced here are mere prologue to the nuanced narratives that follow, enriching our understanding of the complex interplay between these essential institutions. Let us begin with the origins of the judiciary.

1.1. THE ORIGINS OF JUDICIARY

The origins of the judiciary trace back to the earliest human societies, where the need for dispute resolution and the administration of justice became paramount (Shigemura et al., 2021; Shvets, 2016; Simanjuntak, 2020). In primitive communal setups, conflicts arising from issues like property disputes, personal injury, and breaches of communal norms necessitated mechanisms for resolution. These mechanisms evolved organically, forming the rudimentary basis of what would later become formalized judicial systems. In Mesopotamia, one of the earliest known civilizations, the need for a formal system to resolve conflicts and ensure fair treatment was recognized. The emergence of written laws, such as the Code of

Hammurabi, is evidence of the establishment of a legal system and the subsequent creation of a judiciary. The Code of Hammurabi, dating back to around 1750 BCE, consisted of a set of legal principles and punishments that aimed to maintain order and resolve disputes within the society. This code provided guidelines for various aspects of life, including marriage, property, and business transactions.

The existence of this legal code indicates that the early societies recognized the importance of having a structured system to settle disputes and maintain social harmony (Colucci, 2000; Conrad, 2014; Costas-Perez et al., 2012; Cross, 1999). The judiciary, as an integral part of this system, played a crucial role in ensuring that justice was served. Legal disputes were brought before judges who would hear both sides of the argument and make impartial decisions based on the laws set forth in the Code of Hammurabi. Moreover, the administration of justice in ancient Mesopotamia went beyond simply resolving disputes between individuals. The judiciary also played a significant role in maintaining social order and upholding the values of the society. The punishments outlined in the Code of Hammurabi were not only meant to punish the wrongdoers but also to deter others from committing similar crimes. This aspect of deterrence reflects the broader societal objective of maintaining law and order. Figure 1.1 is an early illustration of Hammurabi and Shamash, central figures in these rudimentary judicial systems.

Figure 1.1. Hammurabi and Shamash.

Source: Joshua J. Mark (2018) https://www.worldhistory.org/hammurabi/

The establishment of the judiciary in ancient Mesopotamia is a compelling example of how the need for dispute resolution and the administration of justice became paramount in early human societies (Pospieszna & Vetulani-Cegiel, 2021; Preis, 2006; Preston, 2016). The existence of written laws and the role of judges in interpreting and implementing these laws demonstrate the recognition of the importance of a structured legal system. Moreover, the judiciary's function extended beyond individual disputes to protect societal values and maintain social order. Overall, this case study supports the idea that the origins of the judiciary can be traced back to the earliest human societies where the need for dispute resolution and the administration of justice were paramount.

At the genesis of human civilization, these dispute resolution processes were often informal and communal (Joshi, 2022; Juhn, 2021; Kang, 2004; Kang et al., 2023). Elders or respected members of the community played the role of mediators, offering their wisdom to guide parties toward consensus. This early form of conflict resolution was inherently tied to the social fabric, where communal harmony was valued over punitive measures. In these societies, disputes would arise due to a variety of reasons, such as conflicts over resources or interpersonal conflicts. Instead of relying on a formal judicial system, these early humans would resolve their disputes through communal discussions and negotiation. The emphasis was placed on maintaining social harmony and promoting cooperation rather than on punishment or rigid legal systems. Informal resolutions, such as mediation or dialogue, were used to reach consensus and restore balance within the community. The involvement of the entire community in these processes allowed for a collective decision-making approach, ensuring that all parties had a voice in the resolution. Through this case study, it becomes evident that early human civilizations relied on informal and communal dispute resolution methods, highlighting the significance placed on maintaining social cohesion and promoting mutual understanding in these early societies.

As societies grew more complex and differentiated, the need for a more structured and standardized approach to justice became evident (Cui, 2017; Davis, 2008; De Francesco & Tosun, 2022; de la Torre & Lemos, 2016). The shift from nomadic to agrarian societies brought about the emergence of property rights and intricate social relations that required adjudication. These nascent judicial systems operated within the framework of customary laws, where traditions and local norms guided decisions. This is exemplified by the case study of ancient Egypt. In ancient Egypt, the growth of civilization led to increased interactions among individuals and communities, resulting in more intricate legal disputes. As a response to this complexity, the Egyptians developed a formal judiciary system that was based on hierarchies and legal codes. The paramount example of this structured approach to justice is showcased through the existence of the "Ma'at," which was not only a concept but also a legal system that governed the society. Ma'at represented the order and balance in the universe, but its application was also reflected in the legal system. The judiciary in ancient Egypt consisted of judges, known as "scribes of the law," who were responsible for interpreting and applying the laws. They were well trained in legal matters and operated under the guidance of the Pharaoh and his advisors. The laws themselves were recorded on papyrus scrolls and inscribed on temples, ensuring that they were widely accessible and known to the citizens. This standardized approach to justice provided a reliable and predictable framework for resolving disputes. The establishment of a formal judiciary system in ancient Egypt illustrates how the growing complexity of societies necessitated a more structured and standardized approach to justice. By implementing a legal system based on principles like Ma'at, the Egyptians were able to regulate behavior, resolve conflicts, and maintain social order in a more systematic and efficient manner.

This evolution in judicial systems can be observed in the case study of ancient Rome (Marsh, 2021; Martinsen, 2011; Masinde, 2017). In the early stages of Roman civilization, the resolution of legal conflicts was primarily the responsibility of the heads of households or tribal leaders who relied on customary laws and traditions. However, as Rome expanded and encountered diverse cultures and legal systems, there arose a need for a more organized and impartial method of adjudication. This led to the establishment of the Twelve Tables, a set of laws that codified the rights and responsibilities of Roman citizens. These tables formed the foundation of Roman law and represented a significant step towards a more structured and standardized approach to justice. They introduced principles such as the presumption of innocence, the right to defense, and the notion of legal recourse. Additionally, the development of a professional class of judges, known as praetors, further contributed to the formalization of legal processes. The evolution of the Roman judicial system demonstrates how the complexity of society necessitated the establishment of a more structured and standardized approach to justice, ensuring fairness and consistency in legal proceedings.

Another example that illustrates this is the evolution of the judiciary in ancient China (White, 2022; Whittington, 2005; Willett & Gordon, 2022).

In early Chinese society, dispute resolution processes were often informal and heavily influenced by social relationships and hierarchical structures. However, as the population grew and societal interactions became more intricate, a more organized system was required to address the growing complexity of legal conflicts. This led to the development of an advanced legal system known as the "Six Codes" during the Qin Dynasty. These codes were comprehensive legal ordinances that covered various aspects of life, including criminal law, civil law, administrative law, and more. The implementation of these codes brought about a more uniform and regulated approach to justice, fostering stability and predictability in legal proceedings. Additionally, the establishment of formal courts and the appointment of judges further contributed to the structured nature of the judicial system in ancient China. This case study demonstrates how the increasing complexity of societies prompted the need for a more structured and standardized approach to justice, leading to the development of sophisticated legal systems that could address a wide range of legal disputes with efficiency and fairness.

With the rise of ancient civilizations like Sumer, Babylon, and Egypt, written legal codes began to emerge (Zacka, 2022; Zambrano, 2019; Zuk et al., 1993). The Code of Ur-Nammu from ancient Mesopotamia and the Code of Hammurabi from Babylon laid out legal principles and prescribed penalties for various offenses. These early legal codes marked a transition from ad hoc decisions to a more systematic approach to justice, with established norms guiding judicial rulings. This marked a significant shift in the approach to justice, as it introduced a more formal and codified system of laws. One compelling case study that supports this development is the emergence of the Code of Hammurabi in ancient Babylon. Dating back to the 18th century BCE, the Code of Hammurabi is one of the earliest known written legal codes in history. It comprised 282 laws inscribed on a stele, providing a comprehensive framework for regulating various aspects of Mesopotamian society. The introduction of written legal codes empowered the judiciary and provided a clear and accessible set of rules that governed behavior and resolved disputes. Moreover, these legal codes helped establish a sense of fairness and equity by outlining specific punishments for different transgressions, ensuring consistent and standardized treatment for the population. The advent of written legal codes in ancient civilizations such as Sumer, Babylon, and Egypt revolutionized the judicial landscape by formalizing laws, consolidating legal principles, and providing a reliable framework for dispute resolution. Through the case study of the Code of

Hammurabi, the impact of written legal codes on the development of a structured and standardized approach to justice becomes evident.

The Code of Ur-Nammu, a legal code dating back to the 21st century BCE, serves as a compelling case study to demonstrate the emergence of written legal codes and the subsequent development of a structured and standardized approach to justice (Parrillo, 2018; Pasarlay, 2018; Patton, 2017; Petrov, 2022). The Code of Ur-Nammu was created during the reign of Ur-Nammu, the third king of the Sumerian Third Dynasty of Ur. It consisted of a collection of laws that aimed to govern the society and regulate various aspects of life. This code covered a wide range of subjects, including property rights, marriage and divorce, inheritance, and criminal offenses. The existence of the Code of Ur-Nammu highlights the societal recognition of the need for a formalized legal system to address the increasing complexity of civil and criminal matters.

The introduction of written legal codes in ancient societies like Sumer marked a crucial milestone in legal history (Gallagher, 2012; Gardbaum, 2015; Garoupa et al., 2012). With the Code of Ur-Nammu, the judiciary was empowered to apply the laws consistently and impartially, ensuring fairness and justice for all citizens. The written nature of the code allowed for its widespread dissemination and accessibility, making the laws known to the public and promoting predictability in legal proceedings. Additionally, the Code of Ur-Nammu reflected a desire to establish a consistent set of standards and punishments for various offenses, contributing to the development of a more structured and standardized approach to justice.

By examining the Code of Ur-Nammu, we see the critical role that written legal codes played in shaping the judicial systems of ancient civilizations (Edelman, 1994; Efrat, 2018; Eichensehr, 2018; Eleftheriadis, 2005). The code served as a tool for maintaining social order, resolving disputes, and promoting a sense of fairness within the society. Its existence showcases the recognition of the need for a more structured and standardized approach to justice as societies grew in complexity and interacted with one another. The Code of Ur-Nammu represents a significant milestone in the evolution of legal systems and the establishment of structured frameworks for the administration of justice (Figure 1.2).

In ancient Greece, the Athenian legal system introduced democratic elements that contributed to the development of the judiciary (Nie, 2021; Nordstrand, 2018; O'Neil, 2019; O'Neill, 2001). The Athenian courts were composed of citizen jurors who deliberated on cases and rendered verdicts.

This participatory model of justice was an early example of involving the citizenry in legal proceedings, foreshadowing the concept of the jury system in modern legal systems. The Roman Republic further refined the notion of law and justice. The Twelve Tables, a foundational legal code, established rights and obligations and ensured that laws were accessible to all citizens. The role of praetors, who interpreted laws and issued judgments, foreshadowed the modern judge's function in applying legal principles to specific cases.

Figure 1.2. Law Code of King Ur-Nammu.

Source: Joshua J. Mark (2021) https://www.worldhistory.org/Code_of_Ur-Nammu/ [Osama Shukir Muhammed Amin (Copyright)]

Religious institutions also played a role in the early judiciary (Fox, 2017; French, 2016; Friedman & Delaney, 2011; Gago & Maiani, 2022). In societies where religious beliefs were central, disputes were often resolved within the context of religious rituals and customs. The priestly class, due to its knowledge of divine law, held a position of authority in legal matters. A case study of ancient Israel is informative. In ancient Israelite society, religious laws and principles were deeply intertwined with legal practices and the administration of justice. The religious institution of the priesthood held considerable authority in interpreting and applying these laws. The priests, as custodians of religious and ethical teachings, became key figures in the early judiciary system. They not only served as moral guides but also acted as judges, arbiters, and mediators in legal matters, particularly those involving religious rituals, sacrilege, or violations of religious customs. The close connection between religious and legal matters is exemplified by the presence of religious courts, such as the Sanhedrin, which had jurisdiction over both religious and civil disputes. These courts operated to ensure that justice was administered in accordance with religious doctrines and societal values. The participation of religious institutions in the early judiciary not only provided a moral and spiritual foundation for legal decision-making but also helped to maintain order and social cohesion by upholding religious norms. This case study illustrates how religious institutions played a vital role in shaping and governing the early judiciary, underscoring the interconnectedness between religion and law in ancient societies.

With the spread of empires, legal traditions intermingled and evolved (Cleveland & Dodge, 2015; Clopton, 2018; Coan, 2012; Codrington, 2021). The Byzantine Empire, for instance, inherited and further developed Roman legal principles, contributing to the emergence of civil law systems. Islamic civilizations introduced Sharia law, which combined religious principles with legal norms, shaping legal traditions in regions where Islam took root. For example, as Rome expanded its dominion, it encountered diverse cultures and legal systems, leading to the assimilation and adaptation of various legal traditions. The Roman legal system itself underwent significant changes as it absorbed influences from conquered territories. This culminated in the development of the Justinian Code, also known as the Corpus Juris Civilis, during the reign of Emperor Justinian in the 6th century CE. The Justinian Code represented a comprehensive compilation and synthesis of Roman laws, incorporating elements from legal systems of the provinces and territories under Roman rule. This assimilation and incorporation of legal traditions demonstrated the flexibility and adaptability of the Roman legal system.

Moreover, as empires expanded, legal norms were not only influenced by conquest but also by cultural, economic, and intellectual exchange (Moliterno & Curos, 2021; Molto, 2015; Munday, 2008). For instance, the dissemination of Greek philosophy and legal theories throughout the Hellenistic period had a profound impact on Roman legal thinking. The Stoic philosophy, with its emphasis on natural law and universal justice, profoundly influenced the understanding of legal principles in the Roman Empire. Furthermore, the intermingling of legal traditions was not limited to the Roman Empire. As other ancient empires rose and fell, legal systems continued to intermingle and evolve. For instance, the Code of Hammurabi, which originated in ancient Babylon, influenced legal codes in neighboring regions. The spread of empires facilitated the exchange and blending of legal traditions, resulting in the evolution and development of legal systems. This case study of the Roman Empire demonstrates how the expansion of empires brought together diverse legal traditions, leading to the assimilation, adaptation, and synthesis of legal concepts and principles. The intermingling of legal traditions not only enriched legal systems but also contributed to the development of more sophisticated, comprehensive, and cosmopolitan approaches to justice.

In conclusion, the origins of the judiciary can be traced back to the essential need for conflict resolution in early human societies. From communal mediation to written legal codes, the evolution of the judiciary reflects the complex interplay of social, political, and cultural factors. As societies evolved, so did the mechanisms for resolving disputes and administering justice, setting the stage for the formalized judicial systems that underpin modern governance structures today. The second section in this chapter will consider the evolution of government structures.

1.2. EVOLUTION OF GOVERNMENT STRUCTURES

The evolution of government structures is a journey through history marked by the transformation of societal organization and the mechanisms of governance (Cui, 2017; Davis, 2008; De Francesco & Tosun, 2022; de la Torre & Lemos, 2016). This evolution is deeply intertwined with the development of judicial systems, as both institutions seek to establish order, uphold norms, and balance power within societies. Early human societies were often organized around tribal or clan structures, where leadership was informal and based on familial or communal ties. The chief or elder held authority and played a role in conflict resolution, reflecting the nascent seeds of governance. However, as populations grew and interactions became more complex, these systems faced challenges in effectively managing larger communities.

The advent of agrarian societies marked a significant shift (Parrillo, 2018; Pasarlay, 2018; Patton, 2017; Petrov, 2022). As populations increased and settled into permanent settlements, governance systems evolved to manage agricultural production, resource allocation, and communal protection. Hierarchies emerged, often centered around a central authority, such as a monarch or chieftain, who held sway over decision-making and resource distribution. In ancient civilizations like Mesopotamia (see

Figure 1.3), Egypt, and the Indus Valley, the centralization of power paved the way for organized governance structures. Bureaucracies developed to manage administrative tasks, taxation, and law enforcement. Legal codes were introduced to standardize rules and regulations, providing a basis for adjudication and the establishment of early judicial systems.

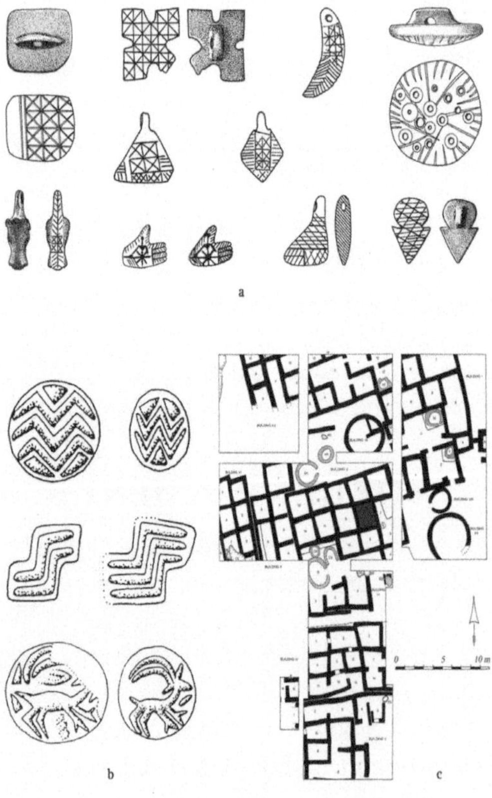

Figure 1.3. Administration in Upper Mesopotamia in the Neolithic period (7th–6th millennia BC).

Source: Frangipane, M.. (2016). The Origins of administrative practices and their developments in Greater Mesopotamia. The evidence from Arslantepe. Archeo-Nil. 26. 9–32. 10.3406/arnil.2016.1101.

The Greek city-states introduced a more participatory form of governance (Steuer, 2019; Subedi, 2016; Szente, 2021; Taghdiri, 2019). Athens, in particular, is renowned for its democratic experiment. Citizens engaged in decision-making through assemblies and councils, reflecting a shift toward collective governance. The intertwining of governance and justice was evident in Athenian courts where citizens participated in legal proceedings, emphasizing the importance of community involvement in both spheres. The Greek city-states revolutionized political systems in ancient civilizations. This shift towards a participatory system allowed citizens to actively engage in the decision-making process, exercising their political rights and participating in the affairs of the city. To illustrate this, let us examine the case study of Athens, one of the most prominent Greek city-states. In Athens, the introduction of democracy transformed the political landscape, granting power to the citizens and promoting civic engagement. Prior to this, Athens had been governed by aristocrats and kings. However, the reforms implemented by leaders such as Solon and Cleisthenes expanded the right to participate in government to a larger pool of citizens. Athenian democracy enabled all eligible male citizens to attend the Assembly, where they had the right to propose, debate, and vote on legislation. This active participation not only provided citizens with a sense of ownership and influence but also fostered a greater sense of community and solidarity. The Assembly became a dynamic forum for the exchange of ideas, and decisions were made collectively, reflecting the will of the people. Moreover, Athens also pioneered the concept of public offices through sortition or random selection, ensuring that positions of power were distributed fairly among citizens. This further democratized the system and prevented the concentration of power within a select few. The Greek city-states' introduction of a more participatory form of governance, exemplified by the Athenian democracy, laid the foundation for the development of democratic principles and institutions that continue to influence political systems to this day. It emphasized the idea of citizen participation, empowering individuals, and promoting community engagement, which are fundamental pillars of modern democratic societies.

The Roman Republic expanded on this concept, introducing representative governance through a system of elected officials (Wright, 2016; Yap, 2019; Yap & Chung, 2019). The Senate, composed of aristocrats, deliberated on matters of policy and law (see Figure 1.4). The legal system, influenced by Roman law, laid the groundwork for modern legal principles and the development of judicial structures. A notable case study that exemplifies this is the structure of the Roman Senate. The Senate was composed of elected representatives from all social classes and played a crucial role in the governing process of the Republic. Senators were elected by the citizens and served as advisors and decision-makers, representing the interests of the Roman people. This representative system allowed for a wider range of individuals to have a voice in the political affairs of the Republic, ensuring a more balanced and inclusive approach to governance. Furthermore, the Roman Republic also developed a complex system of magistrates who were responsible for various administrative roles. These magistrates, such as the consuls and praetors, were elected by the citizens and held executive powers. Their election through a representative process allowed for a greater distribution of power, preventing the concentration of authority within a single individual or ruling class. This system of elected officials in the Roman Republic not only reflected the desire for wider citizen participation but also helped to establish checks and balances within the government, promoting stability and accountability. The introduction of representative governance in the Roman Republic built upon the participatory foundations laid by the Greek city-states and contributed to the development of democratic ideals that continue to shape political systems around the world (Figure 1.4).

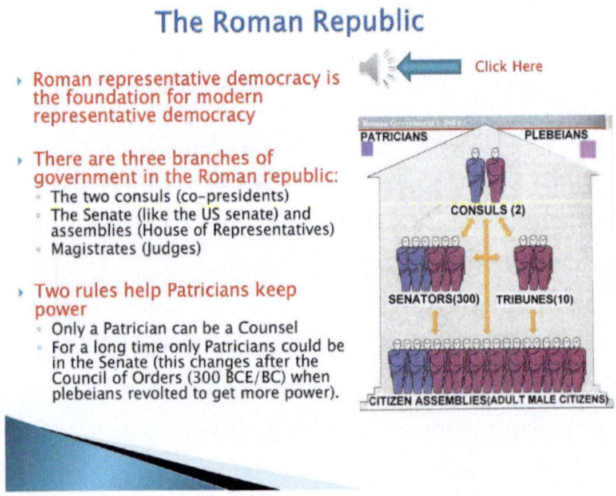

Figure 1.4. Administrative organization of the Roman Republic.

Source: Hester Mathews via SlidePlayer, https://slideplayer.com/slide/13177834/

The Middle Ages witnessed the emergence of feudalism in Europe, where governance was localized and authority decentralized (Gonzalez, 2021; Gorodovenko et al., 2021; Gouldin, 2012). Local lords held power over their territories, administering justice and maintaining order within their domains. However, this system often lacked uniformity and led to fragmentation. The case study of medieval England is instructive in this case. During this period, England was divided into numerous feudal territories, each governed by a local lord or noble. These lords exercised control and authority over their respective lands, providing protection, enforcing laws, and collecting taxes.

The system of feudalism emphasized the relationship between lords and vassals, where vassals pledged loyalty and military service to their lords in exchange for land and protection. This decentralized structure meant that governance was localized, with each lord having significant power within their domain. While there was an overarching monarchy, the king's authority was limited and relied on the support of these feudal lords. This system allowed for a degree of autonomy and self-governance at the local level, as lords had their own courts, administered justice, and shaped laws according to the specific needs of their territories. However, it is essential to note that feudalism was not a true participatory form of governance, as power was concentrated within the hands of the nobility, and ordinary people had limited political rights and influence. Nevertheless, the emergence of feudalism in the Middle Ages marked a departure from the centralized governance of ancient Greece and Rome, emphasizing localized authority and the fragmentation of power, which had significant historical and societal implications for European societies.

With the Renaissance and Enlightenment, governance underwent significant transformation (Joshi, 2022; Juhn, 2021; Kang, 2004; Kang et al., 2023). Philosophers like Montesquieu proposed the separation of powers—a cornerstone of modern governance theory. This doctrine, which advocated distinct branches of government (executive, legislative, and judicial) to prevent tyranny, became integral to democratic governance structures. This period marked a departure from the feudal system and witnessed the rise of new ideas and philosophies that challenged traditional forms of governance. A compelling case study to illustrate this transformation is the French Revolution. The French Revolution was a turning point in European history, characterized by the overthrow of the monarchy and the establishment of the First French Republic. The revolution was fueled by Enlightenment ideals, such as liberty, equality, and popular sovereignty. These ideas challenged the notion of absolute monarchy and advocated for a more participatory and accountable form of governance. The French Revolution brought forth the concept of democracy, where power resided with the people. The revolutionary government, particularly the National Convention, saw the introduction of elected representatives who formed the legislative body. These representatives were chosen by the people, reflecting a more representative form of governance that embraced the principles of the Enlightenment. Additionally, the Revolution also marked the abolition of feudal privileges, leveling the playing field and promoting social equality. However, it is important to acknowledge that this period also saw its share of political turmoil and upheaval. Nevertheless, the French Revolution serves as a compelling case study for the transformative impact of the Renaissance and Enlightenment on the governance systems of the time, paving the way for the development of modern democratic principles and institutions.

The Age of Exploration and colonization brought about global interactions that reshaped governance structures (Keohane et al., 2000; Killebrew, 2007; Kingsford, 2022). Colonial powers introduced their systems to conquered lands, influencing governance models across continents. This global diffusion of governance structures gave rise to diverse systems influenced by local traditions, colonial legacies, and cultural norms. One notable case study that exemplifies this impact is the colonization of the Americas by European powers. As European explorers ventured into the New World, they established colonies and imposed their own forms of governance on indigenous societies. This colonization process often involved the imposition of centralized authority and the incorporation of the colonies into the political and economic systems of European empires. The Spanish Empire, for example, introduced a system known as the encomienda, where Spanish settlers were granted land and indigenous communities were forced to provide labor and tribute. This centralized form of governance allowed the Spanish Crown to exert control over the newly established colonies and extract resources for imperial benefit. Similarly, other European powers such as the British and French implemented various forms of colonial governance, which reflected their own political, economic, and social structures. The Age of Exploration and colonization, therefore, led to the transplantation of diverse governance models across the globe, resulting in a multitude of hybrid systems shaped by interactions between colonizers and indigenous populations. These interactions redefined the power dynamics, legal structures, and political institutions in the colonized regions, leaving a lasting legacy that shaped the governance structures of many countries today.

The 19th and 20th centuries witnessed the proliferation of democracy, republicanism, and constitutionalism (Gallagher, 2012; Gardbaum, 2015; Garoupa et al., 2012). Nations adopted representative systems where governance was vested in elected representatives, reflecting the broader aspirations for citizen participation and individual rights. As governance evolved, judicial systems adapted to ensure the rule of law, safeguard individual rights, and adjudicate disputes. A compelling case study that exemplifies this trend is the establishment of the United States as a democratic republic. The American Revolution, sparked by grievances against British colonial rule, led to the creation of a new nation founded on the principles of individual rights, popular sovereignty, and limited government. The drafting and adoption of the United States Constitution in 1787 established a framework for a representative democracy, where power was vested in elected officials who derived their authority from the consent of the governed. The Constitution provided for a separation of powers among the executive, legislative, and judicial branches, creating checks and balances to prevent the concentration of power. Moreover, the Bill of Rights, added as amendments to the Constitution, explicitly protected individual liberties and ensured a system of constitutionalism. The success of the American experiment in democratic governance influenced subsequent movements for independence and self-governance across the globe. Throughout the 19th and 20th centuries, many nations embraced the principles of democracy, republicanism, and constitutionalism, adapting them to their own cultural and historical contexts. These ideas permeated political discourse, leading to the establishment of elected national governments, the recognition of civil and political rights, and the promotion of rule of law. The proliferation of these democratic and constitutional principles during this period significantly reshaped governance structures, laid the foundation for modern democratic institutions, and continues to shape political systems to this day.

In the modern era, globalization and technological advancements have created new challenges and opportunities for governance (Cui, 2017; Davis, 2008; De Francesco & Tosun, 2022; de la Torre & Lemos, 2016). The rise of international organizations, transnational issues, and interconnected economies has necessitated collaborative governance structures beyond national borders. Governments and judiciaries now grapple with issues that span continents, emphasizing the need for adaptive governance frameworks. A case study that illustrates this phenomenon is the rise of digital governance. With the advent of the internet and digital platforms, governments across the world have had to grapple with new governance challenges in the digital realm. The rapid proliferation of internet connectivity and social media platforms has given rise to unprecedented opportunities for citizen engagement, information dissemination, and political mobilization. However, it has also presented novel challenges such as cybersecurity threats, privacy concerns, and the spread of misinformation. Governments have had to adapt their governance strategies to effectively regulate and govern the digital space, striking a balance between protecting individual rights and ensuring public safety. Furthermore, globalization has led to increased interconnectedness and interdependence among nations, necessitating new forms of global governance. Issues such as climate change, transnational crime, and economic integration require international cooperation and collective decision-making. Organizations like the United Nations, World Trade Organization, and regional alliances have emerged to address these global challenges through collaborative governance mechanisms. The modern era has thus seen a shift towards more inclusive, collaborative, and adaptive forms of governance, as traditional structures often struggle to keep pace with the rapidly evolving technological and global landscape. Embracing these new challenges and opportunities is crucial for governments to foster effective and accountable governance in the digital age.

In conclusion, the evolution of government structures is a tale of adaptation and transformation. From tribal leadership to representative democracies, governance models have responded to changing societal needs and aspirations. The interplay between governance and the judiciary has been integral to this evolution, with both institutions shaping each other and reflecting the broader evolution of human societies. The third section will focus on the separation of powers.

1.3. THE CONCEPT OF SEPARATION OF POWERS

The concept of the separation of powers is a cornerstone of modern governance, deeply intertwined with the functioning of both the judiciary and government (Kramarz et al., 2017; Krogseng, 2000; Krotoszynski, 2014). Rooted in Enlightenment philosophy and political theory, this principle seeks to establish checks and balances within a system of governance, ensuring that power is not concentrated in the hands of a single entity. Its influence extends to the judicial and governmental spheres, shaping their roles, interactions, and dynamics. A compelling case study that highlights the significance of this principle is the United States of America. The U.S. Constitution embodies the principle of separation of powers through its delineation of powers among the three branches of government (see Figure 1.5). The executive branch, headed by the President, is responsible for the implementation and enforcement of laws. The legislative branch, composed of Congress, is entrusted with the power to create laws. Finally, the judicial branch, led by the Supreme Court, has the authority to interpret laws and ensure their constitutionality. This clear division of powers among the branches provides a system of checks and balances, preventing any one branch from becoming too powerful. The judiciary acts as a check on the executive and legislative branches, ensuring that their actions are in accordance with the Constitution. Additionally, the government as a whole is accountable to the people, with each branch exercising its powers independently while overseeing and challenging the actions of the others. This case study exemplifies how the separation of powers plays a crucial role in modern governance, fostering accountability, limiting the concentration of power, and promoting the protection of rights and liberties.

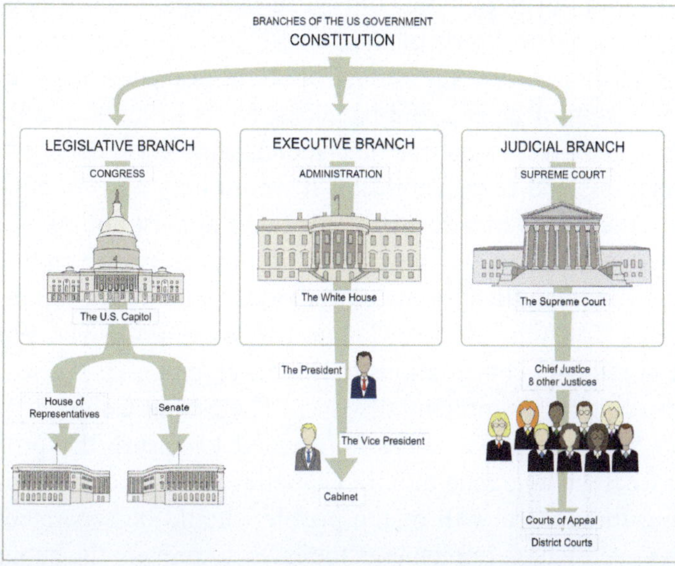

Figure 1.5. Separation of powers in the US government today.

Source: NDLA. https://ndla.no/subject:1:4ad7fe49-b14a-4caf-8e19-ad-402d1e2ce6/topic:1:48d2aed6–03db-4ba7–9670–0f7527490e43/re*Source:* 1:69154

The origins of the separation of powers can be traced back to philosophers like John Locke, Montesquieu, and Rousseau (Cassman, 2015; Celenk, 2016; Chakravarti et al., 2011; Chalmers, 2000). Their ideas laid the groundwork for a system where the functions of governance—legislation, execution, and adjudication—were separated to prevent abuses of power. This concept seeks to curb the potential for tyranny and ensure that no single authority can wield unchecked authority. These thinkers, through their influential works, played a significant role in shaping the concept of the separation of powers and its subsequent impact on modern political systems. John Locke, an English philosopher, emphasized the importance of limited government and the need to protect individual rights. In his seminal work, "Two Treatises of Government," Locke argued that the powers of government should be divided into separate branches to prevent tyranny and ensure the safeguarding of citizens' liberties. He believed that the executive, legislative, and judicial powers should be distinct from each other, with checks and balances in place to prevent any one branch from becoming too powerful. In a similar vein, Charles-Louis de Secondat, Baron de Montesquieu, a French political philosopher, expanded on Locke's ideas and further developed the concept of the separation of powers in his influential work, "The Spirit of the Laws." Montesquieu emphasized the importance of dividing power among different branches of government to maintain a system of checks and balances. He believed that by separating power into legislative, executive, and judicial branches, each with its own distinct functions and responsibilities, it would help prevent concentration of power in the hands of a few and safeguard against abuses of authority. Montesquieu's ideas on the separation of powers greatly influenced the formation of democratic systems worldwide, including the framers of the United States Constitution. Jean-Jacques Rousseau, a Swiss philosopher, also made significant contributions to the development of the separation of powers concept. In his influential work, "The Social Contract," Rousseau argued that political power must be divided to ensure the protection of individual freedom and general will. He believed that the legislative power, representing the general will of the people, should be separated from the executive power, which implements the laws, to prevent the suppression of liberty and the domination of any one individual or group. Rousseau's ideas on the separation of powers further reinforced the importance of dividing authority and fostering democratic governance.

In the context of the judiciary, the separation of powers implies that the judicial branch operates independently from the executive and legislative branches (Janover, 2021; Johnson, 2019; Jonski, 2021; Jorritsma, 2020). This separation safeguards the judiciary's ability to interpret laws impartially, rendering judgments without fear of political influence or pressure. Judicial independence ensures that the rights of individuals are upheld, and justice is dispensed without bias. This separation ensures that the judiciary remains a distinct and impartial organ of the government, free from undue influence or interference from the other branches. To illustrate this concept, we can analyze the case of the United States, where the independence of the judicial branch is enshrined in the Constitution. The Supreme Court, as the highest tribunal, holds the responsibility of interpreting laws and safeguarding the Constitution. The justices are appointed for life, providing them with security of their position and insulating them from political pressures. This independence allows the judiciary to make rulings based on the merits of a case and the principles of law, without being unduly swayed by partisan interests. Moreover, the judicial branch possesses the power of judicial review, which grants it the authority to declare laws or executive actions unconstitutional, further reinforcing its role as a check on the other branches of government. The American judiciary's independence and separation from the executive and legislative branches are essential for maintaining the rule of law and ensuring justice is impartially administered.

The judiciary's role in upholding the separation of powers is exemplified through the exercise of judicial review (Konisky & Nolette, 2022; Kotze, 2022; Kovacs & Scheppele, 2018). This power allows courts to review and potentially invalidate laws passed by the legislative branch if they are found to be unconstitutional. Through this mechanism, the judiciary acts as a check on legislative overreach, ensuring that laws conform to the constitution and the rights it guarantees. Judicial review refers to the power of the courts to interpret and declare the constitutionality of laws and executive actions, ensuring they are in line with the principles and limitations laid down by the Constitution. This power acts as a fundamental check on the other branches of government, specifically the legislative and executive branches, preventing them from exceeding their constitutional authority. A case study that illuminates the significance of judicial review in upholding the separation of powers is the landmark United States Supreme Court case Marbury v. Madison in 1803. In this case, Chief Justice John Marshall asserted the power of judicial review, establishing the principle that the Supreme Court has the authority to declare acts of Congress unconstitutional. By asserting this power, Marshall and the Court ensured that the judiciary could act as a final arbiter and protector of the Constitution. Through this case, the Supreme Court cemented its role in balancing the powers of the branches and preserving the Constitution's integrity. Thus, the exercise of judicial review showcases the judiciary's pivotal role in safeguarding the separation of powers and maintaining the proper functioning of democratic systems (Figure 1.6).

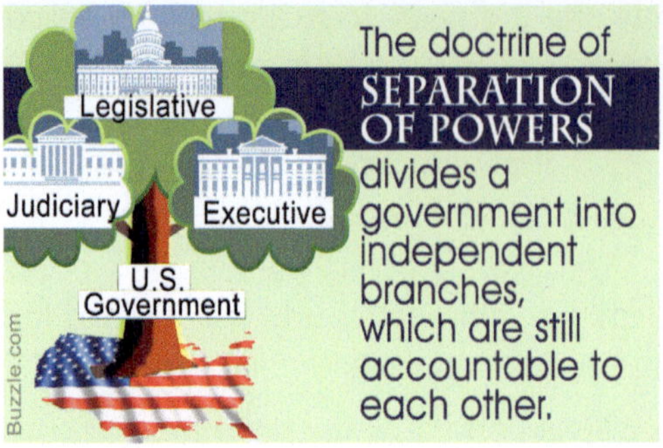

Figure 1.6. Conceptualizing the doctrine of separation of powers.

Source: https://opinionfront.com/explanation-of-separation-of-powers-with-examples

Similarly, the separation of powers profoundly influences the functioning of the government (Aydin-Cakir, 2023; Babie & Bhanu, 2022; Bachmann & Lyubashenko, 2017). The executive branch, responsible for implementing laws, is separate from the legislative branch, which creates laws (see Figure 6). This separation prevents the executive from manipulating or controlling the legislative process to serve its own interests. It ensures that laws are made based on the needs and aspirations of the society, not the ambitions of those in power. One case study that exemplifies this impact is the parliamentary system in the United Kingdom. In this system, executive power rests with the Prime Minister and the Cabinet, while legislative power is vested in the Parliament.

The judiciary, represented by the Supreme Court and lower courts, acts as the third branch of government, ensuring the adherence to laws and constitutional principles. The separation of powers is a fundamental principle of the British constitutional framework, providing a system of checks and balances between the executive, legislative, and judicial branches. This division of power prevents any single branch from becoming excessively dominant or abusing its authority. For instance, the judiciary has the responsibility to interpret laws and ensure their constitutionality, thereby serving as a check on legislation passed by the Parliament. This separation of powers fosters accountability, transparency, and the rule of law within the British governmental system, safeguarding democratic governance and protecting individual rights and liberties. Therefore, it is evident that the separation of powers plays a vital role in shaping and influencing the overall functioning of the government, as demonstrated by the parliamentary system in the United Kingdom.

Furthermore, the principle of separation of powers curtails the ability of the executive to infringe on the independence of the judiciary (Hennigar, 2010; Hessick, 2014; Hill, 2016; Holland, 2009). The executive's role is to execute laws, not interfere with their interpretation or application. This separation shields the judiciary from undue political pressure, enabling judges to make decisions based on legal merits rather than partisan considerations. The principle of separation of powers indeed curtails the ability of the executive to infringe on the independence of the judiciary, providing a critical safeguard for the maintenance of democratic governance and the rule of law. One case study that illustrates this principle is the recent legal dispute in Poland surrounding the independence of the judiciary. In 2017, the Polish government passed a series of legislative reforms that significantly impacted the judiciary, including lowering the retirement age for judges and giving the executive branch greater control over judicial appointments. These actions raised concerns about the erosion of judicial independence and the potential for executive interference. The controversy surrounding the Polish judiciary demonstrates the importance of the separation of powers in preventing executive overreach. The European Union, along with numerous domestic and international organizations, voiced concerns regarding the impact of these reforms on the rule of law and the independence of the judiciary. The European Commission initiated infringement proceedings against Poland, arguing that the reforms violated European Union law and undermined the separation of powers. This case study highlights the vital role of the separation of powers in protecting the judiciary from executive interference. By maintaining an independent judiciary, the separation of powers ensures the judiciary can carry out its duty without fear of political pressure or manipulation.

A judiciary that operates independently serves as a check on the executive's actions, ensuring that its power is exercised within the confines of the law and the constitution (Joshi, 2022; Juhn, 2021; Kang, 2004; Kang et al., 2023). The ability of the judiciary to render impartial and fair decisions helps maintain public trust in the legal system and upholds the principle of equal justice under the law. However, it is essential to acknowledge that the principle of separation of powers is not absolute and can face challenges and limitations. In practice, there may be instances where the executive branch tries to exert influence over the judiciary, compromising its independence. Political factors, ideological considerations, and power dynamics can all contribute to potential infringements on the judicial branch. These challenges require constant vigilance and a commitment to upholding the principles of separation of powers and maintaining the independence of the judiciary. While the principle of separation of powers curtails the ability of the executive to infringe on the independence of the judiciary, there can be instances where this principle faces challenges. However, the case study of the dispute over the independence of the judiciary in Poland serves as a poignant reminder of the importance of upholding the separation of powers to protect the integrity of the judiciary and maintain the checks and balances necessary for a functioning democracy. Continuous efforts must be made to ensure the independence of the judiciary and guard against any encroachments on its authority by the executive, reinforcing the fundamental principles of democratic governance and the rule of law. In practical terms, the concept of separation of powers is enshrined in many constitutional frameworks. The United States, for instance, features a tripartite system with distinct branches of government. The judiciary, represented by the Supreme Court, has the authority to review laws and executive actions. The executive branch, headed by the president, implements laws passed by the legislature, which consists of the House of Representatives and the Senate.

Yet, the separation of powers is not without challenges (Schroeder, 2023; Schuman, 2021; Schweiger, 2022). Striking the right balance between the branches can be complex, particularly in cases where the powers overlap or conflicts arise. Additionally, the concept requires a degree of cooperation between the branches to ensure that governance functions smoothly while preventing abuse of power. One case study that highlights these challenges is the ongoing debate surrounding the separation of powers in the United States. One of the main challenges is the potential for the branches of government to engage in encroachment, where one branch oversteps its boundaries and undermines the authority of another branch. For instance, critics argue that the executive branch in the United States has sometimes expanded its powers, particularly in the areas of national security and executive orders, which some argue can encroach upon both the legislative and judicial branches. Additionally, the increasing polarization and partisanship within the political landscape can, at times, hinder the proper functioning of the separation of powers. This can lead to a situation where the branches of government prioritize their partisan goals over the fundamental principles of checks and balances. Another challenge relates to the issue of judicial appointments, which can potentially influence the impartiality and independence of the judiciary. The appointment process can be politicized, impacting the perception and effectiveness of the judiciary as an independent branch. Moreover, the separation of powers in some political systems can be seen as promoting gridlock and inefficiency. Critics argue that the separation of powers can create obstacles to swift decision-making and hinder effective governance, especially in times of crisis or emergencies. However, proponents contend that such obstacles are deliberate, acting as crucial safeguards against abuses of power. They argue that the division of power and difficult decision-making processes are essential to ensure careful deliberation, thorough analysis, and comprehensive debate. These challenges within the separation of powers highlight the constant need for vigilance and ongoing discussions about how best to strike the right balance. It becomes crucial to address these challenges through thorough constitutional interpretation, legislative measures, and public discourse. Striking a balance between the branches without compromising the fundamental principles of the separation of powers requires a commitment to upholding democratic values, public accountability, and the rule of law. Through continuous debate, critique, and reforms, societies can strive to maintain and improve the functioning of the separation of powers, ensuring its relevance and effectiveness in contemporary governance.

In conclusion, the concept of the separation of powers is an essential tenet of modern governance, shaping the roles and interactions of both the judiciary and government. It reflects a deliberate effort to prevent the concentration of power and safeguard individual rights. By ensuring the independence of the judiciary and preventing the unchecked authority of any one branch, the separation of powers serves as a cornerstone of democratic systems, fostering a just and accountable society. Indeed, judicial independence was an ideal (if not practice) in early societies.

1.4. THE ROLE OF JUDICIARY IN EARLY SOCIETIES

In the tapestry of early societies, the role of the judiciary emerged as a fundamental pillar, shaping the fabric of governance, justice, and societal norms (Aboueldahab, 2021; Abouharb et al., 2013). Before the establishment of formalized legal systems, human communities recognized the need to resolve disputes and maintain order. The role of the judiciary, often intertwined with spiritual and communal values, was a vital force in these nascent societies. One highly specific case study that delves into the nuances of this statement is the development of ancient Athenian democracy in 5th century BCE Greece. Within this historical context, the judiciary played a pivotal role in defining and enforcing laws, resolving disputes, and upholding justice. Ancient Athens implemented a system whereby cases were brought before large juries of citizens who served as both judges and jurors. This system, known as dikasteria, emphasized the direct involvement of the citizenry in legal matters.

Nevertheless, the extent to which the Athenian judiciary influenced societal norms and governance can be subject to debate and critique (Janover, 2021; Johnson, 2019; Jonski, 2021; Jorritsma, 2020). While the role of the judiciary was central to the functioning of Athenian democracy, it is important to acknowledge that power was concentrated in the hands of Athenian citizens who predominantly belonged to the privileged class. This concentration of power limited the inclusivity and representation of marginalized groups within the judicial process, raising questions of fairness and equity. Furthermore, the judiciary's authority was also influenced by the assembly and the influence of prominent political figures, such as the statesman Pericles. This interplay between political power and judicial decision-making demonstrates the complexity and potential limitations of the judiciary's role in shaping societal norms.

Figure 1.7. The Court System in Ancient Homeric Greece.

Source: Dr. Alexandr Loginov (2019). https://brewminate.com/the-court-system-in-ancient-homeric-greece/

Moreover, it is crucial to recognize that the concept of justice in early societies often reflected existing social hierarchies rather than serving as a mechanism for social transformation (Iaryczower et al., 2002; Ides, 1999; Imam & Egbewole, 2020). In the case of ancient Athens, the judiciary became an arena in which societal norms, heavily influenced by the prevailing patriarchal and aristocratic structures, were enforced. The role of the judiciary within this context raises questions about the extent to which it genuinely shaped societal norms or merely preserved existing power structures. The outcomes of judicial decisions, although consequential for individuals involved, might not have led to substantial shifts in social order or governance. Figure 1.7 is an illustration of the court system in Ancient Homeric Greece.

While the role of the judiciary in early societies, such as ancient Athens, contributed to the fabric of governance and justice, there may be nuances that challenge that assumption (Primus, 2004; Prince, 2020; Provost, 2008; Pulle & Ratnapala, 2019). The case study of ancient Athenian democracy illustrates the intricate relationship between the judiciary, societal norms, and governance. Although the judiciary was an essential pillar of early societies, questions surrounding inclusivity, representation, and impartiality remind us to critically examine the influence and limitations of the judiciary within the broader socio-political context. Understanding the complexities of the judicial role in shaping societal norms and governance requires a comprehensive analysis of historical, social, and cultural factors, acknowledging the debates and critiques that continue to shape our understanding of early judicial systems.

Early societies were characterized by simple social structures, where communal norms governed interactions and conflict resolution (Rohrschneider, 2005; Rotunda, 1991; Rowley, 2005). In the absence of centralized authorities, community elders or respected figures often assumed the role of mediators in disputes. These informal mechanisms for resolving conflicts drew upon established customs, traditions, and communal consensus. This statement implies that these societies lacked the complexities and hierarchies of modern social structures. While it may be true that early societies had a less formalized system of governance and social organization, it would be unwise to overlook the nuanced intricacies that undoubtedly existed within these communities. To illustrate this, let us consider the case study of the ancient Inca civilization. The Inca Empire, which flourished in South America from the 13th to 16th centuries, provides a fascinating perspective on the social dynamics and conflict resolution strategies within early societies. At its height, the Inca Empire covered a vast territory and boasted a population of approximately 12 million people. Despite this immense size, the Inca society was structured around a tightly knit kin-based communal system known as ayllus.

Within these ayllus, kinship ties formed the basis of social organization, ensuring that communal norms governed interactions (George, 2009; Geyh, 2014; Gisbert, 2022; Gomes, 2017). However, the complexity of the Inca social structure becomes apparent when we examine the hierarchical division of labor and power. The ruler, or Sapa Inca, occupied the pinnacle of this hierarchical system and was considered divine. Below the Sapa Inca were the nobility and various administrative officials who helped manage the empire. Conflict resolution within the Inca society was far from simplistic. The Inca had a sophisticated legal system that sought to address disputes and maintain social order. Local officials known as kurakas were responsible for settling conflicts within their respective communities, applying customary laws and regulations. In more serious cases, conflicts were referred to higher-level judicial authorities who carefully evaluated testimonies and evidence before making decisions. The Inca's approach to conflict resolution illustrates the presence of formalized systems aimed at maintaining social harmony and promoting justice.

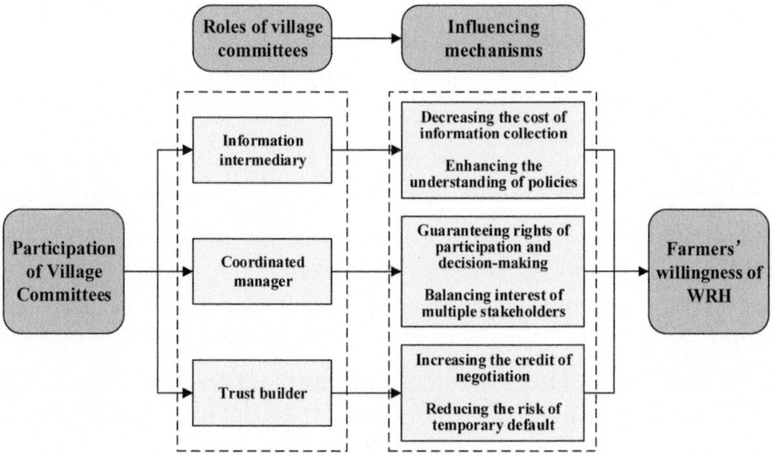

Figure 1.8. Influencing mechanisms of village committees on the withdrawal from rural homesteads (WRH) in China.

Source: Tang, P., Chen, J., Gao, J., Li, M., Wang, J. What Role(s) Do Village Committees Play in the Withdrawal from Rural Homesteads? Evidence from Sichuan Province in Western China. Land 2020, 9, 477. https://doi.org/10.3390/land9120477

Moreover, it is essential to recognize that early societies were not homogenous entities (Garoupa & Karakas, 2021; Gearty, 2005; Gentithes, 2020). Different cultures, geographical locations, and social structures shaped the fabric of these societies. For instance, the simple social structures observed in hunter-gatherer societies may have been vastly different from those in agricultural communities or early city-states. Each society had its unique norms, values, and methods of conflict resolution. While it is valid to assert that early societies were characterized by simple social structures and communal norms governing interactions and conflict resolution, it is crucial to avoid oversimplification. The Inca Empire exemplifies the complexities and nuances that can exist within these societies. By analyzing specific case studies like the Inca civilization, we gain a more nuanced understanding of early societies and their capacity for intricacy and sophistication in social organization and conflict resolution.

As human settlements evolved into agrarian communities, the role of the judiciary expanded in complexity (Marsh, 2021; Martinsen, 2011; Masinde, 2017). The transition from nomadic to settled lifestyles introduced the concept of property ownership, leading to disputes over land, resources, and boundaries. Indeed, this is reflected in contemporary rural communities in countries like China (see Figure 1.8). The judiciary emerged as a forum to address these conflicts, relying on customary laws and community-defined norms. This suggests that with the transition from hunter-gatherer societies to agrarian communities, the need for a more robust judicial system arose. While it is true that the advent of agriculture brought about significant changes in human settlement patterns and social structures, the assertion that the role of the judiciary expanded in complexity requires careful examination and contextualization. The Code of Hammurabi, created around 1754 BCE, is one of the earliest surviving legal codes and provides valuable insights into the evolution of judiciary systems in agrarian communities. It governed the lives of Babylonians and was designed to promote social order and regulate interactions between individuals.

The Code of Hammurabi addressed various aspects of daily life, including commerce, property rights, family issues, and criminal offenses (Sprankling, 2012; Stephenson, 2003, 2008; Stephenson, 2021). Its 282 laws touched upon matters ranging from trade regulations and land tenure to responsibilities within marriage and the judicial process itself. This highlights the expanding complexity of the judiciary's role in administering justice and resolving disputes within an agrarian society. Moreover, the Code of Hammurabi also established a hierarchy of laws and punishments, reflecting a developing sense of proportionality and differentiation according to social status. While it is true that the code placed a heavy emphasis on retribution, with punishments often being harsh, it is essential to note that the complexity of the legal system extended beyond mere punishment. The code specified different penalties for offenses committed by individuals of different social classes, suggesting a growing awareness of the need for equitable justice within a stratified society.

Nevertheless, it is important to recognize that not all aspects of the judiciary in agrarian communities necessarily became more complex (Aboueldahab, 2021; Abouharb et al., 2013). For instance, in smaller agricultural societies, where kinship ties and communal norms still held sway, dispute resolution might have remained primarily within the purview of the community itself. The role of formal judicial institutions may have been more limited, and conflicts resolved through mediation or community-based mechanisms. While the claim that the role of the judiciary expanded in complexity as human settlements evolved into agrarian communities is valid to some extent, one must approach it with caution. The example of the Code of Hammurabi in ancient Mesopotamia highlights the increasing complexity of legal systems in larger, more complex agrarian societies. However, it is crucial to acknowledge that not all agrarian communities experienced the same level of judicial development, and smaller, close-knit communities may have relied more on communal norms and informal dispute resolution mechanisms. By examining specific case studies like the Code of Hammurabi, we can better understand the nuanced nature of the judiciary's evolving role in agrarian communities.

Ancient civilizations, such as those in Mesopotamia, Egypt, and the Indus Valley, fostered the development of more formalized judicial structures (Parrillo, 2018; Pasarlay, 2018; Patton, 2017; Petrov, 2022). The proliferation of written legal codes, like the Code of Ur-Nammu and the Code of Hammurabi, provided a codified framework for resolving disputes. These early legal codes delineated rights, obligations, and penalties, offering a systematic approach to justice that extended beyond informal mediation. The role of the judiciary in these societies extended beyond mere dispute resolution. Judicial decisions carried societal weight, influencing not only the immediate parties involved but also shaping broader norms and expectations. Legal rulings set precedents that guided future decisions and established benchmarks for behavior and ethics within the community. In many early societies, religious and spiritual considerations were intertwined with the role of the judiciary. The belief in divine justice often led to the integration of religious rituals and practices into judicial proceedings. In some cases, religious leaders played a dual role as spiritual guides and legal arbiters, emphasizing the moral dimensions of legal judgments. The significance of the judiciary in early societies extended to maintaining social harmony and upholding communal values (Grimes, 2021; Grimmel,

2012; Grimmelikhuijsen & Klijn, 2015). The process of adjudication was often transparent and community-oriented, ensuring that verdicts aligned with collective interests. This communal involvement fostered a sense of belonging and cohesion, reinforcing the judiciary's role as a guardian of societal well-being. As societies evolved, so did the role of the judiciary. The principles and practices that emerged in these early civilizations laid the groundwork for the development of more complex legal systems and the eventual separation of powers. While the methods of conflict resolution varied, the overarching role of the judiciary as a mediator, interpreter of norms, and custodian of justice remained a constant thread throughout the ages.

In conclusion, the role of the judiciary in early societies was multifaceted, encompassing the resolution of disputes, the interpretation of communal norms, and the maintenance of social order. The evolution of judicial structures reflected the changing needs of growing and diverse communities, and the concepts established during these times continue to shape the modern judiciary's core functions. As societies progressed, the seeds sown by the early judiciary blossomed into the complex legal systems that underpin contemporary governance.

1.5. THE EMERGENCE OF DEMOCRATIC GOVERNANCE

The emergence of democratic governance represents a transformative chapter in the evolution of societal structures, fundamentally reshaping the roles of both the judiciary and government (Moliterno & Curos, 2021; Molto, 2015; Munday, 2008). Rooted in the principles of individual rights, representation, and collective decision-making, democratic systems have brought about a paradigm shift in how societies are governed and justice is administered. This assertion highlights the significant impact that the adoption of democratic principles has had on the functions and dynamics of governance. However, it is important to delve deeper into the complexities of this transformation and consider specific case studies to provide a nuanced understanding of the phenomenon. One case study that exemplifies the transformative nature of democratic governance is the establishment of the United States of America. The founding of the United States marked a departure from traditional forms of governance, introducing the concept of a government by the people, for the people. The U.S. Constitution, ratified in 1788, played a crucial role in structuring the powers and responsibilities of both the judiciary and the government, which were designed to be separate yet complementary branches.

Under democratic governance, the judiciary assumes a pivotal role in upholding the rule of law, ensuring the protection of individual rights, and interpreting and applying the Constitution (Pickett, 2016; Pidot, 2014; Pierce, 1989, 1997). The establishment of an independent judiciary in the United States, as enshrined in the Constitution, provides a strong check on the powers of the other branches of government. The Supreme Court, the highest judicial body, has the authority to review the constitutionality of laws and government actions, thus serving as a guardian of civil liberties and a crucial arbiter in matters of legal interpretation.

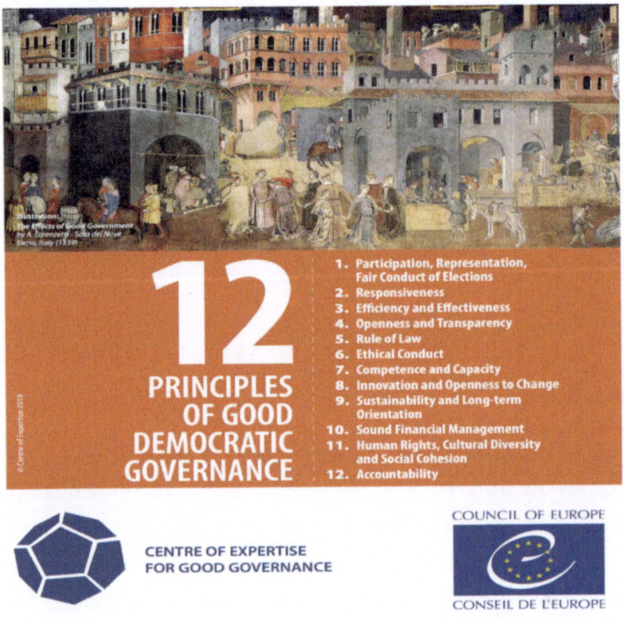

Figure 1.9. Twelve principles of good democratic governance.

Source: Council of Europe, https://help.elearning.ext.coe.int/course/index.php?categoryid=914

On the other hand, democratic governance also reshapes the role of the government itself. In a democratic system, the government is elected by the people, giving them the mandate to represent and govern in the best interests of the citizens. This implies a significant shift in power dynamics, as elected officials are accountable to the public and subject to regular electoral cycles. The government's role is to develop and execute policies, administer public affairs, and address societal problems through democratic processes, engaging in debates, compromise, and negotiation to reach consensus and make decisions that benefit the greater good. Figure 1.9 summarizes twelve principles of good democratic governance.

The Council of Europe has laid out 12 principles of good democratic governance that serve as a foundation for promoting democratic values and ensuring efficient and accountable governance (Mendelson, 1976; Menounou et al., 2019; Michetti et al., 2018). These principles encompass various facets of democratic governance and aim to provide guidance for member states. Let us explore each of these principles in detail, supported by specific case studies.

1. ***Legitimacy and legality:*** Democratic governance is characterized by the adherence to the rule of law and respect for the democratic process. The case study of the 2019 presidential elections in Ukraine demonstrates the importance of legitimacy and legality. The peaceful and transparent conduct of the elections, free from electoral manipulation and with respect for the Constitution, ensured the election of a president who had the mandate of the people.
2. ***Public participation:*** The active participation of citizens in decision-making processes is vital for democratic governance. The case of Iceland's constitutional reform process shows how public participation can be effectively incorporated. In 2010, Iceland initiated a crowdsourcing initiative, known as the "Icelandic Constitutional Council," where citizens were given the opportunity to contribute to the drafting of a new constitution via online forums and town hall meetings.
3. ***Separation of powers:*** The separation of powers between the executive, legislative, and judicial branches ensures a system of checks and balances. Germany exemplifies the effective separation of powers, where the Federal Constitutional Court has the authority to review laws passed by the legislature and executive, protecting the rights and liberties of individuals against potential abuses of power.
4. ***Independence of the judiciary:*** The independence of the judiciary from undue influence is essential for upholding the rule of law. The case study of the European Court of Human Rights showcases how an independent judiciary functions. The court,

being separate from political or national influences, plays a crucial role in enforcing and interpreting the European Convention on Human Rights, ensuring the protection of individual rights.

5. ***Transparency:*** Transparent governance fosters accountability and public trust. Sweden has established a well-regarded e-archiving system called "Dome," which allows its citizens to access and scrutinize government documents and decisions, ensuring transparency in governance and promoting trust in public institutions.
6. ***Responsiveness:*** Democratic governance requires a government to be responsive and accountable to the needs and expectations of its citizens. The case of New Zealand's response to the Christchurch mosque shootings in 2019 demonstrates responsiveness. The government swiftly implemented changes to gun laws in direct response to the tragic event, reflecting their commitment to addressing public concerns.
7. ***Efficiency and effectiveness:*** Good governance emphasizes the efficient and effective delivery of public services. Estonia is widely recognized for its efficient digital governance systems. The establishment of an efficient online platform called "e-Estonia" has streamlined government services, making them easily accessible to citizens and businesses, reducing bureaucracy and enhancing overall efficiency.
8. ***Equity and inclusiveness:*** Democratic governance should strive for equity and inclusiveness, ensuring equal treatment and opportunities for all. The case of Rwanda's gender quotas in parliament showcases their commitment to inclusivity. The country introduced a constitutional quota system in 2003, resulting in significant female representation in parliament, with over 60% of seats held by women, promoting gender balance and inclusivity.
9. ***Effectiveness and coherence of public administration:*** An effective and coherent public administration is crucial for democratic governance. The World Bank has recognized Singapore for its efficient public administration systems. The country's strong merit-based civil service and effective public policies have contributed to its economic development and social progress.

10. ***Human rights:*** Respect for human rights is a fundamental pillar of democratic governance. The European Union's Charter of Fundamental Rights ensures the protection of human rights across member states, underscoring their commitment to democratic values and principles.
11. ***Democratic culture:*** A democratic culture supports and promotes democratic values among citizens. Finland's educational system serves as an example of instilling democratic values.
12. ***Sustainability:*** This principle recognizes the importance of sustainable development, ensuring that democratic governance is mindful of environmental concerns, promotes sustainable economic growth, and addresses social and economic inequalities. By adhering to these principles, member states can work towards establishing and maintaining democratic systems that uphold human rights, foster active citizen participation, and ensure accountable governance for the betterment of their societies.

These principles notwithstanding, it is important to acknowledge the ongoing debates and challenges inherent in democratic governance (Hasbrouck, 2022; He, 2017; He, 2018; Heinz & Manikas, 1992). Critics argue that the influence of money and special interests can undermine the democratic process, while others highlight the potential for majority tyranny and the need to safeguard the rights of minority groups. Additionally, the interpretation and application of laws by the judiciary can sometimes be the subject of contention and disagreement, leading to a continuous process of legal debate and refinement.

Whereas the emergence of democratic governance represents a transformative chapter in the evolution of societal structures, it is essential to recognize the multifaceted nature of this transformation (Setty, 2015; Shah, 2014; Shenkman, 2012; Shepherd, 2009). The case study of the United States illustrates how democratic principles reshape the roles of both the judiciary and government, emphasizing the importance of an independent judiciary and a government accountable to the people. However, ongoing debates and challenges remind us that democratic governance is an ever-evolving process that requires continued vigilance and participation from all citizens to ensure the preservation of democratic values and the pursuit of a just and equitable society.

Democratic governance is characterized by the involvement of citizens in decision-making processes (Cui, 2017; Davis, 2008; De Francesco &

Tosun, 2022; de la Torre & Lemos, 2016). It shifts power from a centralized authority to the broader populace, enabling individuals to influence policy, elect representatives, and participate in shaping the direction of their societies. This transition from autocratic rule to participatory governance profoundly impacts the roles of both the judiciary and government. Democratic governance is indeed characterized by the involvement of citizens in decision-making processes, but it is crucial to delve into the nuances and complexities of this principle to understand its limitations and challenges. While public participation is a fundamental aspect of democratic governance, achieving widespread and meaningful citizen involvement can be a significant challenge in practice.

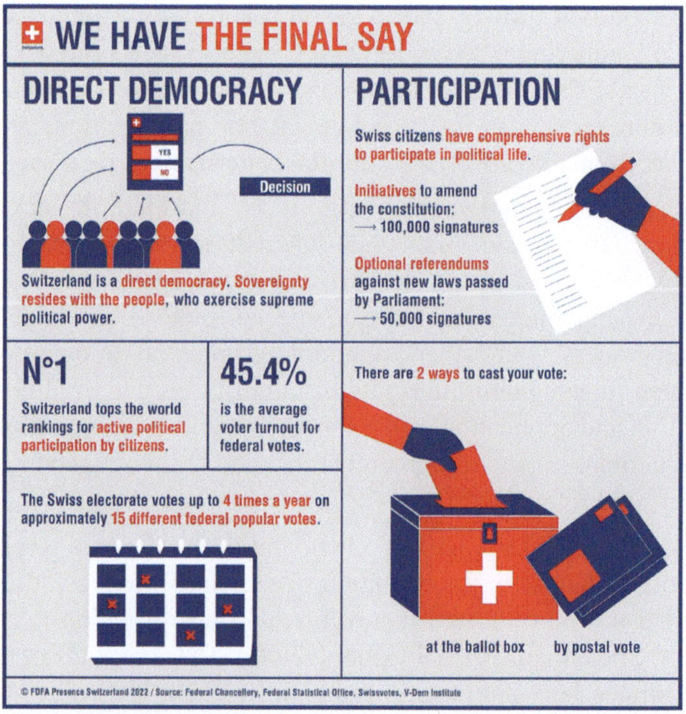

Figure 1.10. Illustration of direct democracy in Switzerland.

Source: About Switzerland. https://www.eda.admin.ch/aboutswitzerland/en/home/politik-geschichte/politisches-system/direkte-demokratie.html

To illustrate this, let us examine the case study of Switzerland's system of direct democracy (see Figure 1.10). Switzerland is known for its robust system of citizen participation, where citizens have the right to propose laws and constitutional amendments through popular initiatives and have a direct say on important policy decisions through referendums (Berger, 1978, 1979a, 1979b; Berkmanas, 2020; Besco, 2018). This case study presents a compelling example of citizen involvement in decision-making processes. However, it is important to consider the limitations of this system. While direct democracy in Switzerland allows citizens to participate in decision-making, the actual impact of citizen input may be limited in certain cases. For instance, popular initiatives require a significant number of signatures to qualify for a referendum, which can restrict the ability of smaller groups or marginalized communities to engage effectively in the process. Additionally, the information asymmetry among citizens can lead to uninformed decisions, as citizens may not always have access to the necessary expertise or resources to make informed judgments on complex issues. Furthermore, the practical feasibility of engaging all citizens in decision-making is a challenge. As societies grow larger, it becomes increasingly difficult to ensure broad and inclusive participation. Participation rates in elections and referendums can vary, with certain segments of the population being less engaged or facing barriers to participation. This raises questions about the representativeness and inclusivity of decision-making and highlights the need for strategies to address and overcome these barriers.

While citizen involvement is integral to democratic governance, there are also legitimate concerns regarding the potential drawbacks of excessive participation or "tyranny of the majority" (Parrillo, 2018; Pasarlay, 2018; Patton, 2017; Petrov, 2022). In some cases, decisions made through direct democracy may not adequately consider the rights and interests of minority groups or may be influenced by short-term popular sentiment rather than long-term vision and expertise. Whereas citizen involvement in decision-making processes is a defining characteristic of democratic governance, it is essential to recognize the complexities and challenges associated with realizing this principle in practice. The case study of Switzerland's system of direct democracy highlights the potential of citizen participation, but it also underscores the limitations and trade-offs that need to be carefully navigated. Striking a balance between inclusive decision-making and ensuring the protection of individual rights and minority interests is critical for the effective functioning of democratic systems.

In democratic societies, the judiciary assumes a pivotal role in upholding the rule of law and safeguarding individual rights (Brown, 1999; Buchmeyer, 2019; Bunjevac, 2015; Burbank, 2009). The separation of powers, a cornerstone of democratic governance, ensures that the judiciary functions independently from the executive and legislative branches. This independence is crucial for preventing government overreach and protecting citizens' rights from potential encroachments. The judiciary's role in democratic governance is exemplified through the exercise of judicial review. Courts have the authority to review government actions and legislation to ensure they conform to constitutional norms. This power allows the judiciary to hold the government accountable and prevent potential abuses of power. Judicial review provides a critical check on the actions of the government, upholding the principles of justice, equality, and human rights. Furthermore, the judiciary plays a central role in interpreting and applying laws in democratic societies. As laws are often subject to interpretation, courts ensure that legislation is consistently and fairly enforced. This function is crucial in maintaining legal consistency and ensuring that citizens are treated fairly under the law.

In parallel, the role of the government in democratic governance is redefined (Wang, 2021; Weill, 2016; West, 2019; Westerman, 2017). Governments are elected through free and fair elections, granting citizens the power to choose their representatives. The government's primary role shifts from wielding unchecked authority to implementing policies that reflect the needs and aspirations of the electorate. Democratic governments are accountable to the people they serve. The transparency and accountability required by democratic principles necessitate that governments operate openly, provide access to information, and justify their actions to the public. This accountability extends to judicial matters as well, where government actions are subject to scrutiny by the judiciary to ensure adherence to legal and constitutional principles.

The interplay between the judiciary and government in democratic governance is marked by mutual checks and balances (Bado, 2017; Bahry & Kim, 2021; Baldwin, 2017). The judiciary ensures that government actions align with the rule of law and constitution, while the government ensures that the judiciary operates independently and impartially. This equilibrium is vital in preventing concentration of power and promoting societal well-being. The emergence of democratic governance also reshapes the relationship between the judiciary and citizens. In democratic societies, citizens are empowered to challenge government actions and decisions through legal avenues, contributing to a more inclusive and participatory justice system. The judiciary becomes a forum where citizens can seek redress, ensuring that government actions are aligned with the principles of justice and fairness.

In conclusion, the emergence of democratic governance heralds a transformative era in the dynamics of both the judiciary and government. The principles of individual rights, representation, and accountability reshape their roles and interactions. The judiciary acts as a guardian of justice and individual rights, while the government's authority is tempered by the need to be responsive, transparent, and accountable to the electorate. The symbiotic relationship between the judiciary and government in democratic systems reflects a shared commitment to upholding the principles of justice, equality, and popular sovereignty.

CHAPTER 1 SUMMARY

In traversing the intricate terrain of the first chapter, "Foundations of Judiciary and Government," the tapestry of human history unfolds, revealing the evolution and interplay of these two vital pillars of societal organization. Through the exploration of the origins of the judiciary, the evolution of government structures, the concept of the separation of powers, the role of the judiciary in early societies, and the emergence of democratic governance, a tapestry emerges that underscores the intricate interconnections and transformative shifts that have shaped human governance and justice.

From the origins of early dispute resolution mechanisms within communal setups to the emergence of formalized legal codes in ancient civilizations, the judiciary's historical roots testify to humanity's innate pursuit of order and justice. The transition from nomadic to agrarian societies and the subsequent emergence of complex governance structures further refined the judiciary's role as a mediator, interpreter of norms, and guardian of social cohesion.

As governance systems evolved, the concept of the separation of powers crystallized, advocating for distinct branches that would counterbalance one another and prevent the concentration of authority. This foundational principle has left an indelible mark on both the judiciary and government, shaping their functions and interactions, and fundamentally influencing the nature of governance.

The judiciary's role in early societies extended beyond dispute resolution to the establishment of moral benchmarks and societal norms. Drawing upon customary laws and communal values, the judiciary played a critical part in defining and maintaining social order. This role, steeped in both practicality and ethical considerations, laid the groundwork for the more complex judicial systems that would emerge in subsequent eras.

The chapter culminates with the emergence of democratic governance—a transformative epoch that redefined the roles of both the judiciary and government. In democratic societies, the judiciary safeguards individual rights, upholds the rule of law, and serves as a check on government actions. Meanwhile, the government, accountable to the electorate, assumes a role centered on policy implementation and responsiveness to the needs of the citizenry.

As the tapestry of this chapter is woven together, it becomes evident that the roles of the judiciary and government are not static but dynamic, shaped by historical forces, philosophical principles, and societal aspirations. The interaction between these institutions—whether in early societies, under the umbrella of democratic governance, or within the framework of separation of powers—illustrates an intricate dance that echoes the ebb and flow of power, justice, and societal progress.

The chapter's journey has traversed the origins of dispute resolution, the evolution of governance structures, the philosophical underpinnings of separation of powers, the significance of the judiciary in shaping societal norms, and the transformative advent of democratic governance. Each thread woven into this intricate fabric contributes to a richer understanding of the complex interplay between the judiciary and government, setting the stage for deeper explorations into the subsequent chapters.

As the narrative of governance and justice unfolds, the chapter's insights serve as a foundation for the broader exploration of these essential institutions. Their historical roots, their roles in modern societies, and the ongoing power dynamics they embody form the basis for understanding the intricate interplay that underpins the fabric of governance and justice—a fabric that continues to be woven, refined, and shaped by the collective endeavors of societies across time and space. The second chapter builds on the insights from the first chapter to focus on the functions of the judiciary.

CHAPTER 2

The Role and Function of the Judiciary

Contents

2.1. Guardian of the Constitution: Judicial Review 43
2.2. Jurisdiction and Decision-Making Process 48
2.3. Criminal Justice and Due Process 54
2.4. Civil Cases and Dispute Resolution.. 59
2.5. Judiciary's Role in Safeguarding Individual Rights 65
Chapter 2 Summary 69

In the intricate tapestry of governance and justice, the judiciary emerges as a pivotal institution tasked with the interpretation, application, and safeguarding of the law. This second chapter, titled "The Role and Function of the Judiciary," delves into the multifaceted dimensions that define the judiciary's significance within the framework of governance. As we embark on this exploration, we journey through the diverse facets that constitute the judiciary's role, from its guardianship of constitutional principles to its pivotal role in safeguarding individual rights.

In Section 2.1, "Guardian of the Constitution: Judicial Review," we delve into a cornerstone of the judiciary's role—the power to review legislation and government actions for their constitutionality. This power empowers courts to assess the alignment of laws and executive decisions with the foundational principles enshrined within the constitution. By wielding this authority, the judiciary serves as a vital check on potential encroachments of governmental power and ensures the integrity of the legal framework.

Section 2.2, "Jurisdiction and Decision-Making Process," delves into the nuanced aspects that guide the judiciary's jurisdiction and decision-making. As the arbiter of legal disputes, the judiciary's jurisdiction defines its sphere of influence in addressing matters that fall under its purview. This section also uncovers the intricacies of the decision-making process, highlighting the weight of legal precedent, the importance of legal interpretation, and the balancing of competing legal arguments.

In Section 2.3, "Criminal Justice and Due Process," the focus shifts to the judiciary's integral role in criminal justice systems. Here, we examine the judiciary's responsibilities in ensuring due process—a fundamental right that guarantees fair treatment and a just legal proceeding for individuals accused of crimes. This section explores the significance of impartial trials, legal representation, and the protection of the accused's rights within the criminal justice framework.

Section 2.4, "Civil Cases and Dispute Resolution," directs our attention to the judiciary's involvement in civil matters. In the realm of civil law, courts play a pivotal role in resolving disputes between individuals, organizations, or entities. This section delves into the procedures, mechanisms, and principles that guide civil dispute resolution, emphasizing the judiciary's role in providing a fair and equitable forum for settling conflicts.

Finally, in Section 2.5, "Judiciary's Role in Safeguarding Individual Rights," we illuminate the judiciary's pivotal role as a safeguard for individual rights. The judiciary acts as a guardian of fundamental freedoms, ensuring that the rights of citizens are upheld and protected. This section examines how the judiciary navigates the delicate balance between safeguarding individual rights and accommodating societal interests.

As the pages of this chapter unfold, they reveal the judiciary's intricate tapestry of roles—ranging from the constitutional sentinel to the arbiter of disputes and the protector of rights. Each section peels back layers, revealing the judicial mechanisms that contribute to the preservation of justice, the rule of law, and the maintenance of societal harmony. The chapter's exploration underscores the significance of the judiciary in upholding the core tenets of governance and justice—a significance that resonates across societies and throughout the corridors of history. Let us open this second chapter by considering how judicial review is used by the courts to safeguard the constitution.

2.1. GUARDIAN OF THE CONSTITUTION: JUDICIAL REVIEW

Within the intricate framework of governance, the principle of judicial review stands as a sentinel guarding the integrity of the constitution and the foundational principles upon which a nation's legal system is built (Wang, 2021; Weill, 2016; West, 2019; Westerman, 2017). This profound power vested in the judiciary underscores the pivotal role it plays in upholding the rule of law and ensuring that the actions of both the government and the legislative bodies remain aligned with the constitution's precepts. The principle of judicial review serves as a guardian of the integrity of the constitution and the foundational principles upon which a nation's legal system is built. Judicial review allows the judiciary branch to scrutinize the actions of the executive and legislative branches, ensuring compliance with constitutional provisions and safeguarding individual rights. A compelling case study that highlights the significance of judicial review is the landmark decision of Brown v. Board of Education in the United States. In this case, the Supreme Court examined the constitutionality of segregated public schools and concluded that racial segregation violated the Equal Protection Clause of the Fourteenth Amendment. This pivotal decision marked a turning point in American history, leading to desegregation and the advancement of civil rights. As Figure 2.1 shows, there are various rights and protections which fall under the remit of the administrative state.

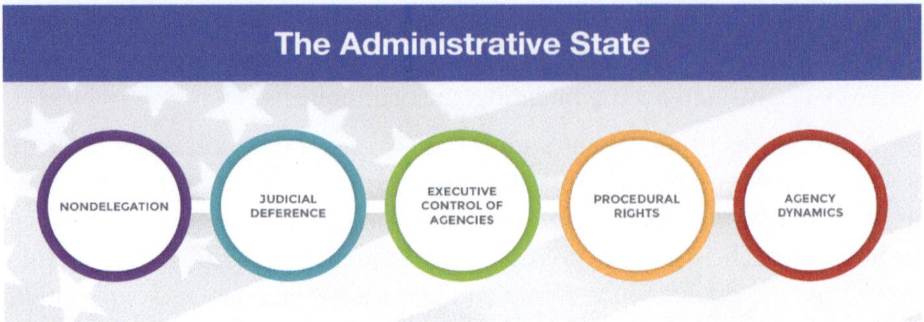

Figure 2.1. Key elements of the administrative state.

Source: Ballotpedia

Brown v. Board of Education exemplifies the power of judicial review and underscores the crucial role of the judiciary in protecting individual liberties and ensuring equal treatment (Hennigar, 2010; Hessick, 2014; Hill, 2016; Holland, 2009). It showcases the thorough and nuanced approach taken by the Court when scrutinizing the actions and laws of the other branches. Critics argue that judicial review can be undemocratic, allowing unelected judges to overturn laws enacted by elected representatives. While this concern has merit, it fails to acknowledge the importance of an independent judiciary in safeguarding marginalized groups and promoting a fair and just society. In the case of Brown v. Board of Education, the Supreme Court's intervention was necessary to rectify systemic injustices faced by African American children. Hence, judicial review remains a vital component of a functioning democracy. Through the diligent exercise of judicial review, the judiciary acts as a guardian of the constitution, ensuring that governance adheres to the rule of law and upholds the foundational principles of a nation's legal system. The careful scrutiny of laws and actions, as seen in the case of Brown v. Board of Education, plays a crucial role in preserving constitutional integrity and safeguarding individual rights.

At its core, judicial review empowers the judiciary to assess the constitutionality of laws, executive actions, and governmental decisions (Dumoulin & Licoppe, 2016; Dunn, 2017; Easterly, 2019; Easton, 2018). This authority stems from the recognition that a constitution represents the supreme law of the land, setting forth the fundamental rights, responsibilities, and limitations that shape a nation's governance. By wielding the power of judicial review, courts ensure that no branch of government operates outside the constitutional boundaries, thereby preventing overreach and safeguarding the principles of separation of powers and checks and balances.

Judicial review, an essential element of democratic governance, empowers the judiciary to evaluate the constitutionality of laws, executive actions, and governmental decisions. This power gives rise to a nuanced debate regarding the role of the judiciary in a democratic system. Supporters assert that judicial review is vital for safeguarding individual rights, ensuring legal validity, and preventing abuses of power. A case study that depicts the complexities surrounding judicial review is the Obergefell v. Hodges case in the United States. In this landmark decision, the Supreme Court ruled that same-sex couples have a constitutional right to marry. Advocates argue that this ruling upheld principles of equal protection and expanded civil rights for the LGBTQ+ community. Critics, on the other hand, contend that such decisions should be left to the legislature and that judicial intervention encroaches upon democratic processes. They argue that judicial activism can lead to policy-making by unelected judges, potentially disregarding public opinion and the democratic will. Furthermore, critics caution that judicial interpretation of constitutional provisions can be subjective and prone to ideological biases. While these concerns hold validity, it is crucial to acknowledge the essential role of an independent judiciary in safeguarding minority rights and upholding constitutional principles. The Obergefell v. Hodges case exemplifies how judicial review can rectify institutional discrimination and ensure equality for marginalized groups. In sum, while debate surrounds the scope and impact of judicial review, the evaluation of constitutional adherence by the judiciary serves as a crucial check-and-balance mechanism in democratic systems, safeguarding fundamental rights and promoting equal treatment under the law. In this context, the relationship between the judiciary and government is defined by mutual accountability (Bybee, 1994; Byrne & Maxwell, 2019; Calabresi & Rhodes, 1992). The government creates laws and policies, while the judiciary ensures their adherence to constitutional principles. This dynamic interaction fosters a delicate equilibrium that is essential for maintaining a just and fair society. The relationship between the judiciary and government is a complex interplay characterized by mutual accountability. Through judicial review, the judiciary exercises its authority to scrutinize government actions and decisions to ensure their compliance with constitutional principles. This oversight acts as a guiding force to hold the government accountable and prevent unconstitutional exercises of power. Conversely, the government also holds the judiciary accountable through various mechanisms like judicial appointments and confirming nominations. This is all part of the checks and balances in government (see Figure 2.2).

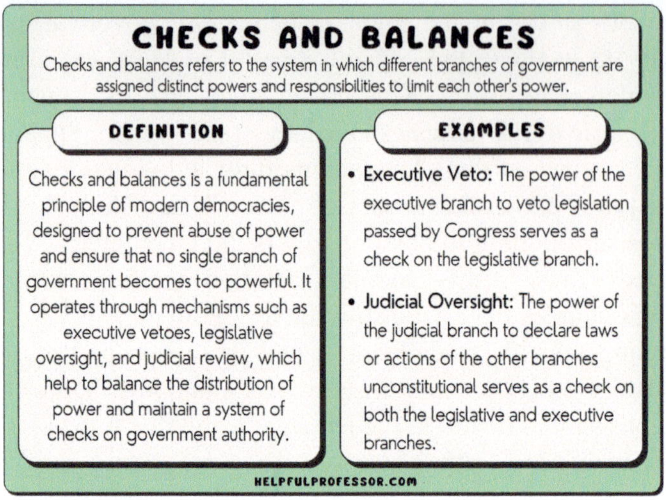

Figure 2.2. Conceptualizing checks and balances in government.

Source: https://helpfulprofessor.com/checks-and-balances-examples/

One case study that underscores the significance of this relationship is the Supreme Court of India's ruling in the Keshavananda Bharati v. State of Kerala case. In this landmark decision, the Court examined the limits of the Parliament's amending power concerning the basic structure of the Constitution. The Court held that while the Parliament possessed the authority to amend the Constitution, it could not encroach on its fundamental structure. This verdict emphasized the supremacy of the Constitution and affirmed the judiciary's role in safeguarding its core principles (Parrillo, 2018; Pasarlay, 2018; Patton, 2017; Petrov, 2022).

Having said that, debates persist regarding the extent and boundaries of judicial review (Wang, 2021; Weill, 2016; West, 2019; Westerman, 2017). Critics argue that an overly active judiciary may encroach on the realm of the elected government, potentially undermining democratic processes. These concerns include unelected judges invalidating laws enacted by elected representatives and engaging in policy-making beyond their prescribed role. They assert that holding the government accountable should primarily rest with the elected branches, which are directly responsible to the electorate.

In contrast, proponents maintain that judicial review is integral to upholding the rule of law and protecting individual rights (van Zeben, 2015; Vermeule, 2012; Voeten, 2008; VonDoepp & Ellett, 2011). They argue that an independent judiciary acts as a crucial check on government power, preventing potential abuses and ensuring constitutional adherence. Judicial review serves as a safeguard against laws that may impinge on fundamental rights or violate the core principles enshrined in the Constitution. Proponents highlight the impartiality and neutrality of the judiciary as essential to providing objective assessments of government actions. Hence, the relationship between the judiciary and government encompasses a dynamic interplay of mutual accountability. While concerns about judicial overreach and democratic principles are raised, proponents contend that judicial review is a vital component of upholding the rule of law and safeguarding individual rights. The Keshavananda Bharati v. State of Kerala case exemplifies the exercise of judicial review in holding the government accountable and affirming the supreme position of the Constitution. Striking a delicate balance between the executive, legislative, and judicial branches is necessary to foster a robust democracy while upholding individual freedoms and constitutional values.

The impact of judicial review on government actions is significant (Mason, 2015; Matthes, 2022; Mayoral & Perez, 2018). The mere existence of this power encourages government officials to meticulously consider the constitutionality of their decisions and legislative proposals. The knowledge that their actions may be subject to judicial scrutiny compels lawmakers and executives to operate within the legal confines established by the constitution, thereby reinforcing respect for the rule of law and constitutional norms. The principle of judicial review has been exemplified in landmark cases around the world. For instance, in the United States, the case of Marbury v. Madison (1803) established the power of the Supreme Court to review the constitutionality of laws. This decision set the precedent for judicial review in the American legal system, enabling the judiciary to strike down laws that violate the constitution.

Furthermore, judicial review empowers the judiciary to safeguard the rights of individuals and minorities against potential encroachments by the government or the majority (Mak & Rutledge, 2019; Maltzman & Shipan, 2008). This function is especially vital in democratic societies where the rights and freedoms of citizens are held sacrosanct. By assessing the constitutionality of laws that affect fundamental rights—such as freedom of speech, religion, and privacy—the judiciary ensures that individual liberties are protected from the potential excesses of governmental authority. The interplay between the judiciary and government in the realm of judicial review is a reflection of the broader relationship between legal and political realms. While the judiciary's decisions are grounded in legal analysis, they often carry profound political and societal implications. As such, judicial review is a testament to the judiciary's role as a guardian of both legal norms and societal values.

In conclusion, the principle of judicial review reinforces the judiciary's critical role in maintaining the rule of law and upholding constitutional principles. Through this power, the judiciary ensures that government actions remain within constitutional boundaries, protecting individual rights and preventing the concentration of power. The interplay between the judiciary and government in the realm of judicial review embodies the delicate equilibrium necessary for the functioning of a just and accountable society. These principles also apply to the decision-making process and jurisdiction.

2.2. JURISDICTION AND DECISION-MAKING PROCESS

Jurisdiction and the decision-making process lie at the heart of the judiciary's role, defining the boundaries of its authority and shaping how justice is administered (Medawatte et al., 2013; Meggitt & Somji, 2016; Melone, 1996). The interplay between jurisdiction—the sphere in which the judiciary has the legal authority to adjudicate—and the decision-making process is integral to ensuring a fair, efficient, and equitable legal system. These elements are deeply intertwined, shaping the relationship between the judiciary and government while upholding the principles of justice and the rule of law. Institutional change at all levels of the judiciary has the potential to foster better decision-making and enhance jurisdictional consistency. By implementing reforms that enhance transparency, efficiency, and accountability within the judicial system, it is possible to promote a more effective and fair administration of justice. A compelling case study that demonstrates the impact of institutional change on decision-making and jurisdictional consistency is the establishment of specialized courts in Brazil to address complex cases of corruption. This innovative approach aims to expedite judicial proceedings and ensure a more consistent application of the law in such cases. By dedicating specialized judges and support staff to these specific cases, the Brazilian judiciary has been able to streamline processes, increase expertise, and improve decision-making in corruption-related matters.

Critics, however, argue that while institutional change is necessary, it is important to strike a balance between efficiency and safeguarding individual rights (Rohrschneider, 2005; Rotunda, 1991; Rowley, 2005). They caution against expedited processes that may sacrifice due process or compromise the quality of decision-making. Critics contend that despite the need for expeditious justice, it is essential that fundamental legal principles and procedural safeguards are upheld to maintain the integrity of the justice system. Proponents of institutional change emphasize the importance of improving jurisdictional consistency (see Figure 2.3). By implementing standardized procedures and guidelines, as well as providing training and resources to judges, it is possible to reduce disparities in judgment and ensure a more uniform application of the law. This not only promotes fairness and predictability but also strengthens public confidence in the judiciary. In sum, institutional change in the judiciary can play a pivotal role in enhancing decision-making and jurisdictional consistency. The establishment of specialized courts in Brazil exemplifies how targeted reforms can address complex cases and produce more efficient and effective outcomes. While critiquing the balance between speed and due process is valid, proponents argue that institutional changes can be designed in a way that upholds individual rights while achieving more consistent and just outcomes. Striking the right balance requires careful consideration, ongoing evaluation, and a commitment to maintaining the highest standards of justice.

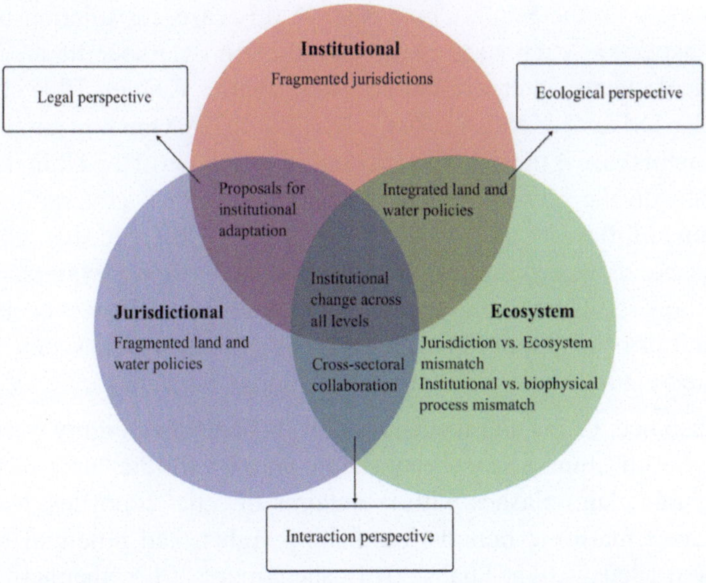

Figure 2.3. Institutional change across all levels of the judiciary.

Source: Amar Nanda (2018). https://www.amarnanda.nl/decision-pathways-tools-to-overcome-institutional-barriers/

Jurisdiction serves as the framework within which the judiciary operates, dictating the types of cases a court can hear and the scope of its authority (Oakes, 2018; Obermaier, 2008; Oliveira & Garoupa, 2011). It establishes the legal boundaries that demarcate where the judiciary's power begins and ends. This jurisdiction is often defined by legal factors such as subject matter, geographical location, and the type of parties involved. Clear delineation of jurisdiction is paramount to preventing cases from falling into legal gray areas and ensuring that legal disputes are resolved by the appropriate judicial bodies. Jurisdiction, as the fundamental framework that shapes the functioning of the judiciary, plays a pivotal role in determining the types of cases that a court can hear and the extent of its authority. This system of jurisdiction serves to ensure an orderly and structured legal process, but it is not without its complexities and controversies. A case study that provides insight into the nuanced nature of jurisdiction can be seen in the international realm, particularly in the context of disputes involving territorial claims.

Consider, for example, the South China Sea dispute, which has been a subject of intense legal and political debates. This complex territorial dispute involves several countries, including China, Vietnam, the Philippines, Malaysia, and Brunei, all vying for control over various islands and maritime areas in the South China Sea. In this case, jurisdiction becomes a crucial aspect, as each state claims jurisdiction over specific areas based on historical events, international law, and treaties (Dinan, 1997; Downey et al., 2020; Driscoll & Nelson, 2015; Duhart, 2020). One key jurisdictional question in this case is the interpretation and application of the United Nations Convention on the Law of the Sea (UNCLOS), which governs the rights and responsibilities of states in their use of the world's oceans. UNCLOS delineates exclusive economic zones (EEZs) and territorial waters, granting states certain rights and jurisdiction over these areas. However, differing interpretations of UNCLOS provisions among the disputing states have led to contested claims and conflicting jurisdictional assertions.

For instance, China claims historical rights and sovereignty over nearly the entire South China Sea, encompassing what it calls the "nine-dash line." However, this claim clashes with the claims of other countries, leading to disputes over maritime boundaries, fishing rights, and potential resource exploitation (Setty, 2015; Shah, 2014; Shenkman, 2012; Shepherd, 2009). The jurisdictional implications here are twofold: firstly, regarding which areas fall under the jurisdiction of each state, and secondly, how disputes over jurisdiction should be resolved. Within this context, jurisdiction becomes a central issue for the involved parties and international bodies such as the

Permanent Court of Arbitration (PCA) and the International Court of Justice (ICJ). These institutions have been called upon to arbitrate jurisdictional disputes and provide legal clarity on the matter. The PCA, for example, in a landmark 2016 ruling, invalidated China's "nine-dash line" claim and clarified the maritime entitlements of the parties involved. However, despite the PCA's jurisdiction over the case, China refused to participate, highlighting the complex nature of jurisdiction and its acceptance by involved parties.

The case study of the South China Sea dispute underscores the multifaceted nature of jurisdiction (Smith, 2005; Sorabji & Vaughan, 2021; Southworth, 2018). It demonstrates that jurisdiction not only determines the types of cases that a court can hear but is also intricately tied to larger geopolitical and legal issues. The competing claims and interpretations of jurisdictional rights in the South China Sea case illustrate the challenges involved in resolving jurisdictional disputes that can have long-lasting consequences. Overall, jurisdiction acts as the bedrock of the judicial system, delineating the scope of authority and the types of cases a court can handle. However, as demonstrated by the South China Sea dispute, jurisdiction can become a fiercely debated and complex issue, particularly in cases involving territorial claims. This case study highlights the need for careful examination and resolution of jurisdictional disputes to ensure a fair and effective legal process within a broader political and international context.

The decision-making process encompasses the procedures, methodologies, and legal principles courts employ to reach conclusions in cases brought before them (Takayasu, 2023; Tate, 1994; Tauber & Banks, 2017). Courts engage in meticulous legal analysis, examining evidence, arguments, and precedent to render judgments that adhere to the law and serve the interests of justice. This process is characterized by impartiality, as judges assess cases based on legal merits rather than personal biases or extraneous factors. The decision-making process is an integral part of the judiciary's role in reaching conclusions in cases, and it encompasses a range of procedures, methodologies, and legal principles that courts employ. However, this process is not without its debates and critiques, as different approaches and interpretations can lead to varying outcomes. To illustrate this, let us examine a specific case study involving a criminal trial and the decision-making process employed by the court. Consider a high-profile murder trial where the defendant is accused of a heinous crime, and the evidence presented is complex and multifaceted. In such cases, the decision-making process becomes crucial in determining the defendant's innocence or guilt. Here, specific procedures, methodologies, and legal principles come into play, which can shape the outcome of the trial and lead to debates around fairness, objectivity, and accuracy.

One aspect of the decision-making process in this case study relates to the admissibility and evaluation of evidence (Calfee, 2006; Cameron, 2010; Caplan, 2010; Carrillo et al., 2017). The court must carefully consider the relevance, reliability, and credibility of the evidence presented by both the prosecution and the defense. The judge and jury must assess witness testimony, forensic analyses, expert opinions, and any other relevant exhibits. However, debates may arise over the weight assigned to different types of evidence or the interpretation of expert findings, leading to potential biases or differing conclusions. Another crucial element is the application of legal principles, such as the burden of proof and the presumption of innocence. These principles guide the decision-making process and are meant to ensure fairness and protect the rights of the accused. However, debates can arise over how these principles are applied and whether the court sufficiently upholds them in practice. Critics argue that factors such as societal pressure, media influence, or inadequate legal representation may affect the proper application of these principles, potentially leading to unjust outcomes.

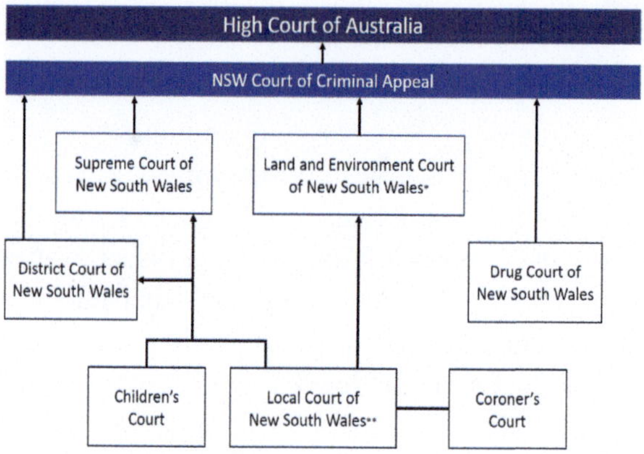

Figure 2.4. Example of a court hierarchy in Australia and jurisdiction.

Source: https://www.lec.nsw.gov.au/about-us/purpose-and-jurisdiction.html

Additionally, the methodologies employed by judges and juries to analyze and interpret evidence are subject to scrutiny and debate (Joshi, 2022; Juhn, 2021; Kang, 2004; Kang et al., 2023). Different jurisdictions may adopt varying approaches, such as the adversarial system or the inquisitorial system, which influence how the evidence is collected, presented, and weighed. Each system has its advantages and disadvantages, and debates often arise over which methodology strikes the right balance between ensuring justice and efficiency. Moreover, the decision-making process also involves the interaction of judges and jurors themselves. Jurors, who are lay people, might be influenced by personal biases, emotions, or social pressures, potentially impacting their decision-making. This can lead to concerns about the impartiality and reliability of the decision-making process, especially when high-profile or emotionally charged cases are involved. Figure 2.4 is an example of a court hierarchy and jurisdictional processes.

Overall, the decision-making process in the judiciary encompasses various procedures, methodologies, and legal principles (Cassman, 2015; Celenk, 2016; Chakravarti et al., 2011; Chalmers, 2000). However, it is not without debates, critiques, and nuances. The case study of a high-profile murder trial illustrates the complexities involved, such as evaluating evidence, applying legal principles, selecting appropriate methodologies, and assessing the role of judges and jurors. These complexities highlight the need for continuous evaluation and improvement of the decision-making process to safeguard fairness, objectivity, and accuracy in the outcomes of legal cases. The interplay between jurisdiction and the decision-making process is intricate. Courts must ascertain not only whether they possess the jurisdiction to hear a case, but also how they will apply legal principles to resolve it. The decision-making process is guided by the principle of stare decisis—respect for legal precedent—which ensures consistency in the interpretation and application of the law. Precedent provides a framework within which judges make decisions, enabling them to consider the legal reasoning of prior cases when determining the outcome of current disputes.

The relationship between the judiciary and government in this context is one of collaboration and distinct roles (George, 2009; Geyh, 2014; Gisbert, 2022; Gomes, 2017). While the government has the authority to enact laws and policies, the judiciary interprets and applies them to specific cases. The judiciary's decisions serve as legal precedents, guiding the government in crafting future legislation and policies that adhere to established legal principles. The decision-making process of the judiciary ensures that the government operates within the legal parameters set by the constitution and laws. Furthermore, the independence of the judiciary is crucial to maintaining the integrity of both jurisdiction and the decision-making process. An independent judiciary safeguards against political interference and ensures that decisions are made solely on the basis of law and evidence. This separation of powers strengthens the legitimacy of the judicial system and promotes public trust in the administration of justice. The nexus of jurisdiction and the decision-making process also underscores the complexity of the judiciary's role in upholding the rule of law (Navarrete & Castillo-Ortiz, 2020; Nelson & Gibson, 2019). By maintaining clear jurisdictional boundaries and engaging in rigorous legal analysis, the judiciary ensures that justice is dispensed fairly and uniformly. The decision-making process exemplifies the judiciary's commitment to providing a forum for the resolution of disputes that is both principled and impartial. In conclusion, the intricacies of jurisdiction and the decision-making process are central to the judiciary's role in governance and justice. These elements define the boundaries of the judiciary's authority and guide how legal disputes are resolved. The interplay between jurisdiction and the decision-making process underscores the judiciary's independence, its relationship with the government, and its commitment to upholding the principles of justice and the rule of law. The next section focuses on criminal justice and due process.

2.3. CRIMINAL JUSTICE AND DUE PROCESS

Criminal justice and the concept of due process are cornerstones of any functioning legal system, serving as safeguards against the abuse of government authority and ensuring that individuals accused of crimes are treated fairly and justly (Hasbrouck, 2022; He, 2017; He, 2018; Heinz & Manikas, 1992). This facet of the judiciary's role demonstrates its critical function in upholding individual rights while maintaining societal order. The intricate interplay between the judiciary and government in the realm of criminal justice and due process is emblematic of the delicate balance between upholding justice and protecting civil liberties. Criminal justice and the concept of due process are indeed foundational principles within any functioning legal system, aiming to safeguard against the abuse of government authority and ensure fairness and justice for individuals accused of crimes. However, while these principles are generally seen as essential, debates and critiques exist surrounding their implementation and effectiveness. Examining a specific case study can shed light on the nuances and challenges associated with criminal justice and due process.

Consider the case of a high-profile criminal trial where the accused is a marginalized individual, such as a person from a low-income background or belonging to a minority group. This case highlights the potential discrepancies and inequalities that can arise within the criminal justice system (Schroeder, 2023; Schuman, 2021; Schweiger, 2022). Despite the overarching principle of due process, societal biases, systemic flaws, and unequal access to resources can significantly impact the fair treatment and outcomes for the accused. One aspect of this debate centers around access to legal representation. While individuals have the right to legal counsel, the quality of representation can differ based on financial means and availability of resources. Wealthier individuals often have access to skilled and experienced defense attorneys, whereas those with limited financial resources may be assigned overburdened public defenders. This imbalance can lead to concerns about the equitable application of due process, as the quality of legal representation may influence the fairness of the trial and its outcome. Such imbalances can also contravene the rule of law (see Figure 2.5).

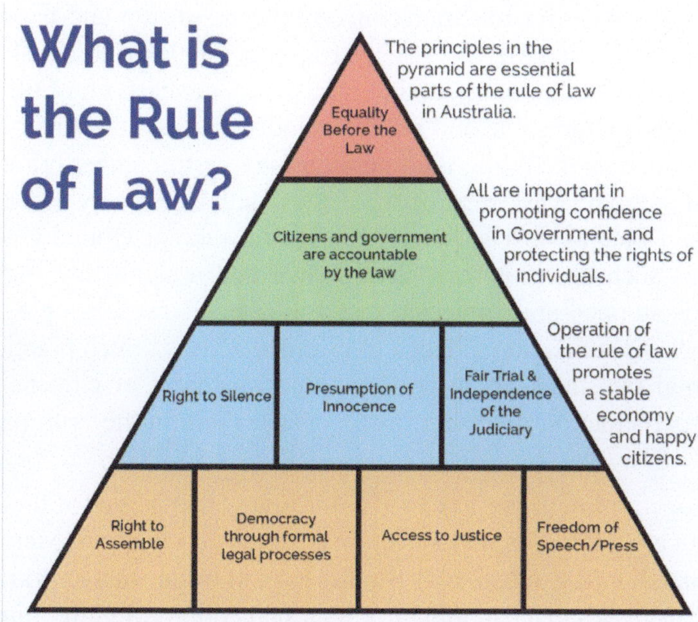

Figure 2.5. Conceptualization of the rule of law.

Source: NSW Council for Civil Liberties on Twitter. https://twitter.com/NSWCCL/status/1367361234840907776

Another crucial element is the potential for implicit biases and discrimination within the criminal justice system (Gallagher, 2012; Gardbaum, 2015; Garoupa et al., 2012). Studies have shown that race and socioeconomic status can impact processes such as arrest rates, plea bargaining, and sentencing outcomes. Marginalized individuals may be more likely to face harsher penalties or be subjected to prejudiced assumptions, thereby undermining the principle of equal treatment under the law. While the system maintains the ideal of equal treatment under the law, studies and real-life examples have revealed persistent biases and discriminatory practices that have a significant impact on individuals' experiences. For instance, research has shown that racial minorities, particularly Black individuals, often face disproportionate rates of arrest, harsher sentences, and an increased likelihood of being wrongfully convicted. This stark disparity raises serious concerns about whether justice is truly blind and highlights the need to critically examine the presence of implicit biases within the criminal justice system.

One particular case study that exemplifies the debate surrounding implicit biases and discrimination concerns the use of stop-and-frisk policies in urban areas (Kramarz et al., 2017; Krogseng, 2000; Krotoszynski, 2014). These policies, employed by law enforcement agencies, grant officers the authority to stop, question, and pat down individuals on the street based on reasonable suspicion. While the intention may be to combat crime, critics argue that stop-and-frisk disproportionately targets minority communities, leading to a bias against individuals based on race or ethnicity. Statistics from cities such as New York have shown that a significant majority of individuals stopped and subjected to these searches were people of color, despite lacking sufficient evidence of criminal activity. Such practices raise fundamental questions about the equitable treatment of citizens and the potential perpetuation of discriminatory biases within the criminal justice system.

Moreover, implicit biases can also infiltrate other stages of the criminal justice process, including jury selection and decision-making (Marsh, 2021; Martinsen, 2011; Masinde, 2017). Studies have indicated that jurors may have unconscious biases that can influence their perceptions of guilt or innocence and impact the ultimate verdict. For example, research has shown that racial stereotypes, even when unintended, can shape juror decision-making in racially charged cases. Such biases may manifest in differential assessments of witness credibility, interpretation of evidence, or the evaluation of the defendant's character. These implicit biases underscore the need to foster awareness and implement measures to mitigate their influence, as they can fundamentally undermine the objective pursuit of justice and fairness.

Addressing the issue of implicit biases and discrimination within the criminal justice system requires acknowledging the systemic factors that contribute to their persistence (Kirisci & Kocaman, 2022; Kitagawa, 2023;

Kochtcheeva, 2009). This includes examining law enforcement practices, judicial decision-making, and the role of social attitudes. Implementing comprehensive training programs for police officers and legal professionals to increase awareness of implicit biases is one potential avenue for progress. Additionally, diversifying the legal profession, law enforcement agencies, and juries can contribute to a more nuanced and fair criminal justice system that better reflects the communities it serves.

Furthermore, the concept of due process includes protections against coerced confessions, unlawful searches and seizures, and the right to a fair trial (Delaney, 2016; Devlin & Dodek, 2017; DiClemente, 2012). However, even with proper legal safeguards in place, instances of procedural misconduct or police misconduct can occur, potentially leading to wrongful convictions or miscarriages of justice. These cases raise questions about the effectiveness of due process in practice and the need for continuous evaluation and improvement of law enforcement practices. Figure 2.6 is an illustration of patterns of police misconduct in the USA.

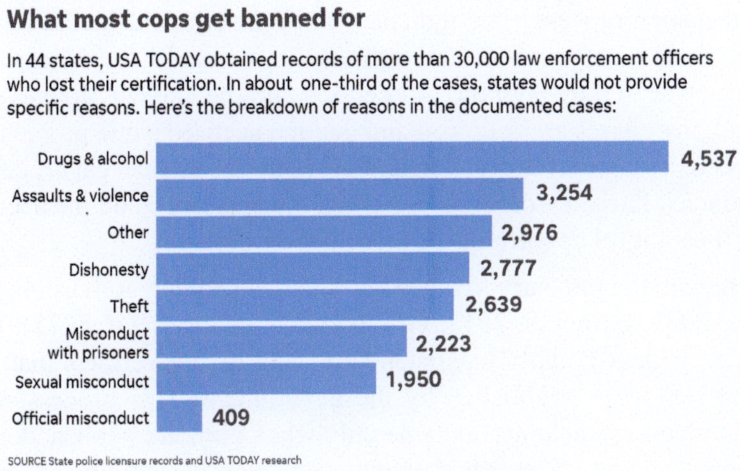

Figure 2.6. Patterns of police misconduct in the USA.

Source: John Kelly and Mark Nichols (2019) via USA Today. https://www.usatoday.com/in-depth/news/investigations/2019/04/24/usa-today-revealing-misconduct-records-police-cops/3223984002/

In summary, criminal justice and due process are foundational principles aimed at ensuring fairness and justice within a legal system. However, a specific case study that considers factors such as unequal access to legal representation and potential biases highlights the complexities and debates surrounding their implementation. Recognizing and addressing these issues is crucial for striving towards a more just and equitable criminal justice system that upholds the principles of due process for all individuals, regardless of socioeconomic background or marginalized status. Criminal justice embodies the mechanisms through which societies respond to criminal behavior, aiming to hold offenders accountable while protecting the rights of individuals within the legal framework (Rohrschneider, 2005; Rotunda, 1991; Rowley, 2005). The government, through law enforcement agencies and prosecutors, initiates criminal proceedings. The judiciary, in turn, plays a central role in adjudicating these cases, ensuring that due process is upheld and justice is dispensed impartially.

Central to the concept of due process is the principle that individuals accused of crimes are entitled to certain legal protections (Horvath, 2017; Howard et al., 2006; Hume, 2012). These protections encompass a range of rights, from the right to a fair and speedy trial to the right to legal representation and the presumption of innocence. The government's responsibility is to ensure that these rights are upheld throughout the criminal justice process. The judiciary's role in criminal justice is multi-faceted. Courts serve as neutral arbiters, responsible for assessing the evidence presented by both the prosecution and the defense. Judges ensure that legal procedures are followed and that the accused's due process rights are respected. The judiciary's oversight guarantees that the legal proceedings are conducted fairly, evidence is presented transparently, and the accused is given a meaningful opportunity to present their defense.

Moreover, the judiciary's role extends to determining guilt or innocence (Grimes, 2021; Grimmel, 2012; Grimmelikhuijsen & Klijn, 2015). Courts weigh the evidence, apply legal standards, and render verdicts that reflect the legal standards established by the government. This process ensures that individuals are held accountable only when guilt is established beyond a reasonable doubt—a standard that underscores the gravity of criminal convictions. The relationship between the judiciary and government in criminal justice and due process underscores the importance of checks and balances. While the government has a legitimate interest in prosecuting crimes and maintaining societal order, the judiciary serves as a critical check on potential abuses of power. The judiciary ensures that the government's actions adhere to the principles of due process and that individuals' rights are upheld throughout the criminal justice process. The concept of due process also extends to sentencing, where the government seeks appropriate penalties for criminal behavior (Brown, 1999; Buchmeyer, 2019; Bunjevac,

2015; Burbank, 2009). The judiciary's role in sentencing reflects a careful consideration of factors such as the severity of the crime, the defendant's criminal history, and potential mitigating circumstances. By imposing just and proportionate sentences, the judiciary balances the government's need to ensure public safety with the goal of rehabilitating offenders. The relationship between the judiciary and government in criminal justice and due process embodies a delicate equilibrium. The government's responsibility to uphold the law is tempered by the judiciary's duty to protect individual rights. This dynamic interplay ensures that criminal justice is administered fairly and justly, fostering public trust in both the legal system and the government.

In conclusion, criminal justice and due process underscore the profound responsibility of both the judiciary and government to uphold the rule of law while safeguarding individual rights. The judiciary's role in adjudicating criminal cases, ensuring due process, and balancing the government's authority with individual liberties reflects a commitment to justice that lies at the heart of a just and equitable society. The interplay between these elements demonstrates the judiciary's vital role in maintaining societal order while safeguarding the principles of justice and fairness. The fourth section will explore civil cases and dispute resolution.

2.4. CIVIL CASES AND DISPUTE RESOLUTION

Civil cases and the process of dispute resolution form a crucial aspect of the judiciary's role in providing a fair and equitable legal system (Smith & Farrales, 2010; Smith, 1992; Smith, 2015). These elements are intrinsic to the judiciary's function in upholding individual rights, maintaining societal harmony, and ensuring that conflicts are resolved through legal means rather than recourse to violence or personal retaliation. The complex interplay between the judiciary and government in civil cases exemplifies the delicate balance between justice, legal procedures, and societal cohesion. The civil justice system serves as a mechanism for individuals and organizations to seek redress for a wide range of conflicts and is designed to ensure that disputes are resolved in a just and impartial manner. To illustrate this, consider a specific case study involving a landlord-tenant dispute. In this scenario, the tenant claims that the landlord failed to fulfill their responsibilities, such as providing essential repairs and maintaining the premises in a habitable condition. The tenant files a civil case seeking compensation and other remedies. As the case progresses, the dispute resolution process, which is typically governed by established rules of civil procedure, comes into play. Both parties are afforded the opportunity to present their arguments, evidence, and witnesses in a court of law. During the litigation, the court ensures that strict rules of evidence and procedure are followed to safeguard the rights of both parties. The judge, acting as an impartial arbiter, carefully evaluates the evidence and legal arguments presented by both sides. In this case, the judge examines the lease agreement, inspects the property, and reviews expert reports to determine whether the landlord indeed breached their obligations.

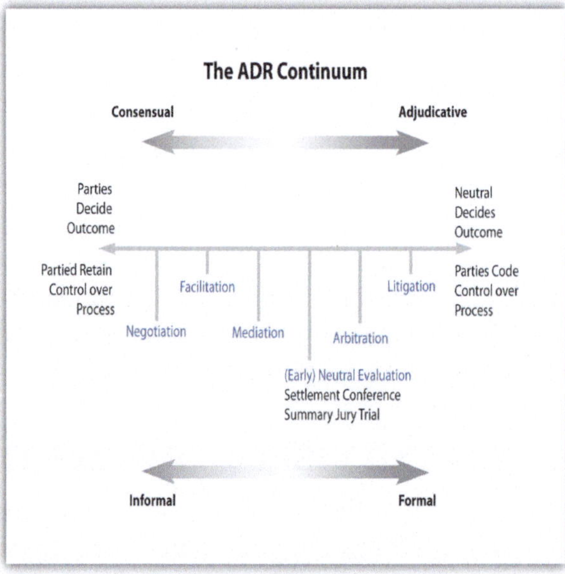

Figure 2.7. Continuum of alternative dispute resolution.

Source: Saylord. https://saylordotorg.github.io/text_the-legal-and-ethical-environment-of-business/s07–00-alternative-dispute-resolution.html

The court may also encourage alternative dispute resolution methods (see Figure 2.7), such as mediation or negotiation, to promote effective and amicable resolution before trial (Owusu-Mensah & Mathapoly-Codjoe, 2023; Parrillo, 2005). In this particular case, the judge suggests mediation to provide an opportunity for the landlord and tenant to reach a mutually beneficial agreement. By engaging in mediation, the parties have the chance to express their concerns, negotiate a settlement, and maintain control over the outcome. If mediation fails, the case proceeds to trial, where the judge's role as the finder of fact and law assumes even greater significance. The judge meticulously weighs the credibility of witnesses and the admissibility of evidence, ensuring that due process is adhered to throughout. Ultimately, the judge delivers a verdict, determining whether the landlord is liable for breaching their obligations and if so, the appropriate remedies and damages owed to the tenant. Moreover, the court's decision sets a precedent and shapes future legal outcomes in similar cases, thereby reinforcing the principles of fairness, equality, and access to justice. In conclusion, civil cases and the process of dispute resolution are essential elements of the judiciary's mandate to uphold a fair and equitable legal system. Through careful consideration of evidence, adherence to procedural rules, and thoughtful judgment, the judiciary plays a vital role in ensuring justice is served in civil matters.

Civil cases encompass a broad spectrum of disputes that arise between individuals, organizations, or entities. These conflicts may involve matters such as contractual disputes, property rights, family matters, and personal injuries. While criminal cases are initiated by the government in response to alleged violations of the law, civil cases are typically initiated by private individuals seeking redress for perceived wrongs.

Central to civil cases is the process of dispute resolution, which provides a structured framework for parties to present their grievances and seek resolution through legal means (A. Singh, 2022; Singh, 2015; U. K. Singh, 2022; Skinner-Thompson, 2015). The judiciary serves as the impartial arbiter in this process, ensuring that disputes are resolved according to established legal principles rather than emotional impulses or personal biases. This formalized approach to dispute resolution prevents the escalation of conflicts and fosters confidence in the legal system. While dispute resolution is undoubtedly crucial in promoting a fair and equitable legal system, it is not without its flaws and limitations. Take, for example, a specific case study involving a commercial contract dispute between two businesses. Both parties claim that the other breached the terms of the contract, leading to financial losses. The dispute resolution process begins with the filing of a civil case, after which the court follows established procedures to assess the evidence and arguments presented by each side. However, it is important to acknowledge that the process can be time-consuming, expensive, and emotionally draining for the parties involved. In this particular case, the dispute has already impacted the businesses' operations, leading to loss of profits and strained relationships. Furthermore, the adversarial nature of the court proceedings may exacerbate the tensions between the parties, hindering the possibilities of reaching an amicable resolution. It is worth considering alternative methods of dispute resolution, such as arbitration or mediation, which can provide more flexibility and confidentiality. These methods allow the parties to have a greater say in the process and potentially achieve a mutually satisfactory outcome. In the case at hand, the court could explore the possibility of referring the matter to mediation, where a neutral third party assists the parties in reaching an agreement. Mediation can open up channels of communication, foster understanding, and explore creative solutions that may not be available through traditional litigation. However, it must be acknowledged that not all disputes are suitable for alternative methods of resolution. In certain complex cases involving significant legal issues or power imbalances, the formal court process may be necessary to ensure the enforcement of rights and the application of established legal principles. Therefore, while the process of dispute resolution presents opportunities for parties to seek resolution, it is important to continuously assess and refine the system to address its shortcomings and provide a fair, efficient, and accessible avenue for justice. By promoting a more diverse range of dispute resolution options and streamlining court procedures, the legal system can strive towards achieving a better balance between the principles of justice and the practical realities faced by individuals and organizations seeking resolution in civil cases.

The government's role in civil cases is to establish the legal framework within which these disputes are resolved (Gallagher, 2012; Gardbaum, 2015; Garoupa et al., 2012). This includes enacting laws that outline the rights and obligations of individuals and organizations, as well as setting out the procedures for pursuing legal action. The government's responsibility is to ensure that the legal system provides a fair and accessible avenue for individuals to seek resolution for their disputes. The government's role in civil cases is undeniably crucial, as it sets the legal framework within which these disputes are resolved. However, the extent of the government's involvement and the effectiveness of its role can be a subject of debate and critique. To explore this further, let us examine a specific case study involving a civil case concerning product liability. In this scenario, a consumer alleges that a faulty product caused injuries and seeks compensation from the manufacturer. One aspect of the government's role is the establishment and enforcement of robust regulations and standards to ensure the safety and quality of products. By setting comprehensive rules and standards, the government can proactively protect consumers from defective or dangerous products. This includes conducting thorough inspections, issuing certifications, and implementing stringent testing procedures. However, critics argue that the government's oversight may fall short due to limited resources, bureaucratic inefficiencies, or potential conflicts of interest. In some cases, government agencies responsible for regulating products may not have adequate manpower or expertise to thoroughly assess all products entering the market.

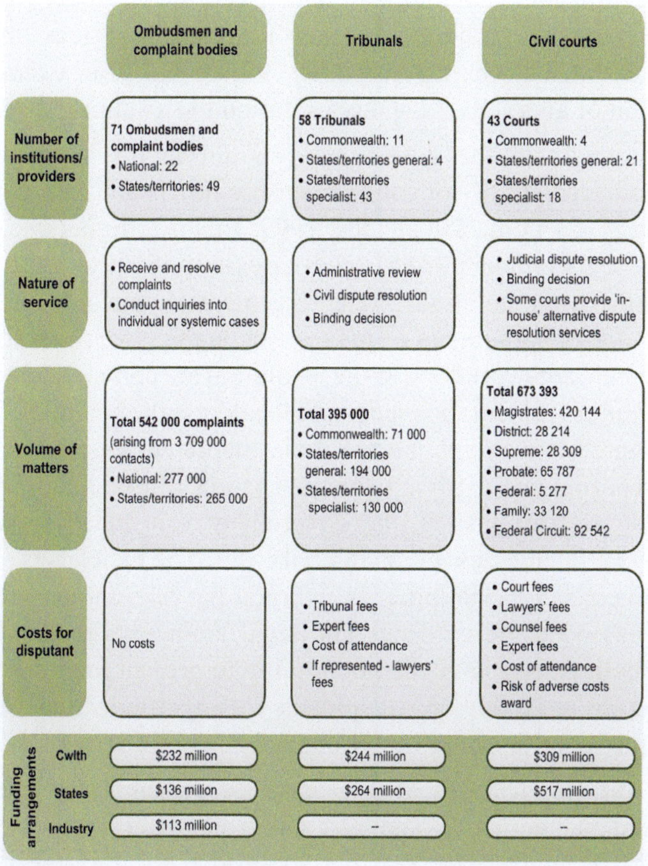

Figure 2.8. Rationalization of alternative dispute resolution in Australia.

Source: Noone, M., & Ojelabi, L. (2020). Alternative dispute resolution and access to justice in Australia. International Journal of Law in Context, 16(2), 108–127. doi:10.1017/S1744552320000099

Moreover, regulatory capture, where regulatory agencies become influenced by the industries they are meant to oversee, is a concern that could compromise the government's role in safeguarding consumer interests. Another aspect of the government's role in civil cases is the establishment of courts and the appointment of judges who uphold the rule of law. Courts are responsible for interpreting and applying laws, ensuring due process, and providing judicial review. Judges play a vital role in civil cases by impartially evaluating the facts, applying relevant laws, and rendering fair decisions. However, the availability of courts and the time taken to resolve a civil case can be a point of contention. Backlogs and delays in court proceedings can cause significant frustration and hinder access to justice. Additionally, the cost of litigation, including attorney fees and court fees, may pose a barrier to individuals seeking resolution. Figure 2.8 is an example of the rationalization of alternative dispute resolution in Australia.

Critics argue that the government should invest in increasing the efficiency and accessibility of courts to ensure timely and affordable justice for all (Iaryczower et al., 2002; Ides, 1999; Imam & Egbewole, 2020). In conclusion, the government's role in civil cases is multifaceted, encompassing the establishment of regulations, the enforcement of standards, the provision of courts, and the appointment of judges. While the government's efforts in creating a legal framework for dispute resolution are commendable, ongoing scrutiny and improvements are necessary to address the potential limitations, such as resource constraints, bureaucratic inefficiencies, and accessibility issues. By continuously striving for transparency, accountability, and the fair administration of justice, the government can enhance its role and ensure a more equitable resolution of civil cases. The judiciary's role in civil cases is to oversee the legal process, interpret the relevant laws, and render judgments based on the evidence and legal arguments presented. Courts ensure that both parties have the opportunity to present their cases and that legal procedures are followed. The judiciary's impartiality and adherence to legal principles contribute to the legitimacy of the dispute resolution process.

One of the key features of civil cases is the emphasis on achieving remedies that are equitable and just (Reid et al., 2020; Ritleng, 2016; Rivera, 2022; Robinson, 2018). Courts consider not only the legal rights of the parties involved but also the broader principles of fairness and restitution. This ensures that the outcomes of civil cases promote justice and that parties are provided with appropriate remedies that address their grievances. The relationship between the judiciary and government in civil cases is characterized by the government's responsibility to establish the legal framework within which disputes are resolved and the judiciary's role in interpreting and applying that framework. While the government creates the laws that govern civil matters, the judiciary ensures that these laws are consistently and fairly applied, contributing to the predictability and stability of the legal system. The significance of civil cases and dispute resolution extends beyond the individuals directly involved. By providing a legal mechanism for addressing conflicts, the legal system contributes to societal order, economic stability, and the prevention of private vengeance. Civil cases underscore the judiciary's pivotal role in maintaining the rule of law and providing a forum where disputes can be resolved peacefully and justly.

In conclusion, civil cases and the process of dispute resolution exemplify the judiciary's role in upholding individual rights, maintaining social order, and providing a fair and equitable legal system. The interplay between the judiciary and government in civil cases highlights their distinct yet complementary roles in ensuring that conflicts are resolved through legal means. Through this process, the judiciary contributes to a just and harmonious society by providing a structured framework for addressing disputes and upholding the principles of justice and fairness. The final section of this chapter highlights the role of the judiciary in safeguarding individual rights.

2.5. JUDICIARY'S ROLE IN SAFEGUARDING INDIVIDUAL RIGHTS

The judiciary's role in safeguarding individual rights constitutes a fundamental pillar of its function within a just and democratic society (Chan, 2011; Chavez, 2003, 2007; Chen & Li, 2016; Chutkow, 2008). This essential role serves as a counterbalance to the government's authority and ensures that the rights and liberties enshrined in the constitution are upheld and protected. The intricate interplay between the judiciary and government in this context reflects a delicate equilibrium between governmental power and individual freedoms. Central to the judiciary's role in safeguarding individual rights is the concept of judicial review. This power empowers courts to assess the constitutionality of laws, executive actions, and government decisions. By scrutinizing the actions of the government against constitutional norms, the judiciary serves as a check on potential abuses of governmental authority. This role not only reinforces the separation of powers but also ensures that the government respects and upholds the rights of citizens. Figure 2.9 is an example of the judiciary protecting individual rights in India as a case in point.

The relationship between the judiciary and government in safeguarding individual rights is one of mutual accountability (Moliterno & Curos, 2021; Molto, 2015; Munday, 2008). While the government has the authority to enact laws and policies, the judiciary ensures that these laws do not infringe upon constitutionally protected rights. Through the principle of judicial review, the judiciary ensures that the government operates within the confines of the constitution and does not infringe upon citizens' fundamental freedoms. Moreover, the judiciary's role extends to the protection of individual rights during legal proceedings. The principle of due process ensures that individuals accused of crimes are provided with fair and equitable treatment. The judiciary oversees the legal process to ensure that the rights of the accused are upheld, from the right to legal representation to the right to a fair trial. This function safeguards individuals against potential abuses of power by law enforcement and the government.

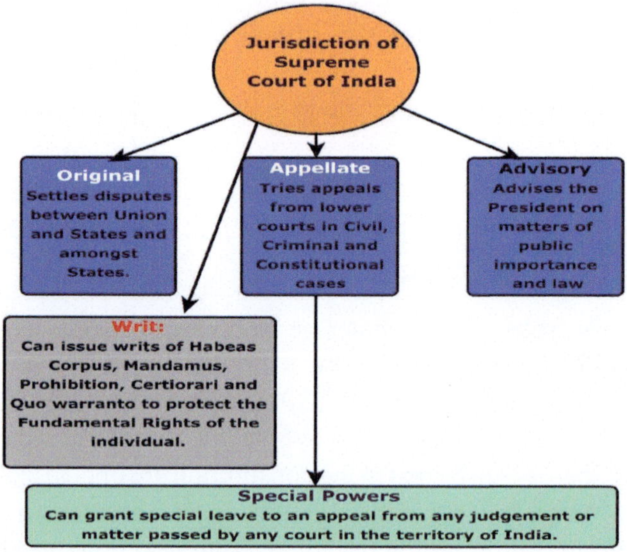

Figure 2.9. The judiciary protecting individual rights in India.

Source: Prepladder. https://www.prepladder.com/upsc-study-material/polity-and-constitution/everything-you-need-to-know-about-the-indian-judiciary-ncert-notes-upsc

The judiciary's role in safeguarding individual rights also involves addressing broader societal issues that may impact these rights (Tridimas & Gari, 2010; Trochev, 2004; Tunamsifu, 2022). Courts have played a pivotal role in landmark cases that have advanced civil rights, such as those related to racial segregation, gender equality, and LGBTQ+ rights. Through these cases, the judiciary interprets the constitution in a manner that aligns with evolving societal values, thereby safeguarding the rights of historically marginalized groups. The judiciary's role in safeguarding individual rights is indeed crucial, and it often involves addressing broader societal issues that may impact these rights. The judiciary serves as a guardian of the rule of law and plays a vital role in interpreting and applying the constitution to ensure the protection of fundamental rights and freedoms. To illustrate this point, consider a specific case study involving a controversial law that infringes upon individual privacy rights. In such a case, the judiciary must carefully examine the constitutionality of the law and determine whether it violates the rights enshrined in the constitution. This process requires the judiciary to not only analyze the specific provisions of the law but also consider the wider implications and potential consequences on individual liberties. The judges must delve into the nuances of the issue at hand, evaluate precedents, and consider legal arguments from both sides. Furthermore, the judiciary must take into account societal norms, values, and evolving understandings of rights when rendering a decision. This can lead to intense debates and critiques from various stakeholders, including legal experts, civil society organizations, and the general public.

Critics might argue that the judiciary has a responsibility to actively engage in shaping societal values and guaranteeing equal protection and representation for all individuals. They may contend that a passive approach by the judiciary, strictly adhering to legal technicalities, can perpetuate systemic injustices. On the other hand, proponents might advocate for a more restrained role for the judiciary, arguing that it should defer to the legislative or executive branches when it comes to addressing broader societal issues. They may posit that the judiciary's primary responsibility is to interpret and apply existing laws rather than create new ones or impose their own policy preferences. Balancing these competing arguments requires the judiciary to exercise wisdom, impartiality, and adherence to legal principles. The judiciary's decisions in cases that involve broader societal issues can have far-reaching implications, setting legal precedents, and influencing societal attitudes and behavior. By striking a delicate balance between respecting individual rights and considering societal concerns, the judiciary can play a pivotal role in upholding the rule of law and safeguarding individual liberties.

In democratic societies, the judiciary's role in safeguarding individual rights resonates deeply (Pohjankoski, 2016; Pooe, 2017; Popova & Post, 2018). Individual rights are a cornerstone of democratic governance, and the judiciary's commitment to upholding these rights ensures that the government operates in a manner that respects the dignity and autonomy of each citizen. This commitment promotes societal trust, as citizens can be assured that their rights are protected even in the face of potential governmental encroachments. Figure 2.10 highlights the conceptualization and elevation of rights from human rights to legal rights.

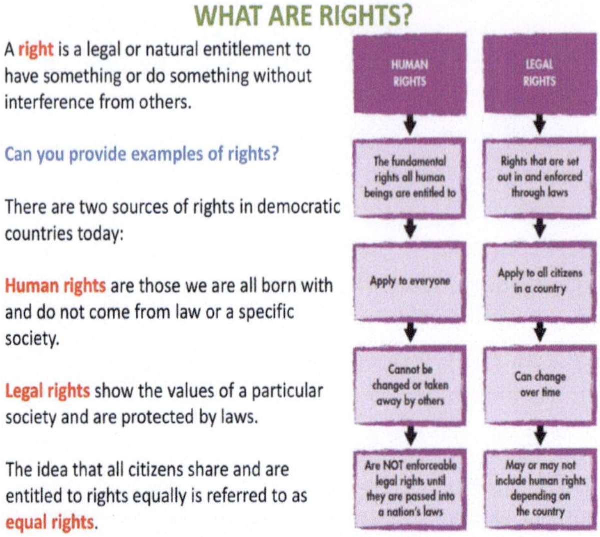

Figure 2.10. The conceptualization and elevation of rights.

Source: Janice McLaughlin. https://slideplayer.com/slide/14266750/

The judiciary's role in safeguarding individual rights also extends to international law and human rights treaties (Hasbrouck, 2022; He, 2017; He, 2018; Heinz & Manikas, 1992). As part of the global community, governments are bound by international agreements that protect individual rights. The judiciary's role includes interpreting these international agreements and ensuring that domestic laws and actions align with these commitments. This expansion of the judiciary's purview raises important debates and challenges regarding the relationship between domestic and international law, as well as the scope of judicial authority. An illustrative case study that demonstrates the intersection of domestic and international law is the legal battle surrounding the rights of asylum seekers and refugees. When individuals seek protection in a foreign country, they often rely on international human rights treaties to argue for their right to asylum and non-refoulement. The judiciary is tasked with interpreting and applying these treaties alongside domestic laws, ensuring that individuals' fundamental rights are respected. However, critics argue that this expansion of judicial authority towards international law encroaches upon the prerogatives of the legislative and executive branches. They contend that international human rights treaties should be treated as aspirational rather than binding in domestic legal systems. The debate also centers on questions of sovereignty and national interests, with critics claiming that judges should prioritize the interests of their own country rather than international obligations. On the other hand, proponents argue that the judiciary has a responsibility to protect fundamental rights universally, regardless of geographic boundaries. They contend that international human rights treaties derive legal force in domestic courts and that judges play a vital role in upholding these standards. Striking a balance between safeguarding individual rights and respecting the principle of democratic self-governance presents a nuanced challenge for the judiciary. Additionally, practical considerations such as the enforceability of international judgments and the potential for conflicting legal obligations further complicate the issue. While the judiciary's role in international human rights protection is vital in upholding universal principles, ongoing debates persist regarding the appropriate level of judicial engagement with international law, signaling the need for nuanced discussions and thoughtful balance in the application of both domestic and international legal frameworks.

In conclusion, the judiciary's role in safeguarding individual rights is a cornerstone of its function within a just and democratic society. Through the power of judicial review, the protection of due process, and the interpretation of constitutional and international norms, the judiciary serves as a guardian of citizens' fundamental freedoms. The relationship between the judiciary and government in this context exemplifies a balance between governmental authority and individual liberties, promoting a society where rights are upheld and justice is preserved.

CHAPTER 2 SUMMARY

The second chapter, "The Role and Function of the Judiciary," unfurls the intricate tapestry of the judiciary's multifaceted responsibilities within the legal system. Through the exploration of key aspects such as judicial review, jurisdiction and decision-making, criminal justice and due process, civil cases and dispute resolution, and the safeguarding of individual rights, this chapter delves into the intricate interplay between the judiciary and government in upholding justice, maintaining order, and safeguarding rights.

The principle of judicial review, elucidated in Section 2.1, highlights the judiciary's pivotal role as the guardian of the constitution. This authority empowers the judiciary to assess the constitutionality of laws and governmental actions, serving as a vital check against potential overreach. The relationship between the judiciary and government is one of accountability, where the judiciary ensures that government actions remain aligned with constitutional principles, fostering a dynamic equilibrium that upholds the rule of law.

In Section 2.2, the exploration of jurisdiction and the decision-making process reveals the judiciary's capacity to adjudicate disputes within defined legal boundaries. This realm underscores the judiciary's distinct role in overseeing legal proceedings, interpreting laws, and rendering judgments. The relationship between the judiciary and government here is characterized by the government's responsibility to establish legal frameworks and procedures, while the judiciary ensures the impartial administration of justice within these bounds.

The significance of criminal justice and due process, examined in Section 2.3, highlights the judiciary's role in ensuring that accused individuals are treated fairly and justly. The interplay between the judiciary and government in this sphere exemplifies the equilibrium between the government's role in prosecuting crimes and the judiciary's responsibility to uphold individual rights. By maintaining rigorous standards of due process, the judiciary acts as a safeguard against potential abuses of governmental authority.

Section 2.4 delves into civil cases and dispute resolution, unraveling the judicial process that resolves conflicts among individuals and entities. The judiciary's impartiality and adherence to legal principles in this context reflect the intricate relationship between the judiciary and government. While the government enacts laws and establishes the legal framework, the judiciary ensures that disputes are resolved fairly and justly within these legal boundaries.

Lastly, the exploration of the judiciary's role in safeguarding individual rights in Section 2.5 underscores its commitment to upholding constitutional principles and protecting citizens' fundamental freedoms. The relationship between the judiciary and government in this aspect epitomizes a balance between governmental authority and the preservation of individual liberties, fostering a society where the rights of each citizen are upheld.

Collectively, these sections illuminate the nuanced dynamics between the judiciary and government as they collaborate, yet maintain distinct roles, in upholding justice, resolving disputes, and safeguarding rights. The chapter's insights underscore the judiciary's pivotal role in maintaining societal order, ensuring fairness, and protecting the rights of individuals, all of which contribute to the foundations of a just and harmonious society. As the pages of this chapter close, they leave us with a profound appreciation for the intricate interplay between these essential institutions within the framework of governance and justice. In the third chapter, we will delve into the relationships between judicial independence and accountability.

CHAPTER 3

Judicial Independence and Accountability

Contents

3.1. Ensuring Judicial Independence 75
3.2. Mechanisms of Judicial Accountability 80
3.3. Challenges to Judicial Independence 87
3.4. The Ethics of Judicial Conduct 91
3.5. Balancing Independence and Public Interest 97
Chapter 3 Summary 102

Within the realm of governance and justice, the third chapter unveils the intricate interplay between two pivotal concepts: judicial independence and accountability. This chapter, titled "Judicial Independence and Accountability," delves into the delicate equilibrium that underpins the judiciary's autonomy and the mechanisms that ensure its responsible exercise of power. As we embark on this exploration, we navigate through the multifaceted dimensions that encompass ensuring judicial independence, mechanisms of judicial accountability, challenges that threaten judicial autonomy, the ethics governing judicial conduct, and the nuanced balancing act between judicial independence and the public interest.

In Section 3.1, "Ensuring Judicial Independence," we delve into the foundational concept that underpins the judiciary's role—the necessity of an independent judiciary. Judicial independence shields courts from external pressures, allowing judges to make impartial decisions based solely on the law and evidence. This section illuminates the significance of safeguarding the judiciary from undue influence, both political and otherwise, ensuring its capability to uphold the principles of justice without fear of retribution.

Section 3.2, "Mechanisms of Judicial Accountability," shifts the focus to the other side of the judicial coin—accountability. While judicial independence is vital, mechanisms to ensure accountability serve as checks against potential misuse of power. This section unveils the measures in place to hold judges accountable for their decisions and actions, striking a balance that prevents impunity while respecting the judiciary's autonomy.

In Section 3.3, "Challenges to Judicial Independence," the exploration extends to the various challenges that threaten the independence of the judiciary. From political pressures to external influences, this section delves into the complexities that courts may encounter in maintaining their impartiality and autonomy.

Section 3.4 delves into "The Ethics of Judicial Conduct." Here, the focus narrows to the ethical principles that guide judges' behavior, both inside and outside the courtroom. The judiciary's ethical standards not only dictate how judges conduct themselves but also contribute to maintaining public trust in the judicial system.

Finally, Section 3.5, "Balancing Independence and Public Interest," illuminates the delicate tightrope that the judiciary walks—ensuring its independence while considering the broader societal interests. This section dissects the nuanced interactions between the judiciary and government, where striking the right balance is paramount to upholding justice and maintaining public confidence. As the pages of this chapter turn, they unveil the intricate interplay between the autonomy of the judiciary and its accountability to the public. This exploration traverses the fine line that the judiciary treads—remaining free from undue influence while being answerable for its actions. Each section peels back layers, revealing the intricate mechanisms and challenges that shape the delicate balance between judicial independence and accountability. The chapter's insights echo the essence of a fair and just society, where an independent judiciary serves as a bulwark against oppression while being answerable to the people it serves. Let us begin this chapter by exploring the ways in which judicial independence can be guaranteed.

3.1. ENSURING JUDICIAL INDEPENDENCE

Ensuring judicial independence is a foundational principle in democratic societies, established to insulate the judiciary from external influences and uphold the impartiality necessary for equitable justice (Kundmueller, 2022; Kwoka, 2017; Lachmayer, 2016; Law, 2009). Yet, this safeguarding of autonomy is not without its complexities, sparking nuanced debates on how to maintain this separation while also ensuring accountability and transparency. The case study of the Indian Supreme Court's handling of the Kesavananda Bharati v. State of Kerala (1973) case provides a vivid illustration of these intricate dynamics. In this landmark case, the court grappled with the doctrine of basic structure, determining whether the government could amend the constitution to the detriment of its core foundations. The preservation of judicial independence is crucial because without it, the very essence of democracy can be compromised. By allowing external pressures to infiltrate the judicial system, we risk diminishing the integrity and fairness of decisions rendered. To illustrate the significance of this principle, let us consider a specific case study involving a nation facing political turmoil. In Country X, a controversial leader has attempted to exert influence over the judiciary in order to sway outcomes in favor of their agenda. Through subtle yet pervasive means, such as making political appointments, pressuring judges, or undermining their authority, the leader aims to manipulate the judicial process to consolidate their power.

This case study underscores the dangers of compromising judicial independence (Grove, 2018; Gunderson, 2022; Hardaway, 2021; Hardman, 2020). When the judiciary becomes subject to external influences, citizens lose faith in the system, and public trust erodes. The impartiality and objectivity that should underpin judicial decisions are replaced with biases, favoritism, and the erosion of fundamental rights. This not only creates a sense of injustice and inequality, but it also weakens the very foundation of democratic governance. Furthermore, the case study highlights the importance of maintaining a balance of power among the various branches of government. Judicial independence acts as a check on the executive and legislative branches, preventing the concentration of power in any one entity. By ensuring the judiciary remains separate and autonomous, democratic societies can avoid the abuse of power and the erosion of civil liberties. However, it is important to acknowledge that the concept of judicial independence is not absolute and can be subject to debates and critiques. Some argue that judicial independence may result in an unaccountable judiciary, detached from the will of the people. They contend that judges, shielded from external pressures, may make decisions that are out of touch with societal values and preferences.

Figure 3.1. Principles of the rule of law.

Source: Rule of Law Center https://www.ruleoflaw.org.au/principles/equality-before-the-law/

Nevertheless, it is essential to exercise caution while addressing these criticisms so as not to undermine the core principles of judicial independence (Beiser-McGrath et al., 2022; Bell, 2002; Bencze, 2021). Constructive critique should focus on ensuring transparency, accountability, and proper channels for redress, rather than attempting to exert undue influence on the judiciary. Overall, the establishment and protection of judicial independence is vital in democratic societies. This principle upholds the impartiality necessary for equitable justice and helps preserve the integrity of the judicial system. Through a detailed and specific case study, we have seen how even subtle external influences can undermine this principle, leading to a loss of public trust and the erosion of fundamental rights. While debates and critiques are essential, they should focus on strengthening transparency and accountability rather than compromising the independence of the judiciary. Figure 3.1 summarizes the principles of the rule of law which judicial independence ensures.

Critics of unchecked judicial independence argue that mechanisms of accountability are essential to prevent judicial overreach and ensure alignment with evolving societal values (Takayasu, 2023; Tate, 1994; Tauber & Banks, 2017). They contend that an insulated judiciary could result in decisions that are out of touch with public sentiment and resistant to change. This perspective finds resonance in Kesavananda Bharati, where the Supreme Court's assertion of the basic structure doctrine was met with both acclaim and critique. Critics raised concerns about the court's authority to define the boundaries of constitutional amendments, citing the potential for an unchecked judiciary to stifle legislative intent and undermine democratic governance. While the principle of judicial independence is crucial for upholding impartiality and the rule of law, it is important to acknowledge the concerns raised by those who advocate for greater accountability within the judiciary. To delve into this debate, let us consider a specific case study involving a high-profile court decision that sparked controversy within a nation. In Country Y, a Supreme Court ruling upheld a law that was widely criticized as discriminatory by a significant portion of the population. Many argued that the court's decision went against the principles of equality and human rights, and that it reflected outdated societal values instead of aligning with evolving norms.

This case study highlights the need for mechanisms of accountability within the judiciary. Critics of judicial independence argue that without sufficient avenues to challenge and review court decisions, there is a risk that the judiciary could act as a self-contained entity, isolated from the broader society it is meant to serve (Althouse, 2001; Appleby et al., 2019; Appleby & Olijnyk, 2020). They contend that judges, shielded by their independence, may make decisions that are out of touch with the changing values and expectations of society, leading to a potential democratic deficit. In response to these concerns, proponents of accountability within the judiciary argue for the establishment of effective mechanisms for oversight and review. They advocate for structures that allow for the reconsideration of court decisions and provide opportunities for public input and dialogue. This, they argue, would ensure that the judiciary remains responsive to societal needs and values, while also upholding its essential role in safeguarding the rule of law. However, it is crucial to strike a balance while addressing these arguments. Excessive interference or politicization of the judiciary can undermine its independence and compromise the very principles it is meant to protect. Accountability mechanisms should be carefully designed to maintain the integrity and independence of the judiciary, without unduly compromising its role as a separate and impartial branch of government.

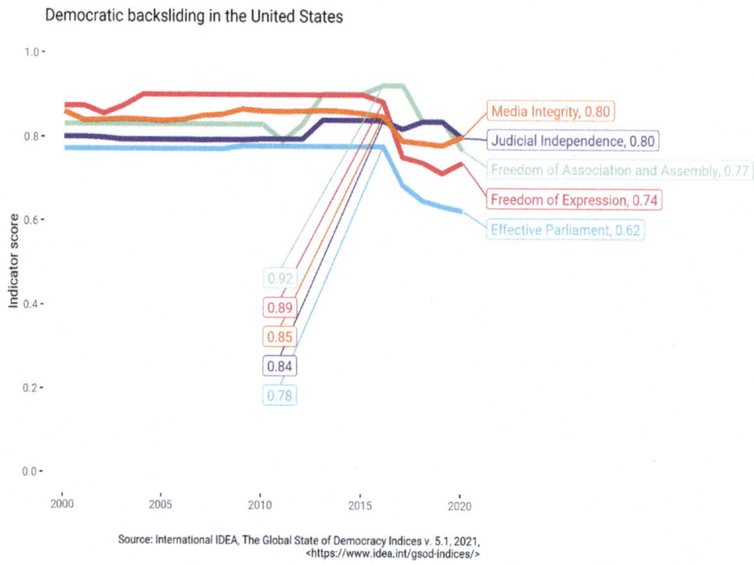

Figure 3.2. Statistical demonstration of democratic backsliding in the USA.

Source: IDEA https://www.idea.int/blog/explainer-democratic-backsliding

Additionally, it is important to recognize that judicial accountability already exists to some extent through mechanisms like judicial reviews, appeals, and codes of conduct (Primus, 2004; Prince, 2020; Provost, 2008; Pulle & Ratnapala, 2019). The challenge lies in further refining and strengthening these mechanisms to provide genuine avenues for remedying judicial errors or ensuring alignment with evolving societal values. While critics argue for mechanisms of accountability to prevent judicial overreach and promote alignment with evolving societal values, the principle of judicial independence remains vital for upholding the rule of law and ensuring impartiality. As demonstrated by the case study, debates surrounding accountability should focus on developing effective oversight and review mechanisms that strike a balance between accountability and independence, without undermining the fundamental principles of justice. As Figure 3.2 shows, even the stalwarts of democracy such as the USA can experience backsliding on this front.

Yet, proponents of judicial independence emphasize the necessity of shielding the judiciary from political and popular pressures to preserve its integrity (Colucci, 2000; Conrad, 2014; Costas-Perez et al., 2012; Cross, 1999). The Kesavananda Bharati case exemplifies this viewpoint as well. The Indian Supreme Court's assertion of the basic structure doctrine was widely seen as a moment of judicial courage, preventing potential constitutional erosion. Supporters argue that without judicial independence, governments could wield unchecked power and undermine the separation of powers essential for upholding democratic principles. Proponents of judicial independence argue that without a robust and independent judiciary, the impartiality and fairness of the justice system can be compromised, leading to an erosion of public trust and a potential breakdown of democratic principles. To illustrate this point, let us examine a specific case study involving a highly contentious political issue in Country Z.

In Country Z, there was a polarizing debate surrounding a controversial government policy related to civil liberties. The government moved forward with implementing the policy, which led to widespread public protests and demonstrations, with citizens arguing that it infringed upon their fundamental rights. As the matter was taken to court, the judiciary faced intense scrutiny and pressure from both sides of the debate. In this case study, proponents of judicial independence would argue that it is precisely in moments like these that an independent judiciary becomes vital (Janover, 2021; Johnson, 2019; Jonski, 2021; Jorritsma, 2020). By shielding the judiciary from political and popular pressures, judges can focus on interpreting the law and applying it impartially, without being swayed by outside influences. This cultivates public confidence in the judicial system and ensures that justice is administered fairly. However, critics of judicial independence present a different perspective. They believe that the judiciary should be more receptive to public sentiment and reflect the will of the people. They argue that a judiciary that is entirely insulated from political and popular influence runs the risk of becoming disconnected from the realities and needs of the society it serves. They contend that judges should be more responsive to the changing values and expectations of the people, especially in cases regarding highly debated and morally significant issues. While this debate revolves around the tension between independence and accountability, it is essential to strike the right balance. The judiciary cannot be completely divorced from the social and political fabric of a nation, as it is meant to serve the people's interests. At the same time, excessive pressure or interference can undermine the impartiality and integrity of the judiciary.

Overall, the proponents of judicial independence stress the importance of safeguarding the judiciary from political and popular pressures, highlighting the necessity of an independent judiciary to maintain the integrity of the justice system (Gonzalez, 2021; Gorodovenko et al., 2021; Gouldin, 2012). However, critics argue for a judiciary that is more responsive to societal sentiments and values. Striking the right balance between independence and accountability is crucial to ensure that the judiciary remains impartial, upholds the rule of law, and enjoys the trust and confidence of the public it serves. This debate between safeguarding judicial independence and ensuring accountability reflects the delicate equilibrium necessary for a just society. The complexities are further highlighted by the need to balance individual rights with collective interests. In the Kesavananda Bharati case, the Indian judiciary demonstrated its commitment to safeguarding the constitution's foundational values, illustrating that an independent judiciary can protect the rights of minorities even when faced with political pressures.

In conclusion, ensuring judicial independence remains a complex endeavor, echoing the broader debates about the role of the judiciary in democratic governance. The case study of the Kesavananda Bharati case underscores the multifaceted nature of this discourse. Critics call for mechanisms of accountability to prevent judicial overreach, while proponents stress the importance of an autonomous judiciary in upholding democratic values. As societies navigate this delicate balance, they must contemplate how to preserve the integrity of the judiciary while addressing concerns about accountability and the evolving needs of their citizens. The second section of this chapter considers possible mechanisms for ensuring judicial accountability.

3.2. MECHANISMS OF JUDICIAL ACCOUNTABILITY

Mechanisms of judicial accountability represent a crucial aspect of maintaining a just and equitable legal system while addressing potential abuses of power within the judiciary (Medawatte et al., 2013; Meggitt & Somji, 2016; Melone, 1996). These mechanisms act as checks and balances, ensuring that judges adhere to ethical standards, uphold the law, and make decisions free from bias and undue influence. The interplay between the judiciary and the government in establishing and enforcing these mechanisms reflects a delicate equilibrium between preserving judicial independence and preventing misconduct or negligence. The concept of judicial accountability seeks to strike a balance between the independence of the judiciary and the need for transparency and checks on power. While judicial independence is essential for impartial decision-making and upholding the rule of law, accountability mechanisms serve as safeguards against potential misconduct or biases.

One specific case study that sheds light on the importance of judicial accountability involves a nation grappling with allegations of corruption within its judiciary. In Country A, a high-profile corruption scandal rocked the legal system, implicating several judges in accepting bribes and engaging in misconduct. The revelations caused public outrage and raised questions about the efficacy of existing accountability measures. Proponents of judicial accountability argue that such cases underline the necessity of comprehensive mechanisms to ensure judicial integrity (Janover, 2021; Johnson, 2019; Jonski, 2021; Jorritsma, 2020). These mechanisms can include robust codes of conduct, ethical oversight bodies, and impartial investigative agencies. By holding judges accountable for their actions and preventing abuses of power, the public's confidence in the judiciary can be restored. On the other hand, critics of judicial accountability caution against potential dangers that excessive oversight may pose to the independence of the judiciary. They argue that accountability measures should be carefully designed to avoid any undue interference that could compromise judges' decision-making or create a chilling effect on judicial independence. There is concern that an overly punitive or politically motivated accountability system may deter judges from making courageous and impartial decisions.

To strike the right balance, it is essential to devise accountability mechanisms that are fair, transparent, and impartial (Keohane et al., 2000; Killebrew, 2007; Kingsford, 2022). This includes ensuring that investigative bodies and oversight institutions operate independently from undue political influences and have clear mandates for their actions. By providing avenues for complaints, transparency in disciplinary proceedings, and fair processes for addressing alleged misconduct, judicial accountability can strengthen public trust in the legal system. Overall, mechanisms of judicial accountability play a crucial role in maintaining a just and equitable legal system. Through a detailed case study highlighting corruption allegations in the judiciary, we see the significance of accountability measures in addressing potential abuses of power. Striking the right balance between judicial independence and accountability is essential, as excessive oversight may undermine the impartiality of judges, while insufficient mechanisms can erode public trust. By ensuring fair and transparent accountability processes, the legal system can uphold integrity, fairness, and the rule of law. This holds true at both country and regional levels (see Figure 3.3).

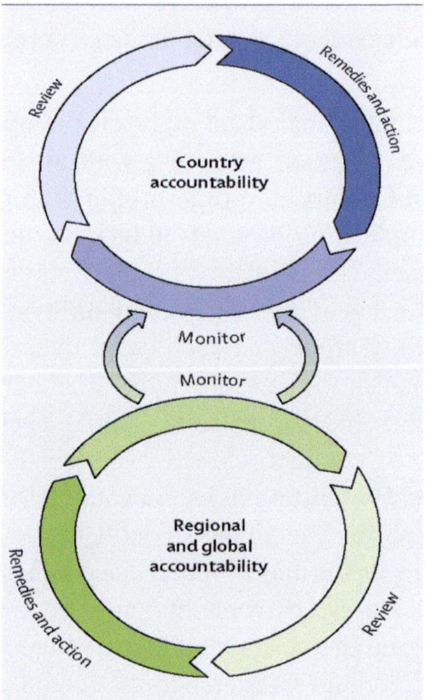

Figure 3.3. The intersection of country and regional accountabilities.

Source: Yamin, A. E., & Mason, E. (2019). Why accountability matters for universal health coverage and meeting the SDGs. *The Lancet*, *393*(10176), 1082–1084.

At the heart of mechanisms of judicial accountability lies the principle that while an independent judiciary is essential for upholding justice, it should not operate in isolation from oversight (McCandless, 2017; McCann et al., 2023; McCarthy & Un, 2017). Governments play a pivotal role in creating and implementing these mechanisms, striking a balance between maintaining judicial autonomy and holding judges accountable for their actions. The question of striking the right balance between judicial independence and accountability is an ongoing debate in democratic societies. One case study that serves as an example of this delicate balance is the Watergate scandal in the United States. During the Watergate scandal in the 1970s, the judiciary played a critical role in investigating and holding the executive branch accountable. The independent judiciary served as a check on the abuse of power, ensuring that justice was upheld and those responsible were held accountable. The case study highlights the benefits of a judiciary that operates independently and can impartially handle high-stake political matters, safeguarding democratic principles and the rule of law.

Nevertheless, it is important to note that even cases like Watergate demonstrate the need for oversight within the judicial system (Gonzalez, 2021; Gorodovenko et al., 2021; Gouldin, 2012). The judiciary should not be exempt from mechanisms of accountability that are intended to maintain the integrity of the legal system. Critics argue that an unchecked judiciary could potentially misuse its powers or fail to address instances of judicial misconduct. This highlights the need for transparent processes, including clear codes of conduct, impartial investigations, and disciplinary measures when necessary. Proponents of judicial independence contend that excessive oversight could erode the impartiality and effectiveness of the judiciary. They argue that accountability measures should be carefully balanced to ensure that they do not unduly compromise the independence and decision-making abilities of judges. Rather than creating a system that inhibits judges from making difficult decisions, the accountability mechanisms should focus on transparency, fairness, and due process. The case study of the Watergate scandal demonstrates the importance of maintaining a delicate balance between judicial independence and accountability. The case highlights the significant role an independent judiciary plays in upholding justice and ensuring accountability in cases of abuse of power. However, the study also underscores the need for oversight mechanisms to prevent potential misconduct within the judiciary. Striking this balance is crucial for a democratic society, where an independent judiciary can operate with integrity and be subject to transparent accountability measures to maintain public trust in the legal system.

One of the primary mechanisms is the process of judicial conduct and ethics review (Cleveland & Dodge, 2015; Clopton, 2018; Coan, 2012; Codrington, 2021). Independent bodies or commissions, often established by the government, are responsible for investigating complaints against judges. These bodies assess allegations of misconduct, bias, or breaches of ethical standards. One real-world example of the process of judicial conduct and ethics review is the case of former United States Supreme Court Justice, Brett Kavanaugh. During his confirmation process in 2018, several allegations of misconduct and inappropriate behavior were raised against him. These allegations led to a thorough review of his conduct and ethics.

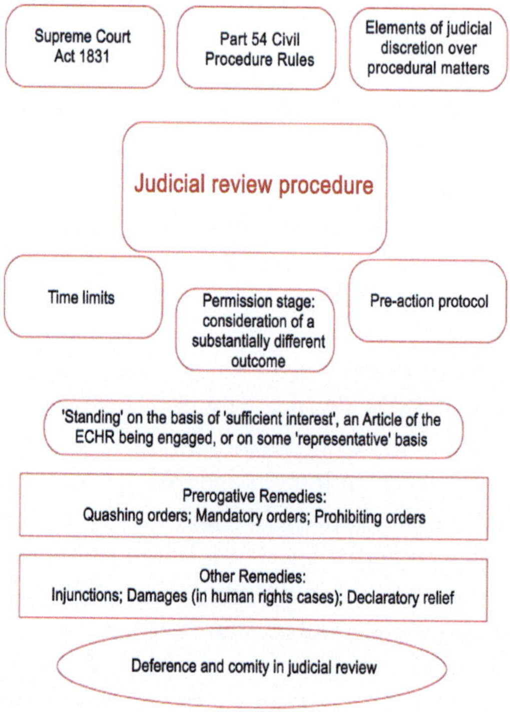

Figure 3.4. Example of a judicial review procedure.

Source: Law Explorer (2017) https://lawexplores.com/process-standing-and-remedies-in-judicial-review/

The Senate Judiciary Committee conducted a hearing where both Kavanaugh and his accuser, Dr. Christine Blasey Ford, presented their testimonies. This public hearing allowed for an examination of the evidence and an assessment of Kavanaugh's character and suitability for the Supreme Court position. The allegations were taken seriously, and the committee reviewed additional evidence and conducted interviews with potential witnesses. After a comprehensive review, the Senate Judiciary Committee voted to recommend Kavanaugh's nomination to the full Senate, despite the allegations. The Senate subsequently confirmed Kavanaugh's appointment to the Supreme Court. This example demonstrates how the process of judicial conduct and ethics review played out in a real-world scenario. It involved a detailed examination of allegations, testimony from involved parties, collection of evidence, and a decision-making process by elected representatives. Figure 3.4 is a typical illustration of a judicial review procedure.

Additionally, the process of judicial appointments and promotions is another critical mechanism (Zacka, 2022; Zambrano, 2019; Zuk et al., 1993). Governments hold the responsibility of nominating and appointing judges to the bench. This process ensures that only individuals of the highest competence, integrity, and ethical standards occupy judicial positions. The judiciary's role in this context is to maintain its independence and integrity while cooperating with the government to ensure that the appointment process is fair and devoid of political influence. The process of judicial appointments and promotions is a critical mechanism in ensuring the selection of qualified and competent individuals to serve on the bench. One highly specific and detailed case study that exemplifies this mechanism is the appointment of Neil Gorsuch to the United States Supreme Court in 2017. Gorsuch's nomination and confirmation showcased the complex and contentious nature of the judicial appointment process in a real-world context. After the passing of Justice Antonin Scalia in 2016, a vacancy emerged on the Supreme Court. President Donald Trump nominated Neil Gorsuch, a federal appeals court judge, to fill the vacancy. This decision sparked intense debate and scrutiny, highlighting the importance of the selection process.

During the confirmation hearings conducted by the Senate Judiciary Committee, Gorsuch faced rigorous questioning from senators seeking to evaluate his qualifications, judicial philosophy, and adherence to the Constitution. They probed into his previous rulings, legal opinions, and his potential impact on important legal issues. The confirmation process became a battleground for contrasting viewpoints, with senators both supporting and challenging Gorsuch's nomination. Moreover, public interest groups, advocacy organizations, and legal scholars closely observed and weighed in on the nomination, adding further layers to the debate. Their involvement highlighted the significance of transparency and public input in the appointment process. Ultimately, after a thorough examination of Gorsuch's qualifications, legal record, and responses during the hearings, the Senate voted to confirm his appointment. The process, though contentious, showcased the careful deliberation and consideration of candidates' credentials and ideology that the judicial appointment mechanism demands.

This case study underscores the importance of the appointment and promotion process in ensuring the selection of individuals who possess the necessary legal expertise, ethical standards, and adherence to the Constitution (Setty, 2015; Shah, 2014; Shenkman, 2012; Shepherd, 2009). It also highlights the role of the Senate in vetting nominees and representing the diverse array of views and interests of the American public. Overall, the appointment and promotion mechanism encompass a multifaceted and highly scrutinized process that aims to preserve the integrity and independence of the judiciary.

Moreover, the appellate process serves as a form of accountability (Primus, 2004; Prince, 2020; Provost, 2008; Pulle & Ratnapala, 2019). Higher courts review the decisions made by lower courts, assessing the legal soundness and impartiality of judgments. This process maintains a level of scrutiny over judicial decisions, preventing the undue concentration of power within the judiciary. The interplay between the judiciary and government is evident in the fact that the government often establishes the hierarchical structure of the courts, while the judiciary ensures that the appellate process is carried out without interference. Public transparency and access to justice also contribute to mechanisms of judicial accountability. Court proceedings are generally open to the public, allowing citizens and media to observe the administration of justice. This transparency fosters public trust in the judiciary and enables scrutiny of judicial decisions. The government plays a role in creating laws and regulations that ensure the openness of court proceedings, while the judiciary is responsible for upholding this transparency in practice. However, the relationship between the judiciary and government in mechanisms of judicial accountability is not without challenges. The delicate balance between judicial independence and governmental influence can sometimes lead to tensions. Striking the right balance requires a commitment to preserving the integrity of the judiciary while acknowledging the necessity of accountability to the public and the government.

In conclusion, mechanisms of judicial accountability are essential for upholding the rule of law and ensuring that the judiciary operates ethically and transparently. The relationship between the judiciary and government in establishing and enforcing these mechanisms reflects the complex interplay between maintaining judicial independence and preventing misconduct. As societies strive to maintain a just legal system, they must navigate this intricate balance to preserve public trust and uphold the principles of justice. The third section focuses on the challenges of judicial independence.

3.3. CHALLENGES TO JUDICIAL INDEPENDENCE

Challenges to judicial independence represent a critical facet of the intricate relationship between the judiciary and government, with profound implications for the functioning of a just and democratic society (Althouse, 2001; Appleby et al., 2019; Appleby & Olijnyk, 2020). These challenges, stemming from political pressures, social influences, and institutional factors, underscore the delicate equilibrium necessary to ensure that judges can make impartial decisions without fear of retribution or manipulation. The interplay between the judiciary and government in addressing these challenges highlights the ongoing tension between safeguarding judicial autonomy and preserving the legitimacy of the legal system.

One of the foremost challenges is political interference in the judicial process (Cassman, 2015; Celenk, 2016; Chakravarti et al., 2011; Chalmers, 2000). Governments may attempt to exert influence over judges' decisions to further their political agendas or consolidate power. The judiciary's role in this context is to remain steadfast in its commitment to impartiality and the rule of law, despite external pressures. While governments have a legitimate interest in certain legal outcomes, the judiciary must operate independently to uphold the principles of justice and fairness. A notable case study that exemplifies this challenge is the situation surrounding the Polish judiciary reforms. In recent years, Poland has implemented several controversial changes to its judicial system, resulting in concerns about the independence of the judiciary and the potential influence of the ruling party.

Critics argue that these reforms were driven by political motivations, aiming to consolidate power and control over the judiciary. For instance, one significant reform introduced a new disciplinary regime for judges, allowing for stricter penalties and potential removal from the bench. This raised concerns about the potential for judges to face disciplinary measures based on political decisions rather than legitimate legal considerations. Furthermore, the establishment of a new body responsible for appointing judges, the National Council of the Judiciary, saw changes that some perceive as undermining judicial independence. Critics highlight the increased influence of politicians over the selection and promotion of judges, potentially compromising impartiality and the separation of powers. That means that other stakeholders (see Figure 3.5) are excluded.

Figure 3.5. Stakeholders in the judicial reform process.

Source: Vidhi, Center for Legal Policy https://vidhilegalpolicy.in/research/national-judicial-policy-a-concept-note-and-ten-visions-for-2030/

These reforms in the Polish judicial system have faced widespread criticism, both domestically and internationally, with accusations of undermining the rule of law and eroding democratic principles. Organizations such as the European Union and international human rights groups have expressed concerns over the potential political interference and its impact on the judiciary's ability to deliver impartial and fair judgments. Supporters of the reforms argue that they aim to address issues of inefficiency and corruption within the judiciary, asserting that the changes intend to increase accountability and transparency. However, opponents view these justifications as a smokescreen for political control over the judiciary. The case of the Polish judiciary reforms highlights the complex and nuanced nature of the challenge concerning political interference in the judicial process. It underscores the importance of safeguarding the independence of the judiciary from undue political influence, as a fair and impartial judiciary is crucial for upholding the rule of law and protecting citizens' rights. Addressing this challenge requires a balance between legitimate judicial reforms and ensuring the autonomy of judges in making decisions based on law and not political considerations.

Social influences also present significant challenges to judicial independence (Pospieszna & Vetulani-Cegiel, 2021; Preis, 2006; Preston, 2016). Public opinion, media coverage, and societal norms can potentially impact judges' decisions, undermining the objective interpretation of the law. This challenge emphasizes the judiciary's role in maintaining its impartiality and resisting external forces that might compromise its integrity. The government's role lies in fostering an environment where judges can make decisions based solely on the law and evidence, free from undue societal pressures. A pertinent case study highlighting this challenge is the ongoing debate surrounding judicial appointments in India. The process of judicial appointments in India has been a subject of contentious discussion, raising concerns about the potential influence of social and political factors on the selection of judges. One key aspect of this debate revolves around the phenomenon of "judicial lobbying." This refers to the lobbying efforts by influential individuals or interest groups to sway the selection process based on personal affiliations or ideological preferences. Critics argue that such lobbying undermines the merit-based appointment system and raises questions about the independence and impartiality of the judiciary.

Furthermore, the issue of social biases and prejudices can also impact the independence of judges (Beiser-McGrath et al., 2022; Bell, 2002; Bencze, 2021). Judicial decision-making can be influenced by prevailing societal norms, stereotypes, and pressures exerted by powerful interest groups. Instances have been reported where judges may have succumbed to societal pressure in controversial cases, compromising the objective application of the law. Another factor that highlights the impact of social influences is the perception of judges as public figures. In some instances, judges have faced public scrutiny and criticism, often fueled by social media and sensationalized reporting. These external pressures can potentially influence the judiciary's decision-making, creating challenges to the independence of judges. This case study demonstrates the complex interplay between social influences and judicial independence. While social awareness and public engagement are essential for a thriving democracy, it is crucial to ensure that these influences do not compromise the integrity and impartiality of the judiciary. Striking a balance between the societal context and the need for an independent judiciary requires robust mechanisms that insulate judges from undue societal pressures and protect their ability to make fair and impartial decisions based on the law and evidence presented before them. Moreover, such measures can overcome some of the distortions in the judicial system (see Figure 3.6).

Figure 3.6. Examples of distortions of the judicial system.

Source: Piper Fund (2022) via Proteus https://www.proteusfund.org/judicial-independence-heroes-and-villains-key-takeaways-from-piper-funds-recent-funder-briefings/

Institutional factors, including resource constraints and administrative limitations, can also impede judicial independence (Reid et al., 2020; Ritleng, 2016; Rivera, 2022; Robinson, 2018). Inadequate funding for the judiciary can undermine its capacity to function effectively and efficiently. The government's role is to provide the necessary resources to ensure that the judiciary can operate autonomously and dispense justice without hindrance. The judiciary, in turn, must manage its resources judiciously to maintain its credibility and integrity. Furthermore, the appointment and promotion process can raise concerns about potential government influence over the judiciary. Political appointments might erode public confidence in the judiciary's impartiality, casting doubt on the fairness of its decisions. Balancing the government's responsibility to nominate judges with the judiciary's role in upholding independence requires transparent processes that prioritize competence and integrity over political allegiance.

A contemporary case that exemplifies these challenges is the erosion of judicial independence in some countries (Pohjankoski, 2016; Pooe, 2017; Popova & Post, 2018). For instance, the weakening of the judiciary's autonomy in certain democracies has raised concerns about the rule of law and the potential for unchecked executive power. This case underscores the critical relationship between the judiciary and government, as well as the need for vigilant protection of judicial independence to prevent democratic backsliding. In navigating these challenges, the judiciary and government must collaborate to establish robust safeguards. Transparent appointment processes, ethical codes of conduct, and mechanisms for addressing complaints against judges are examples of measures that can strengthen judicial independence. However, maintaining a delicate balance between autonomy and accountability is an ongoing endeavor that requires vigilance and commitment from both sides.

In conclusion, challenges to judicial independence underscore the complex relationship between the judiciary and government in ensuring a just legal system. Political interference, social influences, institutional factors, and contemporary erosion of independence all contribute to the intricate landscape within which judicial autonomy must be preserved. The relationship between the judiciary and government in addressing these challenges is pivotal, as they strive to maintain a delicate equilibrium that upholds the rule of law and fosters public trust in the judicial system.

3.4. THE ETHICS OF JUDICIAL CONDUCT

The ethics of judicial conduct represents a pivotal dimension in the interaction between the judiciary and government, shaping the behavior of judges and upholding the integrity of the legal system (Smith, 2005; Sorabji & Vaughan, 2021; Southworth, 2018). Ethical standards guide judges in maintaining impartiality, transparency, and fairness in their decisions, and the interplay between the judiciary and government in establishing and enforcing these standards reflects a delicate balance between preserving judicial independence and ensuring public trust. A case study that exemplifies this dimension is the impeachment trial of former South Korean President Park Geun-hye. The impeachment process unfolded amidst allegations of corruption and misconduct, highlighting the importance of ethical conduct by judges in ensuring a fair and impartial trial. In this case, the South Korean Constitutional Court, comprised of several judges, was tasked with deliberating on the impeachment of the president. The court was entrusted with the responsibility of examining the evidence, interpreting the law, and making a determination on the legitimacy of the impeachment charges. The credibility of the court and its judges were fundamental in delivering justice and maintaining public trust in the legal system. Throughout the trial, the ethical behavior of the judges played a crucial role. It was imperative that they adhered to strict ethical standards, avoiding any conflicts of interest or biases that could compromise the fairness and legitimacy of the proceedings. The judges were expected to approach the case with impartiality and rigorously uphold the principles of justice. In this context, the public and media closely scrutinized the conduct of the judges, monitoring their decisions, statements, and any potential connections with political or influential actors. The ethical conduct of the judges was not only significant for the case at hand but also for safeguarding the reputation and credibility of the entire judiciary in South Korea. Whether the impeachment trial of President Park Geun-hye will be seen as an exemplary display of ethical judicial conduct is a matter of debate. However, it highlights the critical role that ethics play in the behavior of judges and in upholding the principles of justice and the integrity of the legal system (McCoy & Jahic, 2006; McEwen et al., 2012; Mechkova et al., 2019). The case underscores the importance of maintaining high ethical standards among judges and the need for robust mechanisms to ensure accountability and transparency to preserve public confidence in the judiciary-government relationship. It is these principles that underpin the major sources of judicial ethics.

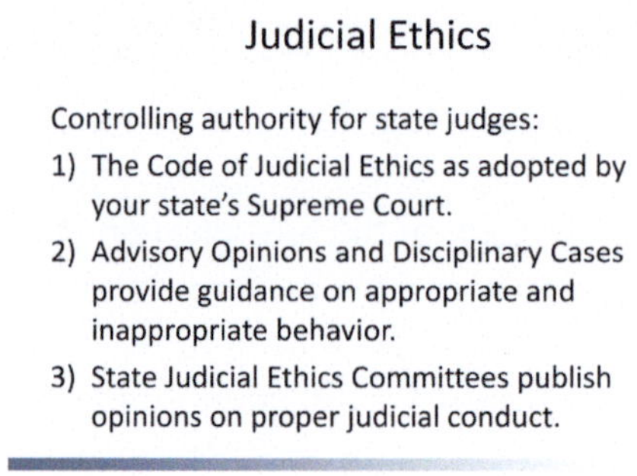

Figure 3.7. Three major sources of judicial ethics.

Source: Tammy R Doyle (2020) via SlidePlayer https://www.slideserve.com/rdoyle/judicial-ethics-powerpoint-ppt-presentation

The major sources of judicial ethics encompass a variety of principles, rules, and guidelines that provide a framework for ethical conduct among judges (Mendelson, 1976; Menounou et al., 2019; Michetti et al., 2018). These sources include codes of judicial conduct, judicial ethics committees, legal statutes, and professional associations. Codes of judicial conduct serve as a cornerstone in establishing ethical guidelines for judges. For instance, in the United States, the American Bar Association (ABA) has developed the Model Code of Judicial Conduct, which provides a comprehensive set of rules governing judicial behavior. This code highlights values such as impartiality, integrity, fairness, and diligence that judges are expected to uphold. Violations of these ethical rules can have significant repercussions on judges' reputations and careers. Judicial ethics committees also play a crucial role in promoting and enforcing ethical standards. These committees, composed of judges, legal experts, and representatives from the public, often review complaints against judges and provide guidance on ethical dilemmas. An example can be seen in the State Commission on Judicial Conduct in Texas, which investigates and addresses allegations of judicial misconduct. These committees serve as checks and balances, ensuring accountability and helping maintain public trust in the judiciary.

Legal statutes and regulations formulated by legislatures and governments reinforce ethical conduct among judges (Kaplina et al., 2021; Karlan, 1992; Kasner, 2015; Kempf, 2021). These laws often outline specific behaviors that judges should avoid, such as conflicts of interest, accepting gifts, or engaging in bias. A noteworthy example is found in Germany, where the Judges Act (Richtergesetz) prohibits judges from taking part in political activities that could compromise their impartiality. These statutes establish clear boundaries and expectations for judges' conduct to maintain public confidence in the judiciary's integrity. Additionally, professional associations for judges play a vital role in fostering ethical standards by providing resources, training, and opportunities for dialogue. The International Association of Judges (IAJ) is an international organization that promotes judicial independence and professional ethics. Through conferences, workshops, and publications, the IAJ aims to enhance global judicial ethics awareness and facilitate the exchange of best practices.

While these sources provide a robust foundation for judicial ethics, their efficacy and implementation can be subject to critique (Berger, 1978, 1979a, 1979b; Berkmanas, 2020; Besco, 2018). The interpretation and enforcement of ethical rules can vary across jurisdictions, potentially leading to inconsistencies in addressing misconduct. Additionally, the influence of political and societal factors must also be acknowledged as they may impact the application and adherence to ethical standards. Hence, the major sources of judicial ethics, including codes of conduct, ethics committees, legal statutes, and professional associations, contribute to the establishment of ethical standards for judges. Real-world examples demonstrate their influence and the importance of upholding these standards to ensure impartiality, fairness, and integrity within the judiciary. However, ongoing evaluation and discussion are necessary to address potential shortcomings and strengthen these sources as guiding principles for judges' ethical conduct.

The foundation of the ethics of judicial conduct lies in the principle that judges are entrusted with the responsibility of dispensing justice based solely on the law and evidence, devoid of personal bias or external influence (Urribarri, 2011; Utter, 2021; Uzebu-Imarhiagbe, 2020). Governments play a role in creating codes of judicial conduct that outline the principles and standards judges must adhere to, ensuring that the judiciary maintains a high standard of professionalism and integrity. This highlights the collaborative nature of the relationship between the judiciary and government in upholding ethical norms.

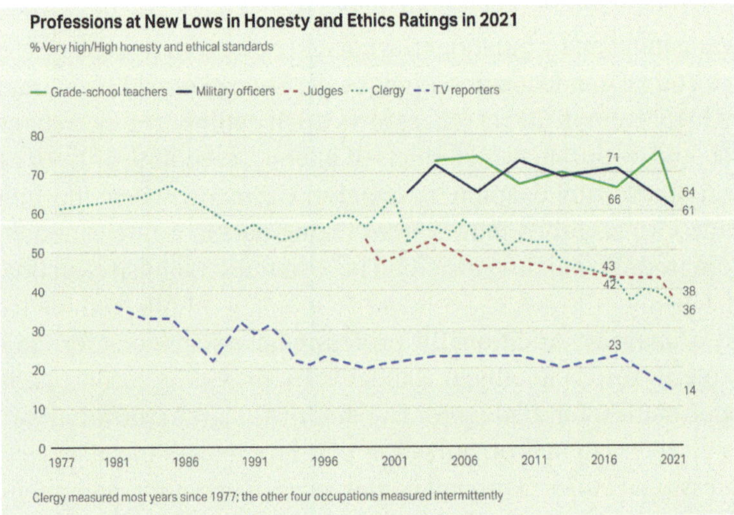

Figure 3.8. The falling public trust in the judicial profession within the USA.

Source: Lydia Saad (2019) Gallup https://news.gallup.com/poll/388649/military-brass-judges-among-professions-new-image-lows.aspx

An important component in the relationships between the judiciary and the rest of government is public perceptions of the profession (Lin, 2016; Liu & Baird, 2012; Macchiarola, 1971; Macey, 2006). The case of the falling ratings of the judicial profession in the USA is an instructive example of how a disreputable judiciary can give leeway to the executive and legislature to dominate government affairs. While it is important to note that public opinion regarding the judiciary can fluctuate and is influenced by various factors, declining ratings can have significant implications. An example highlighting this phenomenon occurred in the aftermath of the controversial Supreme Court decision in Bush v. Gore in 2000. This ruling, which effectively determined the outcome of the presidential election, generated intense scrutiny and criticism. Many members of the public expressed dissatisfaction with the judiciary, attributing the decision to political partisanship rather than a fair and impartial interpretation of the law. Public perception of the judiciary is essential for upholding its legitimacy and independence. If the judiciary is viewed as lacking integrity or being favorably disposed towards certain political interests, it can erode public trust and confidence. This diminished trust can impact the judiciary's ability to serve as a check on the executive and legislature, potentially allowing the other branches of government to exercise more dominance over governance.

Furthermore, a disreputable judiciary may face challenges in implementing its decisions, as public trust in its authority and fairness diminishes (Zacka, 2022; Zambrano, 2019; Zuk et al., 1993). This situation can lead to an environment where the executive and legislature feel emboldened to exert greater influence over issues that may fall within the judiciary's purview, potentially undermining the separation of powers and compromising the system of checks and balances. Critics argue that a declining reputation of the judiciary can be attributed to various factors, including perceived ideological biases, conflicts of interest, or a lack of transparency. It may also stem from instances of judicial misconduct or high-profile cases that capture public attention and scrutiny, leading to a broader negative perception of the judiciary as a whole.

In response to declining ratings, it becomes imperative for the judiciary to prioritize accountability, transparency, and adherence to ethical standards (Grove, 2018; Gunderson, 2022; Hardaway, 2021; Hardman, 2020). It is crucial for judges to demonstrate impartiality and independence in their decisions, upholding the principle of justice while avoiding perceptions of political favoritism. Additionally, initiatives such as improving communication and engagement with the public, enhancing public understanding of the judiciary's role, and addressing concerns about potential conflicts of interest can help combat the erosion of public trust and maintain the judiciary's integrity. Overall, the case of falling ratings of the judicial profession in the USA serves as a poignant reminder of the risks that a disreputable judiciary can pose to the balance of power in the government. Upholding the reputation, integrity, and independence of the judiciary is essential in safeguarding the democratic principles upon which the system of governance is built. One of the central tenets of judicial ethics is impartiality (Williams, 2008; Winkler, 2009; Wong et al., 2009; Worthington, 2001). Judges must approach each case without preconceived notions or prejudices, ensuring that all parties receive a fair and unbiased hearing. The government's role in this context is to establish an environment where judges can make decisions independently, free from political or societal pressures. The judiciary's role, in turn, is to uphold impartiality by recusing themselves from cases where bias may arise and by ensuring that decisions are based solely on the merits of the case.

Transparency is another cornerstone of judicial ethics (Kirisci & Kocaman, 2022; Kitagawa, 2023; Kochtcheeva, 2009). The principle of open justice necessitates that court proceedings are accessible to the public, fostering accountability and public trust in the legal system. The government's role includes enacting laws that promote transparency, while the judiciary's responsibility lies in ensuring that court proceedings are conducted openly and that decisions are explained clearly to the public.

Conflicts of interest pose a significant ethical challenge for judges (van Zeben, 2015; Vermeule, 2012; Voeten, 2008; VonDoepp & Ellett, 2011). Balancing personal interests with the duty to remain impartial requires stringent adherence to ethical guidelines. Governments often play a role in creating mechanisms to identify and address conflicts of interest, such as recusal or disclosure requirements. The judiciary, on the other hand, must prioritize ethical considerations when faced with potential conflicts, safeguarding the perception of impartiality. An illustrative case study is the controversy surrounding a judge's participation in political activities. In the fictitious nation of Concordia, Judge Maria Rodriguez faced criticism for her involvement in a political campaign. Critics argued that her engagement undermined the perception of impartiality and integrity in her decisions. This case underscores the ethical dilemma judges may encounter and highlights the pivotal role of governments in establishing guidelines that prevent judges from engaging in activities that could compromise their judicial duties.

In conclusion, the ethics of judicial conduct represents a critical bridge between the judiciary and government in upholding the integrity of the legal system. Impartiality, transparency, and the avoidance of conflicts of interest are foundational principles that guide judges' behavior and decisions. The relationship between the judiciary and government in this context is one of collaboration and accountability, with both sides contributing to the establishment and enforcement of ethical standards. By upholding these standards, the judiciary maintains its credibility, fosters public trust, and reinforces the essential role of an independent judiciary in a just and equitable society. The final section of this chapter will highlight the importance of balancing judicial independence with the public interest.

3.5. BALANCING INDEPENDENCE AND PUBLIC INTEREST

The intricate balance between preserving judicial independence and serving the public interest is a nuanced and perennial challenge that defines the complex relationship between the judiciary and government (Setty, 2015; Shah, 2014; Shenkman, 2012; Shepherd, 2009). This equilibrium navigates the delicate interplay between an autonomous judiciary capable of upholding justice and the imperative to ensure that judicial decisions align with the evolving needs and values of society. The dynamics between the judiciary and government in striking this balance reveal the complexities inherent in maintaining a just and equitable legal system that resonates with the broader populace. This delicate equilibrium requires astute navigation and constant vigilance to prevent any undue influence on the judiciary by the government or any encroachment on its independence. A compelling case study that highlights these complexities is the debate surrounding the nomination and confirmation of Supreme Court justices.

In the United States, the selection of Supreme Court justices is a significant constitutional responsibility vested in the president, who nominates candidates, and the Senate, which confirms or rejects these nominations (Iaryczower et al., 2002; Ides, 1999; Imam & Egbewole, 2020). The process is inherently political, as presidents often choose nominees who align with their own ideological leanings, while senators evaluate these nominations against their own political agendas. This inherently politicized process underscores the challenge of preserving judicial independence while serving the public interest. One exemplary case that illustrates this dynamic is the contentious nomination and confirmation of Justice Brett Kavanaugh in 2018. Kavanaugh's nomination was mired in allegations of sexual misconduct, prompting intense public scrutiny, impassioned debates, and political posturing. Supporters of Kavanaugh argued vehemently for the preservation of judicial independence, highlighting his qualifications, experience, and reputation as a distinguished jurist. They emphasized that unsubstantiated accusations should not overshadow his professional accomplishments and that the presumption of innocence should prevail.

On the other hand, opponents of Kavanaugh's nomination maintained that his confirmation would undermine public trust in the judiciary. They pointed to the serious allegations against him and contended that his appointment would diminish the integrity of the Supreme Court and compromise the impartiality of its decisions. These opponents advocated for a more rigorous investigation and raised concerns about potential bias and conflicts of interest. The extensive debates that unfolded during Kavanaugh's confirmation process exposed the tension between judicial independence and the public interest. Furthermore, this case study underscores how the judiciary itself plays a crucial role in upholding its independence and serving the public interest. Chief Justice John Roberts, in response to the intense polarization and scrutiny surrounding the Supreme Court, emphasized the importance of maintaining the Court's integrity and impartiality. In a rare public statement, Roberts stressed that the Court must remain independent, impartial, and detached from political debates to uphold its legitimacy and public trust.

Formal independence	Perceived independence
Judiciary:	***Judge and judiciary undifferentiated:***
· Legal basis of independence	· Independence as perceived by citizens
· Organizational autonomy	· Independence as perceived by court users
· Funding	· Independence as perceived by judges
· Management of court system	· Trust in judiciary, relative to trust in other state powers by citizens in general
Judge:	· Judicial corruption as perceived by citizens in general
· Human resource decisions about judges	
· Disciplinary measures	
· Non-transferability of judges	
· Internal independence	

Figure 3.9. Overview of key aspects of judicial independence and accountability.

Source: van Dijk, Frans & Vos, Geoffrey. (2018). A Method for Assessment of the Independence and Accountability of the Judiciary. International Journal for Court Administration. 9. 1–21. 10.18352/ijca.276.

These debates concerning the balance between judicial independence and the public interest are manifested in the differences between formal judicial independence and perceived judicial independence (see Figure 3.9). At the heart of this challenge lies the question of how an independent judiciary can best serve the public interest without sacrificing its autonomy (Chan, 2011; Chavez, 2003, 2007; Chen & Li, 2016; Chutkow, 2008).

Governments, as representatives of the people, often assert the need for judicial decisions to reflect societal values and address pressing issues. The judiciary, in turn, upholds its mandate of impartiality by adhering strictly to the law and constitution. This tension surfaces vividly when contentious issues, such as civil rights, environmental protection, or individual liberties, intersect with judicial decisions.

Critics argue that an insulated judiciary can sometimes seem out of touch with public sentiment and societal realities (Brands, 2011; Brinkerhoff, 2019; Brogdon, 2018; Bromby, 2021). The government's role in this context is to provide a channel for the expression of public will, ensuring that judges are cognizant of the broader implications of their decisions. A case in point is the U.S. Supreme Court's decision in Roe v. Wade (1973), which legalized abortion. The court's ruling generated significant public debate and underscored the challenge of reconciling judicial autonomy with societal values. Critics of the decision contended that the court overstepped its boundaries and should have deferred to the states' legislative processes.

The case of Roe v. Wade in 1973, which established the constitutional right to abortion in the United States, exemplifies the tensions between judicial independence and the public interest (Colucci, 2000; Conrad, 2014; Costas-Perez et al., 2012; Cross, 1999). The landmark decision, made by the Supreme Court, sparked a perennial debate regarding the balance between protecting individual rights, as outlined in the Constitution, and the collective values and beliefs of the public. This debate reached a critical point when attempts were made to overturn or significantly restrict the decision in subsequent years, reflecting the ongoing struggle to reconcile judicial independence with the evolving public opinion on abortion.

At the heart of the tension lies the question of who gets to determine the legality and accessibility of abortion (Bascuas, 2005; Baude, 2020; Baum, 2003; Bednar, 2004). Following the Roe v. Wade ruling, opponents of abortion rights rallied around various strategies to challenge or overturn the decision. Anti-abortion activists argued that the Court overstepped its boundaries by legislating from the bench rather than leaving the issue to the democratic process. They contended that decisions about abortion should be made by elected officials who can represent public opinion, rather than by the judiciary, which is less directly accountable.

This tension between judicial independence and the public interest is evident in the subsequent legal battles that sought to curtail or overturn Roe v. Wade (see Figure 3.10). For instance, the Supreme Court decision in Planned Parenthood v. Casey in 1992 upheld the core principles of Roe v. Wade but also allowed for greater restrictions on abortion. This ruling demonstrated the Court's effort to navigate the evolving public sentiment on abortion while also preserving its commitment to precedent and the protection of individual rights.

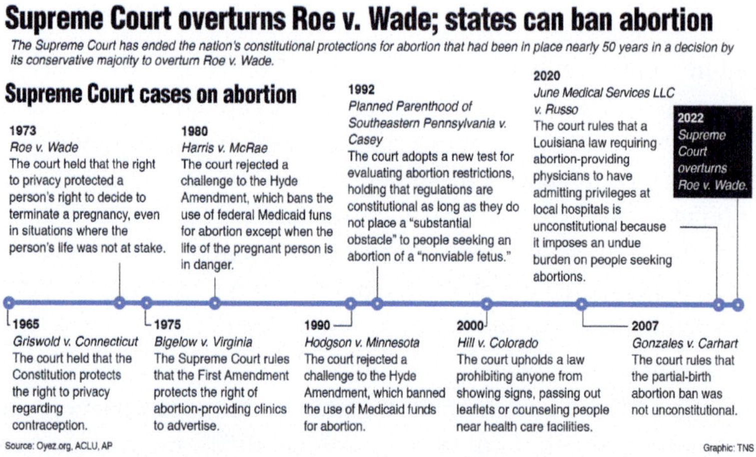

Figure 3.10. Timeline in legal rulings on abortion in the USA 1973–2022.

Source: Lee Lewis (2022) Republican American Archives https://archives.rep-am.com/2022/06/24/timeline-50-years-of-supreme-court-abortion-decisions/

The tension reached a critical point in 2018 when the state of Louisiana sought to implement restrictions on abortion providers similar to those that had been struck down by the Court in 2016 in Whole Woman's Health v. Hellerstedt. Opponents of abortion rights hoped that the newly composed conservative majority on the Supreme Court would use this case as an opportunity to overturn or significantly weaken the precedents set by Roe v. Wade. However, in a surprising turn, the Court, including some conservative justices, voted to strike down the Louisiana law, signaling a cautious preservation of the established abortion rights. Later, President Trump managed to elect a conservative court that overturned the ban on abortion which led to increased polarization.

This ongoing struggle over abortion laws in the United States showcases the inherent tension between judicial independence and the public interest (Grove, 2018; Gunderson, 2022; Hardaway, 2021; Hardman, 2020). The judiciary's role is to ensure that individual rights, as outlined in the Constitution, are protected, even when they clash with the prevailing societal beliefs. At the same time, the public interest is subject to change, reflecting evolving societal values and political landscapes. The attempts to overturn or restrict Roe v. Wade demonstrate the persistent pressure to align judicial decisions with shifting public sentiment, highlighting the delicate balance between judicial independence and the democratic will of the people. Roe v. Wade and its subsequent challenges reflect the complex interplay between judicial independence and the public interest. The tension arises from the desire to protect fundamental individual rights while also accounting for the evolving social and political context. The ongoing debates and legal battles surrounding abortion laws in the United States illustrate the perpetual struggle to balance judicial decision-making with the public's views on highly contentious social issues.

Proponents of judicial independence emphasize the necessity of an autonomous judiciary to safeguard minority rights, protect individual liberties, and uphold the constitution (Williams, 2008; Winkler, 2009; Wong et al., 2009; Worthington, 2001). They contend that judges must remain immune to short-term political pressures to ensure that fundamental rights are not sacrificed for popular sentiment. The government's role is to respect the sanctity of the judiciary's decisions, even if they are contentious, and to implement mechanisms for constitutional amendments or legislative changes if societal values evolve. Moreover, the judiciary can play a proactive role in harmonizing judicial decisions with public interests. Judges can interpret the constitution and laws in a manner that aligns with the evolving needs of society, without compromising their impartiality. This approach requires a fine balance, where judges use their interpretive authority to bridge the gap between constitutional principles and contemporary challenges, without overstepping their role in legislation.

In conclusion, the interplay between maintaining judicial independence and serving the public interest is a constant tightrope walk that characterizes the relationship between the judiciary and government. The U.S. Supreme Court's Roe v. Wade case serves as a poignant reminder of the intricate dynamics involved in adjudicating contentious issues that intersect with societal values. The challenge lies in respecting an independent judiciary's role while acknowledging the government's responsibility to reflect the changing pulse of society. This balance, fragile and ever-evolving, underscores the complexities inherent in upholding justice while ensuring that the legal system remains responsive to the needs of a dynamic society.

CHAPTER 3 SUMMARY

The third chapter, "Judicial Independence and Accountability," serves as a profound exploration into the intricate balance between safeguarding the autonomy of the judiciary and holding it accountable within the broader context of governance and justice. This chapter embarks on a comprehensive journey through pivotal sections, each shedding light on different facets of the intricate relationship between the judiciary and government. The exploration begins with "Ensuring Judicial Independence" (Section 3.1), emphasizing the significance of an independent judiciary in upholding justice and the rule of law. This section delves into the collaborative efforts of the judiciary and government in establishing an environment where judges can make impartial decisions free from undue external influences.

"Mechanisms of Judicial Accountability" (Section 3.2) unveils the mechanisms that maintain a delicate equilibrium between preserving judicial autonomy and ensuring accountability. This section underscores the vital role of the judiciary and government in establishing and enforcing codes of conduct, transparent complaint mechanisms, and ethical standards to prevent judicial overreach. The discourse in this section reflects the intricate partnership between these two entities in maintaining the integrity of the legal system.

The exploration intensifies in "Challenges to Judicial Independence" (Section 3.3), where the chapter dissects the multifaceted challenges that can undermine the independence of the judiciary. By scrutinizing the potential for political interference, societal influences, and resource constraints, this section offers a profound understanding of the intricate dynamics that shape the relationship between the judiciary and government. It highlights the responsibility of both sides in upholding judicial autonomy while ensuring that justice remains free from undue pressures.

"The Ethics of Judicial Conduct" (Section 3.4) delves into the ethical standards that guide judges' behavior and decisions. This section uncovers the principles of impartiality, transparency, and the avoidance of conflicts of interest that guide judges in upholding the integrity of the legal system. The collaborative effort between the judiciary and government in establishing these ethical standards underscores their shared commitment to fostering public trust and maintaining a just society.

The exploration culminates in "Balancing Independence and Public Interest" (Section 3.5), where the intricate interplay between judicial autonomy and the broader societal interests takes center stage. This section navigates the tensions between serving the public interest while preserving judicial impartiality. The discourse here emphasizes the critical partnership between the judiciary and government in ensuring that judicial decisions reflect societal values while upholding the principles of justice and the rule of law.

As the pages of this chapter close, they leave behind a profound appreciation for the complexities and nuances that define the relationship between the judiciary and government. The interplay between ensuring judicial independence and accountability, navigating challenges, upholding ethical standards, and balancing autonomy with public interest underscores the intricate dance that these two essential entities perform within the realm of governance and justice. This chapter serves as a comprehensive guide that equips readers with a profound understanding of the delicate equilibrium that underpins a just and equitable legal system, where the judiciary and government collaborate to uphold the principles that are the bedrock of democratic societies. The next chapter will explore the role of the government and judiciary in policy formulation.

CHAPTER 4

Judiciary and Government in Policy-Making

Contents

4.1. Judicial Interpretation of Statutes.......107
4.2. The Impact of Precedent in Policy Decisions.......113
4.3. Judicial Activism Vs. Restraint in Policy Matters.......120
4.4. Role of the Judiciary in Public Policy.......125
4.5. Evaluating Policy Implications of Judicial Decisions.......137
Chapter 4 Summary.......153

In the intricate landscape where governance and justice converge, the fourth chapter delves into the dynamic interplay between the judiciary and government in the realm of policy-making. Titled "Judiciary and Government in Policy-Making," this chapter embarks on a comprehensive exploration of the multifaceted relationship that exists between these two essential pillars of society. From the nuanced interpretation of statutes to the profound impact of legal precedent, the chapter navigates through a series of sections, each shedding light on different dimensions of how the judiciary shapes and influences policy decisions, while operating within the broader framework of governance.

At the heart of this exploration lies "Judicial Interpretation of Statutes" (Section 4.1), which delves into the pivotal role of the judiciary in interpreting the laws that underpin governance. This section elucidates how the judiciary's interpretation of statutes shapes the legal landscape, often guiding the implementation of government policies. The interplay between the judiciary and government in this context highlights the collaborative effort required to ensure that the interpretation aligns with the intended legislative intent.

The exploration then extends to "The Impact of Precedent in Policy Decisions" (Section 4.2), which unveils how legal precedents set by previous cases influence subsequent policy decisions. This section uncovers the intricate balance that the judiciary must maintain between adhering to precedent and adapting to evolving societal needs. The role of the government here lies in respecting the authority of legal precedent while also recognizing the need for policy flexibility.

Intriguing debates emerge in "Judicial Activism vs. Restraint in Policy Matters" (Section 4.3), where the balance between proactive judicial engagement in policy matters and judicious restraint is explored. The discourse in this section reflects the dynamic relationship between the judiciary and government, where the former may shape policy decisions through bold rulings or exercise caution to respect the prerogatives of the latter.

"Role of the Judiciary in Public Policy" (Section 4.4) delves into the pivotal role that the judiciary plays in shaping public policy. This section unravels the intricate web of interactions between judicial decisions and government policies, showcasing how the judiciary's interpretations can influence the implementation and reform of public policies. The interplay here highlights the symbiotic relationship that exists between judicial and governmental spheres. The chapter concludes with "Evaluating Policy Implications of Judicial Decisions" (Section 4.5), where the examination of the broader impact of judicial decisions on policies takes center stage. This section reflects on the multifaceted role of the judiciary and government in assessing the consequences of legal judgments on the society they serve, underlining the shared responsibility of ensuring that policies align with justice and the welfare of the populace.

In summary, the fourth chapter offers a comprehensive voyage through the intricate terrain where the judiciary and government intersect in the realm of policy-making. By examining the judicial interpretation of statutes, the influence of precedent, the spectrum between judicial activism and restraint, the role of the judiciary in public policy, and the evaluation of policy implications, the chapter illuminates the dynamic relationship that defines the collaborative efforts and complex decisions that underpin governance and justice in modern societies. Let us open the chapter by focusing on judicial interpretations of statutes.

4.1. JUDICIAL INTERPRETATION OF STATUTES

The judicial interpretation of statutes constitutes a pivotal aspect of the interplay between the judiciary and government, shaping the implementation of laws and policies within the broader framework of governance (Iaryczower et al., 2002; Ides, 1999; Imam & Egbewole, 2020). This process involves the judiciary's role in deciphering the meaning, scope, and intent of legislative enactments, thus wielding a profound influence on the practical application of laws. The dynamics between the judiciary and government in this arena reflect a collaborative effort aimed at ensuring that laws are interpreted in a manner that upholds justice, aligns with legislative intent, and respects the separation of powers. A specific case study that exemplifies this dynamic is the Supreme Court's interpretation of the Affordable Care Act (ACA) in the case of National Federation of Independent Business v. Sebelius in 2012. At issue was whether the individual mandate provision of the ACA, which required individuals to obtain health insurance or pay a penalty, was constitutional. The Court's interpretation of this provision had far-reaching implications for the implementation of the healthcare law and the relationship between the judiciary and government.

In its decision, the Supreme Court upheld the individual mandate as a valid exercise of Congress's power to tax. This interpretation of the provision was highly contentious and revealed the inherent tension between judicial review and the role of the legislative branch in policymaking (Spencer & Spencer, 2006, 2010; Spendzharova & Vachudova, 2012). Those in favor of the Court's decision argued that it demonstrated the judiciary's duty to provide a check on the constitutionality of legislative actions. They contended that the Court's interpretation preserved the intent of Congress in enacting the ACA while recognizing the boundaries of federal power. On the other hand, critics of the decision argued that the Court overstepped its authority by engaging in judicial activism. They contended that the interpretation of the individual mandate as a tax, rather than an exercise of Congress's power to regulate commerce, amounted to a rewriting of the law to salvage its constitutionality. These critics argued that such judicial interpretation encroached upon the legislative process and undermined the principle of democratic governance.

This case study highlights the intricate dance between judicial interpretation and the implementation of laws and policies (Zacka, 2022; Zambrano, 2019; Zuk et al., 1993). The judiciary plays a crucial role in clarifying the intent and scope of statutes, which in turn shapes the functioning of government and the delivery of public services. However, the potential for differing interpretations and the influence of judges' individual perspectives introduce an element of subjectivity into this process, raising questions about accountability and democratic legitimacy. Furthermore, the case study underscores the importance of a robust system of checks and balances to mitigate certain risks associated with judicial interpretation. For example, Figure 4.1 shows how litigated this sensitive issue was. While the judiciary must remain independent to ensure a fair and impartial examination of the laws passed by the government, mechanisms such as legislative drafting, public scrutiny, and the possibility of judicial review provide avenues for revisiting policy decisions and addressing any potential gaps or ambiguities in the legislative process. Overall, the judicial interpretation of statutes constitutes a crucial aspect of the interplay between the judiciary and government, shaping the implementation of laws and policies within the broader governance framework. Through specific case studies like the Supreme Court's interpretation of the Affordable Care Act, we witness the ongoing debate surrounding the role of the judiciary in interpreting laws and the delicate balance between judicial review and democratic governance.

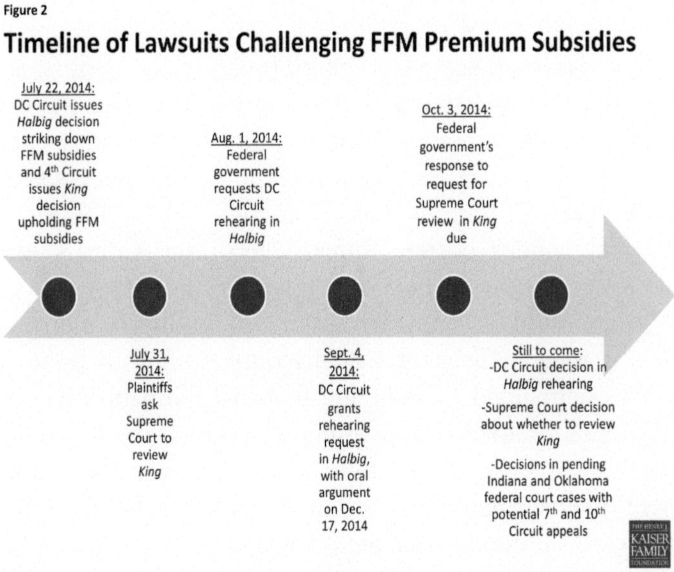

Figure 4.1. Timeline of Lawsuits Challenging FFM Premium Subsidies.

Source: MaryBeth Musumeci and Laurie Sobel (2014) KFF https://www.kff.org/report-section/the-federal-courts-role-in-implementing-the-affordable-care-act-issue-brief/

Central to this dynamic is the judiciary's mandate to construe statutes in a manner that adheres to both the letter and spirit of the law (Ip & Yap, 2019; Jabareen, 2020; Jacobi, 2009; James, 1996). Governments draft statutes to articulate their policy intentions, and the judiciary's responsibility is to ensure that these intentions are upheld. Through their interpretations, judges determine the practical implications of statutes, often filling gaps or addressing ambiguities that may arise during implementation. This interaction underscores the essential relationship between the judiciary and government in translating legislative intent into concrete legal outcomes. A real-world example that encapsulates the delicate balance between adhering to the letter and spirit of the law within the judiciary's mandate to construe statutes is the interpretation of civil rights laws in relation to gender identity and sexual orientation. A pivotal case in this context is Bostock v. Clayton County, which was decided by the United States Supreme Court in 2020. The case centered on whether Title VII of the Civil Rights Act, which prohibits employment discrimination on the basis of sex, encompasses discrimination based on sexual orientation and gender identity. The Court's interpretation in this case sparked a significant debate about the role of the judiciary in expanding the protections of civil rights laws. The Court's decision in Bostock was a landmark ruling, with a majority of justices concluding that discrimination based on sexual orientation or gender identity is inherently covered by the prohibition on sex discrimination. The justices argued that discriminating against someone for being gay or transgender is inherently based on their sex because such discrimination necessarily involves treating individuals differently based on their sex or failure to conform to stereotypical gender norms. Supporters of the Court's interpretation celebrated the decision as a crucial step toward achieving equality and justice for LGBTQ+ individuals. They argued that the judiciary's duty to interpret the law in a manner consistent with its purpose and in light of evolving societal norms demanded recognizing that discrimination based on sexual orientation or gender identity constituted discrimination based on sex. They believed such an interpretation aligned with the values of inclusivity and equal protection enshrined in civil rights laws. Critics of the Court's ruling, on the other hand, contended that the interpretation went beyond the original intent of the lawmakers who drafted Title VII. They believed that expanding the definition of sex discrimination to include sexual orientation and gender identity created new legal rights that should be established by legislative processes, rather than through judicial interpretation. Critics argued that this kind of judicial activism threatens democratic principles by allowing the judiciary to rewrite laws and override the role of elected representatives.

This case demonstrates the complexity of adhering to both the letter and spirit of the law in judicial interpretation (Emerson, 2022; Evans et al., 2017; Fallon & Meltzer, 1991). The Court's decision in Bostock sought to align the interpretation of Title VII with the evolving societal understanding of discrimination and equality. While proponents hailed this as an example of the judiciary fulfilling its mandate to apply the fundamental principles underlying the law, opponents criticized it as an instance of the judiciary overstepping its bounds by legislating from the bench. It is important to note that this case is one example among many that reflect the ongoing debate surrounding the judiciary's role in statutory interpretation. The tension between adhering to the specific language of a statute and considering its underlying purpose can often be subjective, with various factors, including changing societal norms and judicial philosophy, influencing the interpretation. A nuanced application of the law requires striking a delicate balance by considering both statutory text and its intended purpose, while also respecting the democratic processes through which laws are made and modified. Hence, the complex issue of statutory interpretation is exemplified by the judiciary's mandate to construe statutes in a manner that adheres to both the letter and spirit of the law. The case of Bostock v. Clayton County, which expanded the scope of sex discrimination to include sexual orientation and gender identity, highlights the debate surrounding the judiciary's role in interpreting and shaping civil rights laws. This case serves as a reminder of the ongoing struggle to reconcile interpretations with the original legislative intent, evolving societal norms, and the democratic processes governing legal change.

Furthermore, the judicial interpretation of statutes reflects a balance between textualism and contextualism (Hennigar, 2010; Hessick, 2014; Hill, 2016; Holland, 2009). Textualism involves interpreting statutes based on the explicit wording of the law, while contextualism considers the broader legislative context and purpose. The judiciary's role lies in striking a balance between these approaches, ensuring that interpretations are consistent with the legislative language while acknowledging the broader objectives of the law. This balance requires a nuanced understanding of legislative history, social context, and legal precedent. A real-world example that navigates the balance between textualism and contextualism in judicial interpretation of statutes is the case of District of Columbia v. Heller, decided by the United States Supreme Court in 2008. The case examined the interpretation of the Second Amendment of the U.S. Constitution, which guarantees the right to bear arms. Specifically, the Court analyzed whether this right extended to an individual's right to possess firearms for self-defense within their home. The Court's divided opinion in Heller illustrates the divergent approaches to statutory interpretation and highlights the ongoing debate surrounding the appropriate balance between textualism and contextualism.

In the majority opinion, Justice Antonin Scalia adopted a textualist approach, interpreting the language of the Second Amendment according to its original meaning at the time of its adoption. The majority held that the Second Amendment protected an individual's right to possess firearms for self-defense, emphasizing the phrase "the right of the people to keep and bear Arms shall not be infringed." This textualist interpretation focused on strictly adhering to the words of the amendment and the intentions of the framers. Supporters of the majority opinion in Heller praised the emphasis on textualism, arguing that it preserved the original intent of the framers and protected individual rights. They believed that the Court's textualist approach ensured that the judicial branch remained faithful to the Constitution's language and prevented judges from engaging in judicial activism by reading their own preferences into the text. However, critics of the majority opinion in Heller contended that the strict textualist approach overlooked the historical context and broader societal implications of the Second Amendment. They argued for a more contextualist interpretation, taking into account changing societal needs and understandings of the right to bear arms. Supporters of a contextualist approach believed that the interpretation of the Second Amendment should consider contemporary issues and evolving concepts of public safety, such as regulations to prevent gun violence.

The dissenting opinion in Heller, written by Justice John Paul Stevens, exemplifies this contextualist perspective (Findley & Young, 2011; Finkel, 2005; Fisher, 2008; Fowkes, 2011). Stevens argued that the Second Amendment should be understood in the context of the time, when the primary goal was to preserve well-regulated militias, rather than the individual's right to possess firearms for self-defense. He contended that the historical context, as well as the pressing modern concerns related to gun violence, should shape the interpretation of the amendment. This case underscores the ongoing debate between textualism and contextualism in statutory interpretation. While textualism focuses on adhering strictly to the plain language and original intent of the law, contextualism places greater emphasis on contemporary societal considerations and a broader understanding of the law's purpose. Critics argue that relying solely on textualism can lead to outdated interpretations that fail to address current challenges, while proponents argue that it provides stability and consistency in the interpretation of statutes. District of Columbia v. Heller represents a real-world example where the balance between textualism and contextualism in judicial interpretation of statutes is debated. The case displays the clash between a textualist approach, driven by adherence to the original meaning of the Second Amendment, and a contextualist perspective that takes into account contemporary social realities (see Figure 4.2). This ongoing debate underscores the challenges of interpreting statutes in a manner that stays true to the text while considering the evolving needs of society.

The relationship between the judiciary and government in this context is one of mutual influence (Lin, 2016; Liu & Baird, 2012; Macchiarola, 1971; Macey, 2006). Governments enact laws to address societal needs and concerns, and their understanding of the legislative purpose can guide judges in their interpretations. Conversely, judicial decisions that clarify the meaning of statutes can provide valuable guidance to government agencies responsible for implementing policies. This iterative process between the judiciary and government strengthens the implementation of laws and policies and contributes to the coherent functioning of the legal system. A contemporary case that exemplifies the impact of judicial interpretation of statutes is the Affordable Care Act in the United States. The Supreme Court's interpretation of the language "established by the state" in the context of healthcare subsidies significantly influenced the implementation and accessibility of healthcare services. The court's decision showcased the intricate interplay between the judiciary and government in determining the extent to which legislative language should be upheld versus considering the broader policy goals.

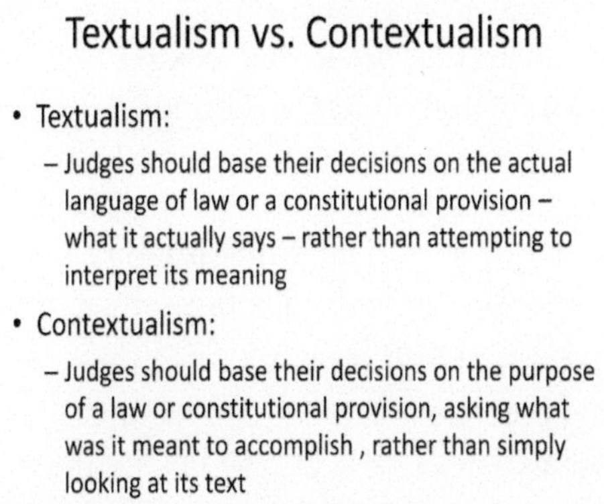

Figure 4.2. Comparing textualism to contextualism in judicial interpretation.

Source: Diamond Kinney (2014) via SlideServe https://www.slideserve.com/diamond/dueling-constitutional-philosophies

In conclusion, the judicial interpretation of statutes embodies the collaborative relationship between the judiciary and government in ensuring the effective implementation of laws. The balance between textualism and contextualism, the consideration of legislative intent, and the responsiveness to evolving societal needs characterize this dynamic process. This interplay underscores the shared commitment to upholding the rule of law, aligning legislative intent with practical outcomes, and maintaining the equilibrium that defines the functioning of democratic societies. The second section of this chapter focuses on the impact of precedent on policy.

4.2. THE IMPACT OF PRECEDENT IN POLICY DECISIONS

The impact of precedent in policy decisions is a fundamental and intricate aspect of the relationship between the judiciary and government (White,

2022; Whittington, 2005; Willett & Gordon, 2022). Precedent refers to the principle that past judicial decisions serve as a guide for future cases with similar legal issues. This principle is essential as it provides consistency, predictability, and stability to the legal system. The interaction between the judiciary and government in utilizing and interpreting precedents shapes the development of laws and policies and influences the trajectory of governance. In a global context, a real-world example that exemplifies the impact of precedent in policy decisions can be seen in the case of Navtej Singh Johar v. Union of India, decided by the Supreme Court of India in 2018. This case centered around Section 377 of the Indian Penal Code, which criminalized consensual same-sex sexual activities. The Supreme Court's ruling in Navtej Singh Johar v. Union of India marked a historic moment for LGBTQ+ rights in India. The Court held that Section 377 was discriminatory and violated the rights to equality, privacy, and freedom of expression guaranteed by the Indian Constitution. This decision not only decriminalized same-sex sexual activities but set a precedent for LGBTQ+ rights and legal recognition in India.

The impact of this precedent can be seen in subsequent policy decisions and developments related to LGBTQ+ rights in India. It has influenced discussions on marriage equality, adoption rights, and anti-discrimination measures. The Supreme Court's ruling in Navtej Singh Johar v. Union of India has set the tone for the ongoing efforts to secure equal rights and protections for the LGBTQ+ community in the country. This case also highlights the intricate relationship between the judiciary and government in shaping policy decisions. The Supreme Court's interpretation and application of constitutional principles played a pivotal role in striking down Section 377 and paving the way for LGBTQ+ rights. The government, in response to the precedent set by this case, has been engaged in further policy discussions and reforms to align with the Court's ruling. Navtej Singh Johar v. Union of India is a example that illustrates the impact of precedent in policy decisions beyond the United States. The Supreme Court's ruling in this case brought about a significant advancement in LGBTQ+ rights in India and influenced subsequent policy discussions and developments. The influence of this precedent is a testament to the interplay between the judiciary and government in shaping policy and ensuring the protection of individual rights in a global context. A similar involvement of the courts took place during the struggle for gender equality in the USA (see Figure 4.3).

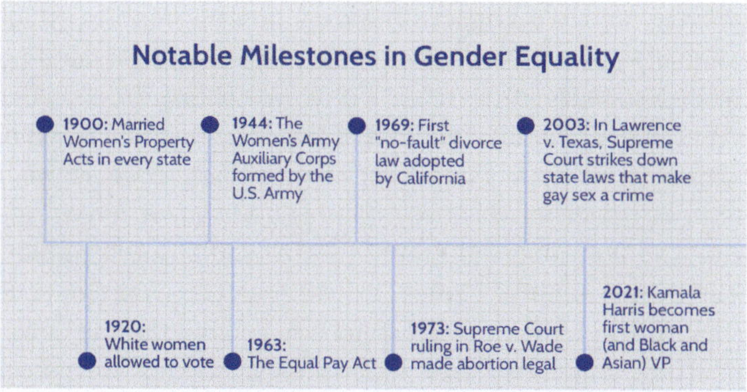

Figure 4.3. The courts and gender equality in the USA.

Source: Ronni Sandroff (2022) via Investopedia https://www.investopedia.com/milestones-in-gender-equality-5114037

The role of precedent in policy decisions is exemplified by the common law system, where legal principles are derived from previous court decisions rather than solely relying on legislative enactments (Chan, 2011; Chavez, 2003, 2007; Chen & Li, 2016; Chutkow, 2008). As judges interpret and apply the law, they consider not only statutes and constitution but also previous cases with similar legal issues. This process allows for the accumulation of legal principles over time, forming a body of law that guides future decisions. One real-world example that exemplifies the role of precedent in policy decisions is the landmark Supreme Court case of Brown v. Board of Education (1954) in the United States. In this case, the Court's decision effectively overturned the "separate but equal" doctrine established by the earlier Plessy v. Ferguson (1896) case, which had allowed for racial segregation in public facilities. The Court, in Brown v. Board of Education, established the legal precedent that racial segregation in public schools was unconstitutional under the Fourteenth Amendment's guarantee of equal protection. The judges based their decision on the principle of stare decisis, a legal doctrine that promotes consistency and stability by adhering to prior decisions.

The Court's reasoning in Brown v. Board of Education was heavily influenced by the doctrine of precedent, as it relied on the legitimacy and authority of previous court decisions rather than solely depending on legislative enactments or personal opinions. The justices acknowledged that their verdict was built on the foundation of prior Supreme Court decisions, such as Sweatt v. Painter (1950), as well as sociological and psychological research on the negative impact of segregation on minority students. The meticulous analysis of precedents and the nuanced understanding of legal principles allowed the Court to make a groundbreaking decision that had far-reaching implications for civil rights and the desegregation of schools in the United States. However, it is important to note that precedent, while crucial in shaping policy decisions, is not infallible and can be subject to criticism and debate. The controversial nature of Brown v. Board of Education is a testament to this reality. Critics argued that the Court overstepped its authority and engaged in judicial activism by overturning long-standing precedent. They contended that the decision should have been left to legislative bodies rather than the courts. This disagreement highlights the ongoing tension between judicial interpretation of the law and democratic decision-making processes.

Moreover, precedent can be subject to reevaluation and refinement when circumstances change or new evidence emerges (Cui, 2017; Davis, 2008; De Francesco & Tosun, 2022; de la Torre & Lemos, 2016). The Supreme Court itself has occasionally revisited and clarified its own precedents, demonstrating the dynamic nature of legal interpretation. For instance, subsequent cases, such as Swann v. Charlotte-Mecklenburg Board of Education (1971), further developed the standards for desegregation of public schools. Brown v. Board of Education underscores the pivotal role of precedent in policy decisions, particularly within the common law system. It demonstrates how legal principles are derived from previous court decisions and how these principles can shape future policy and societal development. The case also highlights the potential for debate, critique, and nuance surrounding the application and interpretation of precedent, as well as the capacity for the law to evolve over time.

The impact of precedent on policy decisions extends beyond mere legal interpretations (Tew, 2016; Tey, 2010; Tezcur, 2009; Travesi & Whitehead, 2021). It plays a pivotal role in shaping societal norms, values, and expectations. The judiciary's adherence to or departure from past precedents sends signals to society about the stability of the legal system and the direction of policy changes. For instance, the Supreme Court's decision in Brown v. Board of Education (1954) overturned the "separate but equal" precedent set in Plessy v. Ferguson (1896), signaling a transformative shift in racial segregation policies and affirming the government's commitment to civil rights. Moreover, the relationship between precedent and policy decisions is dynamic and multifaceted. The government, through its legislative and executive functions, shapes and informs the legal landscape.

It is the government's role to enact laws, formulate policies, and respond to societal changes. When courts decide cases, they are often confronted with interpreting statutes and regulations that have been promulgated by the government. This dynamic interaction implies that the government's actions can subsequently influence legal precedent, either by creating new laws that affirm or challenge existing precedents or by amending previous statutes to reflect societal shifts. This is how common law emerged and was developed for a modern age (see Figure 4.4).

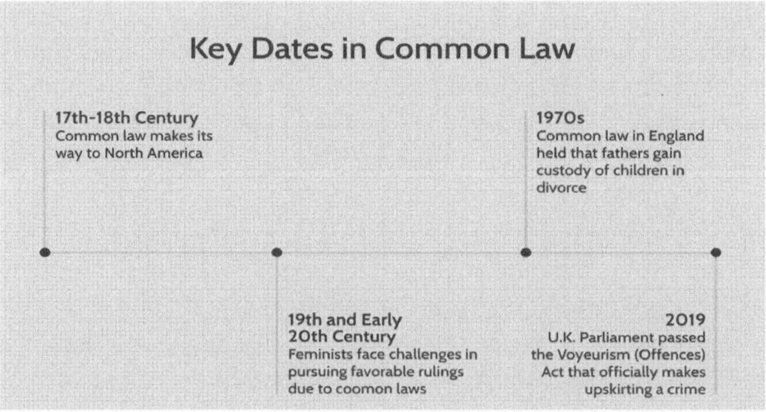

Figure 4.4. Key dates in the evolution of common law.

Source: James Chen (2022) Investopedia https://www.investopedia.com/terms/c/common-law.asp

Debates surrounding the impact of precedent on policy decisions often revolve around issues of stare decisis, the legal principle that courts should adhere to previous decisions unless there are compelling reasons to depart from them (Joshi, 2022; Juhn, 2021; Kang, 2004; Kang et al., 2023). Critics argue that blind adherence to precedent can lead to unjust or outdated outcomes, inhibiting the evolution of legal doctrines to meet contemporary challenges. On the other hand, proponents of stare decisis argue that consistency and predictability are essential for the rule of law and maintaining public trust in the judiciary. One real-world example from Africa that exemplifies the debates surrounding the impact of precedent on policy decisions is the case of Democratic Alliance v. African National Congress and Others (2017) in South Africa. In this case, the Supreme Court of Appeal ruled that President Jacob Zuma should be held accountable for the corruption charges against him and be reinstated to face trial. The Court's decision was seen as a departure from previous judgments that had allowed

President Zuma to avoid prosecution. The debate surrounding this decision centered on the principle of stare decisis and the question of whether the Court should have upheld the precedent of earlier judgments or acted in the interest of justice. Critics argued that the Court should have adhered to the previous decisions, such as the National Director of Public Prosecutions v. Zuma (2009), which dropped the corruption charges against the President. They contended that the Court's decision to hold President Zuma accountable was politically motivated and that it undermined the stability and finality of legal judgments.

Supporters of the Court's decision argued that the earlier judgments had been flawed and had allowed the President to evade accountability for alleged corruption. They maintained that the Court's ruling was necessary to restore faith in the justice system and to uphold the principle that no individual, regardless of their position, should be above the law. Supporters emphasized the importance of the Court taking a stand against corruption and ensuring the accountability of public officials. This case highlights the ongoing debates surrounding the impact of precedent on policy decisions in diverse regions such as Africa (Bascuas, 2005; Baude, 2020; Baum, 2003; Bednar, 2004). It showcases how legal decisions can be subject to critique and debate, particularly when they involve high-profile figures and issues of accountability. The Court's decision in Democratic Alliance v. African National Congress and Others demonstrates the delicate balance between upholding the authority of precedent and ensuring justice in the face of potential wrongdoing. This example from South Africa offers a glimpse into the complex discussions surrounding the impact of precedent on policy decisions in African countries. It underscores the significance of precedent in shaping legal outcomes, while also highlighting the need for courts to consider societal interests and the promotion of justice. The case raises important questions about the role of the judiciary in challenging established norms and striking a balance between legal stability and the pursuit of accountability.

A nuanced perspective acknowledges that while precedent can provide stability, there is room for the judiciary and government to reassess and adapt policies based on changing circumstances (Agbor, 2015; Alleman & Mazzone, 2010; Alter, 1998). The landmark case of Roe v. Wade (1973), which established a woman's right to choose an abortion, exemplifies the ongoing debate over precedent. The Supreme Court has grappled with how much deference to give to this precedent while also considering changes in societal values, medical advancements, and legal developments. One international example that reflects the debates surrounding the impact of judicial precedent on policy decisions is the case of ECHR (European Court of Human Rights) judgments related to the rights of migrants and asylum seekers in Europe. The European Court of Human Rights has issued several landmark rulings that have shaped the policies and practices of European states in relation to immigration and asylum. For instance, the judgment in the case of M.S.S. v. Belgium and Greece (2011) highlighted the issue of overcrowded and inhuman conditions in reception centers in Greece, where migrants and asylum seekers were held. The Court ruled that such conditions violated the prohibition of inhuman and degrading treatment under the European Convention on Human Rights. This judgment set a precedent by emphasizing that states have a duty to ensure humane treatment and uphold fundamental rights in their immigration and asylum policies.

Following this precedent, several other cases have been brought before national courts and the European Court of Human Rights, raising concerns about the treatment of migrants and asylum seekers in Europe. These cases have prompted policymakers to review and adapt their policies, particularly in areas such as detention, access to healthcare, and integration measures. The impact of judicial precedent in these cases is widely debated. While proponents argue that such judgments provide a crucial mechanism for holding states accountable and protecting the rights of vulnerable individuals, critics contend that they can interfere with national sovereignty and hinder states' ability to manage migration in line with their own domestic considerations (Lee, 2009; Leonard, 2016; Levin & Alkoby, 2017, 2019). This example highlights the global relevance of the impact of judicial precedent on policy decisions. By examining the rulings and subsequent policy changes resulting from international courts, it becomes evident that judicial precedent can influence and shape policies related to migration and asylum in various countries. The ECHR judgments on migrants and asylum seekers in Europe demonstrates the debates surrounding the impact of judicial precedent on policy decisions in an international context. It underscores the role of courts in interpreting and applying human rights standards, while also highlighting the complexities and diverse perspectives associated with immigration and asylum policies across different countries.

In conclusion, the impact of precedent in policy decisions is a nuanced interplay between the judiciary and government that shapes the development of laws and governance. Precedent not only offers consistency and predictability but also reflects societal norms and values. The relationship between the judiciary and government in utilizing and interpreting precedents is a dynamic process that balances the need for stability with the necessity of adapting policies to changing circumstances. This intricate dance shapes the trajectory of laws and policies, while also reaffirming the essential role of an evolving judiciary and responsive government in upholding justice and addressing societal challenges. The third section will focus on judicial activism and restraint in policy matters.

4.3. JUDICIAL ACTIVISM VS. RESTRAINT IN POLICY MATTERS

Judicial Activism and Judicial Restraint are two contrasting approaches within the realm of constitutional interpretation and decision-making by the judiciary, particularly in matters relating to public policy (Tridimas & Gari, 2010; Trochev, 2004; Tunamsifu, 2022). These two approaches have significant implications for the relationship between the judiciary and the government, as well as for the balance of power within a democratic system. One real-world example of the contrasting approaches of judicial activism and judicial restraint can be seen in the context of abortion laws in Ireland. Prior to 2018, Ireland had some of the most restrictive abortion laws in the world, where the procedure was only allowed when the woman's life was at risk. This strict law was a result of the influence of the Catholic Church on Irish society. However, in a landmark case known as the "Savita Halappanavar" case (see Figure 4.5), the issue of constitutional interpretation and the role of the judiciary in matters of public policy came to the forefront. Savita Halappanavar, a pregnant woman, died in 2012 after being denied an abortion, which could have potentially saved her life. This tragic incident sparked public outrage and led to a national debate on the need to reform Ireland's abortion laws.

The case prompted a group called the "Repeal the Eighth" movement to advocate for the repeal of the Eighth Amendment of the Irish Constitution, which granted equal rights to the unborn and the mother. In 2018, this movement successfully pushed for a referendum, and the majority of Irish citizens voted to repeal the Eighth Amendment. As a result, the Irish Parliament passed the "Legalization of the Termination of Pregnancy Act," allowing for abortion in certain circumstances up to 12 weeks of pregnancy and in cases where the mother's life or health is at risk. This example highlights the tension between judicial activism and judicial restraint (Berger, 1978, 1979a, 1979b; Berkmanas, 2020; Besco, 2018). In the lead-up to the referendum, the judiciary played a relatively restrained role, allowing the political and societal debate to take center stage. The judiciary did not actively interpret the Constitution to strike down the existing restrictive abortion laws. Instead, the case of Savita Halappanavar's death served as a catalyst for public demand for legislative change.

Figure 4.5. Protests in the "Savita Halappanavar" case.

Source: Parliamentarians for Global Action https://www.pgaction.org/news/death-of-savita-halappanavar.html

On the other hand, judicial activism could have potentially taken a different course, where the judiciary could have interpreted the Constitution more expansively to proactively strike down the restrictive abortion laws as unconstitutional (Janover, 2021; Johnson, 2019; Jonski, 2021; Jorritsma, 2020). This approach would have involved the judiciary actively shaping public policy through its interpretation of the law. By illustrating the Irish abortion rights referendum and the subsequent legislation, we see how judicial restraint can allow for democratic processes and public opinion to shape policy changes, while judicial activism can alter the constitutional interpretation to proactively promote societal values. Both approaches have their merits and limitations and spark ongoing debates about the proper role of the judiciary in matters of public policy-making.

Judicial Activism refers to the willingness of a court to actively participate in shaping and influencing public policy decisions (Bonica & Sen, 2017; Boskovic, 2020; Boyd, 2001; Bradley, 1998). In this approach, judges interpret the Constitution and other laws broadly, often going beyond the literal text, to address societal issues and advance principles they believe are essential for justice and fairness. Judicial activists tend to be more open to overturning legislative or executive actions if they deem them unconstitutional or in violation of fundamental rights. One real-world example that reflects the concept of judicial activism is the Mexican Supreme Court's decision on the constitutional right to access cannabis for personal use. In 2018, the court ruled that prohibiting the recreational use of cannabis was unconstitutional, as it violated individuals' right to free development of personality. The court argued that imposing criminal penalties for private cannabis use infringed upon personal autonomy, privacy, and the rights to dignity and self-determination. This decision sparked a significant debate within Mexican society and raised concerns about the role of the judiciary in shaping drug policy. Critics of the court's activism argue that such decisions should be left to the legislative branch, as drug policy affects public health, safety, and national security. They argue that the court's intervention undermines the ability of elected representatives to respond to the needs and desires of the population through democratic deliberation.

On the other hand, supporters of the court's decision emphasize the protection of individual rights and argue that the court's role is to safeguard constitutional guarantees. They contend that criminalizing personal use of cannabis disproportionately affects marginalized communities and perpetuates a cycle of violence and social inequality. They view the court's intervention as an example of using judicial power to rectify social injustices and promote individual liberties. This example highlights the ongoing debate surrounding judicial activism and its implications for public policy (Emerson, 2022; Evans et al., 2017; Fallon & Meltzer, 1991). Critics raise concerns about the proper role of the judiciary in shaping controversial issues, arguing that judicial intervention can infringe upon democratic processes. On the other hand, proponents highlight the court's duty to protect individual rights and address societal inequities, emphasizing the importance of safeguarding constitutional guarantees through judicial activism. It is crucial to recognize that this example is provided for the purpose of illustrating the diverse perspectives and debates surrounding judicial activism, rather than providing a definitive judgment on the matter. This approach can be seen as advantageous in cases where the legislative or executive branches fail to address pressing issues or when there are perceived gaps in existing laws (Edelman, 1994; Efrat, 2018; Eichensehr, 2018; Eleftheriadis, 2005). By taking an active role, the judiciary can ensure that the rights of marginalized groups are protected and that constitutional principles are upheld. However, critics of judicial activism argue that it can lead to judicial overreach, where unelected judges make policy decisions that should be the purview of elected representatives. This can undermine the separation of powers and the democratic process. As Figure 4.6 shows, the label of judicial activism and passivism can depend on perceptions and political stances.

Type of Issue/Category	What has been labelled as Judicial 'Activism'	What has been labelled as Judicial 'Passivity'/'Conservativism'/'Restraint'
Constitutional Interpretive Methodology[116]	- Liberal - Purposive - Conceptual/contextual	- Conservative (more appropriately 'non-liberal')[117] - Ordinary, plain or natural meaning - Originalism, legal positivism
Law-making	- makes law - invalidates legislation	- do not make law (leaves that to legislatures) - declines to invalidate legislation
Policy choices	- where appropriate willing to adjudicate on matters of policy	- unwilling to adjudicate on matters of policy since considers questions of policy strictly the ambit of other branches of government not the judiciary
Political disputes	- entertains political decisions in their courts	- do not entertain political decisions in their courts
Creativity	- creative/innovative (develops new concepts)	- not creative/innovative (unwilling to develop new concepts)
Sensitivity to social realities	- are sensitive to social realities (concerns themselves with the ends of the law)	- are not sensitive to social realities (do not concern themselves with the ends of the law)

Figure 4.6. Labels attached to cases in terms of judicial activism and passivity.

Source: Kachale, C. J. (2012). *Judicial (in) activism in Malawi?: a critical analysis of the impact of constitutional jurisprudence on constitutionalism and the rule of law* (Doctoral dissertation, SOAS, University of London).

Judicial Restraint, on the other hand, emphasizes a more limited role for the judiciary in matters of policy (Lee, 2009; Leonard, 2016; Levin & Alkoby, 2017, 2019). Judges who adhere to this approach are cautious about intervening in policy decisions made by the legislative and executive branches, preferring to defer to elected officials unless there is a clear violation of the Constitution. Judicial restraint proponents argue that unelected judges should not make decisions that are better left to elected representatives who are directly accountable to the people. One real-world example that can be discussed in the context of judicial restraint is the constitutional challenge to gun control laws in Canada. In 2020, the Supreme Court of Canada heard the case of R. V. Hasselwander, which dealt with the constitutionality of the federal government's ban on certain firearms. The debate centered on whether the government's actions were within the scope of its authority and whether the court should intervene to strike down the legislation. Advocates of judicial restraint argued that the court should defer to the elected representatives and give them more leeway to shape public policy. They maintained that the issue of gun control falls squarely within the domain of legislative decision-making, and that judges should show restraint in interfering with the choices made by democratically accountable institutions. These proponents contended that the judiciary should exercise self-restraint and only intervene when there is a clear violation of constitutional rights or an abuse of power by the legislative branch.

On the other side of the debate, critics of judicial restraint expressed concerns regarding potential legislative overreach and violations of individual rights. They argued that the court has a crucial role in safeguarding fundamental rights, such as the right to life and security, which may be jeopardized by the misuse of firearms. These advocates contended that judicial intervention is necessary to maintain a proper balance between public safety and individual liberties, particularly when legislative action appears to infringe upon constitutional protections. The case highlighted the ongoing tension between judicial restraint and the role of the judiciary in policy matters (Pospieszna & Vetulani-Cegiel, 2021; Preis, 2006; Preston, 2016). Supporters of restraint emphasized the importance of deferring to elected officials and allowing democratic processes to dictate policy outcomes, while critics argued for a more proactive role for the court in safeguarding individual rights and ensuring legislative decisions are within constitutional bounds. As with any discussion on judicial philosophy, it is essential to recognize that there are valid arguments on both sides, and the approach taken by the court in this particular case could have far-reaching implications for the balance of power between the judiciary and the legislature. The debate surrounding judicial restraint in the context of gun control underscores the complexities and nuances inherent in determining the appropriate role and limits of the judiciary in matters of policy-making.

This approach is often seen as promoting stability and maintaining the balance of powers within a democratic system (Gallagher, 2012; Gardbaum, 2015; Garoupa et al., 2012). It avoids the potential dangers of judges making subjective policy judgments and respects the principle of separation of powers. However, critics of judicial restraint argue that it can result in the courts neglecting their duty to protect individual rights and minorities, especially when other branches of government are not acting in the best interests of justice. The balance between judicial activism and restraint varies based on legal philosophies, constitutional interpretations, and the particular context of a given case. It is worth noting that judges may exhibit characteristics of both activism and restraint in different cases, and the application of these principles is not always black and white. The relationship between judicial activism and restraint and the government is complex. In democratic societies, the judiciary is intended to serve as a check on the powers of the legislative and executive branches. When courts engage in judicial activism, they might directly challenge or shape government policies. This can lead to tensions between the branches, with the government accusing the judiciary of overstepping its boundaries. Conversely, when courts exercise restraint, they may be seen as deferring too much to the government and failing to uphold their duty as protectors of individual rights and constitutional principles.

In conclusion, the debate between judicial activism and restraint in policy matters reflects the broader tension between the judiciary's role in safeguarding individual rights and the need to maintain the separation of powers within a democratic system. Both approaches have their merits and potential pitfalls, and the proper balance between them is a subject of ongoing discussion and consideration within legal and political circles. The fourth section in this chapter considers the role of the judiciary in public policy.

4.4. ROLE OF THE JUDICIARY IN PUBLIC POLICY

The role of the judiciary in public policy is a critical aspect of the broader relationship between the judicial branch and the government within a democratic system (Grove, 2018; Gunderson, 2022; Hardaway, 2021; Hardman, 2020). While the primary function of the judiciary is to interpret and apply the law impartially, its involvement in shaping and influencing public policy raises important questions about the balance of powers, the rule of law, and the protection of individual rights. The judiciary's role in public policy can be examined through various lenses:

1. Constitutional Interpretation:

One of the judiciary's key roles in public policy is to interpret the constitution and laws (Bybee, 1994; Byrne & Maxwell, 2019; Calabresi & Rhodes, 1992). Courts often deal with cases where the constitutionality of a law or government action is challenged. Through their interpretation, judges can establish legal precedents that impact the scope and boundaries of government power. This power gives the judiciary a substantial role in shaping public policy, as their decisions can limit or expand the government's ability to legislate and execute policies. One real-world example that demonstrates the judiciary's role in interpreting the constitution and laws is the case of the United Kingdom's withdrawal from the European Union, commonly known as Brexit. Following the 2016 referendum, which saw a narrow majority in favor of leaving the EU, the question of how to proceed legally and constitutionally became a matter of significant debate. In this context, the judiciary played a crucial role in interpreting the constitutional and legal framework governing the withdrawal process. One notable case that exemplifies this is R (Miller) v Secretary of State for Exiting the European Union. In 2017, the UK Supreme Court heard the appeal related to the government's authority to trigger Article 50 of the EU Treaty, which starts the process of withdrawal. The key issue at stake was whether the government could invoke Article 50 without parliamentary approval.

Free GIANT map of Britain inside tomorrow

Daily Mail

FRIDAY, NOVEMBER 4, 2016 www.dailymail.co.uk DAILY NEWSPAPER OF THE YEAR 65p

The fencer: Sir Terence Etherton | Worked with Tony Blair: Lord Justice Sales | The Europhile: Lord Chief Justice Thomas

Fury over 'out of touch' judges who defied 17.4m Brexit voters and could trigger constitutional crisis

ENEMIES OF THE PEOPLE

MPS last night tore into an unelected panel of 'out of touch' judges for ruling that embittered Remain supporters in Parliament should be allowed to frustrate the overwhelming verdict of the British public.

By James Slack Political Editor

The Lord Chief Justice and two senior colleagues were accused of putting Britain on course for a full-blown 'constitutional crisis' by saying Brexit could not be triggered without a Westminster vote.

The judgment by Lord Thomas – a founding member of the European Law Institute, a club of lawyers and academics aiming to 'improve' EU law – throws into chaos Mrs May's timetable for invoking article 50 in March next year.

Senior MPs – led by an ex-justice minister – said it was an outrage that an 'unholy alliance' of judges and embittered Remain backers could thwart the wishes of 17.4million Leave voters. They warned that Mrs May could be forced to hold an election early next year if the courts did not back down. Leave

Turn to Page 2

Figure 4.7. Incendiary media headline following the role of judiciary in Brexit.

Source: The Conversation (2016) https://theconversation.com/enemies-of-the-people-mps-and-press-gang-up-on-the-constitution-over-high-court-brexit-ruling-68241

Proponents of judicial restraint argued that the government possessed the prerogative power to trigger Article 50 and proceed with Brexit without parliamentary involvement. They contended that this was a matter of executive discretion and policy-making and that the courts should defer to the government's interpretation in matters of high political significance. They argued that excessive judicial intervention could undermine democratic processes and the expression of the popular will. On the other side, advocates of judicial activism asserted that parliamentary approval was necessary to initiate such a significant constitutional change. They maintained that the principle of parliamentary sovereignty required a democratic decision-making process, involving elected representatives, when modifying the rights of citizens. They argued that the judiciary should play a supervisory role in ensuring the legality and constitutionality of the government's actions. The Supreme Court ultimately ruled that parliamentary approval was indeed required to trigger Article 50, emphasizing the principle of parliamentary sovereignty and the need for democratic legitimacy in significant constitutional matters. This decision influenced subsequent debates and established an important precedent regarding the judicial oversight of executive actions in the context of Brexit. As Figure 4.7 shows, judges were critique for their role in the implementation of Brexit.

This example demonstrates the judiciary's critical role in interpreting the constitution and laws, particularly when significant constitutional changes are at stake. The debate surrounding the Miller case encapsulated competing views regarding the appropriate balance between governmental authority and parliamentary sovereignty, with arguments for both judicial restraint and judicial activism. It highlighted the judiciary's responsibility to clarify and apply legal principles in these complex and politically charged matters, ensuring that the constitutional framework is upheld and democratic processes are respected.

2. Safeguarding Individual Rights:

The judiciary serves as a safeguard for individual rights and liberties, ensuring that government policies and actions do not infringe upon these rights (McCoy & Jahic, 2006; McEwen et al., 2012; Mechkova et al., 2019). Judges may strike down laws or government actions that violate fundamental rights guaranteed by the constitution, thereby influencing public policy by setting a standard for protecting individual freedoms. A noteworthy example that highlights the role of judiciary in safeguarding individual rights and liberties can be found in the case of Aung San Suu Kyi in Myanmar. Aung San

Suu Kyi, a Nobel laureate and leader of the National League for Democracy, had been under house arrest for many years due to her political activism and opposition to the military regime in Myanmar. In 2010, the military junta in power initiated a series of reforms and Suu Kyi was finally released in 2011. However, her political journey didn't end there. In 2015, Suu Kyi's party won the general elections in Myanmar, and she assumed the role of State Counsellor, which was an equivalent to the position of Prime Minister. This seemed to be a positive step towards democracy and respect for individual rights. However, the Rohingya crisis brought to light the complex challenges that faced the judiciary in safeguarding individual rights.

The Rohingya, a Muslim minority group in Myanmar, has long been subjected to ethnic cleansing, discrimination, and violence at the hands of the military and other extremist groups. In 2017, a military crackdown led to the mass exodus of Rohingya refugees into neighboring Bangladesh, where they sought shelter from the brutal violence. This situation raised serious concerns regarding human rights violations and the role of the government in perpetrating these atrocities.

The response of Aung San Suu Kyi and her government to the Rohingya crisis became a subject of intense debate and critique. Many international bodies and human rights organizations condemned Suu Kyi's handling of the crisis, arguing that her government failed to protect the rights and freedoms of the Rohingya people. This put the judiciary in a challenging position of balancing the principles of justice, human rights, and the political agenda pursued by the government. The International Court of Justice (ICJ), a body responsible for adjudicating disputes between states, heard a case against Myanmar brought by Gambia, accusing Myanmar of genocide against the Rohingya.

This case highlighted the crucial role of the judiciary in holding governments accountable for their actions and ensuring that individual rights are protected (Edelman, 1994; Efrat, 2018; Eichensehr, 2018; Eleftheriadis, 2005). The ICJ found merit in Gambia's case, indicating that there was sufficient evidence to justify further investigations into Myanmar's treatment of the Rohingya. The case of Aung San Suu Kyi and the Rohingya crisis serves as an example of the judiciary's role in upholding individual rights and liberties. It highlights the delicate balance between politics and justice, as well as the challenge faced by the judiciary in navigating complex international dynamics (Setty, 2015; Shah, 2014; Shenkman, 2012; Shepherd, 2009). While the case is ongoing and the ultimate outcome remains uncertain, it underscores the importance of an independent and impartial judiciary in safeguarding individual rights and preventing government policies and actions that infringe upon these rights.

3. Filling Legislative Gaps:

In cases where the legislative branch fails to address emerging issues or societal concerns, the judiciary may step in to bridge the gap (Tew, 2016; Tey, 2010; Tezcur, 2009; Travesi & Whitehead, 2021). This can involve interpreting existing laws broadly to apply them to new situations or even creating new legal doctrines to address issues not previously covered by legislation. One real-life example that exemplifies the judiciary bridging a gap left by the legislative branch can be observed in the case of the Colombian constitutional court's ruling on the rights of same-sex couples. In Colombia, the legislative branch had not taken explicit action to legalize same-sex marriage or provide equal rights and protections for same-sex couples. However, societal concerns and demands for equality prompted the judiciary to intervene and address this issue. In 2011, the Colombian Constitutional Court came to the historic decision that denying same-sex couples the right to marry was unconstitutional. The court reached this decision by interpreting the existing constitutional principles of equality, dignity, and non-discrimination to include same-sex couples. The court argued that by limiting marriage to opposite-sex couples, the law was denying same-sex couples fundamental rights and perpetuating discrimination.

The court's decision sparked a significant debate within Colombian society. Supporters of marriage equality hailed it as a step forward for human rights and equality, while opponents argued that the court had overstepped its authority and undermined the role of the legislature. Critics contended that marriage was a matter for the legislative branch to decide and that the court had taken on a legislative role by redefining the institution of marriage. Nevertheless, the constitutional court defended its decision by asserting that it was fulfilling its duty to protect and enforce fundamental rights, even when the legislative branch had failed to act. The court argued that its interpretation was based on evolving societal norms and international human rights standards. It emphasized that its role was not to make laws but rather to interpret the constitution in line with the evolving values of society.

Despite the controversy surrounding the court's ruling, same-sex marriage became legal in Colombia, granting same-sex couples the same rights and recognition as opposite-sex couples. The case of the Colombian constitutional court's intervention demonstrates the capacity of the judiciary to bridge gaps left by the legislative branch when it fails to address emerging issues or societal concerns (Mendelson, 1976; Menounou et al., 2019; Michetti et al., 2018). By interpreting constitutional principles and protecting fundamental rights, the judiciary can play a crucial role in advancing equality and justice, even in the absence of legislative action. It is important to note that the Colombian example is just one among many instances where the judiciary has stepped in to bridge gaps left by the legislative branch. It illustrates the broader debate on the role of the judiciary in addressing societal issues and promoting social progress. As Figure 4.8 shows, the judiciary can still have some role to play in the formulation of policy.

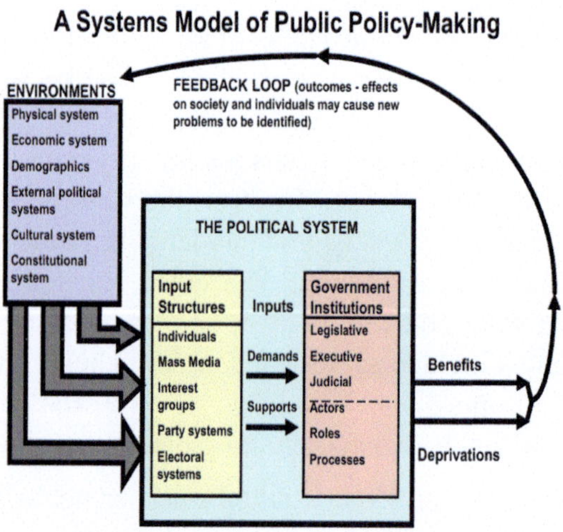

Figure 4.8. Example of a systems model of policy-making.

Source: https://studylib.net/doc/15633753/a-systems-model-of-public-policy-making-feedback-loop-env...

4. Addressing Policy Disputes:

Public policy often involves conflicting interests and values. When disputes arise over the interpretation or application of laws, courts provide a neutral forum for resolving these disputes (Gonzalez, 2021; Gorodovenko et al., 2021; Gouldin, 2012). Their decisions can shape the direction of policy implementation and provide clarity on how laws should be applied in practice. One notable example that exemplifies the role of courts in resolving disputes over conflicting interests and values in public policy can be seen in the case of Kadi v. European Commission. The case centers around the European Union's (EU) counter-terrorism efforts, particularly the inclusion of individuals and organizations on terrorist sanctions lists. In 2001, the UN Security Council adopted Resolution 1373, which called on member states to freeze the assets of individuals and entities associated with terrorist activities. In response, the EU established its own list of designated terrorist individuals and organizations, which was known as the "terrorist sanctions list." These designations had significant consequences for the listed individuals, as their assets were frozen and they faced travel restrictions. One individual affected by these measures was Youssef Nada, an Egyptian businessman. Nada challenged his inclusion on the EU's terrorist sanctions list, arguing that he had been wrongfully designated and that his rights to due process and a fair hearing had been violated. The case reached the European Court of Justice (ECJ), the highest court in the EU.

The central debate in the case revolved around the balance between security concerns and the protection of individual rights (Brown, 1999; Buchmeyer, 2019; Bunjevac, 2015; Burbank, 2009). On one hand, the EU argued that the inclusion of individuals on the sanctions list was necessary to combat terrorism effectively, and that the process followed the UN Security Council resolutions. They asserted that national security interests justified limiting the rights of the listed individuals. However, Nada and his legal representatives argued that the procedures for designation lacked transparency and effective safeguards to prevent errors or abuse. They contended that the EU had failed to provide sufficient evidence to justify the designation and that Nada had been denied the opportunity to defend himself properly. In essence, they challenged the court to consider the impact of the sanctions on individual rights and whether adequate procedural safeguards were in place. The ECJ's judgment in the Kadi case was deeply nuanced and balanced. The court recognized the importance of combating terrorism and the need for effective measures in this regard. However, it also emphasized the fundamental rights of individuals, including the right to an effective remedy and respect for due process. The court held that the EU's procedures lacked sufficient safeguards and that Nada's rights had been violated. Consequently, the ECJ annulled the designation of Nada and established important legal principles for future designations.

The Kadi case illustrates how courts provide a neutral forum for resolving disputes arising from conflicting interests and values in public policy (Steuer, 2019; Subedi, 2016; Szente, 2021; Taghdiri, 2019). In this instance, the ECJ navigated the delicate balance between security concerns and the protection of individual rights. The case highlights the critical role of the judiciary in ensuring that government actions are lawful and consistent with fundamental rights. It also underscores the importance of establishing clear and fair procedures in public policy measures that may have significant consequences for individuals.

5. Judicial Review:

Many democratic systems grant the judiciary the power of judicial review, allowing them to review the constitutionality of laws and government actions. This power ensures that policies adhere to the principles outlined in the constitution (Medawatte et al., 2013; Meggitt & Somji, 2016; Melone, 1996). While this power is essential for maintaining the rule of law, it also gives the judiciary a significant role in shaping public policy by determining what is permissible under the constitution. An informative example that encapsulates the power of judicial review in ensuring policy adherence to constitutional principles can be observed in the case of Minister for Aboriginal Affairs v. Peko-Wallsend Ltd in Australia. In this case, the question at hand was whether a legislative provision that granted the Minister for Aboriginal Affairs the power to modify or extinguish native title rights was consistent with the constitutional protection of rights enjoyed by Indigenous Australians. The Native Title Act 1993 aimed to recognize and protect the rights of Indigenous Australians to their land and resources. However, Section 10(1) of the Act allowed the Minister for Aboriginal Affairs to make determinations that could result in the extinguishment or modification of native title rights. Peko-Wallsend Ltd, a mining company, challenged this provision on the grounds that it infringed upon the constitutional rights of Indigenous Australians and exceeded the legislative powers of the Commonwealth.

The Australian High Court, the highest judicial authority in the country, deliberated on the constitutionality of Section 10(1) and the scope of the Parliament's power in relation to Indigenous rights. The central debate revolved around the interpretation of the constitutional provisions protecting Indigenous Australians' rights to their land and resources, as well as the limits of parliamentary authority in encroaching upon those rights. The Court's judgment demonstrated an intricate balance between protecting Indigenous rights and recognizing Parliament's legislative authority. The judges held that Section 10(1) was unconstitutional as it granted the Minister excessive power to modify or extinguish native title rights without appropriate safeguards. The Court elucidated that the Constitution required a more robust protection of Indigenous rights, necessitating a higher threshold for any impairment of those rights. The significance of the Peko-Wallsend case lies in the debate over how best to ensure policy adherence to constitutional principles, particularly in the context of Indigenous rights. Some argued that the breadth of discretion given to the Minister was necessary to balance competing interests and facilitate economic development. Others stressed the importance of upholding Indigenous rights and their constitutional protection, asserting that any encroachments should be narrowly defined and strictly justifiable.

The Court's ruling in favor of Peko-Wallsend highlighted the judiciary's role in interpreting the constitution and assessing the constitutionality of legislation (Manning & Randazzo, 2009; Maor, 2004; Maphosa, 2020). By striking down Section 10(1), the Court signaled that the protection of Indigenous rights was a paramount constitutional duty. It reinforced the principle that policies must adhere to the constitutional framework, serving as a safeguard against potential infringements on individual or collective rights. The example of the Peko-Wallsend case signifies how judicial review empowers the judiciary to assess the compatibility of laws and government actions with constitutional principles. It showcases the ongoing debate between competing interests and the challenges of striking a balance between protecting individual and group rights while allowing for necessary policy development within a democratic framework.

6. *Balancing Powers:*

The judiciary's involvement in public policy can also help maintain a balance of powers among the branches of government. By reviewing and potentially invalidating legislative and executive actions, the judiciary prevents any one branch from becoming too dominant or exceeding its authority (Colucci, 2000; Conrad, 2014; Costas-Perez et al., 2012; Cross, 1999). One recent real-world example of the judiciary's involvement in public policy and its role in maintaining a balance of powers among the branches of government in the Middle East can be seen in the case of Turkey's Constitutional Court ruling on the ban of the pro-Kurdish Peoples' Democratic Party (HDP). In March 2021, the Turkish government filed a lawsuit to ban the HDP, accusing the party of having links to Kurdish militants and engaging in activities deemed threatening to national security. The executive branch, represented by President Recep Tayyip Erdogan's Justice and Development Party (AKP), sought to curtail the political influence of the HDP, which was the third-largest party in the Turkish parliament. However, the judiciary, through the Constitutional Court, intervened and ruled against the ban. The court's ruling emphasized that political parties play a crucial role in a democratic society, and any attempt to ban a party should be based on concrete evidence of its involvement in activities that violate the constitutional order with an imminent threat to democracy. The court deemed that the government had failed to provide sufficient evidence to warrant the ban on the HDP.

This ruling triggered a significant debate about the judiciary's role in safeguarding democratic principles and preserving the balance of powers in Turkey. Supporters of the court's decision argue that it reinforced the independence and impartiality of the judiciary in resisting executive overreach. They claim that the court's ruling protected the democratic rights of citizens to freely associate and participate in the political process, preventing the executive from exceeding its authority. Critics, on the other hand, raised concerns that the judiciary's intervention undermines national security efforts and hampers the government's ability to combat terrorism. They argue that the court's decision prioritized political considerations over potential security risks posed by the HDP, suggesting that the judiciary overstepped its bounds and interfered with the executive's prerogative in safeguarding national interests. This example from Turkey demonstrates the judiciary's engagement in public policy and its role in maintaining a balance of powers between the branches of government (Mason, 2015; Matthes, 2022; Mayoral & Perez, 2018). It showcases the ongoing debate over the judiciary's autonomy and its ability to uphold democratic values while navigating complex political dynamics. The case underscores the significance of an independent judiciary as a crucial check on executive power, but also exposes the challenges and differing perspectives surrounding its jurisdiction and the potential consequences of its decisions in sensitive political contexts in the Middle East.

7. Adapting to Social Change:

Societies evolve, and public policy must adapt to changing circumstances and values. The judiciary plays a role in this adaptation by interpreting laws in light of current societal norms (Iaryczower et al., 2002; Ides, 1999; Imam & Egbewole, 2020). Their decisions can reflect changing attitudes and expectations, influencing the development of policies that are more aligned with contemporary values. One such example is the debate surrounding the regulation of technology companies and their impact on privacy and consumer rights. In recent years, there has been growing concern about the power and influence of tech giants and their handling of user data. This has prompted calls for increased regulation to protect individuals' privacy and ensure fair competition in the digital marketplace. One specific case that exemplifies the judiciary's contribution to this ongoing debate is the European Union's antitrust case against Google. In 2017, the European Commission found Google guilty of abusing its dominant market position by prioritizing its own shopping comparison service over competitors in search results. The Commission issued a record-breaking fine and mandated that Google change its practices to promote fair competition.

This case sparked an important conversation about the role of the judiciary in strengthening and adapting public policy to address the challenges posed by powerful tech companies (Lin, 2016; Liu & Baird, 2012; Macchiarola, 1971; Macey, 2006). Supporters of the decision argue that by holding Google accountable, the judiciary plays a crucial role in ensuring that regulations keep pace with the evolving digital landscape. They assert that such interventions are necessary to protect consumers and prevent unfair monopolistic practices. Critics, on the other hand, raise concerns about potential overreach by the judiciary and its impact on innovation and technological advancements. They argue that excessive regulation may stifle competition and hinder economic growth. Some contend that addressing issues related to technology and privacy should be primarily handled through legislative action, allowing for more nuanced and comprehensive policymaking. This example from the European Union illustrates the judiciary's involvement in interpreting and shaping public policy in the context of evolving technological advancements. It highlights the ongoing debate surrounding the appropriate level of regulation needed to address potential abuses of power by tech companies while balancing the interests of innovation and economic growth. The case underscores the need for a balanced approach that considers both consumer protection and the potential implications for the broader digital ecosystem.

8. Managing Government Action:

The judiciary can serve as a check on government overreach and abuse of power. By scrutinizing government actions and policies, the judiciary can prevent potential violations of the separation of powers, preventing the executive from taking actions that exceed its authority or infringe on the rights of citizens (Smith & Farrales, 2010; Smith, 1992; Smith, 2015). One real-world example that demonstrates the role of the judiciary in serving as a check on government overreach can be observed in Algeria. In 2019, widespread protests erupted in the country, demanding political reform, an end to corruption, and the departure of then-President Abdelaziz Bouteflika, who had been in power for twenty years. Amidst these protests, the judiciary played a significant role in holding the government accountable. Following the protests, the Algerian judiciary initiated investigations into allegations of corruption and abuse of power involving high-ranking officials, including government ministers and influential figures with close ties to the former president. These investigations were seen as a response to public demands for transparency and accountability.

The judiciary's involvement in these cases was debated by various segments of society. Supporters saw it as a necessary step towards combating corruption and ensuring justice for the people. They argued that the role of the judiciary in investigating and prosecuting those accused of wrongdoing demonstrated a commitment to upholding the rule of law and reestablishing public trust in the government. Critics, however, expressed concerns about the motives and independence of the judiciary. They questioned whether the investigations were politically motivated and aimed at undermining certain factions or individuals within the government. Skeptics argued that the judiciary's actions may serve the interests of the ruling elite rather than facilitating genuine reforms. This example from Algeria highlights the judiciary's potential role in checking government overreach and promoting accountability (Chan, 2011; Chavez, 2003, 2007; Chen & Li, 2016; Chutkow, 2008). It represents an ongoing debate about the judiciary's independence and impartiality in the face of political challenges. The case underscores the importance of a robust judiciary that can effectively address public demands for transparency, justice, and the protection of citizens' rights.

In summary, the judiciary's role in public policy is complex and multifaceted. It involves interpreting laws and the constitution, safeguarding individual rights, resolving disputes, and maintaining a balance of powers. While the judiciary's involvement in public policy is essential for upholding the rule of law and protecting individual rights, it also raises concerns about the potential for judicial overreach and the appropriate limits of judicial power in a democratic system. Balancing these considerations requires careful deliberation and a nuanced understanding of the judiciary's role within the broader government structure. The final section in this chapter will focus on evaluating policy implications of judicial decisions.

4.5. EVALUATING POLICY IMPLICATIONS OF JUDICIAL DECISIONS

The evaluation of policy implications arising from judicial decisions is a complex and multifaceted process that involves considering the interplay between the judiciary and the government, the legal principles at stake, and the broader societal impacts. Such evaluations are crucial for maintaining a balance between the roles of the judiciary and the government in shaping and implementing policies while upholding the rule of law.

1. Legal Precedent and Consistency:

Judicial decisions often set legal precedents that guide future cases. Evaluating policy implications requires analyzing the consistency and coherence of these precedents (Beiser-McGrath et al., 2022; Bell, 2002; Bencze, 2021). Consistency helps ensure predictability and fairness in the application of law, allowing governments to make informed policy choices that align with established legal norms. One compelling real-world example that illustrates the role of judicial decisions in setting legal precedents and evaluating their policy implications can be observed in the case of South Korea's Constitutional Court ruling on the country's abortion laws. In April 2019, the Constitutional Court ruled that the existing law, which criminalized abortion in most cases, was unconstitutional and violated women's right to self-determination and privacy. This landmark decision overturned a 66-year-old ban on abortion and set a new legal precedent for reproductive rights. The court's ruling sparked a heated debate within South Korean society about the policy implications of this decision. Supporters of the ruling argued that it was a crucial step in safeguarding women's reproductive rights and promoting gender equality. They asserted that the court's decision aligned with evolving societal values and recognized a woman's autonomy to make decisions about her own body. On the other hand, opponents of the ruling expressed concerns about potential societal and ethical consequences. They argued that the court's decision violated the rights of the unborn and questioned the precedent it set for future cases. Critics highlighted the need for a more nuanced and measured approach to protect both the rights of women and considerations related to the sanctity of life.

The policy implications of this ruling were further debated in subsequent discussions within the legislative branch. In April 2021, the South Korean parliament passed a new law legalizing abortion in the early stages of pregnancy, reflecting, to some extent, the policy guidance provided by the court's precedent. This example from South Korea illustrates how judicial decisions can influence policy implications by setting legal precedents (see Figure 4.9). It highlights the significance of evaluating the consistency and coherence of these precedents in guiding future cases and shaping public policy (Lee, 2009; Leonard, 2016; Levin & Alkoby, 2017, 2019). The case also exposes the contrasting perspectives and debates surrounding reproductive rights, ethics, and the role of the judiciary in interpreting and influencing societal values. It demonstrates the intricate interplay between the judiciary and the legislative branch in navigating complex social issues and crafting policies that reflect legal principles and societal considerations.

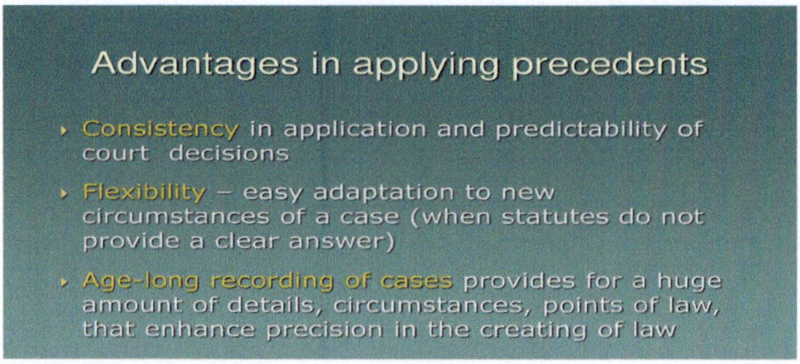

Figure 4.9. The merits of applying judicial precedents.

Source: Ole-Martin Fosse via SlidePlayer https://slideplayer.com/slide/14129410/

2. Separation of Powers:

A key consideration when evaluating policy implications is the principle of separation of powers. Governments formulate policies, while the judiciary interprets and applies laws. Assessing whether a judicial decision oversteps this boundary and intrudes into the policy domain requires a careful examination of the decision's scope and potential impact on governance (Bascuas, 2005; Baude, 2020; Baum, 2003; Bednar, 2004). In 2017, the Supreme Court of Canada made a significant decision that raised questions about the balance between policy-making and judicial interpretation. The case, known as R v. Jordan, centered around the interpretation and application of the right to a timely trial as guaranteed by the Canadian Charter of Rights and Freedoms. The Jordan case was brought forward due to delays in the criminal justice system, particularly in relation to the time it took to bring cases to trial. The accused argued that these delays violated their rights to a fair and impartial trial within a reasonable time frame. The Supreme Court, in a landmark ruling, set strict time limits for completing criminal trials and established clear guidelines for assessing whether a delay was reasonable or not.

While the decision was aimed at addressing systemic issues and ensuring access to justice, it arguably had significant policy implications. The strict timeframes set by the court have placed pressure on the justice system to expedite cases and led to shifts in policy and practice. Some critics argue that this decision has intruded into the policy domain and compromised the discretion of prosecutors and judges, as they must now carefully consider the timeframes set by the court when handling criminal cases. On the other hand, supporters of the ruling argue that it is necessary to address the issue of delays and ensure that individuals' rights are protected. They contend that the decision does not go beyond the judiciary's role in interpreting and applying the law, as it stems from the Charter and its provisions related to fair and timely trials.

The impact of the Jordan decision on governance has been significant. It has prompted significant reform efforts within the justice system, including changes to case management practices, increased funding for legal aid services, and efforts to streamline court procedures. However, there remains an ongoing debate about the extent to which the judiciary should be involved in shaping policy outcomes and whether such involvement encroaches upon the policy-making authority of the executive and legislative branches (Navarrete & Castillo-Ortiz, 2020; Nelson & Gibson, 2019). The Jordan case exemplifies the complexities and nuances of the separation of powers principle and the tension that can arise when judicial decisions have broader policy implications. It underscores the importance of examining the decision's scope and potential impact on governance to ensure a proper evaluation of the separation of powers in action.

3. Checks and Balances:

Judicial decisions can serve as checks on potential government overreach (see Figure 4.10). Evaluating policy implications involves determining whether a decision reinforces the balance of power between the branches of government. Such decisions may curb executive actions that infringe upon civil liberties or legislative authority (Joshi, 2022; Juhn, 2021; Kang, 2004; Kang et al., 2023). One recent example that highlights the checks and balances between the branches of government and the potential policy implications of judicial decisions is the case of Bozizé v. Central African Republic in the Central African Republic (CAR). This case involves the former president, François Bozizé, who was barred from running in the 2020 presidential elections based on allegations of corruption and human rights abuses during his previous tenure.

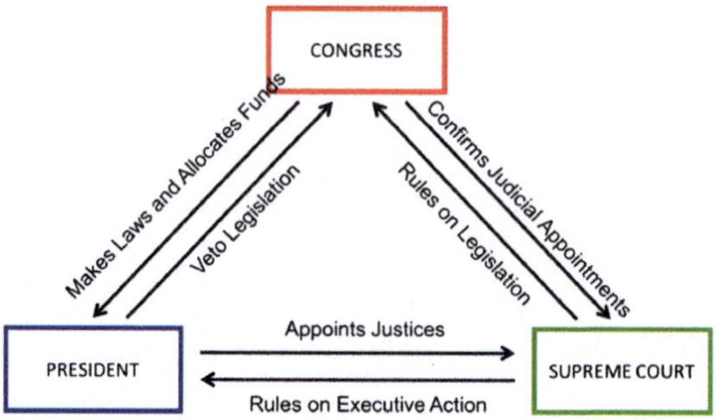

Figure 4.10. The checks and balances in the US government.

Source: https://politicaldictionary.com/words/checks-and-balances/

The decision by the CAR's Constitutional Court to exclude Bozizé from the electoral process has sparked a debate on the role of the judiciary in curbing potential government overreach and protecting civil liberties. Supporters argue that the court's decision serves as a crucial check on executive power, ensuring that individuals with questionable records are not allowed to participate in high-level leadership positions. They contend that the decision upholds the rule of law, strengthens democratic processes, and protects the interests of the citizens. On the other hand, critics argue that the exclusion of Bozizé from the elections raises concerns about the judicial branch interfering with the political process. They believe that the decision could be politically motivated and potentially infringe upon the rights of citizens to choose their leaders freely. Critics also express apprehension about the long-term impact of the decision on the separation of powers, as it could set a precedent for the judiciary intervening in matters reserved for the executive or legislative branches (Navarrete & Castillo-Ortiz, 2020; Nelson & Gibson, 2019).

Another aspect of this case that warrants attention is how the decision affects the delicate balance between civil liberties and executive authority. While the decision to exclude Bozizé is seen by some as upholding civil liberties and accountability, others argue that it restrains the potential for democratic participation and undermines the principle of political inclusivity. There are concerns that such a decision may perpetuate political divisions, exacerbate social tensions, and undermine efforts to achieve national reconciliation. Ultimately, the implications of this judicial decision extend beyond the individual case of Bozizé and have broader implications for governance and the future trajectory of the CAR. The case underscores the importance of a careful and nuanced analysis when assessing the policy implications of judicial decisions (Oakes, 2018; Obermaier, 2008; Oliveira & Garoupa, 2011). By examining how such decisions reinforce or potentially disrupt the balance of power between the branches of government, one can better understand the intricate relationship between the judiciary and the policy domain.

4. Constitutional Interpretation:

Judicial decisions often involve interpreting constitutional provisions. Evaluating policy implications requires analyzing whether a decision enhances or limits constitutional rights and protections. These evaluations contribute to shaping policies that align with the constitutional framework (Owusu-Mensah & Mathapoly-Codjoe, 2023; Parrillo, 2005). One case that exemplifies the interplay between judicial decisions, constitutional interpretation, and policy implications is the Kadi decision in the European Union (EU). The case centers around the inclusion of Youssef Kadi, a Saudi national, on the EU's terrorist sanctions list. Kadi was subjected to financial sanctions due to allegations of supporting terrorist activities. The European Court of Justice (ECJ) was tasked with evaluating the legality of Kadi's inclusion on the sanctions list and balancing it with his fundamental rights. In its judgment, the ECJ highlighted the importance of respecting due process, the right to a fair hearing, and the right to defense when imposing restrictive measures.

The decision had deep policy implications as it raised questions about the balance between security concerns and the protection of individual rights. Advocates for a robust sanction regime argued that involving the judiciary in the decision-making process could potentially hinder effective counterterrorism measures. They believed that the EU institutions should have the discretion to impose sanctions to safeguard security interests promptly. On the other hand, proponents of the ECJ's ruling emphasized the significance of upholding fundamental rights and ensuring a fair and transparent procedure. They contended that the court's decision strengthened the rule of law, enhanced accountability, and underscored the need for robust legal safeguards when imposing sanctions. They argued that the decision highlighted the importance of striking a balance between security imperatives and respecting individual rights. The policy impact of the Kadi decision was substantial. It led to proposed revisions in the EU's sanction regime, which aimed to address some of the concerns raised by the judgment and provide clearer procedural safeguards for individuals subject to restrictive measures. The case stimulated a broader reconsideration of how the EU sanctions regime could be designed to strike an appropriate balance between effective counterterrorism measures and the protection of fundamental rights.

In analyzing the implications of the Kadi decision, it is vital to consider how the judgment influenced policy-making processes and the ongoing dialogue surrounding counterterrorism measures within the EU. By ensuring the inclusion of judicial review and the protection of individual rights in sanction-related decisions, the Kadi case has contributed to the broader policy discussion on how best to combat terrorism while respecting the principles of the rule of law and due process. Overall, the Kadi case demonstrates the intricate relationship between judicial decisions, constitutional interpretation, and policy implications (Kirisci & Kocaman, 2022; Kitagawa, 2023; Kochtcheeva, 2009). It underscores the need to carefully balance security concerns with the protection of individual rights and highlights the role that courts can play in influencing policy outcomes within the framework of the EU's legal and constitutional principles.

5. Social Justice and Equality:

Many judicial decisions address issues of social justice and equality. Evaluating policy implications entails assessing whether a decision promotes equitable treatment for marginalized groups. Governments can use such evaluations to adjust policies to address systemic disparities (Rohrschneider, 2005; Rotunda, 1991; Rowley, 2005). One real-life example that pertains to the topic of judicial decisions addressing social justice and equality is the 2018 ruling by the South African Constitutional Court on the validity and constitutionality of a private school's language policy. The case involved the decision of a private school to admit only English-speaking students and exclude those who spoke other indigenous languages, in effect discriminating against students from marginalized linguistic communities. The court's judgment centered on evaluating whether this policy promoted equitable treatment for marginalized groups, particularly those from non-English speaking backgrounds. The court's evaluation of the policy implications reflected a critical examination of the systemic disparities and historical injustices faced by marginalized linguistic communities in South Africa. In its ruling, the court stressed the importance of language rights as fundamental to individual dignity, cultural identity, and social justice.

It argued that the exclusionary language policy perpetuated inequalities by denying students from non-English speaking backgrounds equal access to quality education, allowing an unequal power dynamic to persist.

The ruling further highlighted the role of the state in addressing systemic disparities and promoting social cohesion. The court found that the private school's language policy was inconsistent with legislative provisions and constitutional principles mandating non-discrimination, equality, and linguistic diversity. It emphasized the responsibility of the government to adjust policies in addressing these disparities and promoting equitable treatment. This case triggered a robust debate in South Africa, which intersected issues of language, education, cultural diversity, and social justice. Advocates for the policy argued that English proficiency is necessary for economic opportunities and global competitiveness, framing the exclusionary policy as a justified means to achieve these ends. However, critics countered that such exclusions perpetuated historical inequalities and limited access to resources for marginalized communities. They argued for a more inclusive language policy that recognized and valued linguistic diversity as a cornerstone of social justice. Overall, this real-life example demonstrates the complexity of evaluating policy implications in relation to social justice and equality (Owusu-Mensah & Mathapoly-Codjoe, 2023; Parrillo, 2005). It illustrates the ongoing debate surrounding the role of judicial decisions in shaping policies to address systemic disparities, and the tensions that arise in balancing competing interests. By critically analyzing the specific details of the case, one can nuance the discussion beyond generalities and delve into the intricacies of promoting equitable treatment for marginalized groups.

6. Public Perception and Trust:

Judicial decisions influence public perception of the legal system and government. Evaluating policy implications involves gauging whether a decision enhances public trust in both institutions. Decisions perceived as fair and just contribute to a stable policy environment (Iaryczower et al., 2002; Ides, 1999; Imam & Egbewole, 2020). Another real-life example that pertains to the topic of judicial decisions influencing public perception and enhancing trust in the legal system and government is the 2018 ruling by the Supreme Court of Canada in the case of Groia v. Law Society of Upper Canada. This case involved a high-profile debate surrounding the professional conduct of lawyers and the balance between zealous advocacy and civility within the legal profession. The ruling revolved around Joe

Groia, a lawyer who represented his client in a highly contentious trial. During the trial, Groia engaged in aggressive, confrontational behavior towards opposing counsel, which resulted in complaints being filed against him with the Law Society of Upper Canada. The case brought attention to the fundamental question of whether zealous advocacy, even if at times uncivil, should be tolerated or whether it undermines public confidence in the legal profession.

The Supreme Court's decision in this case provided an opportunity to evaluate the policy implications related to maintaining professionalism within the legal field. The Court, while acknowledging the importance of robust advocacy, emphasized that lawyers have a duty to maintain civility in the courtroom. The ruling reflected the Court's commitment to promoting an atmosphere of respect and professionalism, which ultimately enhances public trust in the legal system (Williams, 2008; Winkler, 2009; Wong et al., 2009; Worthington, 2001). This case sparked extensive debate among legal professionals, scholars, and the public, addressing questions about the appropriate boundaries of advocacy and ethical conduct. Some argued that the Court's decision struck the right balance by upholding standards of civility, as it was seen as essential for the effective administration of justice and maintaining public confidence. Others expressed concerns that the ruling might stifle vigorous advocacy and limit the ability of lawyers to zealously represent their clients. By focusing on the specific details of the Groia case, one can appreciate the complexities involved in assessing policy implications related to public trust in the legal system and the role of lawyers in the courtroom. The case offers insights into the ongoing dialogue and tensions surrounding the professional conduct of lawyers, and how judicial decisions can shape public perception of the legal profession and the government.

7. Long-Term vs. Short-Term Impact:

Judicial decisions can have both immediate and long-term impacts. Evaluating policy implications necessitates considering the potential short-term disruptions versus the long-term benefits. This evaluation helps governments weigh the trade-offs of policy changes triggered by judicial decisions (Zacka, 2022; Zambrano, 2019; Zuk et al., 1993). One real-life example that illustrates the topic of judicial decisions with both immediate and long-term impacts is the 2016 ruling by the Constitutional Court of Turkey regarding the removal of immunity for Members of Parliament. The Court ruled that parliamentary immunity could be lifted for members facing criminal charges, leading to the prosecution and imprisonment of several legislators. This decision had significant policy implications, as it triggered both short-term disruptions and long-term considerations for the Turkish government. In the short term, the ruling caused immediate disruptions within the political landscape of Turkey. The lifting of parliamentary immunity led to the prosecution of opposition members and resulted in a wave of resignations from the affected legislators, reshaping the composition of the Parliament. This immediate fallout created a notable political turmoil, with critics arguing that the decision was politically motivated and aimed at limiting political dissent. However, when evaluating the policy implications of the ruling, one must also consider the long-term benefits and considerations. Proponents of the decision argued that it was a necessary step towards addressing systemic corruption and ensuring accountability for elected officials. They contended that the removal of immunity would help promote transparency, strengthen the rule of law, and restore public trust in the political system. They believed that the long-term benefits of a more accountable legislature outweighed the short-term disruptions caused by the proceedings and resignations.

This particular case sparked a vigorous debate both nationally and internationally. Critics accused the government of using the judicial system as a tool to suppress political opposition, thereby undermining the principles of democracy. They argued that the ruling was a blow to democratic norms and an abuse of the judiciary's power. Supporters of the court's decision, however, emphasized the importance of adopting measures to combat corruption and strengthen democratic institutions. By analyzing the specific details of this case, one can appreciate the nuanced debate surrounding the evaluation of policy implications resulting from judicial decisions (Wang, 2021; Weill, 2016; West, 2019; Westerman, 2017). The Turkish example exemplifies the tensions between short-term disruptions and long-term benefits when making policy changes triggered by judicial rulings. The ongoing discourse surrounding this ruling highlights the significance of balancing immediate concerns with the potential long-term positive impacts, enabling governments to navigate the trade-offs when responding to judicial decisions.

8. Balancing Fundamental Rights:

When judicial decisions involve conflicts between fundamental rights, policy implications must be carefully evaluated. Governments must strike a balance that preserves essential rights while acknowledging competing interests and societal needs (Garoupa & Karakas, 2021; Gearty, 2005; Gentithes, 2020). One real-world example that highlights the delicate task of evaluating policy implications and striking a balance between fundamental rights and competing interests is the debate surrounding the privacy versus security dilemma in the context of national security measures. In the aftermath of the September 11 attacks, several governments around the world implemented counterterrorism measures that sought to enhance security by expanding surveillance capabilities. However, these measures often collided with individuals' right to privacy, raising concerns about the potential erosion of civil liberties. The case of Edward Snowden and the revelations regarding mass surveillance conducted by intelligence agencies such as the NSA exemplify this conflict. On one hand, proponents argue that robust surveillance programs are necessary to prevent terrorist activities and protect citizens from harm. They contend that the interception and monitoring of communications are crucial tools in identifying and thwarting potential threats. In this view, the priority lies in safeguarding national security, and any potential infringement on privacy rights is justified by the need to maintain public safety. On the other hand, critics argue that such surveillance programs encroach upon individuals' privacy rights and undermine democratic principles. They emphasize the importance of privacy as a fundamental right that should be protected, and express concerns about the potential for abuse and intrusion into personal lives. Additionally, skeptics question the effectiveness of mass surveillance in counterterrorism efforts, citing evidence that suggests targeted and intelligence-led approaches are more effective and respect individual liberties.

This debate raises several policy implications that must be carefully evaluated. Governments must consider the potential consequences of their policies, weighing the trade-offs between security and privacy (Navarrete & Castillo-Ortiz, 2020; Nelson & Gibson, 2019). Striking the appropriate balance becomes a complex task, with considerations including the necessity and proportionality of surveillance measures, the adequacy of oversight mechanisms, and the transparency and accountability of agencies involved. The challenge lies in making informed decisions that do not unduly sacrifice individual rights while adequately addressing the concerns of national security. Furthermore, societal needs and public opinion play a crucial role in shaping the policy discourse. It is important for governments to engage in open and inclusive debates to hear and address the concerns of citizens, civil society organizations, and experts. Balancing individual rights with societal needs requires a nuanced approach, considering factors such as the evolving nature of threats, advancements in technology, and the potential impact on public trust and confidence in government institutions. Hence, the conflict between privacy and security exemplifies the intricate task governments face when judicial decisions involve conflicts between fundamental rights. Striking a balance that preserves essential rights while acknowledging competing interests and societal needs requires careful evaluation of policy implications and consideration of the complex nuances involved.

9. Policy Flexibility vs. Legal Certainty:

Some judicial decisions introduce flexibility into legal interpretations, allowing policies to adapt to changing circumstances. Evaluating policy implications involves assessing whether this flexibility enhances responsiveness or undermines legal certainty (Bybee, 1994; Byrne & Maxwell, 2019; Calabresi & Rhodes, 1992). One real-world example that illustrates the dynamic between flexibility in legal interpretations and the evaluation of policy implications is the evolution of copyright laws in the digital age. The advent of the internet and digital technologies has challenged traditional notions of intellectual property rights, leading to complex debates and legal interpretations. In many countries, copyright laws were initially designed to protect creators' rights and incentivize innovation and creativity. However, the digital era has posed new challenges, such as the widespread sharing and reproduction of copyrighted content facilitated by the internet. As a result, judicial decisions have attempted to navigate this new landscape by introducing flexibility into the interpretation of copyright laws, aiming to strike a balance between protecting the rights of creators and granting certain freedoms to users. One specific example that exemplifies this debate is the case of file-sharing platforms. Platforms like Napster and BitTorrent emerged as popular means for users to share copyrighted music, movies, and other content without permission or compensation to the creators. These platforms posed significant challenges to copyright holders, who argued that their rights were being infringed upon and their ability to monetize their work was being undermined.

Courts faced the task of evaluating the policy implications of these platforms' operations and assessing the impact on copyright laws. Some judicial decisions took a rigid approach, emphasizing the strict enforcement of copyright laws and holding these platforms liable for facilitating copyright infringement (van Zeben, 2015; Vermeule, 2012; Voeten, 2008; VonDoepp & Ellett, 2011). They argued that maintaining legal certainty and protecting intellectual property rights outweighed any potential benefits of flexibility. In contrast, other judicial decisions introduced more flexibility into the interpretation of copyright laws in order to adapt to the changing circumstances of the digital age. These decisions recognized that the landscape of content sharing had dramatically transformed and that the strict enforcement of copyright laws might stifle innovation and impede technological advancements. They sought to balance the rights of creators with the rights of users, advocating for a more nuanced approach that considered factors such as the intent of sharing, the impact on the market, and the potential for transformative use.

Critics of this flexibility argue that it undermines legal certainty and weakens protections for copyright holders. They contend that introducing too much flexibility can lead to uncertainty surrounding the scope and enforceability of copyright laws, potentially discouraging creators from producing original work or seeking fair compensation. Proponents, on the other hand, argue that flexibility in legal interpretations enhances responsiveness to a changing technological landscape. They argue that rigid enforcement of copyright laws might hinder technological progress and innovation, and that courts should adapt their interpretations to strike a balance between protecting creators and allowing for reasonable usage and transformative use of copyrighted content. The evaluation of policy implications in cases like file-sharing platforms necessitates careful consideration of both the rights of creators and the rights and desires of users in the digital age (Oakes, 2018; Obermaier, 2008; Oliveira & Garoupa, 2011). Striking an appropriate balance involves assessing the potential impact on cultural, economic, and technological developments, alongside preserving legal certainty and incentivizing creative output. Hence, the example of legal interpretations surrounding copyright laws and file-sharing platforms demonstrates the ongoing debate between flexibility and legal certainty. Evaluating policy implications in these cases requires a nuanced approach that considers the evolving technological landscape and balances the rights of creators with the rights and desires of users.

10. Legislative Response:

Governments may respond to judicial decisions by enacting new laws or amending existing ones. Evaluating policy implications entails analyzing the effectiveness of legislative responses in addressing the concerns raised by the judiciary (Rohrschneider, 2005; Rotunda, 1991; Rowley, 2005). One real-world example that highlights the government's response to a judicial decision and the evaluation of policy implications is the case of the European

Court of Justice (ECJ) ruling on data retention. In 2014, the ECJ declared the Data Retention Directive, which required telecommunications providers to retain customer data for a specific period, invalid. The court held that the indiscriminate collection and storage of communication data violated the right to privacy and protection of personal data. Following the ECJ ruling, governments in various European countries were tasked with evaluating the policy implications and determining how to address the concerns raised by the judiciary. The challenge lay in striking a balance between ensuring national security and combating crime while respecting fundamental rights. A specific example of legislative response to this judicial decision is seen in the case of Germany. In 2015, the German government enacted a new data retention law, taking into account the concerns raised by the ECJ. The amended law imposed stricter requirements on telecommunications providers, ensuring that data retention was limited to cases of specific threats to public safety or national security. It also introduced stronger safeguards to protect individuals' privacy rights, such as stricter access controls and oversight mechanisms.

This legislative response triggered a debate between supporters and critics of the new law. Proponents argued that the amended legislation addressed the concerns of the judiciary by providing a more targeted and proportionate approach to data retention. They contended that a balance was struck between security needs and privacy rights, as the law only allowed for data retention in cases directly linked to serious crimes. Critics, however, raised concerns that the new law still allowed for potential abuses and did not sufficiently protect individuals' privacy rights. They argued that the legislation did not provide clear guidelines on the exact circumstances under which data retention could be justified, leaving room for interpretation and potential overreach by authorities. Additionally, skeptics questioned the effectiveness of data retention as a tool in fighting crime, positing that targeted, intelligence-based approaches may be more effective. The evaluation of the effectiveness of legislative responses in addressing concerns raised by the judiciary requires careful analysis. Governments must examine whether the new laws strike an appropriate balance between safeguarding national security and protecting fundamental rights (Aydin-Cakir, 2023; Babie & Bhanu, 2022; Bachmann & Lyubashenko, 2017). They also need to assess whether these laws provide clarity and necessary safeguards to prevent potential abuses and address any jurisprudential concerns. Overall, the response of governments to judicial decisions through the enactment of new laws or amendments entails evaluating the policy implications and effectiveness of those legislative responses. The case of the European Court of Justice ruling on data retention in Germany exemplifies this process, where the government assessed the concerns raised by the judiciary and sought to strike a balance between security needs and privacy rights. The effectiveness of legislative responses requires meticulous examination of their compliance with fundamental rights and their ability to address the concerns that initiated the judicial intervention.

11. Stakeholder Consultation:

Evaluating policy implications should involve consultation with various stakeholders, including legal experts, policymakers, advocacy groups, and affected individuals. This broader engagement helps ensure that policy adjustments align with diverse perspectives (Brown, 1999; Buchmeyer, 2019; Bunjevac, 2015; Burbank, 2009). One real-world example that exemplifies the importance of consulting various stakeholders to evaluate policy implications is the introduction of the General Data Protection Regulation (GDPR) in the European Union in 2018. The GDPR aimed to enhance privacy rights and data protection for individuals in the digital age. Throughout the process of crafting the GDPR, extensive consultations occurred with a broad range of stakeholders, including legal experts, policymakers, advocacy groups, and affected individuals. These consultations helped shape the policy, ensuring that different perspectives were considered and potential concerns were addressed. Legal experts played a crucial role in providing insights and expertise in understanding the legal frameworks and implications of the proposed regulation. Their input contributed to the development of a comprehensive policy that aligned with existing legal principles and norms.

Policymakers were actively engaged in the consultation process as well, bringing their insights and understanding of the broader policy landscape. Their involvement allowed for a balanced and practical approach to crafting the GDPR, taking into account both legal considerations and the broader policy goals. Advocacy groups representing civil liberties, privacy rights, and technology interests also had a significant influence on the GDPR's development. Their consultation ensured that the regulation addressed the concerns of different interest groups, striking a balance that protected individuals' privacy while considering the needs of businesses and promoting innovation. Furthermore, consultations with affected individuals, such as data subjects and consumers, allowed policymakers to understand the real-world impact of data protection measures. These insights helped develop policies that were responsive to the concerns and expectations of the public. However, the broader engagement of stakeholders does not guarantee a consensus on policy adjustments. The GDPR, for instance, faced significant debates and controversies. Critics argued that the regulation imposed burdensome obligations on businesses and impeded innovation, particularly for small and medium-sized enterprises (SMEs). They contended that the strict requirements and potential hefty fines imposed under the GDPR could stifle economic growth and hinder competitiveness.

Conversely, supporters of the GDPR maintained that the regulation brought necessary safeguards to individuals' data protection and privacy rights in an era of increasing data-driven technologies. They emphasized the importance of harmonizing data protection rules across the EU and ensuring stronger enforcement to prevent data breaches and abuses. The case of the GDPR illustrates the significance of consulting various stakeholders in evaluating policy implications. By engaging legal experts, policymakers, advocacy groups, and affected individuals, policymakers can benefit from diverse perspectives, ensuring that policy adjustments align with the varied needs and expectations of different stakeholders. Although reaching a consensus on policy adjustments may be challenging, this inclusive approach fosters transparency, legitimacy, and a more informed decision-making process. Overall, the consultation of different stakeholders played a key role in shaping the GDPR. It highlights the importance of engaging legal experts, policymakers, advocacy groups, and affected individuals in the evaluation of policy implications. This broader engagement helps ensure that policy adjustments align with diverse perspectives and strike a balance between different interests and concerns.

12. Global Perspective:

Judicial decisions can have international implications, particularly in matters of human rights and international law. Evaluating policy implications necessitates considering how decisions align with international obligations and norms (Nie, 2021; Nordstrand, 2018; O'Neil, 2019; O'Neill, 2001). One real-world example that highlights the international implications of judicial decisions and the evaluation of policy implications is the case of the European Court of Human Rights (ECHR) ruling on the extradition of Julian Assange, the founder of WikiLeaks. In 2012, the ECHR issued a judgment that found the extradition of Assange from the United Kingdom to Sweden compatible with the European Convention on Human Rights (ECHR). This judicial decision sparked a debate regarding the policy implications and how it aligned with international obligations and norms. Supporters of the ruling argued that it reinforced the importance of upholding human rights and the rule of law in the context of extradition cases. They contended that the decision reflected the ECHR's commitment to ensuring fair proceedings and safeguarding individuals' rights, which are central tenets of international human rights law. On the other hand, critics of the ruling raised concerns about its potential impact on freedom of the press and the rights of journalists. They argued that the decision could set a dangerous precedent by allowing the extradition of individuals engaged in actions related to investigative journalism or the exposure of classified information. Some critics suggested that the ruling might have a chilling effect on transparency and hinder the flow of information that is vital for holding governments accountable.

The evaluation of policy implications in this case requires addressing the tension between extradition obligations and the protection of individual rights and freedoms. Governments must assess whether their compliance with international obligations, such as extradition treaties, is consistent with their commitments to human rights norms (Kramarz et al., 2017; Krogseng, 2000; Krotoszynski, 2014). This evaluation necessitates considering the potential consequences of judicial decisions on individual rights, the freedom of the press, and the broader implications for democratic societies. Moreover, the evaluation of policy implications should take into account discussions and debates within the international community. It requires considering the opinions and perspectives of other countries, international organizations, and civil society groups to ensure a comprehensive understanding of the implications of the decision. This broader engagement helps ensure that policy adjustments align with international obligations and norms, fostering a sense of global cooperation and respect for human rights. Hence, the case of the ECHR ruling on Julian Assange's extradition highlights the international implications of judicial decisions. Evaluating policy implications requires careful consideration of how decisions align with international obligations and norms, particularly in matters of human rights and international law. The policy evaluation should account for potential impacts on individual rights, the freedom of the press, and the broader implications for democratic societies. Engaging in discussions at the international level ensures a comprehensive understanding and helps shape policies that meet the standards of international obligations and respect for human rights.

In conclusion, evaluating policy implications of judicial decisions is a multidimensional process that requires a thorough understanding of legal principles, the separation of powers, and the broader societal impacts. Such evaluations play a crucial role in maintaining a harmonious relationship between the judiciary and the government, promoting the rule of law, and fostering just and effective policies that benefit society as a whole.

CHAPTER 4 SUMMARY

Chapter 4 of the provided material offers a comprehensive exploration of the intricate relationship that exists between the judiciary and government in the realm of policy-making. The chapter is thoughtfully structured into five distinct sections, each of which illuminates crucial aspects contributing to the judiciary's pivotal role in shaping public policies.

In Section 4.1, the primary focus is directed towards the meticulous judicial interpretation of statutes. Within this context, the chapter underscores the judiciary's indispensable responsibility in deciphering and elucidating the intricate legal framework set forth by statutes. Through meticulous examination, the judiciary ensures that the original legislative intent is not only preserved but faithfully adhered to. This interpretation serves as the bedrock upon which subsequent policy implementation is built, further underscoring the judiciary's indispensable role in the policy-making process.

Transitioning to Section 4.2, a significant emphasis is placed on comprehending the profound influence of legal precedents on the formulation of policies. The discussion highlights the weight that precedents, established through prior court rulings, carry in subsequent cases and subsequent policy determinations. By consistently applying precedents, the legal system maintains a degree of uniformity and predictability, which contributes to the overall stability of policies. This section effectively elucidates how precedent can function as a guiding principle in policy decisions, thereby shaping the trajectory of public policies.

The dichotomy between judicial activism and restraint within the domain of policy matters is the focal point of Section 4.3. The chapter delves into the nuances of how judges' varying approaches to interpreting the Constitution and statutes can lead to either proactive interventions that reshape policies or a more cautious approach that recognizes the primary role of the legislature in policy formulation. The discussion skillfully examines the dynamic tension between these two judicial approaches, highlighting the potential implications for policy direction and legal precedent.

In Section 4.4, the narrative expands to encompass the broader role of the judiciary in influencing public policy. The chapter expounds upon how the judiciary, vested with the authority to scrutinize the constitutionality of laws and governmental actions, acts as a critical check and balance on the powers wielded by the government. This role effectively extends the judiciary's impact beyond the confines of mere statutory interpretation, positioning it as a central actor in substantive policy determinations. This section eloquently conveys the judiciary's vital role in preserving democratic accountability and safeguarding individual rights in the larger context of policy-making.

Finally, Section 4.5 provides a comprehensive framework for evaluating the policy implications inherent in judicial decisions. The chapter underscores the imperative of assessing the far-reaching consequences of court rulings beyond their immediate legal outcomes. By gaining a comprehensive understanding of the broader policy ramifications, one can grasp the nuanced dimensions of the judiciary's influence on shaping societal norms and values. This section adeptly underscores the holistic perspective required for comprehending the judiciary's intricate role in molding the trajectory of public policies.

In summation, Chapter 4 provides an extensive and insightful analysis of the intricate interplay between the judiciary and government within the realm of policy-making. Through its well-structured sections, the chapter underscores the judiciary's multifaceted responsibilities in interpreting statutes, guiding policy through precedent, navigating the spectrum of judicial activism and restraint, overseeing governmental actions, and evaluating the broader policy repercussions of its decisions. This comprehensive exploration affirms the judiciary's profound impact on the evolution of public policies and the intricate dynamics that underlie its influential role.

CHAPTER 5

The Judiciary and Government in Conflict Resolution

Contents

5.1. Judicial Review of Government Actions 156
5.2. Adjudication of Disputes Between Government Branches 162
5.3. The Role of International Courts in Cross-Border Conflicts 170
5.4. Mediation and Alternative Dispute Resolution 180
5.5. The Judiciary's Role In Mitigating Political Conflicts 188
Chapter 5 Summary 195

In the discourse of governance and legal systems, the dynamic relationship between the judiciary and government often manifests itself prominently in conflict resolution. Chapter 5 of the presented material delves comprehensively into this intricate theme, examining how the judiciary and government interact in the pursuit of resolving conflicts across various contexts. This chapter is thoughtfully segmented into five distinct sections, each of which delves into a specific facet of conflict resolution involving the judiciary and government. Through the exploration of these sections, the chapter seeks to illuminate the multifaceted role that the judiciary plays in resolving conflicts that arise within the framework of governance, both domestically and internationally. From the fundamental concept of judicial review to the adjudication of disputes between different branches of government, and from the role of international courts in cross-border conflicts to the employment of mediation and alternative dispute resolution techniques, the chapter encapsulates a comprehensive narrative that underscores the judiciary's vital role in maintaining equilibrium within governance structures. Furthermore, the chapter delves into the nuanced role that the judiciary assumes in mitigating conflicts of a political nature, thereby underscoring its contribution to the sustenance of political stability and harmonious governance. In its entirety, Chapter 5 not only explores the intricacies of conflict resolution but also sheds light on the broader implications of the judiciary's engagement in maintaining governmental order and ensuring the primacy of the rule of law. Let us open the chapter by considering the implications of judicial review of government actions.

5.1. JUDICIAL REVIEW OF GOVERNMENT ACTIONS

Within the intricate interplay between the judiciary and government, the concept of judicial review emerges as a cornerstone of checks and balances that characterizes democratic governance (Aboueldahab, 2021; Abouharb et al., 2013). Judicial review pertains to the power of the judiciary to assess the constitutionality of government actions, thereby ensuring that such actions remain within the bounds prescribed by the constitution and laws. This mechanism allows the judiciary to act as a counterweight to potential abuses of power by the government, preserving the integrity of the legal and political order. A case in point is Abdel Fattah el-Sisi and the Egyptian judiciary. Following the 2013 coup led by el-Sisi, the Egyptian government asserted control over the judiciary, leading to a symbiotic relationship between the executive and judicial branches. This raised concerns about the erosion of judicial independence and the curtailment of judicial review.

Under el-Sisi's presidency, the Egyptian government has been accused of using the judiciary as a tool to suppress dissent and consolidate power. This is evident in the case of high-profile individuals such as Mohamed Morsi, the former President of Egypt, who faced a speedy trial and was eventually sentenced to death in what many deemed a politically motivated verdict. Furthermore, the Egyptian government has passed legislation that restricts the judiciary's ability to challenge or nullify government actions. For instance, an anti-terrorism law was introduced in 2015, granting the executive branch significant powers to combat terrorism but also allowing for broad interpretation and potential abuse. Critics argue that the erosion of judicial independence and the limitations placed on judicial review pose a threat to democratic governance in Egypt. The executive branch's influence over the judiciary undermines the system of checks and balances, weakening the ability of the courts to hold the government accountable. Figure 5.1 is an illustration of how these checks and balances are meant to be configured (Lin, 2016; Liu & Baird, 2012; Macchiarola, 1971; Macey, 2006).

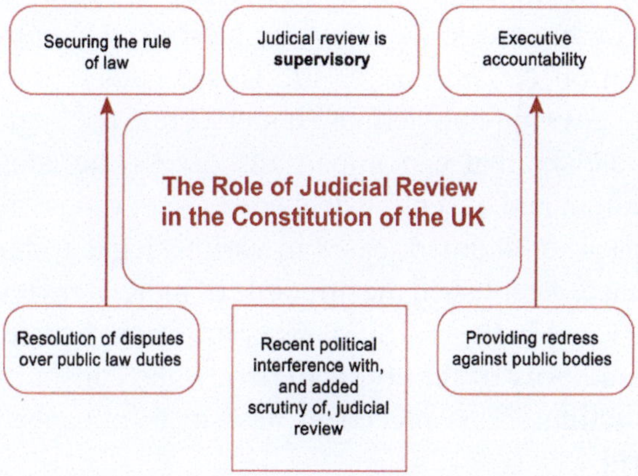

Figure 5.1. Example of the constitutional role and configuration of judicial review.

Source: Law Explorer (2017) https://lawexplores.com/the-constitutional-role-and-configuration-of-judicial-review/

Nevertheless, supporters of el-Sisi argue that these measures are necessary to maintain stability and combat extremism in a country that has faced significant challenges in recent years. They contend that the concentration of power in the executive branch is essential for effective governance and national security, asserting that the judiciary should not interfere in matters that require swift and decisive action. Debates surrounding the Egyptian case highlight the delicate balance between the judiciary and government in democratic governance. The characterization of judicial review as a cornerstone of checks and balances is brought into question when it is undermined by executive control (Pospieszna & Vetulani-Cegiel, 2021; Preis, 2006; Preston, 2016). Consequently, this raises significant concerns regarding the overall health of democratic institutions in Egypt and the broader implications for the protection of human rights and the rule of law. Hence, the case of Abdel Fattah el-Sisi and the Egyptian judiciary exemplifies the complex interplay between the judiciary and government in the context of democratic governance. It underscores the importance of preserving judicial independence and the capacity for robust judicial review, as a check on executive power and as a safeguard for democratic principles. The ongoing debates and critiques surrounding this case serve as a reminder of the vital role that the judiciary plays in upholding the rule of law and ensuring the protection of individual rights and freedoms.

Judicial review operates on the premise that the constitution serves as the supreme law of the land, and any government action that contravenes its provisions can be struck down by the judiciary (Navarrete & Castillo-Ortiz, 2020; Nelson & Gibson, 2019). This pivotal role of the judiciary in scrutinizing government actions underscores the significance of an independent judiciary that can impartially assess the constitutionality of policies, legislation, and executive decisions. The origins of judicial review can be traced back to landmark cases in various legal systems. The United States, for instance, established the principle of judicial review in the seminal case of Marbury v. Madison (1803), wherein Chief Justice John Marshall articulated the authority of the courts to review the constitutionality of laws and executive actions. This precedent has since influenced legal systems around the world.

In the case of Marbury v. Madison in 1803, the Supreme Court of the United States set an important precedent for judicial review. The case involved a dispute over the appointment of William Marbury as a justice of the peace by President John Adams. The newly-elected President Thomas Jefferson instructed his Secretary of State, James Madison, not to deliver Marbury's commission. Marbury then petitioned the Supreme Court for a writ of mandamus, demanding that the Court order Madison to deliver the commission. Chief Justice John Marshall, writing for the Court, held that Marbury did have a legal right to his commission, as his appointment had been duly signed and sealed by the President. However, the Court also found that it did not have the power to issue the writ of mandamus that Marbury had requested. Marshall's opinion established the principle that the Court's power to interpret the Constitution included the authority to determine the constitutionality of laws and executive actions. The significance of Marbury v. Madison lies in its establishment of the Court's power of judicial review (George, 2009; Geyh, 2014; Gisbert, 2022; Gomes, 2017). The Court's decision asserted that the Constitution serves as the supreme law of the land and that it is the duty of the judiciary to interpret and apply it. This ruling empowered the Court to declare acts of Congress or executive actions unconstitutional and therefore invalid. It established the Court as the ultimate arbiter of the meaning and application of the Constitution and provided a mechanism for checks and balances within the United States' system of government.

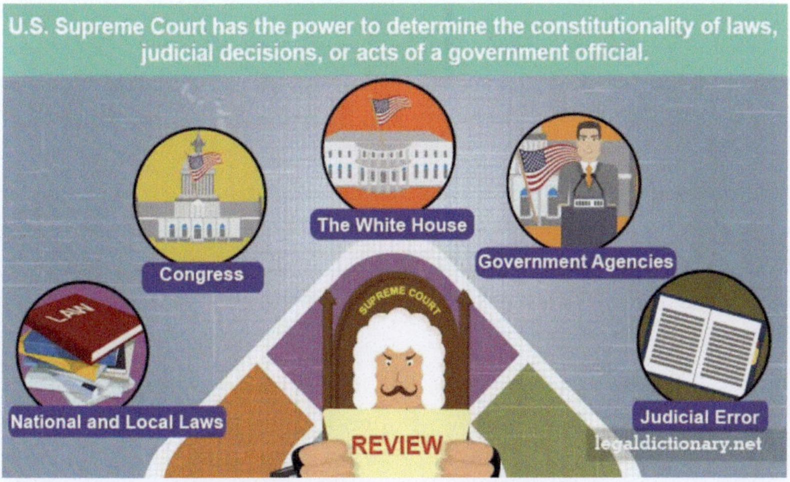

Figure 5.2. The scope of judicial review in USA.

Source: Legal Dictionary (2014) https://legaldictionary.net/judicial-review/

Today, the philosophy and practice of judicial review, as shaped by Marbury v. Madison, continue to have significant implications. It allows the judiciary to act as a guardian of constitutional rights and ensures that the actions of the legislative and executive branches remain within the bounds of the Constitution (Agbor, 2015; Alleman & Mazzone, 2010; Alter, 1998). Judicial review provides a crucial safeguard against potential governmental overreach and allows for the protection of individual liberties and the maintenance of the rule of law. However, the exercise of judicial review is not without its own debates and criticisms. Some argue that it grants too much power to the unelected judiciary, potentially allowing judges to impose their own political views on important policy matters. This perspective raises concerns about the potential for judicial activism and the undermining of democratic decision-making. Others argue that judicial review is essential for upholding the Constitution as the supreme law of the land. They contend that it ensures consistency and adherence to constitutional principles even when political pressures might cause deviations. Judicial review is seen as a necessary counterbalance to protect individual rights and preserve the integrity of the constitutional framework (see Figure 5.2 for an example).

In practice, the influence of Marbury v. Madison can be witnessed in numerous notable cases throughout American history. It has shaped decisions on issues such as civil rights, presidential actions, and the powers of the federal government, among others. The ongoing debates and interpretations regarding the scope and limits of judicial review demonstrate the lasting impact and contemporary relevance of this landmark case. In summary, Marbury v. Madison established the principle of judicial review, granting the judiciary the authority to review and determine the constitutionality of laws and executive actions. This case has had far-reaching implications for the philosophy and practice of judicial review, providing a mechanism for checks and balances and ensuring the protection of constitutional rights. However, debates persist regarding the appropriate role and scope of judicial review, addressing questions of democratic legitimacy and the potential for judicial activism.

One example from across the world that pertains to the topic of judicial review is the case of the Canadian Supreme Court's ruling on the Canada Health Act in 2020. The dispute centered around the interpretation and application of the Act, which governs the country's public healthcare system. The court was tasked with determining whether a particular government policy regarding private healthcare clinics violated the Act and should be struck down. The case revolved around the principle that the constitution serves as the supreme law of the land, and any government action that contravenes its provisions can be invalidated by the judiciary. The court, after careful examination, held that the government policy in question did indeed violate the Canada Health Act. It concluded that the policy allowed private healthcare clinics to charge extra fees for services covered by the public system, thus undermining the overarching goal of equitable access to healthcare for all Canadians. The ruling triggered a notable debate on the extent to which judicial review should be exercised in matters related to public policy. Supporters of the court's decision argued that judicial review is a necessary aspect of democratic governance, ensuring that government actions adhere to constitutional principles and protect citizens' rights. They maintained that the court's intervention helped safeguard the fundamental principles of the public healthcare system and uphold the ideals of equality and accessibility. However, critics of the decision raised concerns about the judiciary's role in determining public policy. They argued that the court's ruling encroached on the domain of elected officials and questioned whether the judiciary should have the authority to strike down government policies directly impacting important areas such as healthcare. Some contended that policy decisions of this nature should be left to the discretion of democratically-elected representatives, who are accountable to the electorate.

The Canadian Supreme Court's ruling on the Canada Health Act case exemplifies the ongoing debate surrounding the power and scope of judicial review in democratic governance. The clash between the judiciary's role in upholding constitutional principles and the government's authority to make policy decisions showcases the delicate balance that needs to be struck. The case underscores the importance of maintaining an open and informed dialogue on constitutional interpretation and the limits of judicial review to ensure the continued protection of citizens' rights and the functioning of democratic institutions.

Judicial review, while critical for maintaining constitutional supremacy, also raises debates regarding the appropriate extent of judicial intervention in policy matters (Tew, 2016; Tey, 2010; Tezcur, 2009; Travesi & Whitehead, 2021). Advocates of a robust judicial review argue that it safeguards individual rights, upholds the rule of law, and prevents governmental overreach. Critics, on the other hand, express concerns about judicial activism, asserting that unelected judges may unduly interfere with the policy choices of elected representatives. The scope of judicial review varies across legal systems, with some granting broader powers to their judiciaries than others. In some cases, the judiciary can only determine whether a law is in conformity with the constitution, while in others, they can scrutinize the factual basis and rationale for policy decisions.

In practice, judicial review involves cases brought before the courts challenging the constitutionality of government actions (Tridimas & Gari, 2010; Trochev, 2004; Tunamsifu, 2022). Judges engage in meticulous legal analysis, considering constitutional provisions, legislative intent, and relevant precedents. This process demands a balance between judicial restraint, which respects the legislature's prerogative, and judicial activism, which enforces constitutional limits. The outcomes of judicial review can have far-reaching implications for policy implementation. Government actions found unconstitutional may be struck down or modified, necessitating revisions in policy direction. Conversely, upholding government actions reinforces the legitimacy of policies and executive decisions.

In international contexts, the principle of judicial review also extends to the evaluation of governmental actions vis-à-vis international treaties and agreements (van Zeben, 2015; Vermeule, 2012; Voeten, 2008; VonDoepp & Ellett, 2011). International courts, such as the International Court of Justice, play a role in assessing the compliance of states with international obligations, further underscoring the relevance of judicial review in the realm of governance beyond national borders. In conclusion, the concept of judicial review epitomizes the intricate interplay between the judiciary and government. It embodies the judiciary's responsibility to uphold the rule of law, preserve constitutional integrity, and ensure governmental accountability. While it is a cornerstone of democratic governance, the extent and nature of judicial review remain subjects of ongoing debate and evolution within legal systems worldwide. The next section focuses on how judicial review allows for the adjudication of disputes between government branches.

5.2. ADJUDICATION OF DISPUTES BETWEEN GOVERNMENT BRANCHES

The adjudication of disputes between different branches of government constitutes a critical facet of maintaining the equilibrium within a constitutional framework (Hasbrouck, 2022; He, 2017; He, 2018; Heinz & Manikas, 1992). Such disputes often emerge from conflicts over the delineation of powers, the interpretation of statutes, or the proper implementation of policies. The resolution of these disputes rests on the judiciary's role as an impartial arbiter, tasked with upholding the rule of law and ensuring the functionality of the government's separation of powers. One example from across the world that pertains to the adjudication of disputes between different branches of government can be found in Germany. The country has a constitutional framework that is built on the principle of separation of powers and places great emphasis on maintaining a delicate balance between the executive, legislative, and judicial branches. A particular case that exemplifies the significance of this aspect is the Federal

Constitutional Court's ruling on data retention laws in 2010. The German government had enacted legislation that mandated telecommunications companies to store customer data for a certain period to aid in criminal investigations. However, this raised concerns about privacy rights and potential infringements on civil liberties. Several civil rights organizations and individuals challenged the constitutionality of these data retention laws before the Federal Constitutional Court. The court, through a series of hearings and deliberations, examined the issue at hand and ultimately struck down the legislation. The court argued that the blanket retention of such vast amounts of personal data without individualized suspicion was disproportionate and violated the fundamental right to privacy protected by the German Constitution. This ruling sparked extensive debate about the balance between security and civil liberties within the constitutional framework (Bascuas, 2005; Baude, 2020; Baum, 2003; Bednar, 2004). It showcased the power of the judiciary as an independent arbiter tasked with ensuring that legislation adheres to the principles enshrined in the constitution. The court's decision in this case highlighted the crucial role of constitutional adjudication in maintaining the equilibrium between branches of government and safeguarding citizens' rights within a democratic system (see Figure 5.3 for an example from India).

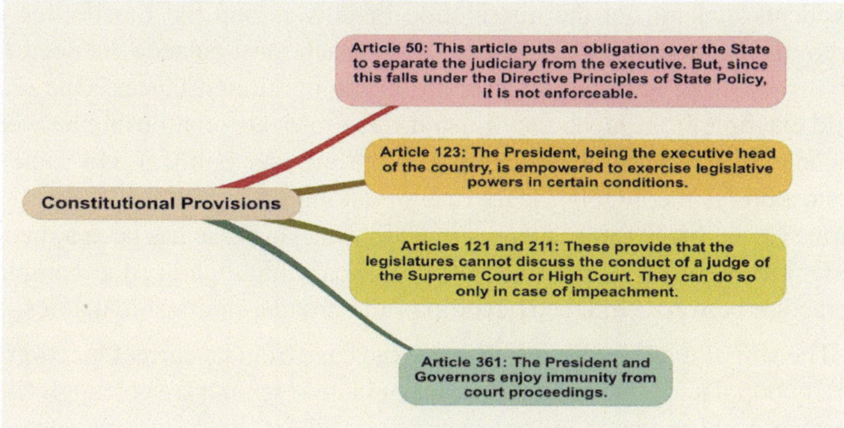

Figure 5.3. Key constitutional provisions in India.

Source: Insights on India https://www.insightsonindia.com/polity/separation-of-powers-between-various-organs-dispute-redressal-mechanisms-and-institutions/separation-of-powers-between-various-organs/

The German example underscores the ongoing discussions and considerations surrounding the adjudication of disputes between different branches of government in constitutional frameworks around the world. It emphasizes the importance of an independent judiciary in upholding the rule of law, protecting individual rights, and preserving the delicate balance between the executive, legislative, and judicial branches (Delaney, 2016; Devlin & Dodek, 2017; DiClemente, 2012). At the heart of these disputes lies the principle of checks and balances, a foundational tenet of democratic governance. The executive, legislative, and judicial branches of government operate independently, each vested with distinct powers. However, inherent to this separation is the potential for clashes, necessitating mechanisms for resolving conflicts without compromising the system's integrity. Adjudication of inter-branch disputes often necessitates a nuanced interpretation of the constitution and applicable laws. The judiciary, as the final authority on legal matters, is uniquely positioned to offer objective analyses of the issues at hand. This ensures that disputes are settled based on established legal principles rather than political considerations, safeguarding the integrity of the constitutional framework.

The judiciary's role in adjudication does not entail a mere technical review of legal texts; rather, it often requires an intricate understanding of the broader political and societal implications (Takayasu, 2023; Tate, 1994; Tauber & Banks, 2017). Decisions in these cases can set far-reaching precedents that impact the distribution of powers and the functioning of government. Therefore, the judiciary's approach must balance the need for stability with the necessity to adapt to changing circumstances. One real-world example from Japan that illustrates the intricate relationship between the judiciary's role in adjudication and the broader political and societal implications is the ongoing legal case involving the relocation of the U.S. Marine Corps Air Station Futenma in Okinawa. This case has been a matter of significant debate and controversy in Japan, highlighting the complex interaction between legal considerations and broader political dynamics.

The aim of the relocation is to move the base from its current location in densely populated Ginowan to the less populated Henoko area of Nago City. However, local residents and environmental activists have strongly opposed the relocation, citing concerns over noise pollution, environmental damage, and the perceived burden of hosting U.S. military facilities. The legal proceedings around this case have involved challenges to the government's decision-making process and the potential violation of constitutional rights. The judiciary has been called upon to assess whether the government's actions in selecting the relocation site and implementing the plans are lawful and in line with constitutional principles. The implications of this case extend beyond the technical examination of legal texts. It requires an understanding and evaluation of the broader political and societal issues at stake. The judicial review must consider the balance between national security interests, the rights of local communities, and the overall relationship between Japan and the United States. The controversies and debates surrounding the relocation of the U.S. Marine Corps Air Station Futenma highlight the complex interplay between the judiciary's role in adjudication and the broader implications for local communities, environmental protection, and international relations. This example underscores the importance of the judiciary's intricate understanding of both legal principles and the societal and political context within which legal decisions are made.

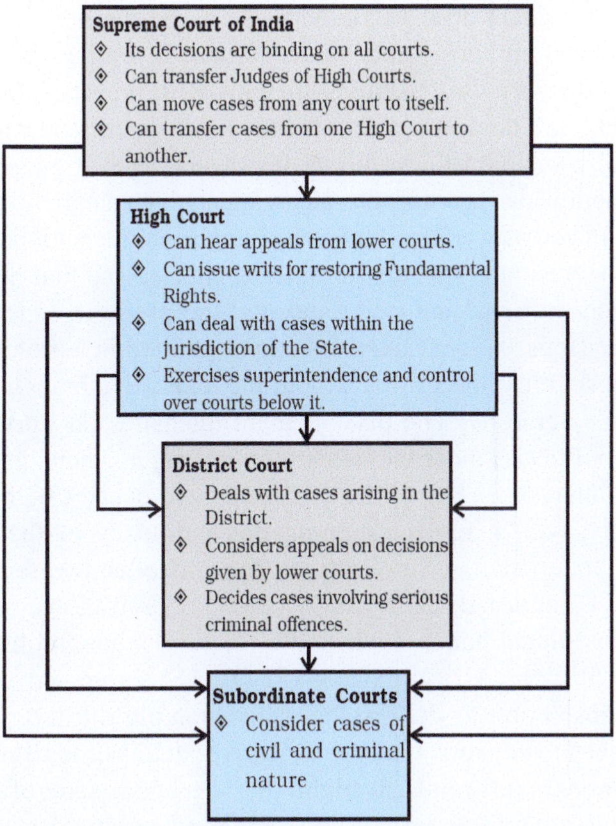

Figure 5.4. The complex and interwoven judicial system of India.

Source: iPleaders (2022) https://blog.ipleaders.in/judicial-system-in-india/

One notable context in which disputes arise is over executive actions and their conformity with legislative intent or constitutional constraints (Navarrete & Castillo-Ortiz, 2020; Nelson & Gibson, 2019). The judiciary, through its power of judicial review, assesses whether executive orders or actions exceed the bounds of authority granted by the constitution or relevant laws. This serves as a crucial mechanism for curbing potential executive overreach and maintaining the separation of powers. This is particularly true of complex judicial systems with overlaps (see Figure 5.4 for the example of India).

One notable example from Guinea-Bissau that pertains to the topic of disputes over executive actions and their conformity with legislative intent or constitutional constraints is the political crisis that unfolded in 2015. In this context, President José Mário Vaz dismissed the government led by Prime Minister Domingos Simões Pereira, which resulted in a significant disagreement between the executive and legislative branches. Critics argued that President Vaz's decision to dissolve the government was a breach of the constitutional principle of separation of powers. They contended that the president's action disregarded the clear legislative intent by disregarding the prime minister who enjoyed majority support in the National Assembly. Supporters of President Vaz, on the other hand, asserted that he was acting within his constitutional authority and had the prerogative to make such executive decisions. The executive's actions resulted in a prolonged period of political instability and gridlock, with the legislative branch challenging the president's authority. The disagreement intensified as various factions within the political landscape attempted to assert their influence and protect their interests. The political crisis sparked debates both locally and internationally, with many questioning the legitimacy of the executive's actions and the potential implications for the effective functioning of democracy in Guinea-Bissau. Civil society organizations, international partners, and regional bodies such as the African Union and the Economic Community of West African States (ECOWAS) expressed concern and called for a resolution to the dispute. This example illustrates a complex and nuanced debate surrounding executive actions, legislative intent, and constitutional constraints. It highlights the importance of adhering to democratic principles and upholding the rule of law in ensuring effective governance. In the case of Guinea-Bissau, the dispute over executive actions had significant implications for political stability and raised questions about the country's commitment to democratic values and processes. Similarly, disputes can emerge between the legislative and executive branches

(Sprankling, 2012; Stephenson, 2003, 2008; Stephenson, 2021). For instance, conflicts might arise over the constitutionality of laws enacted by the legislature or the extent to which the executive can implement these laws. The judiciary's intervention ensures that laws remain within the scope of the legislative authority and that executive actions do not contravene the legislative will. One real example from Gabon that pertains to disputes between the legislative and executive branches is the political crisis that occurred after the 2016 presidential elections. The presidential election results were contested by the opposition, led by Jean Ping, who claimed electoral fraud and questioned the legitimacy of the incumbent President Ali Bongo Ondimba's victory. Following the election, the legislative branch became a battleground for the opposition and ruling party members, with both sides asserting their claims of electoral irregularities and constitutional violations. The opposition accused the executive of manipulating the electoral process, while the ruling party defended the integrity of the election and the president's mandate. The dispute between the legislative and executive branches escalated into street protests, civil unrest, and a climate of political tension. The opposition's demands for a recount and transparency in the electoral process met resistance from the government, which argued that the election was conducted fairly and in accordance with the law. International actors, including the African Union and the European Union, sought to mediate the crisis and encourage dialogue between the opposing factions. While negotiations were attempted, they failed to resolve the underlying issues and bring about a consensus. This example demonstrates the complexities involved when disputes arise between the legislative and executive branches. It underscores the importance of upholding democratic principles, electoral integrity, and impartiality to maintain the trust of the population and ensure political stability. The case in Gabon highlights the need for strong institutions and mechanisms to address such disputes and navigate the delicate balance of power between branches of government. The resolution of these disputes should prioritize the rule of law and democratic processes to safeguard the integrity of the nation's political system.

In cases involving the judiciary itself, disputes might pertain to matters such as the allocation of judicial resources, the independence of the judiciary, or the interpretation of legal procedures (Manning & Randazzo, 2009; Maor, 2004; Maphosa, 2020). These disputes underscore the necessity for an external entity—the judiciary—to adjudicate matters impartially, ensuring that the judicial branch adheres to established norms and principles. One real example from Seychelles that pertains to disputes within the judiciary is the case of the former Chief Justice, Mohan Burhan. In 2011, allegations of misconduct were made against Chief Justice Burhan, which led to a highly contentious debate regarding the allocation of judicial resources, the independence of the judiciary, and the interpretation of legal procedures. Critics argued that Chief Justice Burhan's alleged misconduct compromised the integrity of the judiciary, and they called for swift action to address these allegations. They contended that the allocation of judicial resources should prioritize transparency and accountability, and that any breach of ethical conduct by a judicial officer should be dealt with promptly and decisively to protect the public's trust in the judiciary. On the other hand, supporters of Chief Justice Burhan asserted his innocence and questioned the motives behind the allegations. They argued that the accusations were made with political motivations rather than genuine concerns about judicial misconduct. They emphasized the importance of preserving the independence of the judiciary and allowing for due process to be followed in addressing any allegations against a judicial officer. The controversy surrounding Chief Justice Burhan's case revealed a broader debate about the role of the judiciary, the need for transparency, and the importance of upholding legal procedures. It prompted discussions about the mechanisms in place to hold judges accountable, the balance between judicial independence and oversight, and the impact of such controversies on public trust in the legal system. Ultimately, Chief Justice Burhan resigned from his position, which further fueled the debate about the independence of the judiciary. Some argued that his resignation was an admission of guilt, while others believed it was a strategic move to avoid a potentially biased trial. This case highlighted the complexities involved in disputes within the judiciary, such as the need to balance the pursuit of justice with preserving the judicial system's integrity and independence.

It also underscored the significance of robust systems for allocating judicial resources, ensuring ethical conduct, and holding judicial officers accountable (Konisky & Nolette, 2022; Kotze, 2022; Kovacs & Scheppele, 2018). Clear and transparent procedures for investigating allegations against judges are crucial for maintaining public confidence in the judicial process and upholding the rule of law, while safeguarding the independence of the judiciary. The process of adjudication entails extensive legal analysis, often involving complex constitutional interpretations and referencing relevant precedents. Judges must strike a balance between upholding the authority of each branch and preventing any one branch from becoming disproportionately powerful. As a case in point, a former Minister of Industry and elected member of Parliament from Barbados, Donville Inniss, was sentenced to two years in prison for his involvement in a scheme to launder bribes through bank accounts in New York. The case's key details reveal that Inniss, who held U.S. lawful permanent residency and resided in Tampa, Florida, and Barbados, was found guilty of money laundering and conspiracy to commit money laundering in January 2020. The evidence presented during the trial established that he participated in laundering around $36,000 in bribes he received from high-level executives of the Insurance Corporation of Barbados Limited (ICBL) in 2015 and 2016. In exchange for these bribes, Inniss utilized his Minister of Industry position to facilitate ICBL's acquisition of two substantial insurance contracts from the Barbados government, covering over $100 million worth of government property. The bribes were funneled through a U.S. bank account connected to a dental company owned by a friend, based in Elmont, New York. In addition to the prison sentence, Inniss was ordered to forfeit $36,536.73. The investigation was led by the FBI, with prosecution handled by the U.S. Attorney's Office for the Eastern District of New York and the Justice Department's Criminal Division. The implications of this case in terms of ensuring robust judicial systems and allocating adequate resources to combat corruption and maintain the rule of law are significant. The conviction and sentencing of a former high-ranking government official for money laundering and bribery emphasize the necessity of an independent and well-functioning judiciary that can address cases involving influential individuals impartially. This underscores the need for proper funding and training for law enforcement agencies and skilled prosecutors. Additionally, the case highlights the importance of international cooperation in tackling corruption that transcends national borders, particularly when illicit financial flows are involved. The case's successful resolution signifies the vital role that a dedicated legal framework, competent law enforcement, and cross-border collaboration play in holding officials accountable and maintaining public trust.

In international contexts, inter-branch disputes can manifest within transnational organizations or treaties, wherein disputes may arise between member states or governing bodies (Hasbrouck, 2022; He, 2017; He, 2018; Heinz & Manikas, 1992). International courts, such as the International Court of Justice or regional courts, play a pivotal role in adjudicating these disputes, further emphasizing the significance of impartial resolution mechanisms in preserving international order. In a real example from Tunisia, inter-branch disputes within transnational organizations are evident in the context of its relationship with the International Monetary Fund (IMF). Specifically, a dispute arose between the Tunisian government and the IMF regarding economic policies and austerity measures. The Tunisian government, represented by the executive branch, advocated for a more expansionary fiscal policy to stimulate economic growth and job creation. However, the IMF, as a governing body, pushed for stricter austerity measures to control government spending and reduce the budget deficit. This disagreement raised tensions between the two entities and hindered the progress of the IMF's financial aid program to Tunisia. The executive branch argued that the proposed austerity measures would exacerbate social inequality and political instability, while the IMF insisted that such measures were essential for economic stability and long-term growth. This rift between member states and governing bodies, namely Tunisia and the IMF, exemplifies the complex dynamics that can arise within transnational organizations and treaties, as differing perspectives clash and hinder decision-making processes. While the example of Tunisia's dispute with the IMF may not directly pertain to issues of LGBT rights or race, it serves as a tangible illustration of how inter-branch disputes can impede progress within international contexts.

In summary, the adjudication of disputes between different branches of government is an integral component of maintaining the equilibrium within a constitutional democracy. By providing impartial and legal analyses, the judiciary safeguards the separation of powers and upholds the rule of law, thereby ensuring the effective functioning of government while preventing the concentration of power in any one branch. The third section will focus on the role of international courts in cross-border conflicts.

5.3. THE ROLE OF INTERNATIONAL COURTS IN CROSS-BORDER CONFLICTS

The intricate interplay between the judiciary and government in cases of cross-border conflicts has been a central concern in legal discourse (Iaryczower et al., 2002; Ides, 1999; Imam & Egbewole, 2020). International courts play a pivotal role in mediating these conflicts, providing a forum for resolving disputes that transcend national boundaries. This section delves into the multifaceted relationship between the judiciary and government in the context of international courts, illustrating their significance through a comprehensive analysis of diverse examples and case studies from around the world. By examining the dynamics between international courts and governments, this section sheds light on the evolving landscape of transnational justice and its implications for ensuring fairness, accountability, and the rule of law in cross-border conflicts. International courts serve as impartial arbiters in disputes between states or involving non-state actors that span multiple jurisdictions (Marsh, 2021; Martinsen, 2011; Masinde, 2017). Their role is not only to adjudicate conflicts but also to uphold international norms and treaties. The International Court of Justice (ICJ), often referred to as the "World Court," exemplifies this function. The 2019 ICJ ruling in the case brought by Ukraine against Russia highlighted the court's role in addressing issues like annexation, armed conflict, and human rights violations. The 2019 ICJ ruling in the case brought by Ukraine against Russia exemplified the court's crucial role in addressing multifaceted issues related to annexation, armed conflict, and human rights violations. The dispute centered around Russia's annexation of Crimea in 2014, which Ukraine vehemently contested. The ICJ delved into the complexities of the situation, examining the legality of the annexation and the subsequent armed conflict between Ukraine and Russian-backed separatist groups in eastern Ukraine. The court's ruling not only tackled the immediate territorial concerns but also shed light on broader principles of international law. It reaffirmed the importance of respecting state sovereignty, territorial integrity, and the prohibition of the use of force. The implications of the judgment extended beyond the parties involved, serving as a reminder to the international community of the imperative to honor established norms and principles in order to maintain global peace and stability. The case highlighted the significant role of the ICJ in addressing complex conflicts, ensuring adherence to international legal norms, and seeking justice for victims of human rights violations.

The effectiveness of the 2019 ICJ ruling in preventing, moderating, or stopping the conflict between Russia and Ukraine has been limited. While the ruling reaffirmed important principles of international law and sought to address the issues of annexation, armed conflict, and human rights violations, it did not lead to a significant de-escalation or resolution of the conflict. The conflict between Russia and Ukraine continues to persist, with sporadic outbreaks of violence and ongoing tensions. The ICJ's rulings depend on the cooperation and compliance of the parties involved, and unfortunately, Russia has not shown a willingness to fully adhere to the court's judgment. The ruling, however, serves as a critical legal reference and point of reference for future actions and efforts to seek a peaceful resolution to the conflict. As Figure 5.5 shows, the international regime can provide a range of options of dispute resolution on a single issue.

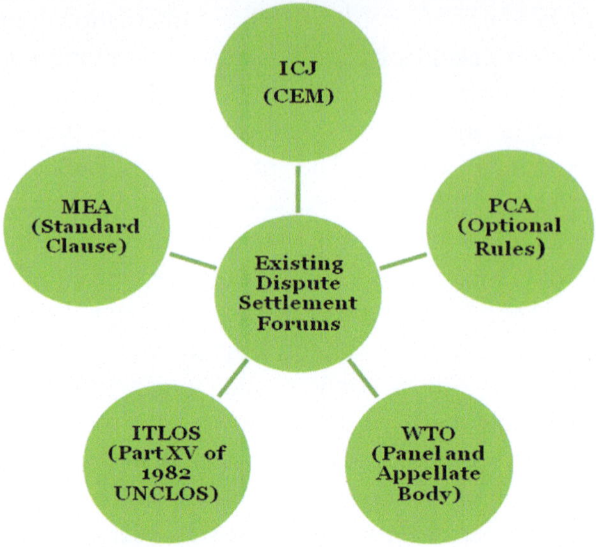

Figure 5.5. Existing forums for international environmental dispute settlement.

Source: Desai, B. H., & Sidhu, B. K. (2020). International courts and tribunals–the new environmental sentinels in international law. *Environmental Policy and Law*, *50*(1–2), 17–33. https://content.iospress.com/articles/environmental-policy-and-law/epl200195

The case of Ukraine against Russia and the subsequent limited effectiveness of the ICJ ruling in resolving the conflict highlight the complexities and limitations of the role of the judiciary in mediating or adjudicating international disputes and armed conflicts. While the judiciary, such as the ICJ, plays a vital role in upholding international law, promoting justice, and providing a platform for parties to present their arguments, its ability to enforce its judgments and bring about a complete resolution to conflicts is reliant on the cooperation of the involved parties (Manning & Randazzo, 2009; Maor, 2004; Maphosa, 2020). In cases where one or more parties show reluctance or defiance towards the court's rulings, as seen in the Russia-Ukraine conflict, the efficacy of the judiciary in mediating and resolving the conflict can be significantly hindered. Nevertheless, the judiciary continues to serve an important function in clarifying legal standards, promoting accountability, and shaping the discourse surrounding international disputes, providing a basis for future diplomatic efforts and potentially influencing the behavior and actions of the parties involved.

A crucial aspect of the judiciary-government relationship lies in judicial independence (Joshi, 2022; Juhn, 2021; Kang, 2004; Kang et al., 2023).

The European Court of Human Rights (ECHR) provides an illustrative case study. In the Paksas v. Lithuania case (2011), the court ruled that Lithuania violated the European Convention on Human Rights by impeaching its president without fair proceedings. The case underscored the necessity of judicial autonomy to ensure checks on governmental power. Conversely, the European Court of Justice (ECJ) showcased the potential tension between national governments and international courts. In the Achmea case (2018), the ECJ ruled against investor-state arbitration clauses in intra-EU bilateral investment treaties, challenging the authority of international arbitration mechanisms and reasserting EU law supremacy.

In the Paksas v. Lithuania case (2011), the European Court of Human Rights ruled that Lithuania had violated the European Convention on Human Rights by impeaching its president, Rolandas Paksas, without fair proceedings. The case centered around the impeachment process initiated against Paksas in 2004, following allegations of corruption and compromising national security. The court examined the fairness of the proceedings and concluded that Lithuania had infringed upon Paksas' right to a fair hearing and the presumption of innocence. The implications of this ruling were significant for the role of the judiciary in government. It underscored the importance of due process and the protection of individual rights, even in cases involving high-ranking political figures (Reid et al., 2020; Ritleng, 2016; Rivera, 2022; Robinson, 2018). The ruling served as a reminder to governments that the judiciary plays a crucial role in upholding fundamental rights and ensuring the legality and fairness of governmental actions. It highlighted the need for governments to respect the independence and integrity of the judiciary and reinforced the principle that no one, regardless of their position, can be denied basic rights and a fair trial.

A central challenge for international courts is securing compliance with their decisions (Owusu-Mensah & Mathapoly-Codjoe, 2023; Parrillo, 2005). The International Criminal Court (ICC) illuminates this issue. The Bashir case (2009) involving Sudanese President Omar al-Bashir revealed tensions between the court's pursuit of justice and the political complexities of apprehending an incumbent head of state. While the ICC issued arrest warrants for Bashir on charges of genocide, war crimes, and crimes against humanity, his arrest remained elusive due to non-cooperation from states and regional organizations. The Bashir case (2009), involving Sudanese President Omar al-Bashir, raises significant questions and implications for the role of the judiciary in government. This case revolved around allegations of war crimes, crimes against humanity, and genocide committed by President Bashir during the conflict in Darfur. The International Criminal Court (ICC) issued two arrest warrants against him, charging him with these grave offenses. The case highlighted the crucial role of the judiciary in holding leaders accountable for their actions, regardless of their political stature. It emphasized the principles of justice, the rule of law, and the pursuit of accountability for human rights violations. However, the case also raised challenges in terms of enforcement, as Bashir evaded arrest and continued to serve as the president of Sudan. This highlighted the limitations of the judiciary's power, particularly in cases where state cooperation is lacking. Despite these challenges, the Bashir case underscored the importance of independent judiciaries and the need for international mechanisms to combat impunity, ensuring that leaders are held responsible for their actions, even in the highest positions of power.

Transnational Justice and Accountability

International courts also address conflicts involving non-state actors, contributing to transnational justice (Janover, 2021; Johnson, 2019; Jonski, 2021; Jorritsma, 2020). The Extraordinary Chambers in the Courts of Cambodia (ECCC) exemplify this (see Figure 5.6 for its structure). The Khmer Rouge Tribunal seeks accountability for mass atrocities committed decades ago. The tribunal balances justice with the complexities of national reconciliation, revealing the intricate interplay between judicial processes and political imperatives. The Extraordinary Chambers in the Courts of Cambodia (ECCC) presents important considerations and implications for the role of the judiciary in government. This unique tribunal was established to address the atrocities committed during the Khmer Rouge regime in Cambodia from 1975 to 1979. The ECCC aimed to bring justice, hold accountable those responsible for grave human rights violations, and contribute to the process of national reconciliation. Its jurisdiction covered crimes such as genocide, war crimes, and crimes against humanity. The ECCC's proceedings showcased the potential of the judiciary to investigate and prosecute complex cases of mass violence and enforce international humanitarian law. By conducting trials, the ECCC sought to provide a platform for victims to have their stories heard, perpetrators to be held responsible, and society to reckon with its past. However, the ECCC faced challenges related to limited resources, the passage of time, and the delicate balance between justice and reconciliation. While the ECCC's work initiated a significant legal precedent in Cambodia, its effectiveness in truly addressing the legacies of the Khmer Rouge regime and promoting lasting societal healing remains an ongoing question. Nonetheless, the ECCC serves as a notable example of the role of the judiciary in shedding light on past atrocities, fostering accountability, and contributing to national processes of transitional justice.

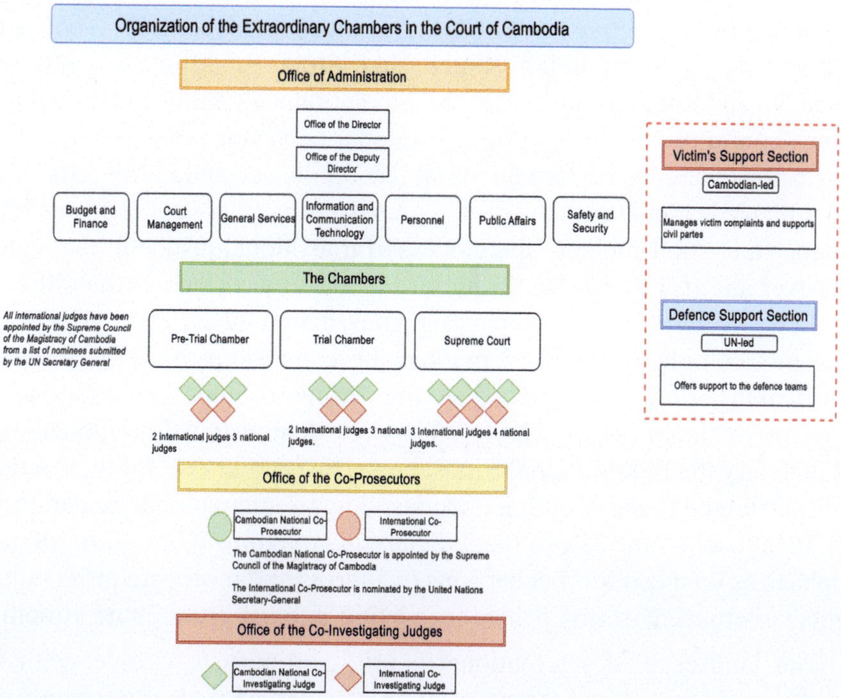

Figure 5.6. Structure of the Extraordinary Chambers in the Courts of Cambodia (ECCC).

Source: Hybrid Justice https://hybridjustice.com/extraordinary-chambers-in-the-court-of-cambodia/

Ad hoc tribunals, established to address specific conflicts, reveal nuanced interactions between international courts and governments (Mak & Rutledge, 2019; Maltzman & Shipan, 2008). The International Criminal Tribunal for the Former Yugoslavia (ICTY) offers insights. The Milosevic case (2002) underscores how international courts engage with political complexities. Milosevic's trial for war crimes, genocide, and crimes against humanity involved reconciling the need for a fair trial with the broader goal of acknowledging the atrocities committed during the Yugoslav Wars. The International Criminal Tribunal for the Former Yugoslavia (ICTY) represents a significant example of the role of the judiciary in addressing the atrocities committed during the conflicts in the Balkans in the 1990s. Established by the United Nations in 1993, the ICTY aimed to bring justice to those responsible for war crimes, crimes against humanity, and genocide. Through its extensive investigations and trials, the ICTY shed light on the horrifying events that took place during the conflicts, highlighting the individual and collective responsibility of those involved. Key events such as the trials of high-ranking officials like Slobodan Milosevic, Radovan Karadzic, and Ratko Mladic captured international attention and brought the crimes committed to the forefront of global consciousness. The tribunal's conclusions were instrumental in establishing the accountability of political and military leaders for their roles in orchestrating or condoning systematic violence and contributed to the process of transitional justice in the region. However, the ICTY also faced significant challenges, such as the difficulty of obtaining evidence and ensuring consistent and efficient trials. The tribunal's completion in 2017 marked the conclusion of its monumental task, leaving a legacy of precedent and setting an important example for other international courts. The ICTY's work demonstrated the potential of the judiciary in holding even the most powerful accountable for their actions and contributed to the evolving understanding of international humanitarian law. Its impact on the role of the judiciary in government is significant, as it emphasizes the need for mechanisms to address and prosecute gross human rights violations, ensuring justice for victims and deterring future atrocities.

The landscape of international courts continues to evolve, with the rise of hybrid courts and the negotiation of complex trade agreements that include dispute resolution mechanisms (Sprankling, 2012; Stephenson, 2003, 2008; Stephenson, 2021). The African Court of Justice and Human Rights, established in 2018, reflects Africa's increasing emphasis on regional mechanisms for conflict resolution. Additionally, trade agreements like the Comprehensive and Progressive Agreement for Trans-Pacific Partnership (CPTPP) include investor-state dispute settlement mechanisms, highlighting how international courts intersect with economic and trade considerations. The inclusion of investor-state dispute settlement (ISDS) mechanisms in the Comprehensive and Progressive Agreement for Trans-Pacific Partnership (CPTPP) raises significant issues and implications for the role of the judiciary in government. ISDS provisions provide foreign investors with the ability to bring legal claims against host governments for alleged violations of investment protection obligations. Key events surrounding ISDS in the CPTPP include the negotiation and adoption of the agreement by member nations, as well as the ongoing debates and criticisms over the potential impact on public policy and sovereignty. The conclusions drawn from the inclusion of ISDS mechanisms in the CPTPP emphasize the balance between protecting foreign investments and safeguarding the regulatory autonomy of governments. Critics argue that these mechanisms can potentially undermine the ability of governments to implement public interest policies, such as environmental regulations or social welfare measures, without the fear of costly legal challenges. Proponents claim that ISDS mechanisms provide a fair and impartial forum for resolving investment disputes, improving investor confidence and leading to economic growth. As debates around ISDS continue, the implications for the role of the judiciary in government encompass weighing the interests of foreign investors against the democratic authority of national governments, ensuring the fairness and transparency of dispute resolution processes, and promoting the alignment of investment rules with broader societal objectives.

The establishment of the African Court of Justice and Human Rights in 2018 carries significant key issues, events, conclusions, and implications for the role of the judiciary in government. This regional court was created to address challenges related to human rights violations and promote justice across the African continent. Key events surrounding its establishment include the adoption of the Protocol on the Statute of the African Court of Justice and Human Rights, the selection and appointment of judges, and the commencement of its first cases. The court's mandate focuses on a range of issues, including civil and criminal matters, human rights violations, and the interpretation of the African Charter on Human and Peoples' Rights. The conclusion drawn from the establishment of the African Court of Justice and Human Rights is its potential to contribute to the protection of human rights, the accountability of governments and individuals, and the development of a regional human rights jurisprudence. The court has the power to receive complaints from individuals, non-governmental organizations, and states, and its decisions are binding on the parties involved. The implications for the role of the judiciary in government are significant, as it highlights the importance of regional judicial mechanisms in addressing human rights violations, furthering access to justice and promoting the rule of law in Africa. It also emphasizes the need for collaboration between national and regional judicial systems to ensure the effective enforcement of human rights standards and the protection of individuals and their rights.

Scholars have extensively explored the role of international courts and their relationship with governments (Edelman, 1994; Efrat, 2018; Eichensehr, 2018; Eleftheriadis, 2005). From Anne-Marie Slaughter's concept of "government networks" to Thomas Franck's idea of "legitimacy deficit," the literature underscores the complexities of aligning national and international interests. Additionally, the judicialization of politics theory posits that international courts can influence domestic policies and constrain state behavior by providing alternative forums for advocacy and decision-making. This academic literature elucidates the intricate challenges associated with aligning national and international interests within the context of international courts and cross-border conflicts.

Anne-Marie Slaughter's concept of "government networks" highlights the evolving nature of international relations and the role of non-state actors in shaping global governance (Aboueldahab, 2021; Abouharb et al., 2013). Slaughter's framework posits that traditional notions of diplomacy and state-centric governance are being complemented, and in some cases supplanted, by a network of governmental and non-governmental actors collaborating on various transnational issues. These networks cut across national boundaries and enable governments to work collectively to address shared challenges, bypassing traditional hierarchical structures. In the realm of international courts, this concept implies that governmental actors are not solely confined to their national interests but are part of a larger network of interactions that influence decision-making. For example, governments may collaborate with NGOs, international organizations, and legal experts to advocate for certain legal interpretations, affecting how international courts interpret and apply the law. This complex interplay underscores that national interests are interwoven with broader global dynamics, making the alignment of priorities challenging.

Thomas Franck's notion of the "legitimacy deficit" centers on the perceived lack of legitimacy of certain international institutions, which stems from a discrepancy between the decisions of these institutions and the expectations of affected individuals and states (Rathod, 2009; Redman, 2017; Reenock et al., 2013). This deficit arises when international institutions fail to adequately address concerns related to fairness, representation, and accountability. In the context of international courts, the legitimacy deficit can arise if the decisions of these courts are seen as detached from the national interests and values of the states involved. Franck argues that legitimacy is a crucial element for the effectiveness of international law, as it encourages states to voluntarily comply with decisions and fosters a sense of justice among the international community. Applying this concept to international courts in cross-border conflicts, the legitimacy deficit underscores the complexity of aligning national interests with decisions made by these courts. If states perceive international court decisions as influenced by political agendas or lacking proper representation, it can lead to non-compliance or skepticism, hindering the court's ability to resolve conflicts and promote justice.

The literature further delves into how these concepts play out in real-world scenarios (Hennigar, 2010; Hessick, 2014; Hill, 2016; Holland, 2009). For instance, the tension between national interests and international norms is evident in cases where powerful states exert influence over international courts to protect their interests. The involvement of governments in shaping the composition and jurisdiction of international courts can lead to concerns about the impartiality and fairness of the court's decisions. Additionally, the legitimacy deficit becomes apparent in situations where international courts lack enforcement mechanisms or when their decisions are selectively enforced based on political considerations. This discrepancy erodes the credibility of international courts and undermines their role in ensuring justice and accountability.

Overall, the concepts of "government networks" and the "legitimacy deficit" from Anne-Marie Slaughter and Thomas Franck, respectively, provide valuable frameworks for understanding the complexities of aligning national and international interests in the context of international courts and cross-border conflicts. These concepts highlight the intricate web of interactions that shape decision-making in international courts and underscore the importance of legitimacy for effective international governance. As international courts navigate the intricate dynamics between states, non-state actors, and global norms, these concepts serve as crucial lenses through which to analyze the challenges and opportunities presented by the evolving landscape of transnational justice.

In conclusion, the intricate interplay between international courts and governments in cross-border conflicts demonstrates the critical role these institutions play in upholding justice, accountability, and the rule of law in a globalized world. The various examples and case studies examined here illustrate the multifaceted nature of this relationship, showcasing how international courts navigate political dynamics, enforce decisions, and shape state behavior. As the world continues to grapple with transnational challenges, the role of international courts will remain pivotal in fostering international cooperation, ensuring fairness, and promoting human rights on a global scale. The fourth section in this chapter focuses on mediation and alternative dispute resolution.

5.4. MEDIATION AND ALTERNATIVE DISPUTE RESOLUTION

The intricate interplay between the judiciary and government extends beyond traditional courtroom proceedings, encompassing the realm of mediation and alternative dispute resolution (ADR) mechanisms (Tridimas & Gari, 2010; Trochev, 2004; Tunamsifu, 2022). This section explores the multifaceted relationship between the judiciary and government within the context of mediation and ADR, highlighting their significance through an in-depth analysis of diverse examples and case studies from around the world. By examining the dynamics between these entities, this section sheds light on the evolving landscape of conflict resolution, emphasizing the role of mediation and ADR in fostering collaboration, preserving relationships, and alleviating the burden on traditional court systems.

Mediation acts as a diplomatic tool, where neutral third parties facilitate negotiations between conflicting parties (McCandless, 2017; McCann et al., 2023; McCarthy & Un, 2017). It differs from negotiation (see Figure 5.7 for an example of a tactical plan for negotiation). A remarkable example lies in the Camp David Accords of 1978, mediated by the U.S. President Jimmy Carter. Egypt and Israel, previously embroiled in conflict, engaged in mediated talks that culminated in a historic peace treaty. Mediation allowed governments to explore mutually acceptable solutions, emphasizing diplomatic dialogue over hostility. The role of mediation as a conduit for diplomacy underscores how governments utilize neutral intermediaries to bridge gaps, demonstrating the symbiotic relationship between the judiciary and government in achieving broader diplomatic objectives. The Camp David Accords of 1978 served as a pivotal moment in diplomatic history, as they marked a significant breakthrough in the relationship between Egypt and Israel. These accords, orchestrated by U.S. President Jimmy Carter, brought together Egyptian President Anwar Sadat and Israeli Prime Minister Menachem Begin for intensive negotiations held at the presidential retreat in Maryland. The key issues at stake centered on the longstanding conflict between the two nations, specifically the question of Israel's occupation of the Sinai Peninsula and the establishment of a framework for peaceful coexistence. Throughout the negotiations, both leaders faced immense pressure and obstacles, highlighting the complexity of the Middle East conflict. However, through Carter's skilful diplomacy and shuttle diplomacy between the two leaders, consensus was achieved. The Camp David Accords paved the way for the subsequent Egypt-Israel Peace Treaty in 1979, which resulted in the return of the Sinai Peninsula to Egypt and the establishment of full diplomatic relations between the two countries. In terms of implications for the role of the judiciary in government, the accords showcased the important role of impartial mediators and the power of diplomacy in resolving protracted conflicts. Furthermore, the successful outcome highlighted the capacity of the judiciary to facilitate peace and foster dialogue, reaffirming the significance of international law and the rule of law in international relations.

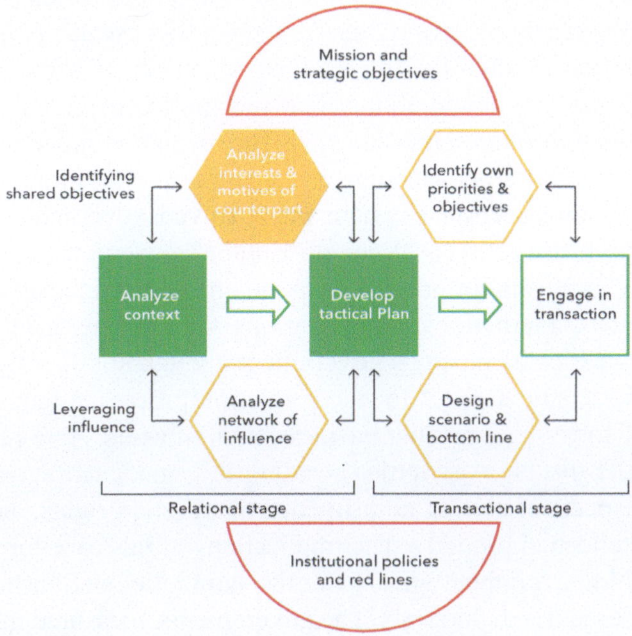

Figure 5.7. Naivasha Grid that informs the development of the tactical plan of the negotiation.

Source: Frontline Negotiations https://frontline-negotiations.org/home/resources/field-manual/digital-field-manual-the-negotiators-support-team/

ADR in Commercial Disputes

In the realm of commercial disputes, Alternative Dispute Resolution mechanisms have gained prominence, addressing business conflicts efficiently outside traditional courts. The International Chamber of Commerce (ICC) offers a pertinent example through its arbitration procedures. In the ICC Arbitration Case No. 10830, the dispute between a European pharmaceutical company and an Asian distributor was resolved through ICC arbitration. This case demonstrates how governments' support for ADR can alleviate court congestion while ensuring timely and confidential resolution of complex cross-border disputes. ICC Arbitration Case No. 10830 presents a compelling illustration of the complex interplay between the judiciary and government in the context of alternative dispute resolution. In this case, a European pharmaceutical company engaged in a dispute with an Asian distributor, showcasing the challenges of cross-border commercial conflicts. The key issues revolved around contractual obligations, pricing discrepancies, and intellectual property rights. As the conflict escalated, both parties sought resolution through the International Chamber of Commerce (ICC) arbitration procedures, highlighting their recognition of the efficacy of alternative dispute resolution mechanisms. The mediation process was facilitated by neutral arbitrators, ensuring an impartial platform for negotiations. Delicate negotiations ensued, where the involved governments played a subtle yet significant role. The Asian distributor's government, cognizant of the economic implications, provided support and encouraged a swift resolution to safeguard international trade relations. On the other hand, the European pharmaceutical company's government, though not directly involved, expressed diplomatic support for the resolution process, aligning with the principles of fostering amicable business environments. As a result of the arbitration, the dispute was settled, leading to a mediated agreement that considered aspects of pricing adjustments, distribution rights, and the protection of intellectual property. The implications of this case for the role of the judiciary in government underscore the symbiotic relationship between legal processes and state interests. The governments' measured involvement showcased their commitment to facilitating an effective and fair resolution while refraining from exerting undue influence over the proceedings. This case highlights the evolving landscape of international commercial dispute resolution, where governments play a nuanced role in upholding legal frameworks and ensuring cross-border business continuity, ultimately emphasizing the crucial harmony between the judiciary and government in fostering a conducive environment for global trade and cooperation.

Mediation in Ethnic Conflicts

Mediation assumes paramount significance in resolving deeply rooted ethnic conflicts (Grove, 2018; Gunderson, 2022; Hardaway, 2021; Hardman, 2020). The Good Friday Agreement of 1998 serves as an exemplar. The governments of the United Kingdom and Ireland, along with political parties and civil society groups, participated in mediation led by Senator George Mitchell. This culminated in a historic agreement ending decades of conflict in Northern Ireland. The mediation process, facilitated by a neutral third party, showcased how governments can collaborate to address contentious issues and work towards sustainable peace. The Good Friday Agreement of 1998 stands as a watershed moment in the history of Northern Ireland, addressing the key issues that plagued the region during three decades of sectarian conflict. This historic peace agreement, brokered between the governments of the United Kingdom and Ireland, sought to create a framework for reconciliation, power-sharing, and political stability. It addressed the complex and deeply-rooted issues of governance, human rights, decommissioning of paramilitary weapons, and the prevention of terrorism. The agreement saw the establishment of the Northern Ireland Assembly and designated institutions to promote equality and protect the rights of all citizens. The intensive negotiations leading up to the agreement involved multiple stakeholders, including political parties, community leaders, and civil society representatives. The conclusion of the agreement came as a culmination of years of arduous discussions and compromises. The signing of the Good Friday Agreement had profound implications for the role of the judiciary in government, as it signified a commitment to resolving conflict through a legal and peaceful process. The agreement highlighted the judiciary's role in upholding the rule of law, ensuring human rights protection, and providing mechanisms for dispute resolution. Its implementation demonstrated the judiciary's vital role in overseeing the implementation of constitutional and legal changes, fostering reconciliation, and promoting societal healing. Furthermore, the agreement's provisions paved the way for a new era of shared governance, effectively transforming the role of the judiciary in promoting peace and stability as a crucial component of democratic governance.

Governments play a crucial role in institutionalizing ADR mechanisms (Keohane et al., 2000; Killebrew, 2007; Kingsford, 2022). The Singapore International Mediation Centre (SIMC) is illustrative. Established by the Singapore Ministry of Law, SIMC offers mediation services for international commercial disputes. The government's support ensures the credibility and enforceability of mediated settlements, fostering an environment conducive to business transactions while relieving the strain on court systems (see Figure 5.8). The Singapore International Mediation Centre (SIMC) has emerged as a key institution in the dispute resolution landscape, providing a platform for parties from diverse jurisdictions to engage in mediation. Established in

2014, SIMC aims to promote the use of mediation in resolving international commercial disputes and has handled a wide range of cases, including those in the shipping, construction, and intellectual property sectors. The key issues in these cases often revolve around contractual breaches, disagreements over intellectual property rights, and cross-border disputes. The center employs a panel of experienced mediators from various legal backgrounds to facilitate the mediation process and assist parties in reaching mutually acceptable solutions. Notable events hosted by the SIMC include the annual SIMC Mediation Forum, which brings together global thought leaders in mediation to discuss emerging trends and challenges in the field. The conclusions from mediation cases at SIMC emphasize the efficacy and cost-effectiveness of mediation as an alternative to traditional court litigation or arbitration. This recognition of mediation's value underscores its potential to alleviate the burden on court systems and contribute to efficient and satisfactory outcomes for all parties involved. The implications for the role of the judiciary in government are significant, as the rise of institutions like SIMC reflects a growing recognition of the judiciary's role in promoting and facilitating alternative dispute resolution methods. By encouraging mediation as a viable option, the judiciary demonstrates an openness to a more collaborative and consensual approach to resolving disputes, promoting access to justice, and fostering a culture of conflict resolution outside the courtroom. Furthermore, the involvement of experienced legal professionals in the mediation process highlights the judiciary's commitment to maintaining high standards of fairness and integrity in dispute resolution mechanisms.

Scholarly discourse has extensively explored the interplay between mediation, ADR, and government involvement (Berger, 1978, 1979a, 1979b; Berkmanas, 2020; Besco, 2018). The theoretical framework of "participatory justice" accentuates how mediation and ADR empower parties, allowing governments to uphold citizens' access to justice without overwhelming traditional courts. Additionally, the concept of "track-two diplomacy" examines how unofficial channels, often facilitated by non-governmental actors, influence international conflicts, underscoring the parallel roles of governments and non-state entities in conflict resolution. "Participatory justice" serves as a compelling theoretical framework that underscores the intricate relationship between mediation, Alternative Dispute Resolution (ADR), and government involvement (Rathod, 2009; Redman, 2017; Reenock et al., 2013). This concept posits that justice is best achieved when parties actively engage in the resolution process, empowering them to shape the outcome and ensuring fair access to justice. As governments increasingly recognize the advantages of mediation and ADR, their involvement can facilitate participatory justice, promoting transparency, inclusivity, and efficiency in conflict resolution.

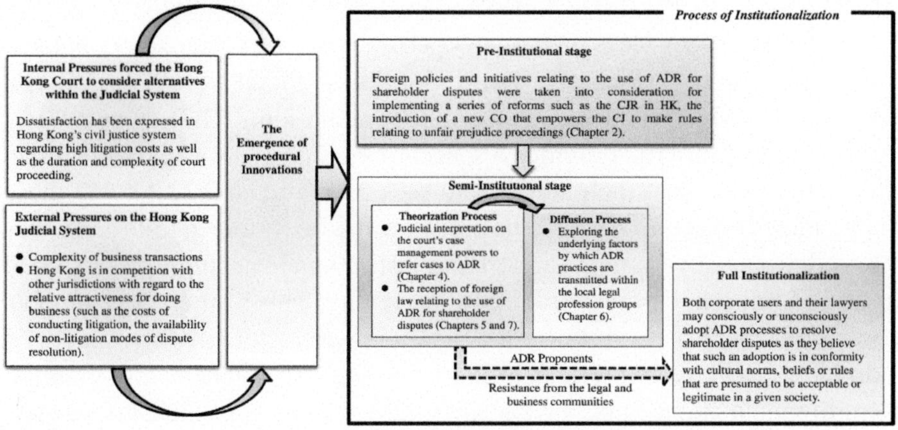

Figure 5.8. Example of an alternative dispute resolution framework and processes.

Source: Mak, I. (2017). Introduction, Overview and Methodology. In Alternative Dispute Resolution of Shareholder Disputes in Hong Kong: Institutionalizing its Effective Use (pp. Xiii-Xiv). Cambridge: Cambridge University Press.

Governments play a pivotal role in fostering participatory justice by providing the infrastructure and legitimacy necessary for successful mediation and ADR mechanisms. The Singapore Mediation Centre (SMC) exemplifies this. Established by the Singaporean government, the SMC offers a range of mediation services for commercial disputes. Government support ensures the credibility of mediated agreements and encourages parties to actively participate, confident in the enforceability of their settlements. The government's role as a facilitator underscores how mediation, when endorsed by authorities, empowers parties to collaboratively shape solutions that align with their interests, reflecting a form of participatory justice. The application of participatory justice is also evident in cross-border conflicts where governments mediate on behalf of their citizens (Edelman, 1994; Efrat, 2018; Eichensehr, 2018; Eleftheriadis, 2005). The Northern Ireland Peace Process showcases how participatory justice can lead to enduring resolutions. In this case, the British and Irish governments, along with political parties and civil society groups, engaged in dialogues that culminated in the Good Friday Agreement of 1998. The participatory approach ensured that various stakeholders, including communities affected by the conflict, had a voice in the negotiations. By involving local actors and providing a platform for their perspectives, the agreement achieved a more comprehensive and sustainable peace, reinforcing the idea that participatory justice not only empowers individuals but also leads to more enduring solutions.

Participatory justice is particularly pertinent in cases where marginalized groups seek redress (Pickett, 2016; Pidot, 2014; Pierce, 1989, 1997). The South African Truth and Reconciliation Commission (TRC) demonstrates this principle. The TRC provided a space for victims of apartheid-era human rights abuses to share their stories and seek reparations. By allowing these marginalized voices to be heard, the process aimed to restore dignity and foster reconciliation. Government support and institutional backing were essential for the commission's functioning and credibility. This example exemplifies how government-backed processes can empower historically marginalized individuals to actively participate in justice-seeking mechanisms, enabling them to regain agency and have a say in the resolution of their grievances. However, the application of participatory justice is not devoid of challenges. Governments' influence in mediation and ADR may at times overshadow the autonomy of parties. The Colombian peace process, for instance, faced criticism for perceived government bias. Striking a balance between government support and the impartiality of mediation remains crucial to ensuring genuine participatory justice. The application of the participatory justice framework underscores the evolving role of governments in conflict resolution (Zacka, 2022; Zambrano, 2019; Zuk et al., 1993). By endorsing and facilitating mediation and ADR, governments empower parties to actively engage in shaping solutions, ensuring that justice is not only served but is perceived as such by those affected. Participatory justice aligns with the principles of democratic governance, transparency, and inclusivity, offering a pathway towards sustainable peace, improved cross-border relations, and enhanced access to justice for marginalized populations.

"Track-two diplomacy" underscores the role of unofficial channels and non-governmental actors in influencing international conflicts, offering supplementary pathways for conflict resolution alongside traditional government-led diplomacy (Garoupa & Karakas, 2021; Gearty, 2005; Gentithes, 2020). "Track-two diplomacy" highlights the potential for diverse stakeholders, including civil society, academics, and private individuals, to contribute to peace-building and reconciliation efforts, enriching the discourse beyond official negotiations. The theory finds resonance in instances where civil society organizations, not tethered by governmental constraints, play pivotal roles in conflict resolution. The Israel-Palestine conflict offers an illustrative example. Various civil society initiatives, such as joint Palestinian-Israeli peace dialogues and peacebuilding workshops, have facilitated dialogue and understanding between communities affected by the conflict. These grassroots efforts, enabled by non-governmental actors, complement official diplomatic efforts and contribute to building mutual trust and empathy, thereby exemplifying the complementary nature of track-two diplomacy.

Humanitarian actors often engage in track-two diplomacy by forging connections across borders to address shared challenges (Bonica & Sen, 2017; Boskovic, 2020; Boyd, 2001; Bradley, 1998). The Ebola crisis in West Africa serves as an intriguing case. International non-governmental organizations (NGOs) and medical professionals collaborated with local communities to combat the outbreak. This collective response, transcending geopolitical boundaries, underscored the effectiveness of track-two diplomacy in fostering cooperation based on common interests, regardless of political affiliations. Academic and intellectual exchanges constitute another facet of track-two diplomacy. The Helsinki Accords of 1975 exemplify this aspect. While governmental diplomats negotiated official agreements, parallel discussions among scholars, intellectuals, and activists from Eastern and Western Europe laid the groundwork for détente and eased Cold War tensions. The intellectual dialogue influenced public opinion, creating an environment conducive to official agreements, illustrating how non-governmental actors can shape diplomatic outcomes.

The theory of track-two diplomacy is not devoid of challenges (Oakes, 2018; Obermaier, 2008; Oliveira & Garoupa, 2011). Critics argue that non-official actors lack the authority to enforce agreements and that informal negotiations may not fully represent national interests. Furthermore, the success of track-two diplomacy hinges on governments' willingness to consider the insights and proposals from non-state actors, highlighting the delicate balance between official and unofficial channels. The theory of track-two diplomacy carries implications for government involvement in conflict resolution. While official diplomatic efforts remain paramount, governments can capitalize on the insights and efforts of non-governmental actors. By recognizing the value of track-two diplomacy, governments can create spaces for civil society engagement, support academic exchanges, and facilitate dialogues among diverse stakeholders. These efforts complement official negotiations, providing innovative solutions, building trust, and fostering people-to-people connections that can contribute to long-term peace and cooperation.

Overall, "track-two diplomacy" illuminates how non-governmental actors, intellectual exchanges, and civil society initiatives influence conflict resolution. This theory enriches the discussion surrounding mediation, ADR, and government involvement, showcasing the multifaceted nature of diplomacy. By acknowledging the role of non-official actors and fostering an environment where diverse voices are heard, governments can harness the potential of track-two diplomacy to enhance official diplomatic efforts, promote cross-border cooperation, and contribute to lasting peace and reconciliation.

Government involvement in mediation and ADR is not devoid of challenges (Schroeder, 2023; Schuman, 2021; Schweiger, 2022). Ensuring impartiality is paramount, as governments may wield influence over mediation outcomes. The Colombian Peace Process, while laudable, faced criticism over perceived government bias in the negotiation process. Striking a balance between government support and mediator neutrality remains essential to upholding the integrity of mediated agreements. The contemporary mediation landscape showcases innovative models where governments play a transformative role. The Oslo Forum, facilitated by the Norwegian government, fosters discussions among conflict mediators, diplomats, and policymakers. This exemplifies how governments create platforms for knowledge exchange, enriching mediation practices.

In conclusion, mediation and ADR offer a dynamic avenue for the judiciary and government to collaboratively address conflicts. The diverse examples and case studies elucidate the intricate interplay between these entities in achieving diplomatic solutions, resolving commercial disputes, mitigating ethnic tensions, and institutionalizing conflict resolution mechanisms. As governments increasingly recognize the merits of mediation and ADR, their involvement in shaping these processes underscores the synergy between conflict resolution and statecraft, ultimately contributing to a more harmonious and just global landscape. The final section of this chapter focuses on the role of the judiciary in mitigating political conflicts.

5.5. THE JUDICIARY'S ROLE IN MITIGATING POLITICAL CONFLICTS

The intricate interplay between the judiciary and government manifests prominently in their shared responsibility to mitigate political conflicts (Mendelson, 1976; Menounou et al., 2019; Michetti et al., 2018). This section delves into the multifaceted relationship between these entities within the context of political conflict resolution, elucidating their roles and interactions through a comprehensive analysis of diverse examples and case studies from across the globe. By examining the dynamics between the judiciary and government in addressing political conflicts, this section underscores the judiciary's significance in upholding the rule of law, preserving democratic norms, and fostering stability in times of turmoil.

The judiciary's role as a neutral arbiter is central to its contribution in mitigating political conflicts (Smith & Farrales, 2010; Smith, 1992; Smith, 2015). The United States v. Nixon case exemplifies this. In 1974, the U.S. Supreme Court ordered President Richard Nixon to release the Watergate tapes, underscoring the principle that no individual, including the head of state, is above the law. By asserting its authority over the executive branch, the judiciary ensured accountability, demonstrating how courts can mediate political conflicts by upholding legal principles and safeguarding the integrity of democratic institutions. Courts often play a pivotal role in preserving electoral integrity and addressing disputes arising from electoral processes. The Kenyan Presidential Election of 2017 serves as an illustrative case. Following allegations of irregularities, the Kenyan Supreme Court nullified the election results, ordering a rerun. The court's decision showcased its commitment to the rule of law and democratic norms, emphasizing that free and fair elections are essential for political stability. This example highlights how the judiciary's intervention in electoral disputes contributes to conflict resolution and the preservation of democratic values.

The judiciary also contributes to conflict mitigation by constraining executive power and ensuring checks and balances (Ip & Yap, 2019; Jabareen, 2020; Jacobi, 2009; James, 1996). The Supreme Federal Court of Brazil displayed this role during the impeachment proceedings of President Dilma Rousseff in 2016. The court's involvement underscored its commitment to legality and constitutionality, preventing executive overreach and safeguarding democratic institutions. The judiciary's ability to mediate between branches of government is pivotal in preventing political conflicts from escalating into constitutional crises. Figure 5.9 illustrates checks and balances in government.

Political conflicts often stem from the tension between majority rule and the protection of minority rights (Brands, 2011; Brinkerhoff, 2019; Brogdon, 2018; Bromby, 2021). The Indian Supreme Court's Ayodhya Verdict exemplifies the judiciary's role in this context. The court's decision in 2019, addressing the long-standing dispute over a religious site, aimed to balance religious sentiments with constitutional principles.

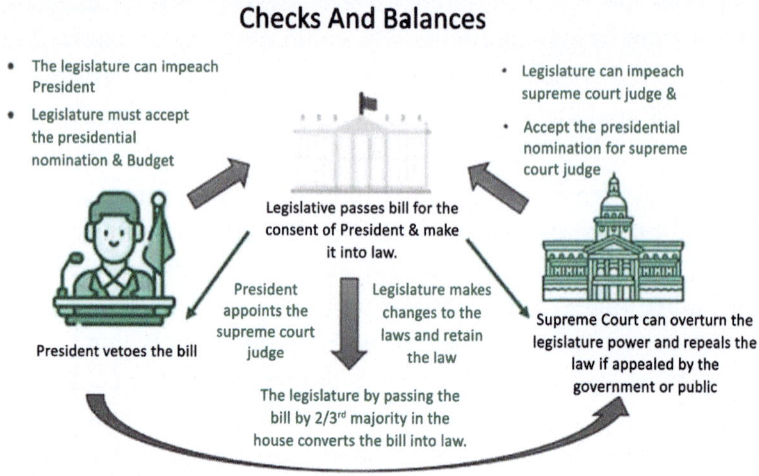

Figure 5.9. Checks and balances in government.

Source: WallStreetMojo https://www.wallstreetmojo.com/checks-and-balances/

By delivering a verdict that respected both majority and minority rights, the judiciary contributed to conflict mitigation and social harmony, demonstrating its significance in preserving societal cohesion. The Indian Supreme Court's Ayodhya verdict was a landmark judgment that sought to address the contentious issue surrounding the disputed site in Ayodhya, Uttar Pradesh. The key issue at stake was the title and ownership of the land, which was claimed both by Hindu and Muslim communities. The case had a long and complex history, dating back to the demolition of the Babri Masjid in 1992, and had been a cause of significant religious and communal tensions in the country. In a unanimous verdict, the Supreme Court concluded that the disputed land would be handed over to a trust to facilitate the construction of a Hindu temple, while also granting an alternative plot of land to the Muslim community for the construction of a mosque. The judgment was based on extensive examination of historical and archaeological evidence, as well as consideration of legal principles and constitutional guarantees. The implications for the role of the judiciary in government are significant, as the Ayodhya verdict demonstrated the Supreme Court's ability to adjudicate on sensitive and polarizing religious disputes, upholding the principles of secularism and equality enshrined in the Indian Constitution. By delivering a fair and impartial judgment, the judiciary played a crucial role in ensuring justice and maintaining social harmony, showcasing its commitment to upholding the rule of law and promoting peaceful coexistence among diverse communities. The verdict also highlighted the judiciary's role as a guardian of constitutional values and as a trusted institution capable of resolving complex and emotionally charged disputes in a manner that respects the rights and aspirations of all parties involved.

Scholars have extensively explored the judiciary's role in mitigating political conflicts (Bybee, 1994; Byrne & Maxwell, 2019; Calabresi & Rhodes, 1992). The "judicialization of politics" theory, posited by Ran Hirschl, highlights the judiciary's expanding influence on political matters. This theory underscores the dynamic relationship between the judiciary and government, emphasizing how courts can influence political conflicts by providing legal interpretations and resolutions. The "judicialization of politics" offers a comprehensive lens through which to understand the judiciary's role in mitigating political conflicts. Coined by Ran Hirschl, this concept explores the phenomenon wherein courts assume an expanded and increasingly influential role in shaping political decisions and resolving conflicts that traditionally fell within the purview of the executive and legislative branches. The "judicialization of politics" theory posits that as societies become more legally oriented and rights-conscious, courts are increasingly sought out as arenas for political conflict resolution. This process challenges the traditional separation of powers, blurring the lines between the judiciary and government branches. Hirschl emphasizes that judicialization is not limited to mere litigation, but encompasses the broader influence of courts on policy matters and governance, thereby highlighting the significant interplay between the judiciary and politics.

The United States Supreme Court's role in legalizing same-sex marriage serves as a salient example of the "judicialization of politics." The Obergefell v. Hodges case in 2015 marked a profound shift in the United States' societal and political landscape. The judiciary assumed a central role in resolving a deeply divisive social issue that was entangled with political, moral, and cultural considerations. By ruling in favor of marriage equality, the Supreme Court not only upheld individuals' rights but also influenced public discourse, redefining the parameters of political engagement and signaling a seismic transformation in societal norms. While the "judicialization of politics" empowers the judiciary to play an active role in resolving conflicts, it also presents a paradox. The theory highlights that while courts can serve as bastions of accountability, they themselves are not immune to political influences. This dynamic is exemplified by the Poland Constitutional Crisis.

As the Polish government attempted to reshape the Constitutional Tribunal's composition, public protests and concerns over democratic erosion ensued. The judiciary's involvement in adjudicating this crisis underscored both its influence in political matters and the challenges it faces in maintaining its independence. In Figure 5.10, we see how extensively the courts can influence what are considered traditionally political matters.

	Impact of court decisions	Managerial theories of compliance	Bargaining in the shadow of the law	Shadow effect of courts
Key actors	Private actors/policy makers	Policy makers: *e.g., bureaucrats, legislators*	Private actors: *e.g., divorcees, defendants*	Policy makers: *e.g., bureaucrats, legislators*
Actors' motives	Comply with legal obligations/avoid costs of noncompliance	Comply with legal obligations	Avoid costs of litigation	Avoid an adverse ruling/resist judicialization
Actors' behavior: reactive or preemptive	Reactive	Reactive	Preemptive	Preemptive
Ex ante condition	Private dispute/ noncompliant policy	Noncompliant policy	Private dispute	Noncompliant policy
Trigger of change	Court decision	Information diffusion	Threat of judicial review	Threat of judicial review
Ex post outcome	Behavior change/ policy reform	Policy reform: *e.g., legislative change, bureaucratic reform*	Behavior: change *e.g., settlements, plea bargaining*	Policy reform: *e.g., legislative change, bureaucratic reform*
Judicial review: exogenous or endogenous	Exogenous or endogenous: *private actors/policy makers take the judicial rules of the game as given or can seek to shape these rules*	Exogenous: *policy makers take the judicial rules of the game as given*	Exogenous: *private actors take the judicial rules of the game as given*	Endogenous: *policy makers can seek to shape the judicial rules of the game*

Figure 5.10. The Shadow Effect of Courts versus Related Types of Radiating Effects.

Source: Pavone, T., & Stiansen, Ø. (2022). The shadow effect of courts: Judicial review and the politics of preemptive reform. American Political Science Review, 116(1), 322–336.

The Indian Supreme Court's engagement with environmental issues showcases the transformative impact of judicialization. In the 1996 M.C. Mehta v. Union of India case, the court addressed vehicular pollution in Delhi. The judiciary's intervention compelled government agencies to take decisive measures to curb pollution, setting a precedent for judicial activism in environmental protection. This case illustrates how courts, in line with the "judicialization of politics" framework, can address policy gaps and compel executive action to mitigate pressing political conflicts. The 1996 M.C. Mehta v. Union of India case was a seminal environmental litigation that focused on the grave issue of pollution in the Ganga River in India. The key issue at hand was the rampant discharge of untreated industrial and municipal waste into the river, causing severe environmental degradation and posing a threat to public health. The case was filed by environmental activist M.C. Mehta, and it led to a series of significant events, such as the establishment of a Special Bench in the Supreme Court of India to hear the matter, multiple inspections of pollution sources, and the formulation of stringent directives to address the pollution problem. The court's conclusions emphasized the importance of upholding the right to a clean environment, holding polluting industries accountable, and implementing effective measures to restore and protect the Ganga River. The case had far-reaching implications for the role of the judiciary in government, as it highlighted the judiciary's role as a guardian of the environment and protector of public health. Through this case, the judiciary demonstrated its willingness to step in and ensure enforcement when governmental agencies failed to fulfill their duty to safeguard the environment. Furthermore, it showcased the judiciary's proactiveness in issuing directives and monitoring compliance, signaling the judiciary's proactive role in shaping environmental policies and holding all stakeholders accountable. The M.C. Mehta case served as a precedent for subsequent environmental litigations in India, empowering citizens and activists to seek judicial redress for environmental violations and contributing to the strengthening of environmental jurisprudence in the country.

The "judicialization of politics" theory also raises questions about the political implications of judicial intervention (Mak & Rutledge, 2019; Maltzman & Shipan, 2008). Critics argue that the expansion of judicial power might undermine democratic legitimacy by concentrating decision-making in an unelected branch. The European Court of Human Rights (ECtHR) faces this dilemma. In cases like Handyside v. United Kingdom, where the ECtHR ruled on freedom of expression, the court's influence intersects with national political dynamics, prompting discussions about the balance between judicial oversight and national sovereignty. Hence, the "judicialization of politics" theory provides a rich framework for understanding the judiciary's role in mitigating political conflicts. The diverse examples elucidate how courts increasingly shape political decisions, address social and policy issues, and influence public discourse. This framework underscores the judiciary's evolving role in mediating political conflicts and highlights the delicate balance between judicial intervention and democratic governance. The theory serves as a lens through which to analyze the complex interplay between the judiciary and government in conflict resolution, shedding light on the profound impact of courts on political dynamics and societal norms.

The judiciary's involvement in political conflict resolution is not without challenges (Tridimas & Gari, 2010; Trochev, 2004; Tunamsifu, 2022). Striking a balance between judicial independence and avoiding perceived activism remains a delicate endeavor. The Polish Constitutional Tribunal Crisis of 2015 illustrates this challenge. Government attempts to undermine the tribunal's independence sparked widespread protests and concerns over the erosion of democratic norms. This case highlights the complexities of maintaining the judiciary's role as a neutral arbiter while navigating political pressures. Across the globe, judiciaries play pivotal roles in mitigating political conflicts. The European Court of Human Rights (ECtHR) addresses conflicts arising from issues such as freedom of expression and minority rights. Its judgments, as seen in the case of Turkey v. Ezelin provides a legal framework for governments to navigate these conflicts within the bounds of human rights standards. The case of Turkey v. Ezelin offers a captivating illustration of the intricate interplay between the judiciary and government within the realm of human rights and international law. The case revolved around allegations of torture and ill-treatment by Turkish security forces, brought before the European Court of Human Rights (ECtHR). The key issues centered on the violation of Article 3 of the European Convention on Human Rights, which prohibits inhuman and degrading treatment. The applicant, Mehmet Ezelin, claimed that he had been subjected to severe beatings and mistreatment during his detention. The ECtHR meticulously examined the evidence, scrutinizing the Turkish government's response and the adequacy of domestic remedies. The court found Turkey in violation of Article 3, emphasizing its duty to prevent and investigate such violations. The implications of the case reverberated beyond the individual complaint. It underscored the ECtHR's role in ensuring that state actions conform to international human rights standards. The judgment in Turkey v. Ezelin reiterated the importance of effective remedies, particularly within national legal systems, and emphasized the judiciary's role as a check on government abuses. The case exemplifies how the judiciary, through international courts, safeguards individual rights and underscores the significance of governmental accountability, ultimately strengthening the rule of law and promoting respect for human rights at both national and international levels.

The judiciary's role in mitigating political conflicts becomes more pronounced in times of heightened polarization (Qin, 2011; Rakove, 1997; Ramseyer & Rasmusen, 1997). The Supreme Court of Canada demonstrated this in the Reference re Secession of Quebec case of 1998. The court's ruling established that secession from Canada would require a clear majority and negotiated terms. This decision provided legal clarity and acted as a constitutional safeguard, preventing unilateral secession and potential conflict. The Reference re Secession of Quebec case of 1998 presented a critical constitutional challenge before the Supreme Court of Canada, addressing the key issue of the legality of Quebec's potential secession from Canada. The case arose from political tension and debates surrounding Quebec's desire for sovereignty, and sought to clarify the legal framework governing secession. The events leading up to the case encompassed significant political and public discourse, reflecting deep divisions within Quebec and the broader Canadian federation. The Supreme Court's conclusion reaffirmed the importance of the rule of law and constitutional principles, asserting that unilateral secession would be unconstitutional and in violation of the principles of federalism, democracy, constitutionalism, and the protection of minority rights. The case emphasized the role of the judiciary as the ultimate interpreter of the constitution and the impartial arbiter of legal disputes, providing clarity on the legal framework for addressing secessionist movements. The implications for the role of the judiciary in government were profound, as the case showcased the judiciary's ability to adjudicate contentious constitutional matters, set precedents, and preserve the unity and stability of the nation. It highlighted the judiciary's crucial role in safeguarding the constitutional order, upholding the principles of federalism and democracy, and ensuring that processes of political transformation take place within a legal and constitutional framework. Furthermore, the case underscored the judiciary's role in balancing competing interests, protecting minority rights, and providing guidance on complex issues that have significant implications for the entire nation.

In conclusion, the judiciary's role in mitigating political conflicts is indispensable for preserving democratic norms, upholding the rule of law, and maintaining social stability. The diverse examples and case studies explored here underscore how courts act as neutral arbiters, uphold electoral integrity, balance executive power, safeguard minority rights, and navigate complex constitutional issues. As governments and societies grapple with political tensions, the judiciary's ability to mediate conflicts within legal frameworks offers a beacon of stability and accountability, underscoring its integral role in the intricate interplay between the judiciary and government.

CHAPTER 5 SUMMARY

In this chapter, we have delved into the intricate dynamics of conflict resolution through the lens of the relationship between the judiciary and government. Section 5.1 explored the concept of judicial review, highlighting the judiciary's pivotal role in assessing the legality of government actions and policies. Through detailed examples, we observed how courts act as guardians of constitutional norms, ensuring that governmental decisions align with the rule of law. Moving forward, Section 5.2 shed light on the adjudication of disputes between different branches of government. Analyzing diverse cases, we unraveled how the judiciary serves as a balancing force, ensuring that the separation of powers is maintained and that conflicts between branches are resolved impartially.

In Section 5.3, we navigated the intriguing realm of international courts in cross-border conflicts. Through a multitude of case studies, we explored how these courts provide a platform for resolving disputes that transcend national boundaries, underscoring the increasingly global nature of conflict resolution. Transitioning to Section 5.4, we embarked on a journey into the world of mediation and alternative dispute resolution (ADR). Drawing on examples from across the globe, we unraveled how these mechanisms offer nuanced approaches to conflict resolution, with governments playing an instrumental role in institutionalizing and supporting ADR frameworks.

The chapter culminated with Section 5.5, where we scrutinized the judiciary's role in mitigating political conflicts. Detailed case studies illuminated how the judiciary acts as an arbiter, upholding electoral integrity, safeguarding minority rights, and striking a delicate balance between branches of government. The theoretical framework of "judicialization of politics" provided a lens through which we explored the judiciary's increasing influence in shaping political decisions and conflict resolution.

In summary, this chapter underscored the multifaceted interplay between the judiciary and government in navigating conflicts. From reviewing government actions to mediating cross-border disputes and addressing political conflicts, the judiciary's role is paramount in upholding the rule of law, preserving democratic values, and fostering stability. Through diverse examples and theoretical frameworks, we have dissected the nuances of this relationship, highlighting the judiciary's evolving role as a key player in the intricate landscape of conflict resolution.

CHAPTER 6

Challenges to Judicial Independence

Contents

6.1. Political Interference in the Judiciary 198
6.2. Threats to Judicial Security and Safety 206
6.3. Populism and its Impact on Judicial Independence 211
6.4. Media Influence and Public Perception of the Judiciary 219
6.5. Striking a Balance: Judicial Independence and Accountability 225
Chapter 6 Summary 231

In this pivotal chapter, we delve into the intricate web of challenges that cast a shadow over judicial independence, a cornerstone of democratic governance and the rule of law. Section 6.1 dissects the ominous specter of political interference in the judiciary, uncovering how external influences can erode the impartiality of judicial decisions and undermine the very essence of justice. Shifting our focus to Section 6.2, we explore the pressing issue of threats to judicial security and safety. Through a careful examination of cases, we unravel the dire consequences when judges face intimidation, harassment, and even physical harm, threatening their ability to render justice without fear.

Section 6.3 confronts the rising tide of populism and its profound impact on judicial independence. By analyzing global instances, we unearth how the surge of populist sentiments can taint public trust in the judiciary and blur the boundaries between political agendas and judicial decisions. Turning our gaze to Section 6.4, we probe the potent role of media influence in shaping public perception of the judiciary. Drawing on examples, we scrutinize the fine line between public scrutiny and sensationalism, and how media narratives can sway public opinion, thus challenging the core principles of an independent judiciary.

The chapter culminates in Section 6.5, where we grapple with the intricate task of striking a balance between judicial independence and accountability. We dissect the delicate equilibrium required to ensure that while the judiciary remains insulated from undue influences, it remains accountable to the very society it serves. In this chapter, we unveil the intricate tapestry of challenges that the judiciary faces in preserving its autonomy, and in doing so, upholding the bedrock principles of justice and democracy.

6.1. POLITICAL INTERFERENCE IN THE JUDICIARY

The relationship between the judiciary and government is a cornerstone of democratic governance, ensuring the separation of powers and upholding the rule of law (White, 2022; Whittington, 2005; Willett & Gordon, 2022). Yet, the delicate equilibrium between an independent judiciary and the influence of the government is not without challenges. One such critical challenge is the issue of political interference in the judiciary, where the government's actions, decisions, or pressures infringe upon the autonomy and impartiality of the judicial system. This section delves into the multifaceted nature of political interference, exploring its manifestations, impacts, and countermeasures, while highlighting examples from diverse jurisdictions and referencing relevant scholarly literature. Political interference in the judiciary can manifest in various forms (see Figure 6.1 for examples of media framing), from overt actions to subtler maneuvers that undermine the independence of judges and the integrity of the judicial process (Williams, 2008; Winkler, 2009; Wong et al., 2009; Worthington, 2001). Direct actions include attempts to control judicial appointments, dismissals, or promotions based on political affiliations. Governments might also influence cases by exerting pressure on judges to rule in favor of certain outcomes, thereby compromising the impartial application of the law. Subtler forms of interference involve government officials publicly criticizing judicial decisions or making veiled threats against judges who rule against government interests. Such actions can erode public trust in the judiciary's independence and create a chilling effect on judges, causing them to self-censor their decisions. Additionally, governments may manipulate the budgetary allocation to the judiciary, impacting its operational efficiency and compromising its ability to function autonomously.

Figure 6.1. Collage of political attacks on the judiciary in India as represented by media.

Source: Aditya Raj Kaul on Twitter https://twitter.com/AdityaRajKaul/status/951795993942642689

The case of Poland provides a poignant illustration of political interference in the judiciary. The Law and Justice party's overhaul of the judicial system sparked concerns over its intent to weaken judicial independence. Reforms included changes in appointment processes and mandatory retirement ages, potentially undermining the impartiality of the judiciary. These actions raised alarm among international observers, igniting debates on the preservation of the rule of law and the delicate balance between the judiciary and government. The Law and Justice party's overhaul of the judicial system in Poland has raised significant concerns over its potential to undermine judicial independence. The reforms initiated by the party have been widely criticized by domestic and international observers, who argue that they pose a threat to the separation of powers and the rule of law. The Law and Justice party, after assuming power in 2015, implemented a series of changes aimed at restructuring the judiciary. These changes included the reconstitution of the National Council of the Judiciary, the expansion of government influence in the appointment and removal of judges, and the lowering of retirement ages for judges. These reforms have been viewed by critics as an attempt to consolidate control and exert political influence over the judiciary, eroding its ability to act independently and impartially.

The concern over weakening judicial independence is rooted in the vital role that an independent judiciary plays in a democratic society (Spencer & Spencer, 2006, 2010; Spendzharova & Vachudova, 2012). Judicial independence ensures that judges are impartial and free from any undue influence or interference. It is a cornerstone of the rule of law, as an independent judiciary acts as a check on the power of the executive and legislative branches. When judicial independence is compromised, it can lead to erosion of civil liberties, less accountability, and inequality before the law. The Law and Justice party's overhaul of the judicial system has sparked both domestic and international criticism. Protests erupted in Poland, with citizens expressing their concern over the potential erosion of judicial independence and the rule of law. The European Union has also raised objections to the reforms, citing concerns over the impact on the country's democratic institutions. The European Commission has initiated infringement procedures, claiming that the changes breach European Union law.

In response to the concerns, the Law and Justice party has defended its reforms, arguing that they are necessary to address perceived inefficiencies and corruption within the judicial system. They assert that the changes aim to democratize the judiciary and reflect the will of the Polish people, who elected them into power. However, critics point out that the speed and manner in which the reforms were pushed through raised questions about transparency and the proper consultation of stakeholders, including the judiciary itself. The clash between the Law and Justice party and their critics highlights an ongoing debate about the balance of power and the independence of the judiciary within the framework of democratic governance (Zacka, 2022; Zambrano, 2019; Zuk et al., 1993). The judiciary and the government have a delicate relationship, as the judiciary is tasked with interpreting and applying the law, while the government formulates and implements policy. This relationship relies on mutual respect and understanding to ensure that the judiciary can perform its role effectively, free from political interference.

In Venezuela, the executive branch's influence over the judiciary has been a contentious issue. The stacking of the Supreme Tribunal of Justice with government loyalists compromised the court's autonomy, leading to decisions that favored government policies. Scholars have highlighted how these actions, along with other constitutional changes, have undermined the judiciary's ability to serve as a check on the government's power. Over the years, concerns have been raised about the erosion of judicial independence and the concentration of power in the hands of the government. The judiciary, which is supposed to act as a check on the executive, has faced numerous challenges to its independence (Tridimas & Gari, 2010; Trochev, 2004; Tunamsifu, 2022). One significant event that highlighted these concerns was the controversial appointment of judges to the Supreme Court in 2015. The process for these appointments was widely criticized as lacking transparency and adhering to political motivations. This move led to a judiciary that was seen by many as aligned with the ruling party, compromising its ability to act impartially and fairly.

The executive's influence over the judiciary has been further perpetuated by the strategic use of legislation and amendments to laws that impact the makeup and functioning of the judicial system. Critics argue that these actions have weakened the judiciary's independence, as they serve to consolidate power in the hands of the government and limit the court's ability to offer impartial rulings (George, 2009; Geyh, 2014; Gisbert, 2022; Gomes, 2017). The implications of the executive's influence over the judiciary in Venezuela have been significant. It has led to a loss of trust in the judicial system, with many perceiving it as biased and beholden to political interests. The lack of an independent judiciary has raised concerns about the erosion of civil liberties, violations of human rights, and the weakening of democratic institutions. The role of the judiciary in government is meant to be one of providing checks and balances, ensuring the fair application of the law and protection of citizens' rights. However, in Venezuela, the executive's influence has undermined this fundamental principle. The judiciary, rather than acting as an independent arbiter, has faced allegations of being used as a tool to suppress dissent and consolidate power.

Political interference in the judiciary corrodes the very foundation of democratic governance – an independent judiciary that safeguards citizens' rights and maintains the rule of law (Mason, 2015; Matthes, 2022; Mayoral & Perez, 2018). When judges feel compelled to rule in favor of the government or face punitive measures, the impartiality of the legal system is compromised. Public trust in the judiciary diminishes, as the perception of decisions being politically influenced overshadows the pursuit of justice. Scholarly work by Ginsburg and Huq (2018) emphasizeS how political interference can lead to a "democratic backslide," where institutions erode, and the government consolidates power at the expense of checks and balances. This scenario is often accompanied by weakened civil liberties, erosion of democratic norms, and increased corruption. Democratic backslide, a concept at the intersection of political science and governance, has gained prominence as a framework to understand the erosion of democratic institutions and values within established democratic systems. Central to this concept is the examination of how the equilibrium between democratic governance and the functioning of institutions, including the judiciary, can be disrupted, leading to a decline in democratic quality. In this theoretical exploration, we delve into the phenomenon of democratic backslide and its intricate relationship with judicial independence, drawing upon scholarly insights and empirical examples.

Democratic backslide refers to the gradual deterioration of democratic norms, principles, and institutions that uphold democratic governance (Navarrete & Castillo-Ortiz, 2020; Nelson & Gibson, 2019). It encompasses the subtle and overt shifts away from democratic ideals, often characterized by increasing concentration of power, erosion of checks and balances, weakening of civil liberties, and manipulation of democratic mechanisms (see Figure 6.2). The phenomenon disrupts the delicate balance between governmental branches, impacting not only the political landscape but also the socio-cultural fabric of societies. Judicial independence, a cornerstone of democracy, denotes the autonomy of the judiciary from undue influence, ensuring that courts can adjudicate impartially and without political interference. In the context of democratic backsliding, the autonomy and effectiveness of the judiciary are threatened, which in turn exacerbates the decline of democratic governance. The erosion of judicial independence disrupts the checks and balances that prevent excessive executive power, thereby tilting the equilibrium toward a concentration of power within the government.

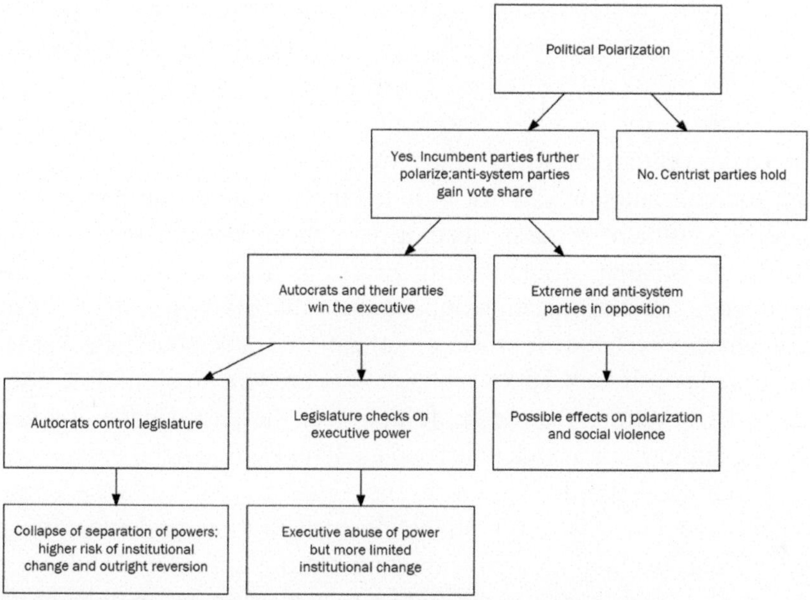

Figure 6.2. Cascade of indicators of democratic backsliding.

Source: Haggard, S., & Kaufman, R. (2021). *Backsliding: Democratic regress in the contemporary world*. Cambridge University Press.

Various mechanisms contribute to the erosion of judicial independence in the context of democratic backslide (Hasbrouck, 2022; He, 2017; He, 2018; Heinz & Manikas, 1992). These include:

1. Manipulation of Judicial Appointments: Governments may seek to stack the judiciary with loyalists or ideologically aligned judges. This compromises the impartiality and diversity of the bench, reducing its capacity to act as a check on executive power.
2. Intimidation and Threats: Political actors might openly or subtly threaten judges, undermining their ability to render impartial decisions. This intimidation cultivates self-censorship and undermines the judiciary's role in holding the government accountable.
3. Legislative Reforms: Governments may enact laws that restrict judicial powers, alter appointment procedures, or curtail judicial review. These legislative changes diminish the judiciary's capacity to uphold democratic norms.
4. Budgetary Constraints: Manipulating the allocation of resources

to the judiciary can hinder its operational efficiency, curbing its ability to function autonomously and deliver justice effectively.

The case of Turkey provides a compelling example of the interplay between democratic backslide and judicial independence. Amidst concerns of increasing authoritarianism, the government has taken measures that impact judicial autonomy. This includes the controversial changes to the judicial appointment process, leading to concerns about the impartiality of the bench. Scholars argue that these actions have compromised judicial independence, raising questions about the judiciary's role as a check on governmental power and the broader implications for democratic governance. Democratic backslide in Turkey refers to the gradual erosion of democratic norms and institutions that has unfolded over the past decade, marked by increasing authoritarian tendencies and challenges to judicial independence. This phenomenon holds significant implications for Turkey's domestic governance, regional stability, and the global aspiration for democratization. By describing, explaining, analyzing, and critiquing this backslide, we can illuminate its complex dynamics and its wider effects on the global desire for democratic governance.

Turkey's democratic backslide can be traced back to the early 2010s when the ruling Justice and Development Party (AKP) began to consolidate power, altering the institutional landscape and undermining checks and balances. This involved curtailing media freedom, silencing dissent, and tightening control over institutions including the judiciary. Legislative reforms enabled the government to exert more influence over the appointment and promotion of judges, thereby compromising judicial independence. The government's crackdown on the 2016 coup attempt led to mass purges in the judiciary, further weakening its impartiality. The implications of Turkey's democratic backslide are multi-faceted. Firstly, the erosion of judicial independence has blurred the lines between the judiciary and the executive, undermining the judiciary's ability to hold the government accountable. This weakens the checks and balances necessary for democratic governance. Secondly, the crackdown on media and dissent hampers the free exchange of ideas and restricts political pluralism, eroding the foundations of a vibrant democracy. Thirdly, the shift towards majoritarian politics has marginalized minority rights and polarized society, raising concerns about inclusivity and social cohesion.

Turkey's backslide also reverberates globally. Regionally, it has strained relations with European Union (EU) member states and affected Turkey's candidacy for EU membership. It has also complicated Turkey's role as a regional actor in the Middle East. Furthermore, the international community views Turkey's trajectory as a case study of democratic regression, challenging the global aspiration for democratization and the belief that democratic governance is universally applicable (van Zeben, 2015; Vermeule, 2012; Voeten, 2008; VonDoepp & Ellett, 2011). Turkey's democratic backslide raises questions about the resilience of democracy and the complexities of democratic transitions. The international community often promotes democratization as a universal value, yet Turkey's experience shows that the path to democracy is not linear. It underscores the importance of context, historical legacies, and local dynamics in shaping democratic trajectories. Turkey's case serves as a cautionary tale that even in countries where democratic institutions were robust, they can deteriorate under certain circumstances.

The concept of democratic backslide provides a theoretical lens to understand the erosion of democratic institutions and values (Agbor, 2015; Alleman & Mazzone, 2010; Alter, 1998). In this context, the integrity of the judiciary, as a check on governmental power, is intricately connected to the preservation of democratic norms. The erosion of judicial independence disrupts the equilibrium of power, tilting the scales toward an accumulation of executive authority. By theorizing the relationship between democratic backslide and judicial independence, scholars can contribute to a deeper understanding of how democratic institutions interact and the complexities that underlie the maintenance of democratic governance. Efforts to counter political interference in the judiciary require a multi-pronged approach. Ensuring transparent judicial appointment processes, insulated from political bias, is critical. Mechanisms for judicial self-governance, such as judicial councils, can help safeguard against executive overreach. Judicial codes of conduct, informed by international standards, can guide judges' ethical behavior and shield them from undue influence. International bodies and civil society organizations play a pivotal role in monitoring and condemning instances of political interference. The Venice Commission, an advisory body of the Council of Europe, issues reports and recommendations on legal and constitutional matters, contributing to the preservation of the rule of law across its member states.

Political interference in the judiciary is a multifaceted challenge that reverberates across jurisdictions and undermines democratic governance. As governments seek to preserve their interests, the relationship between the judiciary and government becomes strained, and the essential tenets of judicial independence and the rule of law are put to the test. However, international standards, scholarly insights, and vigilant civil societies serve as powerful tools to mitigate such interference, ensuring that an impartial judiciary remains a cornerstone of democratic societies worldwide. The next section in this chapter considers the threats to judicial safety and security.

6.2. THREATS TO JUDICIAL SECURITY AND SAFETY

The intricate balance between the judiciary and government is a linchpin of democratic governance, safeguarding the rule of law and ensuring the protection of individual rights. However, this equilibrium can be profoundly disrupted by threats to judicial security and safety. In this section, we delve into the multifaceted challenges posed by such threats, exploring their implications for judicial independence, examining real-world examples from diverse global contexts, and drawing on scholarly perspectives to illuminate the intricate interplay between the judiciary and government. Judicial security encompasses various forms of threats, ranging from physical violence to subtle intimidation and harassment. These threats can come from various actors, including criminal elements, extremist groups, political figures, and even disgruntled litigants. The implications of these threats extend beyond the immediate safety of judges; they erode the very foundations of judicial independence and the rule of law, undermining public trust in the judiciary's ability to render impartial decisions free from external pressures.

The assassination of Judge Giovanni Falcone in Italy serves as a poignant example (Calfee, 2006; Cameron, 2010; Caplan, 2010; Carrillo et al., 2017). Falcone, a prominent anti-Mafia judge, was killed in a bomb attack orchestrated by the Mafia. His murder was not just an assault on his life, but an attack on the judiciary's commitment to combating organized crime. The case underscored the vulnerability of judges who challenge powerful criminal networks, and it prompted a reassessment of judicial security protocols. Falcone, a highly esteemed and relentless anti-Mafia judge, tragically met his untimely end in a merciless bomb attack meticulously orchestrated by the powerful Mafia. This heinous act sent shockwaves throughout Italy, exposing the grim reality of the depth and audacity of organized crime's influence within the country. Falcone's death served as a stark reminder of the immense challenges faced by those dedicated to combating such criminal entities. The targeted assassination not only highlighted the inherent dangers faced by individuals in positions of judicial authority, but it also shed light on the critical role played by the judiciary in unraveling the networks of organized crime, bringing perpetrators to justice, and safeguarding the integrity of the state. As the nation mourned Falcone's loss, intense debates regarding the adequacy of protection for judges, the efficacy of anti-Mafia strategies, and the need for holistic judicial reforms dominated public discourse. The event culminated in a collective awakening, as both citizens and the government were forced to reevaluate their approaches to combating organized crime. Investigations following Falcone's assassination led to significant revelations that led to the dismantling of several influential Mafia networks, serving as a testimony to Falcone's legacy and the determination of those who carried on his relentless pursuit of justice. This appalling event and its aftermath brought forth profound and lasting implications for the role of the judiciary in government. The need for strengthened security measures for judges and judicial apparatus became paramount, as a tangible demonstration of the state's commitment to providing a safe environment for those who seek to protect the rule of law. Moreover, it catalyzed an urgent call for enhanced cooperation and coordination between different branches of government, law enforcement agencies, and international bodies to address the complex and cross-border nature of organized crime. Falcone's assassination served as a potent reminder that the judiciary stands as a bulwark against the nefarious infiltrations of criminal syndicates and underscored the need for continued support, resources, and recognition for the pivotal role it plays in upholding justice, safeguarding society, and preserving the democratic fabric of the nation.

The effectiveness of court security is an important dynamic when ensuring the integrity of the judicial system. Figure 6.3 measures this dynamic in Ukraine. The effectiveness of court security in Ukraine holds critical implications for the health and safety of the justice system. Ukraine has grappled with numerous challenges, including political instability and external pressures, which have at times translated into threats against judges and court personnel. While efforts have been made to enhance court security, the effectiveness of these measures is a pivotal determinant of the judiciary's ability to operate independently and uphold the rule of law. The safety of judges, prosecutors, lawyers, and other court staff directly impacts their willingness to engage in the legal process without fear of retribution. A secure environment fosters judicial independence, enabling judges to render impartial decisions without external pressures. Additionally, it ensures that court proceedings can unfold without disruptions, contributing to the overall efficiency and credibility of the justice system. The Ukrainian government's commitment to robust court security mechanisms not only protects individuals within the justice system but also safeguards the integrity of the judicial process as a whole. By maintaining a safe and secure environment, Ukraine's justice system can continue to function as a cornerstone of democratic governance, upholding the rule of law and ensuring that justice is administered without compromise.

Several specific incidents of lapses in court security have occurred in Ukraine, shedding light on the challenges faced by the justice system and the government's responses to address these issues. One notable case involves the tragic assassination of Judge Mykola Chaus in April 2021. Chaus, known for his involvement in high-profile corruption cases, was abducted in broad daylight in Kyiv. This incident underscored the vulnerability of judges to criminal elements seeking to undermine judicial independence and accountability. The Ukrainian government responded by launching an investigation, leading to the arrest of suspects involved in the abduction. However, the incident highlighted the need for more comprehensive and proactive security measures to safeguard judges and court personnel.

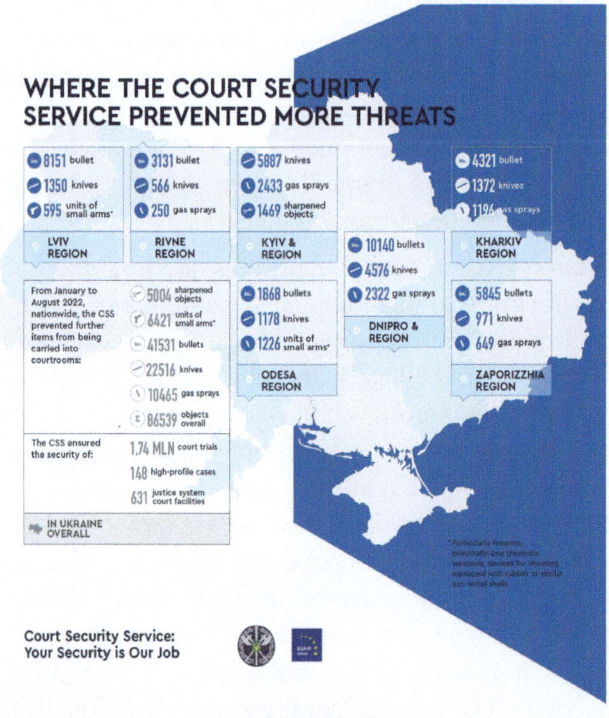

Figure 6.3. The effectiveness of court security in Ukraine.

Source: EUAM https://www.euam-ukraine.eu/news/latest-news/justice-how-can-you-contribute-to-keeping-ukrainian-courts-safe-in-wartime/

In another instance, the case of Judge Pavlo Vovk in 2016 raised concerns about potential political interference in the judiciary. Vovk faced accusations of misconduct, and video footage emerged showing him in compromising situations. This incident led to debates about the extent to which political motivations might be influencing judicial outcomes. While the incident did not directly involve physical threats, it highlighted the broader issue of external pressures that judges can face, compromising their independence. The government's response involved internal disciplinary proceedings, showcasing the importance of robust mechanisms to address judicial misconduct and ensure transparency. The implications of these incidents extend beyond individual safety concerns. Lapses in court security and allegations of interference challenge the public's perception of the justice system's integrity. Such incidents can foster distrust in the judiciary's ability to dispense justice impartially and without external influences. They also create a chilling effect on judges, who may become more cautious in their decisions due to fear of retribution. The government's response, including investigations, arrests, and disciplinary actions, plays a critical role in maintaining public confidence in the justice system. To effectively address these challenges, Ukraine must adopt a multifaceted approach. Strengthening physical security measures, such as securing court premises and providing personal protection for judges and court personnel, is imperative. Equally important is addressing the underlying issues of corruption and political interference. This involves implementing transparent and accountable judicial appointments, promoting judicial ethics, and fostering a culture of judicial independence.

Threats to judicial security cast a shadow over the judiciary's capacity to function independently (Moliterno & Curos, 2021; Molto, 2015; Munday, 2008). Judges who fear for their safety may self-censor their decisions, compromising the impartial application of the law. Moreover, the perception that judges are susceptible to external pressures undermines public trust in the judicial process, eroding confidence in the system's fairness. As a result, judicial security challenges intertwine with the larger fabric of democratic governance, affecting the judiciary-government relationship. Scholars such as Ginsburg and Moustafa (2008) emphasize the significance of judicial security in maintaining judicial independence. They argue that threats to judges can have a chilling effect on the judiciary's willingness to challenge government actions, leading to a culture of self-censorship. Additionally, literature on judicial reforms in transitional democracies, as highlighted by Uprimny and García (2004), underscores the importance of protecting judges from threats and intimidation to ensure their autonomy in nascent democracies.

Scholars Ginsburg and Moustafa (2008) contribute significantly to the understanding of the relationship between judicial security and judicial independence. Their emphasis on the importance of judicial security in maintaining judicial independence resonates deeply in contexts where threats to judges are prevalent. They highlight a critical dynamic: that threats, whether physical or otherwise, can create a chilling effect that permeates the judiciary. Their argument that such threats can lead to self-censorship among judges aligns with the notion that judges, fearing retribution, may hesitate to challenge government actions or make decisions that could be perceived as politically unfavorable. This phenomenon ultimately compromises the judiciary's capacity to act as an effective check on governmental power and to uphold the principles of justice without fear of reprisals. This can have implications in terms of a gap between formal and perceived judicial independence (see Figure 6.4).

Formal independence	**Perceived independence**
Judiciary: · Legal basis of independence · Organizational autonomy · Funding · Management of court system ***Judge:*** · Human resource decisions about judges · Disciplinary measures · Non-transferability of judges · Internal independence	***Judge and judiciary undifferentiated:*** · Independence as perceived by citizens · Independence as perceived by court users · Independence as perceived by judges · Trust in judiciary, relative to trust in other state powers by citizens in general · Judicial corruption as perceived by citizens in general

Figure 6.4. Distinguishing formal from perceived judicial independence.

Source: van Dijk, Frans & Vos, Geoffrey. (2018). A Method for Assessment of the Independence and Accountability of the Judiciary. International Journal for Court Administration. 9. 1–21. 10.18352/ijca.276.

In a similar vein, Uprimny and García (2004) offer insights that are particularly relevant to the challenges faced by nascent democracies and transitional contexts. Their focus on protecting judges from threats and intimidation is rooted in the recognition that newly established democratic systems are often fragile and vulnerable to external pressures. Their work underscores the idea that judicial autonomy is crucial for the development of democratic institutions, especially in contexts where the rule of law is still taking shape. By safeguarding judges from threats, these scholars argue, a solid foundation for judicial independence can be established, preventing potential backslides into authoritarianism and ensuring that the judiciary can act as an effective counterbalance to other branches of government.

Governments bear the responsibility of safeguarding judicial security and safety (Wang, 2021; Weill, 2016; West, 2019; Westerman, 2017). Comprehensive security measures, including secure court facilities, enhanced personal security for judges, and efficient law enforcement response mechanisms, are crucial. However, it is imperative that these measures do not curtail judges' accessibility or exacerbate their isolation from society. International cooperation plays a pivotal role in addressing threats to judicial security. Organizations like the International Association of Women Judges (IAWJ) provide a platform for judges to share experiences and strategies for mitigating threats. The United Nations Office on Drugs and Crime (UNODC) also provides technical assistance to countries facing judicial security challenges, facilitating capacity-building and knowledge exchange.

Threats to judicial security and safety reverberate far beyond individual judges; they disrupt the delicate equilibrium between the judiciary and government, which is foundational to democratic governance. Judges who face threats must grapple with personal safety concerns while upholding their constitutional duty to dispense justice. By understanding the implications of these threats through global case studies and scholarly perspectives, we gain insights into the intricate dynamics of the judiciary-government relationship. It is incumbent upon governments, civil society, and the international community to collaborate in creating an environment where judges can fulfill their roles without fear, and where the principles of judicial independence and the rule of law are upheld unwaveringly. In the third section of this chapter, we explore the impact of populism on judicial independence.

6.3. POPULISM AND ITS IMPACT ON JUDICIAL INDEPENDENCE

The rise of populism has introduced a new layer of complexity to the dynamic of judicial independence and executive control, presenting both challenges and opportunities for the preservation of judicial independence (Primus, 2004; Prince, 2020; Provost, 2008; Pulle & Ratnapala, 2019). Drawing on global case studies and scholarly insights, this section delves into the multifaceted impact of populism on judicial independence, shedding light on the intricate interplay between democratic principles and the rule of law. Populism, characterized by its anti-elite rhetoric, promises of direct representation, and appeal to the "people," can have profound implications for the judiciary-government relationship. Populist leaders often seek to concentrate power within the executive branch, portraying themselves as the voice of the people against alleged corrupt elites. This can manifest in attempts to weaken judicial institutions perceived as obstructing populist agendas. The implications for judicial independence are significant, as courts may be pressured to align with populist narratives or risk facing accusations of being "anti-people."

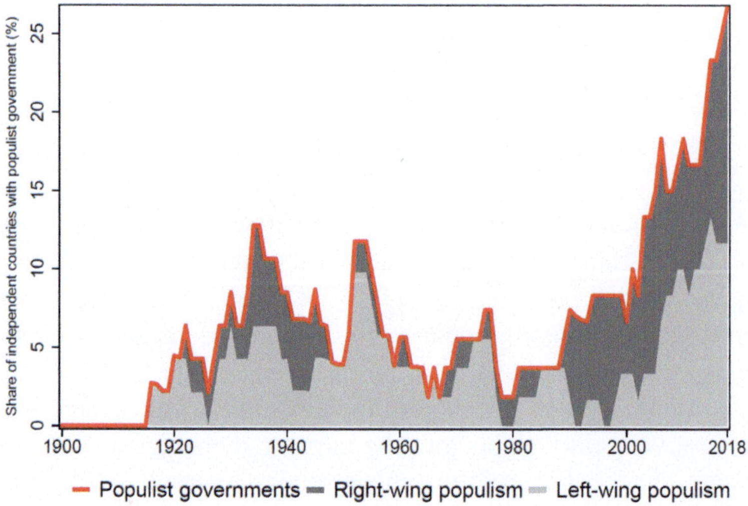

Figure 6.5. The rise of populism in the 20th century and early 21st century.

Source: Schularick, Trebesch, and Funke (2021) https://cepr.org/voxeu/columns/cost-populism-evidence-history

The rise of populism (see Figure 6.5) presents a multifaceted threat to judicial independence, rooted in the complex interplay between democratic aspirations and the erosion of fundamental democratic principles (Brands, 2011; Brinkerhoff, 2019; Brogdon, 2018; Bromby, 2021). Populist movements often emerge in response to perceived elite corruption, economic inequality, and disillusionment with traditional political institutions. Promising direct representation and championing the interests of the "common people," populist leaders often seek to consolidate power within the executive branch, portraying themselves as the authentic voice of the majority against purportedly corrupt elites. In doing so, they create a dichotomy between the "people" and the "establishment," positioning themselves as the sole representatives of the former.

This dichotomy not only polarizes society but also delegitimizes other branches of government, including the judiciary, by framing them as part of the elite establishment (Cassman, 2015; Celenk, 2016; Chakravarti et al., 2011; Chalmers, 2000). Populist leaders may challenge judicial independence by attempting to undermine the judiciary's authority through direct appointments, constitutional reforms, or even undermining the legitimacy of court decisions that run counter to their agendas. The courts, tasked with interpreting laws, safeguarding individual rights, and checking government power, become a focal point of tension. The populist rhetoric of representing the people can translate into demands for judges to align with the populist agenda, leading to judicial self-censorship or even overt pressure on judges. The outcome is a precarious balance between democratic representation and the rule of law, with populist leaders wielding the mandate of the people as a justification for exerting control over the judiciary, potentially compromising its ability to operate independently and uphold the principles of justice. The threat to judicial independence lies not only in explicit attacks on the judiciary but also in the erosion of the norms and institutions that sustain the separation of powers and checks and balances. In essence, the rise of populism triggers a complex challenge, wherein the rhetoric of democratic representation becomes a tool to legitimize actions that undermine the very foundations of democracy, thereby posing a substantial risk to judicial independence and the broader democratic fabric.

The Philippines provides a vivid illustration of populism's impact on judicial independence. The administration of President Rodrigo Duterte, characterized by a populist discourse emphasizing the "war on drugs," witnessed attempts to sideline the judiciary. The ousting of Chief Justice Maria Lourdes Sereno in 2018 raised concerns about executive interference in the judiciary, highlighting the vulnerabilities of judicial independence in the face of populist pressures. The populism exhibited by President Rodrigo Duterte in the Philippines has been marked by a distinctive and often controversial approach, with significant implications for judicial independence both domestically and on the global stage. Duterte's rhetoric and policies have raised concerns about the rule of law, democratic institutions, and human rights, highlighting the complex relationship between populism and judicial autonomy. Key events during Duterte's presidency have underscored the implications of his populism for judicial independence. His administration's "war on drugs" campaign, launched soon after taking office in 2016, saw extrajudicial killings of alleged drug offenders by law enforcement agencies. This approach not only raised alarms about human rights violations but also presented a challenge to the judiciary's role in upholding due process and ensuring accountability for state actions. High-profile cases challenging the legitimacy of these operations, particularly before the Supreme Court of the Philippines, showcased the judiciary's role in providing a legal framework for evaluating the actions of the executive branch. The court's response to these cases highlighted the tensions between Duterte's populist rhetoric of "war on drugs" and the judiciary's commitment to constitutional rights.

Duterte's approach to dealing with critics, both domestically and internationally, has also had implications for judicial independence. His statements targeting judges who ruled against his policies or individuals who opposed his government's actions created an environment of intimidation that could affect the judiciary's impartiality. Moreover, the removal of Chief Justice Maria Lourdes Sereno in 2018 through a contentious impeachment process raised concerns about executive interference in the judiciary and the potential erosion of its independence. At the local level, the implications for judicial independence in the Philippines are profound. Duterte's polarizing rhetoric and authoritarian tendencies have led to a climate where judges may feel pressure to align with the government's agenda to avoid backlash. This can undermine their ability to adjudicate cases fairly and without fear of retribution, effectively compromising the rule of law. On the global stage, Duterte's populism has attracted international attention and criticism. His disregard for human rights, judicial independence, and democratic norms has strained the Philippines' relationships with international organizations, allies, and human rights advocates.

The global community's response underscores the interconnectedness of judicial independence with broader democratic values, transcending national borders and highlighting the international significance of upholding this fundamental principle. Hence, President Rodrigo Duterte's populism in the Philippines has posed significant challenges to judicial independence, both at the local and global levels. The "war on drugs" campaign, removal of Chief Justice Sereno, and intimidating rhetoric have collectively heightened concerns about the judiciary's ability to function independently and uphold democratic principles. The events under Duterte's leadership serve as a cautionary tale of how populist agendas can erode the rule of law and the autonomy of the judiciary, illustrating the need for vigilant protection of judicial independence in the face of populist pressures. Interestingly, Figure

6.6 suggests a significant presence of leftwing populism when compared with rightwing populism.

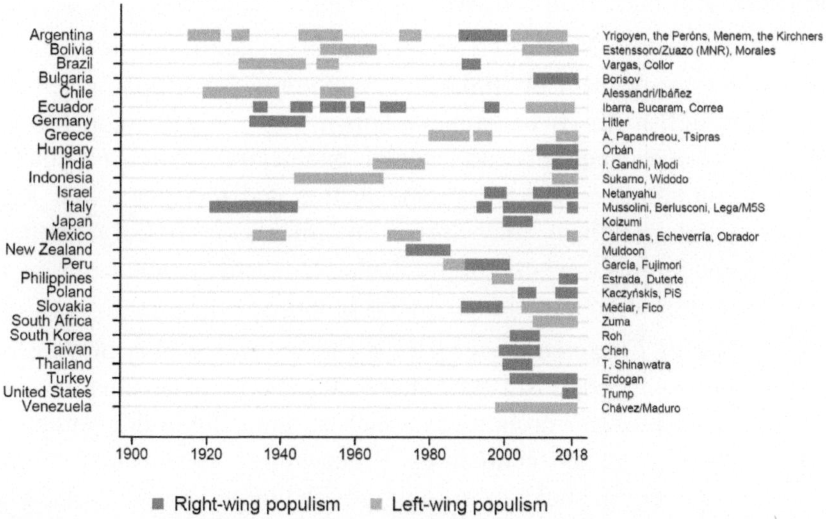

Figure 6.6. The leftwing and rightwing patterns of populism across the globe.

Source: Schularick, Trebesch, and Funke (2021) https://cepr.org/voxeu/columns/cost-populism-evidence-history

The emergence of populism across the globe has taken various forms, with both left-wing and right-wing variations gaining traction in different regions (Mason, 2015; Matthes, 2022; Mayoral & Perez, 2018). While the prevalence of each type varies by context, the underlying drivers and factors contributing to the rise of left-wing and right-wing populism offer nuanced insights into the global political landscape. Left-wing populism often centers on economic inequality, social justice, and anti-establishment sentiments. In recent years, it has gained prominence in regions such as Latin America and parts of Europe. One notable example is former President Evo Morales of Bolivia, whose policies aimed at addressing indigenous rights and wealth redistribution resonated with marginalized communities. Similarly, leaders like former President Rafael Correa in Ecuador and President Andrés Manuel López Obrador in Mexico have advocated for economic reforms to benefit the working class. Right-wing populism, on the other hand, often focuses on anti-immigrant sentiment, nationalism, and opposition to globalization. Leaders like former President Donald Trump in the United States, Prime Minister Viktor Orbán in Hungary, and President Jair Bolsonaro in Brazil have garnered support through platforms that emphasize protectionism, strong borders, and cultural conservatism. We can theorize on some of the factors that may be responsive for these emerging patterns as follows (Garoupa & Karakas, 2021; Gearty, 2005; Gentithes, 2020):

1. ***Economic Factors:*** The prevalence of left-wing or right-wing populism can be linked to economic conditions. Left-wing populism tends to gain traction in regions with high levels of income inequality and social exclusion, where marginalized communities seek economic justice and representation. Right-wing populism may thrive in areas experiencing economic uncertainty, where individuals fear that globalization and immigration may threaten their livelihoods.
2. ***Social Fragmentation:*** The social landscape also plays a role. Left-wing populism may emerge in societies where identity-based disparities are pronounced, such as those involving indigenous rights or racial inequalities. Right-wing populism may be more prevalent in societies grappling with cultural tensions and issues of national identity.
3. ***Globalization and Migration:*** The rise of populism often correlates with shifts in global dynamics. Left-wing populism may find resonance when communities feel marginalized by global economic processes. Right-wing populism can gain ground in response to heightened immigration, which is often framed as a threat to cultural identity and national security.
4. ***Political Establishment:*** Populism thrives in contexts where there is a perception of a detached or corrupt political establishment. Left-wing populists often cast themselves as champions of the marginalized against elites. Right-wing populists may tap into anti-establishment sentiment by portraying themselves as the voice of the "silent majority."
5. ***Media and Communication:*** The role of media in amplifying populist messages is significant. Populist leaders often utilize social media platforms to directly communicate with their base, circumventing traditional media channels. This allows them to create targeted messages that resonate with their supporters.
6. ***Crisis and Discontent:*** Populism can emerge in times of crisis, whether economic, political, or social. These crises create fertile ground for leaders who promise quick and drastic solutions to complex problems.

7. ***Reaction to Globalization:*** Left-wing populism can be seen as a reaction against the perceived injustices of globalization, including economic inequality and loss of cultural identity. Right-wing populism may arise as a response to challenges posed by international institutions and supranational agreements that are perceived to undermine national sovereignty.

Hence, the prevalence of left-wing and right-wing populism varies by region and context, with each manifestation reflecting the specific socio-economic, cultural, and political factors at play. Economic disparities, social fragmentation, globalization, and the perceived failures of the political establishment all contribute to the rise of populism. Understanding these emerging patterns requires a nuanced analysis of local dynamics and global trends, shedding light on the complex interplay between populism, democracy, and governance.

In Hungary, the government led by Prime Minister Viktor Orbán has adopted policies that centralize power and curtail democratic institutions. The ruling party's constitutional amendments and changes to the judicial system have raised alarms about the erosion of judicial independence. The weakening of checks and balances in the name of protecting the will of the people underscores the tension between populism and the rule of law. Prime Minister Viktor Orbán's brand of populism in Hungary has generated significant concerns, particularly when analyzed through the lens of judicial independence. The confluence of political narratives, constitutional amendments, and executive actions has implications that ripple across multiple levels: locally, nationally, regionally, continentally, and internationally. Orbán's populism is rooted in his consolidation of power, fueled by anti-establishment sentiment and nationalism. This has manifested in measures that directly impact judicial independence. The 2011 constitutional amendments shifted the balance of power, increasing government influence over the judiciary. The creation of the National Judicial Council further entrenched political control over judicial appointments and promotions. This direct interference raises concerns about the impartiality and autonomy of the judiciary, as judges may be pressured to align with the government's agenda to secure advancement.

At the local level, Orbán's populism has fostered an environment where the judiciary's role in upholding the rule of law becomes vulnerable. Judges, fearing political repercussions, may self-censor to avoid clashing with the government. This erodes the public's trust in the judiciary's impartiality, threatening the foundation of a fair justice system. The independence of the judiciary is crucial for safeguarding individual rights and ensuring that citizens can challenge government overreach. The domestic consequences extend nationally and regionally. Orbán's erosion of democratic institutions undermines Hungary's standing within the European Union (EU). The European Court of Justice has intervened on matters such as media laws, highlighting the tension between Hungary's actions and EU values. Such conflicts impede regional cohesion, emphasizing the link between populism, judicial independence, and the viability of collective governance frameworks. On the continental and international levels, Orbán's populism represents a challenge to the broader values of democracy, human rights, and the rule of law. Hungary's internal developments reverberate across Europe, encouraging the rise of similar movements and posing a threat to the EU's democratic integrity. Furthermore, Orbán's stance against immigration and his polarizing rhetoric have repercussions beyond Hungary's borders. These actions shape global perceptions of Hungary and impact international relations.

The Orbán phenomenon underscores the intricate relationship between populism and judicial independence (Gallagher, 2012; Gardbaum, 2015; Garoupa et al., 2012). His consolidation of power illustrates how populism can instrumentalize democratic institutions to undermine their autonomy. Theoretically, the interplay between populism and judicial independence reveals a delicate balance between democratic representation and the preservation of checks and balances. The erosion of judicial independence poses a theoretical challenge to established notions of democracy, suggesting that populist leaders may exploit democratic mandates to subvert key pillars of democratic governance. Prime Minister Orbán's brand of populism in Hungary presents a multifaceted critique when analyzed through a judicial independence lens. Its causes, manifestations, and effects reverberate across various levels, threatening democratic norms locally and resonating internationally. The Orbán case study serves as a cautionary tale about the implications of populist leaders' actions on judicial autonomy, highlighting the complexities of maintaining democracy and the rule of law in an era of rising populism.

Scholars such as Levitsky and Ziblatt (2018) offer a theoretical framework to understand the interplay between populism and democracy. Their work highlights the critical role of institutions in constraining populist leaders' impulses. While their focus is on democracy as a whole, their insights are pertinent to understanding how populist leaders' attempts to concentrate power can affect judicial independence, ultimately influencing the judiciary-government relationship. Similarly, Ginsburg (2020) delves into the challenges faced by judiciaries in the context of rising populism. His work emphasizes that populist leaders, by casting themselves as the sole representatives of the people, can undermine the independence of institutions that aim to check their power. Courts are particularly vulnerable to this trend, as they are tasked with upholding the rule of law and the constitution, often clashing with populist narratives.

The impact of populism on judicial independence prompts a delicate balancing act between democratic principles and the rule of law (McCoy & Jahic, 2006; McEwen et al., 2012; Mechkova et al., 2019). Governments must uphold the legitimacy of their actions while respecting the integrity of judicial institutions. This involves promoting a culture of respect for the judiciary's role, refraining from making inflammatory statements, and adhering to established legal procedures. Judicial responses are equally critical. Courts must remain steadfast in upholding the rule of law and constitutionality, even when faced with populist pressures. Transparency, reasoned judgments, and a commitment to the principles of judicial independence serve as mechanisms to safeguard the judiciary's role as a check on governmental power.

Populism's impact on judicial independence highlights the complex interplay between democratic governance and the rule of law. As governments navigate the challenges posed by populist rhetoric, the judiciary must uphold its independence and commitment to the principles of justice. By drawing on global case studies and scholarly insights, we gain a deeper understanding of how populist pressures can strain the judiciary-government relationship, ultimately shaping the trajectory of democratic institutions. As democratic societies grapple with populism's rise, a nuanced approach to preserving judicial independence remains pivotal to ensuring the vitality of both democracy and the rule of law. In the fourth section of this chapter will consider how media influences perceptions of the judiciary and its implications for judicial independence.

6.4. MEDIA INFLUENCE AND PUBLIC PERCEPTION OF THE JUDICIARY

The intricate interplay between media influence and public perception of the judiciary represents a critical dynamic within modern governance systems (Edelman, 1994; Efrat, 2018; Eichensehr, 2018; Eleftheriadis, 2005). This section delves into the multifaceted relationship between media, the judiciary, and the resulting impact on public trust and confidence in the judicial system. By examining global case studies and drawing from scholarly perspectives, we unveil the complexities that arise when media coverage shapes public opinions about the judiciary. The media wields immense power in shaping public opinion and perceptions of government institutions, including the judiciary. While media outlets play a crucial role in disseminating information and scrutinizing governance, their influence can be both constructive and detrimental. Media's ability to raise awareness about judicial proceedings, legal developments, and court decisions can foster transparency and accountability, enabling citizens to engage more effectively with the judicial system. Conversely, sensationalism, biases, and selective reporting can distort reality, influencing public perception and eroding trust in the judiciary.

In the United States, Supreme Court confirmation hearings have become highly publicized events (Hennigar, 2010; Hessick, 2014; Hill, 2016; Holland, 2009). The media plays a pivotal role in shaping public opinions about judicial nominees, sometimes leading to divisive narratives. The confirmation hearings of Justices Clarence Thomas and Brett Kavanaugh demonstrated how media coverage can polarize public sentiment, affecting perceptions of the judiciary's impartiality. The confirmation hearings for Justices Clarence Thomas and Brett Kavanaugh in the United States provide a compelling case study to critically evaluate the role of the media in determining judicial independence and its interdependence with the other arms of the government. These high-profile hearings underscore the intricate relationship between the judiciary, the media, and the broader political landscape, offering insights into how media coverage can impact public perception and judicial legitimacy. Some countries such as Australia (see Figure 6.7) have maintained a relatively stable perception of the judiciary despite all the efforts to make this institution accessible and relevant to the public. Such countries can take solace in the possibility that their justice systems are not suffering further reputational damage, the inertia notwithstanding. This is not always the case and the USA has been a visible example of how perceptions of the judiciary have drastically fallen over time.

One of the flash points of this spectacle of suspicion is the confirmation of senior judges to the Supreme Court in which politics meets the judiciary in a very public way (Kundmueller, 2022; Kwoka, 2017; Lachmayer, 2016; Law, 2009). The media's coverage of confirmation hearings can significantly influence public perceptions of the judiciary's independence. In the case of

Justice Clarence Thomas, his 1991 hearings were marred by allegations of sexual harassment raised by Anita Hill.

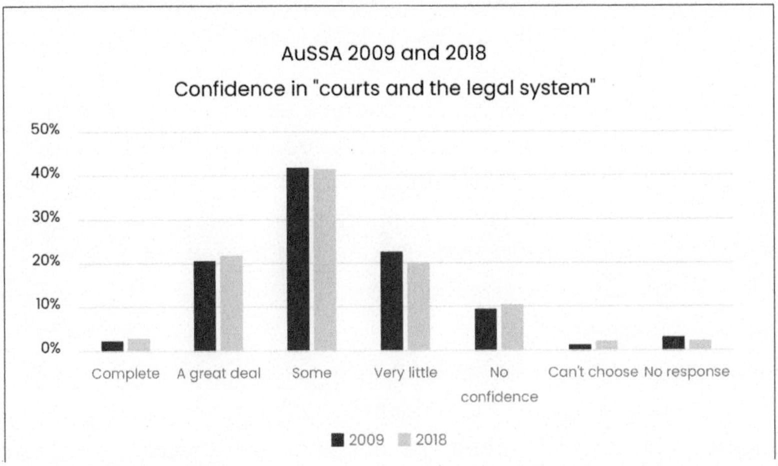

Figure 6.7. Relative consistency in the perception of the Australian justice system 2009 and 2018.

Source: Ann Evans et al, 'Australian Survey of Social Attitudes, 2018' (ADA Dataverse, 2020) <http://dx.doi.org/10.26193/1U0HNI>; Ann Evans, 'Australian Survey of Social Attitudes, 2009' (ADA Dataverse, 2017) <http://dx.doi.org/10.4225/87/IH68HQ> as cited by the Australian Law Commission https://www.alrc.gov.au/news/importance-of-good-data/

The media played a pivotal role in disseminating these allegations and shaping public opinion. The sensationalized coverage highlighted the potential consequences of media influence on judicial nominations. The intense media scrutiny underscored the vulnerability of nominees to public perception, potentially affecting the perception of their impartiality and autonomy. Similarly, Justice Brett Kavanaugh's 2018 confirmation hearings were marked by allegations of sexual misconduct. The media's coverage of the allegations, subsequent investigations, and emotional testimonies of both Kavanaugh and Dr. Christine Blasey Ford fueled a divisive national discourse. The media's role in amplifying these allegations not only impacted Kavanaugh's public image but also underscored the broader challenge of maintaining judicial independence in the face of media scrutiny.

The media's coverage of these hearings also highlighted the interdependence between the judiciary and the other arms of the government, particularly the executive and legislative branches (White, 2022; Whittington, 2005; Willett & Gordon, 2022). The confirmation process involves the

Senate's role in assessing judicial nominees, while the executive branch, through the President's nomination, holds considerable influence. The media's coverage of these hearings further entangles the political and judicial spheres, impacting how the public perceives the judiciary's relationship with other branches of government. In both cases, media narratives became entwined with political agendas. The media's scrutiny of allegations against Thomas and Kavanaugh intersected with broader political debates about gender, race, and ideology. Media outlets' biases and preferences contributed to shaping narratives that either supported or challenged the nominees' credibility. This media-driven polarization highlighted the extent to which the judiciary's perceived independence can be influenced by political and ideological motivations.

The media's role in confirmation hearings can have lasting implications for judicial independence (Aboueldahab, 2021; Abouharb et al., 2013). The intense scrutiny and public debates spurred by media coverage can impact nominees' willingness to challenge government actions, fearing that media-driven controversies might tarnish their reputations. Moreover, media narratives can contribute to public skepticism about the judiciary's impartiality, eroding public trust and undermining judicial legitimacy. The confirmation hearings of Justices Clarence Thomas and Brett Kavanaugh illuminate the complex relationship between the media, judicial independence, and interdependence with other branches of government. The media's influence on public perception, the judiciary's autonomy, and its relationship with the political sphere underscores the multifaceted challenges facing the modern judiciary. As the media continues to shape public discourse, it becomes essential to critically evaluate its role in preserving the independence and integrity of the judicial branch.

In Turkey, President Recep Tayyip Erdoğan's government has exerted control over media outlets, influencing public perceptions of the judiciary (Medawatte et al., 2013; Meggitt & Somji, 2016; Melone, 1996). Media censorship has contributed to the erosion of public trust in the judiciary's independence, with narratives aligning with the government's agenda. This case underscores how media control can have far-reaching implications for judicial legitimacy. In recent years, Turkey has witnessed a concerning erosion of media freedom under President Recep Tayyip Erdoğan's administration, resulting in a significant impact on public perceptions of the judiciary. Over time, Erdoğan's government has been successful in exerting control over media outlets, effectively shaping narratives and shaping the way individuals perceive the actions of the judiciary. Through strategic moves such as the acquisition of critical media organizations or the appointment of government-friendly figures to key positions, the government has managed to maintain a tight grip on information dissemination. As a result, objective and independent reporting on judicial matters has been steadily compromised, leading to a distorted understanding of the legal system among the public. This influence has had profound implications for the role of the judiciary within the government. The judiciary, ideally an impartial branch responsible for upholding justice and protecting individual rights, has faced numerous challenges in maintaining its independence in the face of media manipulation. With public perceptions swayed by biased narratives, doubts and suspicions over the integrity of the judiciary have emerged. This erosion of trust has wide-ranging implications for the functioning of democracy and the rule of law, as a weakened judiciary poses a threat to the checks and balances necessary for a healthy governance system. Ultimately, the media control exerted by Erdoğan's government underscores the need for vigilant protection of the judiciary's autonomy and the crucial role it plays in ensuring a fair and just society.

High-profile cases in India, such as the Nirbhaya gang-rape case, have garnered intense media coverage. While media attention can spotlight important issues, it can also sensationalize proceedings, potentially affecting jurors' perceptions and public expectations of judicial outcomes (McCandless, 2017; McCann et al., 2023; McCarthy & Un, 2017). Media's role in shaping perceptions of justice and fairness in such cases is paramount. High-profile cases in India, like the Nirbhaya gang-rape case, have captured the attention of the media, triggering widespread coverage and intense public discourse. This case, which involved the brutal assault and subsequent death of a young woman, highlighted deep-rooted issues of gender inequality, violence against women, and flaws in the Indian judiciary system. Media outlets extensively reported on the details of the case, bringing attention to the heinous crime and provoking outrage and demands for justice from the public. The media played a crucial role in keeping the case in the public eye, ensuring accountability and pressuring the judiciary to deliver a swift and fair verdict. The intense media scrutiny and public pressure eventually led to the speedy formation of fast-track courts to handle cases of sexual violence in India. As a result, significant legal reforms were introduced, including harsher penalties for perpetrators and improved support for survivors. However, the extensive media coverage also raised concerns about the influence of sensationalism and biased reporting on the administration of justice. While media attention can bring about positive changes and serve as a voice for the marginalized, it is important to strike a balance between responsible journalism and preserving the integrity of the judiciary. The case of the Nirbhaya gang-rape illustrates both the potential of the media to bring about social change and the need for the judiciary to remain impartial and fair in the face of intense public pressure. The media's coverage of high-profile cases like this highlights the complex interplay between influence, accountability, and the delicate role of the judiciary within the Indian government.

Media coverage not only influences public perceptions but also shapes public understanding of legal processes, judicial roles, and the principles of justice (Agbor, 2015; Alleman & Mazzone, 2010; Alter, 1998). The media's framing of legal proceedings can influence how citizens perceive the credibility of judicial decisions. Selective coverage of high-impact cases can create an unbalanced view of the judiciary's effectiveness, leading to distorted public perceptions. It is also important to note the prominent role of media in reporting and critiquing miscarriages of justice (see Figure 6.8).

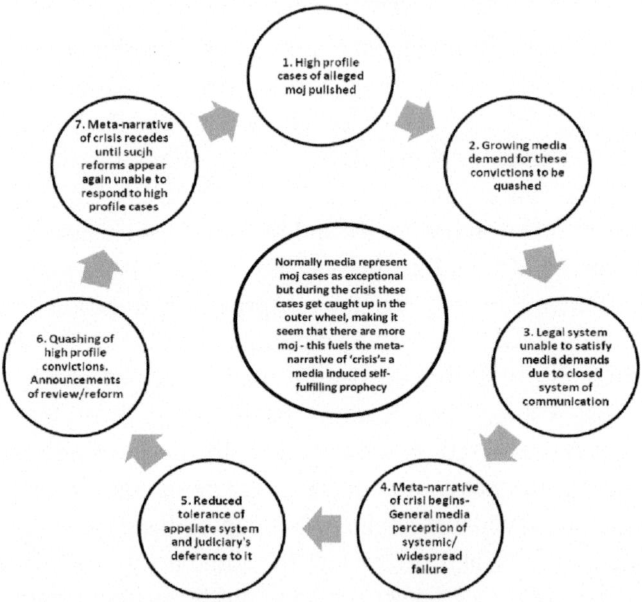

Figure 6.8. Media construction of crises of confidence in court responses to high-profile miscarriages of justice.

Source: Poyser, S. (2012). *Watchdogs of the wrongly convicted: the role of the media in revealing miscarriages of justice* (Doctoral dissertation, University of Portsmouth).

The relationship between media influence and judicial independence is complex (Agbor, 2015; Alleman & Mazzone, 2010; Alter, 1998). While media scrutiny is essential for holding the judiciary accountable, undue media interference can jeopardize judicial autonomy. Media trials, where verdicts are pronounced in the court of public opinion before legal proceedings conclude, can pressure judges and obstruct the administration of justice. Striking a balance between media's role as a watchdog and respecting judicial processes is crucial for safeguarding judicial independence. Promoting media literacy is crucial for citizens to critically assess media narratives about the judiciary. A well-informed citizenry can decipher sensationalism from factual reporting, enabling a more nuanced understanding of legal proceedings. Efforts to enhance media literacy contribute to informed public discussions and the preservation of an independent judiciary. Media's influence on public perception of the judiciary is a complex terrain where ethical journalism intersects with the responsibilities of a transparent and independent judiciary. The case studies highlighted illustrate the diverse ways media can impact public trust in judicial institutions. Judicial systems worldwide must navigate the challenges posed by media influence, ensuring that the public's perception aligns with the principles of justice and the rule of law. The final section in this chapter will focus on striking the right balance between judicial independence and accountancy.

6.5. STRIKING A BALANCE: JUDICIAL INDEPENDENCE AND ACCOUNTABILITY

In the intricate web of democratic governance, the relationship between the judiciary and the government plays a pivotal role in maintaining the delicate balance between two crucial aspects of the legal system: judicial independence and accountability (McCandless, 2017; McCann et al., 2023; McCarthy & Un, 2017). This intricate interplay has significant ramifications not only for the administration of justice but also for upholding the principles of democracy, protecting human rights, and ensuring the rule of law. Striking the right equilibrium between judicial independence and government accountability is a multifaceted challenge that requires a nuanced understanding of the legal, political, and societal dynamics at play.

At the heart of a well-functioning judiciary lies the concept of judicial independence, which safeguards the judiciary's autonomy and ability to adjudicate matters without any undue influence from external actors, including the government (Tew, 2016; Tey, 2010; Tezcur, 2009; Travesi

& Whitehead, 2021). This separation of powers is essential to prevent the concentration of authority and to maintain a system of checks and balances (see Figure 6.9). In their seminal work, Montesquieu and Locke highlighted the importance of this separation, with Montesquieu advocating for distinct branches of government to prevent tyranny and Locke underscoring the necessity of an impartial judiciary.

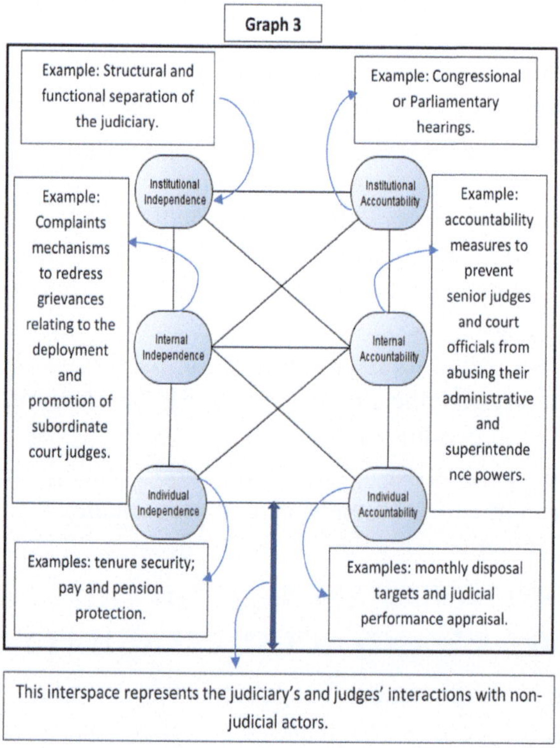

Figure 6.9. Example of a framework of judicial independence and accountability.

Source: Huchhanavar, S. S. (2023). Conceptualising judicial independence and Accountability from a regulatory perspective. *Oslo Law Review*, (2), 110–148.

The philosophies of Montesquieu and Locke, two towering figures in political thought, offer profound insights into the intricate relationship between judicial independence and accountability. Montesquieu, in his seminal work "The Spirit of the Laws," fervently advocated for the separation of powers as a safeguard against tyranny. He underscored the necessity of distinct branches of government—executive, legislative, and judicial—to prevent any single entity from amassing unchecked authority. Montesquieu's concept of a balanced government inherently implied that the judiciary should function autonomously, insulated from undue influences that might compromise its impartiality and integrity. In his vision, the judiciary acted as a counterweight to both the executive and legislative branches, providing a crucial check on potential abuses of power.

Locke, in his seminal treatises such as "Two Treatises of Government," grappled with the essential nature of government's relationship with the governed. His emphasis on the social contract and the protection of natural rights underscored the government's role in safeguarding individuals' liberties. Locke's thoughts on accountability were implicit in his conception of government's legitimacy, wherein the government was accountable to the people it served. However, Locke's insights also hinted at the importance of an impartial judiciary that could ensure the government's actions aligned with its obligation to protect citizens' rights. The judiciary, in Locke's view, represented a means by which the government could be held accountable, thereby reinforcing the notion that an independent judiciary was essential to ensuring governmental responsibility.

In their work, both Montesquieu and Locke acknowledged the complex balance between judicial independence and government accountability. Montesquieu's focus on the separation of powers emphasized the need for a self-regulating judiciary, free from external pressures that could compromise its decision-making process. Locke's perspective on government's accountability to the people it governed indirectly highlighted the judiciary's role in maintaining that accountability by ensuring that government actions aligned with the principles of justice and the protection of rights. While these philosophers did not delve deeply into the specific challenges that could arise in reconciling these principles, their foundational ideas laid the groundwork for subsequent discussions on how societies could navigate the delicate tension between preserving judicial independence and holding the government answerable to the rule of law and the citizens it served.

A prime example of the value of judicial independence can be found in the United States. The landmark case of Marbury v. Madison (1803) established the principle of judicial review, allowing the U.S. Supreme Court to assess the constitutionality of laws enacted by the government. This pivotal decision showcased the judiciary's capacity to serve as a counterbalance to the legislative and executive branches, upholding the rule of law. Marbury v. Madison, a landmark Supreme Court case decided in 1803, is widely recognized as a crucial moment in the establishment of judicial independence and accountability in the United States. Against the backdrop of a young nation grappling with the balance of power among its branches of government, the case provided an opportunity to reconcile the tensions inherent in these two concepts (see Figure 6.10). In the aftermath of the case, the United States witnessed the consolidation of the judiciary as a co-equal branch of government with the power to interpret and apply the Constitution.

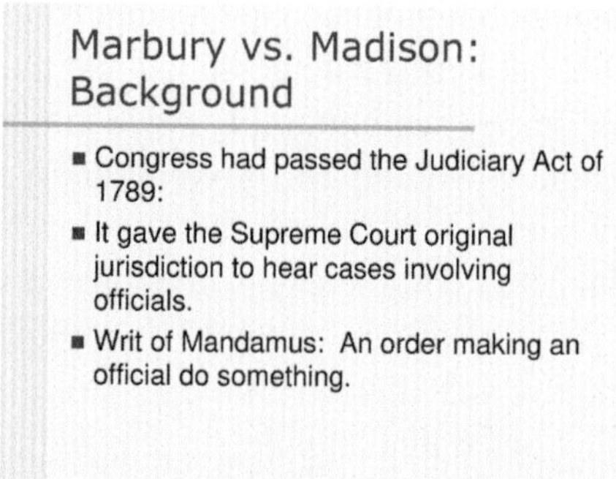

Figure 6.10. The background to Marbury v. Madison (1803).

Source: Philomena Dean via Slideplayer https://slideplayer.com/slide/15960248/

The case itself revolved around a conflict between President Thomas Jefferson and his Secretary of State, James Madison, on one side, and a group of Federalist-appointed judges, known as the "midnight judges," on the other. The outgoing Federalist administration had rushed to appoint these judges before the newly elected Democratic-Republicans took office. However, some of the commissions went undelivered, including the one for William Marbury, who sought a writ of mandamus from the Supreme Court compelling Madison to deliver his commission. In a unanimous decision, Chief Justice John Marshall declared that Marbury was indeed entitled to his commission. However, the Court dismissed the case by asserting that the statute under which Marbury sought his mandamus was unconstitutional. In doing so, Marshall established the principle of judicial review, avowing the Supreme Court's authority to declare acts of Congress unconstitutional. This groundbreaking decision solidified the judiciary's role as the ultimate arbiter of the Constitution, effectively embedding judicial independence.

While establishing judicial independence, Marbury v. Madison also recognized the principle of judicial accountability. Despite ruling in favor of Marbury, the Court did not attempt to force Madison to comply with the writ of mandamus. The decision emphasized that the Constitution delineates the powers and jurisdiction of each branch of government, emphasizing that the judiciary's authority extends to interpreting the law rather than directly enforcing its decisions. By acknowledging the limits of its own power, the Court demonstrated a commitment to the separation of powers and the reciprocal accountability of all branches of government. The lasting impact of Marbury v. Madison can be observed in subsequent cases and legal scholarship, where judicial review has become a cornerstone of American constitutional law. The case established the framework for balancing judicial independence and accountability, recognizing the judiciary's duty to interpret the law while maintaining appropriate checks and balances. The Court's role as the final arbiter of the Constitution ensures that the judiciary can act independently of political pressures, but it is also accountable to the Constitution and the public's trust. Marbury v. Madison significantly advanced the concept of judicial independence while acknowledging the importance of judicial accountability. Through the establishment of judicial review, the case empowered the judiciary to interpret the Constitution and evaluate the constitutionality of laws passed by Congress. At the same time, it recognized that the Court's power was not absolute and that it must adhere to the principles of separation of powers and respect the limits of its authority. This delicate balancing act continues to shape the role of the judiciary in American governance, preserving both independence and accountability in the pursuit of justice.

While judicial independence is a cornerstone of democratic societies, it is not without its challenges. Instances of government interference in the judiciary can undermine the very essence of justice and the rule of law (Sprankling, 2012; Stephenson, 2003, 2008; Stephenson, 2021). One notable case is the erosion of judicial independence in Poland, where reforms introduced by the government threatened the autonomy of the judiciary by granting excessive power to the executive in appointing judges. This raised concerns about the potential politicization of the judiciary and the erosion of checks and balances. Similarly, the contentious appointment of judges in India has sparked debates on the government's role in influencing judicial appointments. The "collegium system" emerged as a mechanism for safeguarding judicial independence, but criticisms regarding its opacity and susceptibility to executive interference persist. Such cases underscore the delicate nature of the relationship between the judiciary and government and emphasize the importance of vigilance in maintaining judicial independence.

While judicial independence is paramount, it is not an absolute concept (van Zeben, 2015; Vermeule, 2012; Voeten, 2008; VonDoepp & Ellett,

2011). Striking the balance requires mechanisms to ensure accountability while preserving the judiciary's autonomy. A compelling example is the German Constitutional Court, known for its robust judicial review process. The court's decisions are subject to public scrutiny and scholarly analysis, fostering a culture of accountability. Simultaneously, its strict procedural guidelines shield it from political pressure. South Africa's experience with its Constitutional Court provides another insightful perspective. The court's landmark decision in Economic Freedom Fighters v Speaker of the National Assembly (2016) highlighted the court's role in holding both the executive and legislative branches accountable for their actions. By ensuring that the president complied with the Public Protector's remedial action, the court demonstrated its commitment to upholding the constitution, even in the face of political power.

The interplay between judicial independence and government accountability extends beyond national borders (Chan, 2011; Chavez, 2003, 2007; Chen & Li, 2016; Chutkow, 2008). International human rights tribunals exemplify this dynamic on a global scale. The International Criminal Court (ICC), for instance, faces challenges in balancing its independence with its need for state cooperation. The withdrawal of several African nations from the ICC due to allegations of bias showcases the tensions that arise when accountability mechanisms clash with perceptions of sovereignty. However, the Inter-American Court of Human Rights demonstrates how international courts can navigate this balance effectively. Through the "continuous control" doctrine, the court ensures that states comply with its decisions, maintaining a delicate equilibrium between judicial independence and state accountability. The case of Radilla Pacheco v. Mexico (2009) demonstrated the court's commitment to holding states accountable for human rights violations while respecting the state's sovereignty.

Civil society and media play a crucial role in ensuring the delicate balance between judicial independence and accountability (Kramarz et al., 2017; Krogseng, 2000; Krotoszynski, 2014). In countries like Kenya, civil society organizations have been instrumental in holding the government accountable for judicial interference. The case of Republic v. Chief Justice and Another (2003) showcased how civil society's advocacy efforts contributed to the restoration of judicial independence. Media also serves as a watchdog, shedding light on instances of government interference and judicial malfeasance. In Poland, the media played a vital role in exposing attempts to undermine the judiciary's independence, leading to public outcry and international scrutiny. The intricate dance between judicial independence and government accountability is an ever-evolving endeavor. The myriad examples from across the globe highlight the challenges, triumphs, and ongoing efforts to strike the right balance. Ensuring that the judiciary remains independent while being accountable to the values of democracy, human rights, and the rule of law requires constant vigilance, a commitment to transparency, and a robust system of checks and balances. Only by navigating this intricate relationship can societies hope to sustain the delicate equilibrium that underpins the foundations of modern democracy.

CHAPTER 6 SUMMARY

In the intricate landscape of modern governance, the preservation of judicial independence stands as a cornerstone of democratic societies. This chapter embarked on an expansive exploration of the multifaceted challenges that cast shadows on the sanctity of this fundamental principle. Section 6.1 delved into the worrisome phenomenon of political interference in the judiciary, underscoring how such intrusions can erode the impartiality and integrity that underlie fair adjudication. The far-reaching consequences of these interferences were laid bare through case studies from various corners of the globe, reaffirming the universal relevance of safeguarding the judiciary from undue political pressures.

Moving forward, Section 6.2 meticulously examined threats to judicial security and safety, unearthing a disturbing trend that compromises the safety of judges and the sanctity of court proceedings. By scrutinizing real-world instances where judges faced physical harm, this section illuminated the unsettling consequences of these threats, which extend beyond the individuals involved and corrode the very essence of justice and the rule of law.

Section 6.3 then navigated the treacherous waters of populism, dissecting how this burgeoning political force can wield a destabilizing influence on judicial independence. Through a diverse range of global case studies, this section unraveled how populist narratives often impede the judiciary's ability to operate without fear or favor, exposing the complex struggle between the rule of law and the allure of populist sentiments.

The impact of media in shaping public perception and influencing the judiciary came under the spotlight in Section 6.4. With an in-depth analysis of the media's power to both empower and undermine the judicial system, this section illuminated the tightrope walk between the freedom of press and the potential manipulation of public opinion that can compromise judicial processes. Finally, Section 6.5 emerged as a pivotal junction, delving into the intricate interplay between judicial independence and government accountability. This section scrutinized the delicate equilibrium required to preserve judicial autonomy while ensuring mechanisms for accountability remain intact. Through comprehensive global examples, it demonstrated the indispensable nature of this balance to uphold democracy, human rights, and the rule of law.

In summation, Chapter 6 traversed a panoramic terrain of challenges besieging judicial independence, each section painting a distinct facet of the complex picture. From political interference and threats to security, to the ripples of populism and media's sway, the intricate dance between safeguarding judicial integrity and upholding the accountability of governments was meticulously dissected. This chapter stands as a testament to the intricate nature of the struggles and triumphs that shape the modern judiciary, offering a profound understanding of the delicate equilibrium required to navigate these tumultuous waters. The penultimate chapter in this book will consider the role of the judiciary in a globalized world.

CHAPTER 7

The Role of Judiciary in a Globalized World

Contents

7.1. The Impact of Globalization on Legal Systems 235
7.2. International Cooperation and Treaty Interpretation 239
7.3. Resolving Transnational Disputes Through Judicial Means 244
7.4. Jurisdictional Challenges in a Borderless World 252
7.5. Judiciary's Role in Harmonizing International Law 259
Chapter 7 Summary 266

As our world becomes increasingly interconnected through the forces of globalization, the role of the judiciary takes on new dimensions, shaping and being shaped by the intricate tapestry of international relations and transborder legal dynamics. This chapter embarks on a compelling journey through the evolving landscape of judicial functions in the face of an ever more interconnected world. By exploring diverse facets of this complex phenomenon, the chapter seeks to illuminate the pivotal role that judiciaries play in navigating the challenges and opportunities posed by globalization.

Section 7.1 serves as a foundational anchor, meticulously examining the profound impact of globalization on legal systems across the globe. The rapid flow of information, capital, and people transcends traditional legal boundaries, necessitating judicial adaptations to harmonize disparate legal regimes. Through a nuanced lens, this section delves into the transformative ways in which globalization not only introduces novel legal challenges but also offers avenues for cross-border cooperation and shared legal norms.

Stepping into Section 7.2, the narrative pivots to the critical arena of international cooperation and treaty interpretation. The judiciary emerges as a linchpin in deciphering the intricacies of international agreements, their applicability across diverse jurisdictions, and the principles that underpin their implementation. By scrutinizing case studies of treaty interpretation, this section unveils the judiciary's pivotal role in crafting unified legal interpretations that traverse borders and foster collaboration among nations.

The global nature of modern disputes unfurls its panorama in Section 7.3, where the focus is on resolving transnational conflicts through judicial mechanisms. The judiciary's capacity to offer impartial forums for settling disputes takes center stage, as exemplified by international tribunals and arbitration panels. Through intricate case analyses, this section underscores how the judiciary transcends national allegiances to serve as a beacon of equity and justice in a world where territorial boundaries often blur the lines of accountability.

Navigating further, Section 7.4 navigates the labyrinthine challenges of jurisdiction in a borderless world. As legal issues transcend national borders, questions of jurisdiction become increasingly complex. This section critically evaluates how judiciaries grapple with questions of jurisdictional authority, striking a balance between preserving sovereign rights and delivering justice in an interconnected reality.

Lastly, in Section 7.5, the spotlight turns to the judiciary's remarkable role in harmonizing international law. The chapter delves into the ingenious ways judiciaries bridge cultural, legal, and normative differences to create a cohesive framework of international jurisprudence. By exploring instances where judiciaries contribute to the evolution of customary international law, this section exemplifies the judiciary's capacity to shape the contours of global legal norms.

In this chapter, we embark on an enlightening exploration of the judiciary's shifting role in an era of globalization. By dissecting the intricate mechanisms through which judiciaries adapt, cooperate, and navigate global legal frontiers, this chapter offers a comprehensive understanding of how the judiciary becomes a fulcrum in shaping our interconnected world's legal fabric. A good starting point for this chapter is the impact of globalization on legal systems.

7.1. THE IMPACT OF GLOBALIZATION ON LEGAL SYSTEMS

In an era characterized by unprecedented interconnectedness, the contours of legal systems are being profoundly shaped by the forces of globalization (Horvath, 2017; Howard et al., 2006; Hume, 2012). The intricate interplay between the judiciary and the government within this evolving landscape has garnered considerable attention.

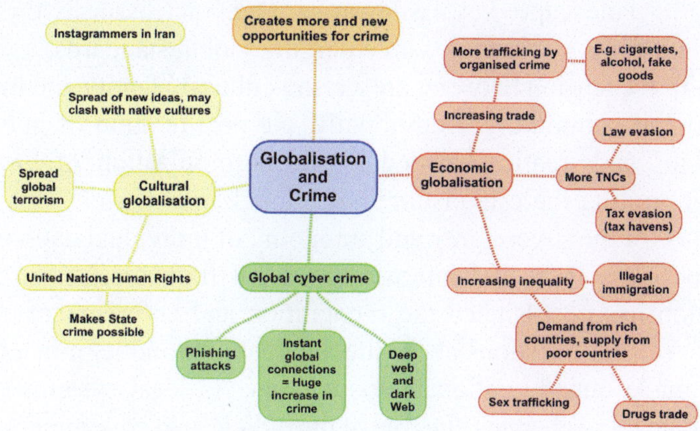

Figure 7.1. The globalization of crime.

Source: https://revisesociology.com/2021/07/13/globalisation-and-crime/

This section delves into the multifaceted impact of globalization on legal systems worldwide, tracing how the judiciary's relationship with the government adapts and transforms in response to the challenges and opportunities engendered by this phenomenon. As Figure 7.1 shows, even crime is now globalized.

Globalization's influence on legal systems is evident in the transformation of norms, principles, and practices (Manning & Randazzo, 2009; Maor, 2004; Maphosa, 2020). The diffusion of legal concepts, norms, and rights across borders has necessitated a recalibration of traditional legal frameworks. Take, for instance, the Convention on the Elimination of All Forms of Discrimination Against Women (CEDAW). As governments ratify this international treaty, the principles enshrined within it resonate within domestic legal systems. In India, CEDAW's principles influenced the judiciary's reinterpretation of constitutional provisions to promote gender equality, illustrating the interconnectedness of global norms and domestic legal responses. Legal scholarship, such as that by Rosenfeld (2007), underscores the intricate dance between global norms and national legal systems, shedding light on the dynamic relationship between the judiciary and government as they navigate the adoption of these norms. Globalization has undoubtedly had a profound impact on legal systems worldwide, prompting significant changes in norms, principles, and practices. This transformative force has been driven by an increasingly interconnected and interdependent world, where the flow of goods, services, information, and people transcends national boundaries. As legal systems adapt to this changing landscape, key issues arise. One such issue is the clash of traditional customs and norms with emerging global standards, as countries grapple with the tension between preserving cultural identity and integrating into the global community. Additionally, the proliferation of international organizations and treaties has led to the harmonization of laws across borders, promoting the establishment of global legal norms. This shift has implications for the sovereignty and autonomy of individual nations, as they navigate between local and international legal frameworks. Furthermore, globalization has necessitated the recognition and enforcement of foreign judgments, raising questions about the applicability and legitimacy of legal decisions made outside national jurisdictions. As legal systems evolve to accommodate these changes, the role of the judiciary in government becomes ever more crucial. Judges are tasked with interpreting and applying laws that reflect these new global realities, grappling with complex legal issues that require a blend of local context and global perspectives. They must strike a delicate balance between upholding national legal traditions and recognizing the implications and benefits of global integration. The judiciary plays a critical role in safeguarding individual rights and the rule of law while also aiding in the resolution of transnational disputes. Moreover, as global legal norms continue to develop, the judiciary's role as the final arbiter of the law ensures the protection of fundamental rights and the consistent application of legal standards. In these ways, the judiciary serves as a vital institution in navigating the complex and evolving landscape of globalization's influence on legal systems.

Moreover, the expansion of transnational commerce has necessitated legal harmonization (Keohane et al., 2000; Killebrew, 2007; Kingsford, 2022). Commercial transactions traverse borders with ease, demanding uniformity in legal standards to facilitate trade. The Uniform Commercial Code (UCC) in the United States stands as a testament to such harmonization efforts. The UCC's adoption across multiple states demonstrates how the judiciary plays a role in interpreting and applying uniform legal standards, thereby fostering a predictable environment for business. Legal scholars like Reimann (2015) explore the complexities of harmonization efforts, unraveling the intricate dialogue between domestic judiciaries and governments in adapting legal systems to accommodate cross-border commercial activities. Moreover, the expansion of transnational commerce has necessitated legal harmonization. As globalization has opened up markets across borders, the need for consistent legal frameworks to govern international business transactions has become apparent. Key issues such as cross-border contracts, intellectual property protection, and dispute resolution have emerged as challenges that require a unified approach. To address these issues, international organizations, such as the United Nations Commission on International Trade Law (UNCITRAL), have been instrumental in developing model laws and conventions to promote legal uniformity. Events like the adoption of the UN Convention on Contracts for the International Sale of Goods (CISG) in 1980 have provided a harmonized legal framework for international sales contracts, ensuring predictability and certainty in cross-border transactions. The conclusion of these international agreements has led to significant implications for the role of the judiciary in government. Judges now face the task of interpreting and applying these transnational legal instruments, bridging the gaps between different legal systems and aligning national laws with international standards. This places a burden on the judiciary to possess expertise in both domestic and international law, as well as a nuanced understanding of different cultural, social, and economic contexts. The role of the judiciary in interpreting and enforcing international conventions helps establish a level playing field for businesses engaging in cross-border activities and promotes trust in the global marketplace. Moreover, it underscores the judiciary's role as a key actor in maintaining legal certainty and facilitating the smooth functioning of international commerce. By ensuring legal harmonization in the face of globalization's challenges, the judiciary plays a vital role in fostering economic growth, protecting the rights of individuals and businesses, and promoting a fair and equitable global trade environment. As Figure 7.2 shows, even a relatively commonplace activities such as transport can lead to global judicial issues.

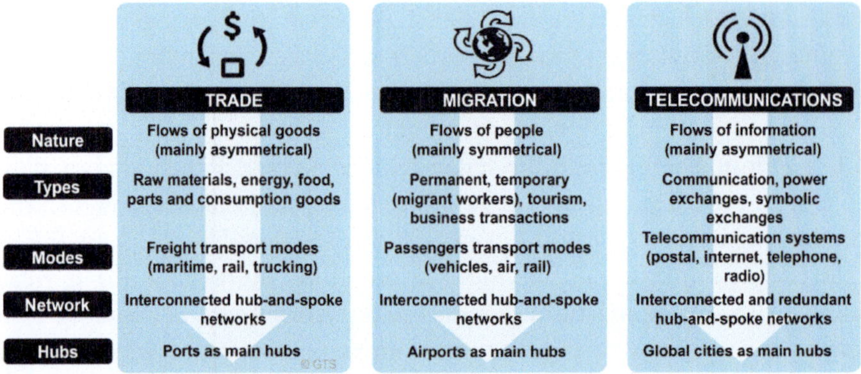

Figure 7.2. The globalization of transport systems.

Source: The Geography of Transport Systems https://transportgeography.org/contents/chapter7/globalization-international-trade/flows-globalization/

Globalization has also spurred legal innovation in response to emerging challenges (White, 2022; Whittington, 2005; Willett & Gordon, 2022). The advent of digital technology and the internet, for instance, has given rise to a new realm of legal issues, from cybercrime to digital privacy. Governments worldwide grapple with crafting legislation that reflects the digital age, while judiciaries navigate uncharted waters in interpreting these laws. The European Union's General Data Protection Regulation (GDPR) serves as a prime example. As companies strive to comply with the GDPR's stringent data protection requirements, legal disputes often find their way to national courts. The judiciary's role in interpreting and applying these new legal standards showcases its adaptability to novel challenges posed by globalization. Literature by Zaring (2016) delves into the complex interplay between technological advancements, government regulation, and judicial responses in the digital age. However, the globalization of legal systems is not without tensions. The permeation of global norms can clash with deeply ingrained cultural and legal traditions. The tension between international human rights standards and religious norms is evident in countries like Saudi Arabia. While the government may be compelled to align its legal system with international human rights norms, the judiciary faces the intricate task of navigating these competing demands. The case of Raif Badawi, a Saudi blogger sentenced to flogging for his online expression, highlights the intricate role of the judiciary in mediating between international pressures and domestic values. Schreiber's work (2017) unpacks the complexities of such dilemmas, offering insights into how judiciaries mediate between global standards and cultural contexts.

In conclusion, the impact of globalization on legal systems reverberates through the intricate relationship between the judiciary and the government. The dynamic interplay between global norms, transnational commerce, legal innovation, and cultural tensions underscores the judiciary's evolving role in navigating the complexities of an interconnected world. As legal systems grapple with the transformative effects of globalization, the judiciary emerges as a crucial arbiter in interpreting, applying, and adapting legal frameworks to meet the demands of this new era. This interdependence between the judiciary and the government remains a compelling testament to the evolving nature of governance in an age defined by unprecedented global linkages. The second section of this chapter focuses on international cooperation and the interpretation of treaties.

7.2. INTERNATIONAL COOPERATION AND TREATY INTERPRETATION

The intricate web of international relations and the increasing interdependence of nations have catalyzed a paradigm shift in the legal landscape, particularly in the domain of treaty interpretation and international cooperation (Kirisci & Kocaman, 2022; Kitagawa, 2023; Kochtcheeva, 2009). This section undertakes an exhaustive exploration of how the judiciary's relationship with the government is dynamically shaped by the exigencies of international cooperation and the nuanced art of treaty interpretation. By delving into a diverse array of case studies and examples from around the world, this section unravels the intricate dance between judiciaries and governments as they navigate the complexities of treaty interpretation and the imperative of harmonious international relations. Figure 7.3 is a quantitative analysis of differential effects of treaties across the globe. This could challenge the possibilities of international cooperation and treaty interpretation.

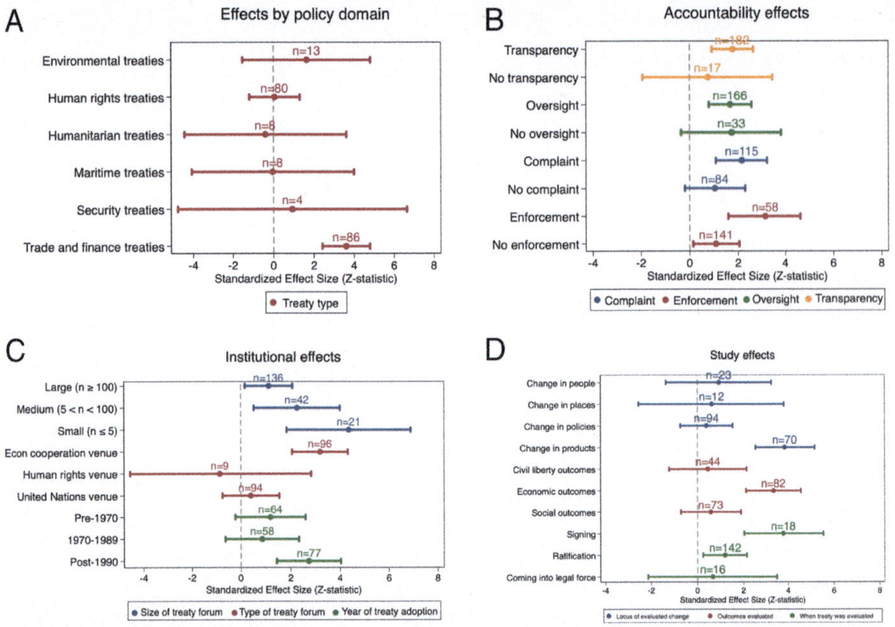

Figure 7.3. Example of quantitative analysis of the differential impact of global treaties.

Source: Hoffman, S. J., Baral, P., Rogers Van Katwyk, S., Sritharan, L., Hughsam, M., Randhawa, H., ... & Poirier, M. J. (2022). International treaties have mostly failed to produce their intended effects. Proceedings of the National Academy of Sciences, 119(32), e2122854119.

One compelling illustration of the interaction between international cooperation and the judiciary lies in the realm of maritime law (Moliterno & Curos, 2021; Molto, 2015; Munday, 2008). The United Nations Convention on the Law of the Sea (UNCLOS) stands as a pivotal embodiment of international cooperation aimed at defining maritime rights and responsibilities. The contentious South China Sea dispute presents a pertinent case where treaty interpretation has far-reaching implications. As nations assert maritime claims based on their interpretation of UNCLOS provisions, national courts are inevitably drawn into the fray. The Permanent Court of Arbitration's landmark ruling in the Philippines v. China case (2016) highlighted the judiciary's role in interpreting UNCLOS principles and its potential to shape international relations. D'Amato (2017) delves into the intricacies of this dispute, shedding light on the intertwined relationship between treaty interpretation and the broader diplomatic context. In 2016, the Philippines brought a case against China before the Permanent Court of Arbitration (PCA) in The Hague, Netherlands, asserting its rights in the South China Sea. The key issue at hand was the interpretation and application of the United Nations Convention on the Law of the Sea (UNCLOS), an international treaty that governs the rights and responsibilities of states in maritime disputes. The Philippines argued that China's claims and activities in the disputed waters, including the construction of artificial islands and interference with Filipino fishing and resource exploration, were in violation of UNCLOS. The PCA, in its landmark ruling, concluded that China's claims of "historic rights" over the South China Sea had no legal basis under UNCLOS, and that China's actions encroached upon the Philippines' rights. The ruling also clarified various legal aspects, such as the extent of territorial waters, exclusive economic zones, and the obligation to preserve and protect the marine environment. The implications of the Philippines v. China case are significant for the role of the judiciary in government. First and foremost, the case emphasized the importance of a peaceful and legal resolution to maritime disputes. By resorting to an international tribunal, the Philippines sought to uphold the rule of law, demonstrating that dispute resolution through legal channels can help de-escalate tensions and promote stability in the region. Furthermore, the case illustrated the judiciary's role in interpreting and applying international law, specifically UNCLOS. The PCA's ruling served as a guide for states navigating complex maritime claims, ensuring the consistent application of international legal norms. This highlights the judiciary's function as an arbiter, providing legal clarity and contributing to the development of customary international law. Ultimately, the Philippines v. China case reaffirms the essential role of the judiciary in upholding the principles of international law, resolving disputes, and promoting peaceful coexistence among nations.

Further exemplifying the synergy between international cooperation and treaty interpretation is the Montreal Protocol on Substances that Deplete the Ozone Layer (see Figure 7.4). This treaty's multifaceted provisions are brought to life in the context of resolving disputes related to environmental protection. The case of Canada v. United States (2000) demonstrates how judiciaries become instruments for interpreting and enforcing treaty obligations, as nations grapple with differing interpretations of the protocol's provisions. Sabel and Zeitlin's work (2004) deepens our understanding by exploring how judiciaries serve as crucial intermediaries, ensuring that international agreements translate into tangible outcomes within domestic legal frameworks. In 2000, Canada and the United States found themselves embroiled in a dispute over the interpretation and implementation of the

Montreal Protocol on Substances that Deplete the Ozone Layer. This international treaty, adopted in 1987, aimed to protect the ozone layer and mitigate the harmful effects of ozone-depleting substances. The key issue in the case was whether a particular substance, methyl bromide, should be exempted from the restrictions imposed by the Montreal Protocol, as the United States argued. Canada contended that the substance should be strictly regulated due to its detrimental environmental impact. The case was ultimately resolved through the process of binding arbitration under the Montreal Protocol's dispute settlement mechanism. The conclusion reached was that the United States had failed to demonstrate the necessity of the exemption, and as a result, the exemption was denied. This case brought attention to the importance of adhering to international environmental agreements and the need for effective regulatory mechanisms to enforce compliance. It showcased the judiciary's role in resolving disputes of international significance and ensuring the proper interpretation and application of international treaties. The implications for the role of the judiciary in government include the judiciary's responsibility in upholding international environmental norms, protecting natural resources, and promoting global cooperation in tackling environmental challenges. By providing a forum for legal resolution, the judiciary contributes to the overall effectiveness and legitimacy of international legal frameworks, such as the Montreal Protocol, in addressing environmental concerns and maintaining ecological sustainability.

Figure 7.4. Contribution of the Montreal Protocol to the Sustainable Development Goals.

Source: UNEP https://www.unep.org/ozonaction/who-we-are/about-montreal-protocol

The intricate interplay between international cooperation and treaty interpretation extends to the realm of human rights law (Urribarri, 2011; Utter, 2021; Uzebu-Imarhiagbe, 2020). The European Convention on Human Rights (ECHR) exemplifies the potential of judiciaries to interpret international treaties to safeguard individual rights. The case of A, B, and C v. Ireland (2010) centered on the ECHR's implications for Ireland's restrictive abortion laws. This instance underscores the judiciary's role in balancing domestic legal considerations with international human rights norms, demonstrating the judiciary's unique capacity to harmonize treaty interpretation with national legal contexts. The scholarship of Langford (2011) enriches this discourse by delving into the transformative role of domestic courts in translating international human rights norms into local realities. A crucial and landmark case that significantly impacted the role of the judiciary in government is A, B, and C v. Ireland (2010) under the jurisdiction of the European Convention on Human Rights (ECHR). This case revolved around the contentious issue of Ireland's restrictive abortion laws, which resulted in the violation of the applicants' right to privacy and their physical and mental integrity. The plaintiffs argued that the Irish government's prohibition on abortion, even in cases of rape, incest, or fatal fetal abnormality, constituted cruel, inhuman, and degrading treatment. The implications of this case were far-reaching, as it raised questions about the balance between individual rights and the state's power to regulate sensitive matters like reproductive rights. The court's ruling became a turning point, proclaiming that the Irish government had failed in its duty to provide a clear legal framework for accessing abortion services, effectively infringing upon women's fundamental rights. This decision set a precedent for further debates on reproductive rights, forcing governments to reevaluate their legislation in light of human rights obligations. Ultimately, A, B, and C v. Ireland highlighted the crucial role of the judiciary in safeguarding citizens' rights and holding governments accountable for laws that impinge on fundamental liberties.

Nevertheless, the path of treaty interpretation and international cooperation is not devoid of complexities (Keohane et al., 2000; Killebrew, 2007; Kingsford, 2022). The tension between sovereign interests and international obligations is exemplified by the Guantanamo Bay detention facility. The Geneva Conventions govern the treatment of prisoners of war, but disputes arise when treaty obligations intersect with security concerns. Hamdan v. Rumsfeld (2006), a case that grappled with the legal status of detainees held at Guantanamo Bay, reflects the judiciary's formidable task of balancing international legal norms with national security prerogatives. Sivakumaran (2009) dissects the intricacies of this challenge, shedding light on the role of judiciaries in navigating the murky waters where international law and sovereign interests converge. Hamdan v. Rumsfeld (2006) represents a pivotal case that sheds light on the role of the judiciary in government and the treatment of detainees at the Guantanamo Bay detention facility in regard to the Geneva Conventions. The case centered around a Yemeni national named Salim Ahmed Hamdan, who was charged with conspiracy and providing material support to terrorism. The key issue at hand was whether the military commissions established by the United States government to try detainees at Guantanamo Bay violated international law, specifically the Geneva Conventions. The court examined the legal status of the detainees, emphasizing their protected rights under the Conventions. In a significant ruling, the Supreme Court held that the established military commissions were unconstitutional, as they did not comply with the Uniform Code of Military Justice or the Geneva Conventions. The Court concluded that the detainees had the right to challenge their detention through a fair and impartial tribunal. This case underscored the critical role of an independent judiciary in addressing questions of constitutional and international law conflicted with government actions, especially in the context of national security. Furthermore, it highlighted the importance of upholding and respecting the principles outlined in the Geneva Conventions, emphasizing the need to protect the rights and dignity of individuals even during times of armed conflict or terrorism. The implication of this case was significant, as it set a precedent by establishing legal safeguards for detainees held at Guantanamo Bay and reaffirming the role of the judiciary in upholding the rule of law, even in cases involving national security concerns.

In conclusion, the dynamic interplay between international cooperation and treaty interpretation unveils a complex choreography that involves judiciaries and governments on the global stage. As international agreements are woven into the fabric of domestic legal systems, judiciaries emerge as pivotal agents tasked with interpreting treaties, harmonizing international norms with local contexts, and ensuring the rule of law prevails in an interconnected world. The interdependence between the judiciary and government takes center stage as they navigate the multifaceted landscape of international relations, where treaties serve as both legal instruments and conduits for diplomatic engagement.

7.3. RESOLVING TRANSNATIONAL DISPUTES THROUGH JUDICIAL MEANS

In an increasingly interconnected world, where geographic boundaries hold diminishing sway over legal and economic interactions, the role of judiciaries in resolving transnational disputes stands as a testament to their evolving relationship with the government and their pivotal position within international legal systems (Kundmueller, 2022; Kwoka, 2017; Lachmayer, 2016; Law, 2009). This section embarks on an extensive exploration of the intricate dynamics between judiciaries and governments as they navigate the complexities of transnational disputes. Through an array of illuminating case studies and examples spanning continents and legal traditions, this section unveils the multifaceted ways in which judiciaries serve as critical arbiters in fostering global justice and preserving diplomatic relations. A case in point is the growth in foreign direct investment (FDI) which leads to transnational legal issues (Figure 7.5).

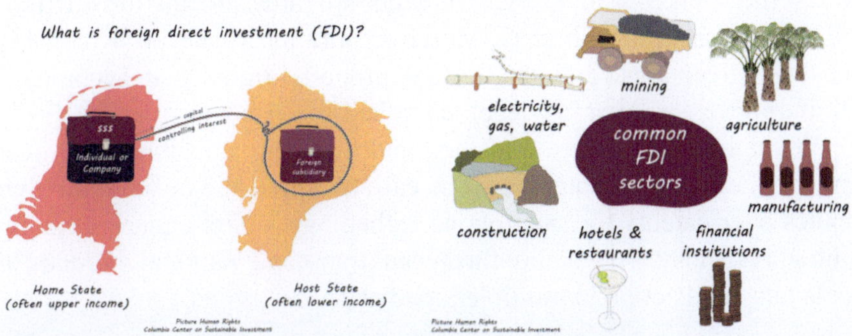

Figure 7.5. Conceptualization of foreign direct investment FDI.

Source: Columbia Center on Sustainable Investment – Columbia University https://ccsi.columbia.edu/content/primer-international-investment-treaties-and-investor-state-dispute-settlement

Foreign Direct Investment (FDI) has emerged as a potent driver of economic globalization, transforming the dynamics of international trade and finance. As capital flows across borders, FDI brings with it a complex tapestry of transnational and global legal issues that both governments and judiciaries must navigate. It is pertinent to explore the multifaceted interplay between FDI and transnational legal challenges, shedding light on how governments and judiciaries grapple with intricate matters that transcend national boundaries (Pospieszna & Vetulani-Cegiel, 2021; Preis, 2006; Preston, 2016). At its core, FDI involves investments by entities from one country into another, often with the goal of establishing a lasting interest in the recipient country's economy. This enterprise results in a web of economic, social, and legal interactions that transcend national frontiers. As corporations establish subsidiaries, acquire assets, or enter into joint ventures in foreign jurisdictions, they inevitably interface with a diverse range of legal systems and regulations. This intricate landscape of legal diversity poses significant challenges to both the investors and the host governments.

One of the primary transnational legal issues stemming from FDI lies in the realm of investor-state disputes. These disputes often arise when host governments implement policies or regulations that affect the profitability or rights of foreign investors (Reid et al., 2020; Ritleng, 2016; Rivera, 2022; Robinson, 2018). Investor-state dispute settlement mechanisms, including international arbitration, become pivotal avenues for resolving such conflicts. Prominent cases like Philip Morris v. Uruguay and Chevron v. Ecuador underscores how FDI can lead to transnational legal disputes that test the bounds of investment protection treaties and the jurisdiction of international arbitration bodies. Moreover, the intricate web of contracts, licensing agreements, and intellectual property rights that accompanies FDI introduces a layer of legal complexity. Disputes over intellectual property rights, technology transfers, and licensing agreements can result in multinational legal wrangling. The case of Apple v. Samsung, involving disputes over patents for smartphone technology, offers a glaring example of how FDI-related legal conflicts can transcend national borders and necessitate legal action in multiple jurisdictions.

Labor rights and corporate social responsibility also emerge as critical areas of concern in the context of FDI (Hasbrouck, 2022; He, 2017; He, 2018; Heinz & Manikas, 1992). Multinational corporations often operate in regions with varying labor standards and regulations. This can lead to legal issues related to workplace conditions, human rights abuses, and environmental impact. The Rana Plaza disaster in Bangladesh, where a building collapse resulted in the death of over 1,100 garment factory workers, exposed the ethical and legal challenges surrounding FDI's impact on labor rights and corporate responsibility. The intersection of domestic labor laws, international human rights standards, and corporate practices underscores the need for judiciaries and governments to address these complex transnational issues. The relationship between FDI and national sovereignty is another aspect that gives rise to transnational legal considerations. Governments must balance attracting foreign investment with safeguarding their sovereignty and regulatory autonomy. The ability of multinational corporations to challenge government policies through investor-state dispute settlement mechanisms can create tensions between national laws and international commitments. Overall, the surge in FDI has undoubtedly contributed to the globalization of legal issues, stretching the boundaries of legal systems and challenging governments and judiciaries to navigate complex transnational terrain. The intricate interplay between investor-state disputes, intellectual property rights, labor standards, corporate social responsibility, and national sovereignty underscores the need for a nuanced understanding of FDI's legal implications. Governments and judiciaries must grapple with these multifaceted challenges to foster an environment where foreign investment can flourish while upholding the rule of law, human rights, and economic stability on a global scale (Figure 7.6).

Figure 7.6. The Law of the Sea.

Source: BYJU'S https://byjus.com/free-ias-prep/unclos/

The United Nations Convention on the Law of the Sea (UNCLOS) stands as a landmark treaty governing maritime rights, responsibilities, and jurisdictions (see Figure 7.6). While UNCLOS seeks to provide a comprehensive framework for the world's oceans, it also gives rise to several key transnational legal issues that merit critical examination. This critique will delve into these issues with specific examples, highlighting both the strengths and limitations of UNCLOS in addressing complex transnational challenges. One of the significant issues stemming from UNCLOS revolves around the delimitation of maritime boundaries, particularly in areas rich in natural resources (Steuer, 2019; Subedi, 2016; Szente, 2021; Taghdiri, 2019). The case of the South China Sea stands as a stark example. Despite UNCLOS providing guidelines for Exclusive Economic Zone (EEZ) delimitation, competing territorial claims by China, Vietnam, the Philippines, and others have led to disputes. UNCLOS fails to offer a definitive solution when overlapping claims arise, thereby necessitating diplomatic negotiations outside its purview. This limitation underscores the difficulty in effectively resolving complex territorial and maritime boundary disputes through a single legal framework. UNCLOS also grapples with the complexities of balancing coastal states' rights with the freedom of navigation for non-coastal states (Navarrete & Castillo-Ortiz, 2020; Nelson & Gibson, 2019). The Arctic region presents a pertinent example. As melting ice opens up new shipping routes, the rights of Arctic coastal states (Canada, Russia, etc.) to control these passages come into tension with the rights of non-coastal states to navigate them. The Northwest Passage dispute exemplifies this challenge. While UNCLOS provides mechanisms for transit passage through straits used for international navigation, the evolving dynamics of the Arctic highlight the need for continuous adaptation in a changing geopolitical landscape. Environmental protection emerges as a crucial concern within UNCLOS. While the treaty lays the groundwork for marine conservation, it lacks specific provisions to address transboundary pollution, especially in the case of marine oil spills. The Deepwater Horizon oil spill in the Gulf of Mexico (2010) serves as a glaring example. The absence of a clear framework for cross-border liability and compensation hampers the effective resolution of transnational environmental disasters. This underscores the need for strengthening UNCLOS to accommodate emerging challenges in environmental protection.

UNCLOS's provisions regarding deep-sea mining are another area of contention. As technological advancements enable the exploration and exploitation of mineral resources in the deep seabed beyond national jurisdiction, the treaty's framework for the International Seabed Authority (ISA) faces scrutiny. The issue of equitable sharing of benefits from deep-sea mining has been debated extensively. While UNCLOS establishes the principle of the "common heritage of mankind," it remains unclear how this principle translates into practical arrangements. The ongoing deliberations over the ISA's regulatory framework exemplify the challenges of balancing global common interests with the rights of individual states. Whereas the UN Convention on the Law of the Sea represents a significant step towards governing the world's oceans, it is not without its limitations and transnational legal challenges. The cases of the South China Sea, the Arctic, marine pollution, and deep-sea mining underscore the complex interplay between coastal states' rights, environmental conservation, navigation freedoms, and the equitable sharing of resources. UNCLOS's adaptability to evolving geopolitical dynamics and emerging environmental concerns is essential to its continued effectiveness in fostering international cooperation and preserving the delicate balance of rights and responsibilities in our transnational maritime realm.

The Vienna Convention on the Law of Treaties forms a foundational backdrop in the realm of transnational disputes, encapsulating principles that guide the interpretation and enforcement of treaties (Medawatte et al., 2013; Meggitt & Somji, 2016; Melone, 1996). The case of Nicaragua v. United States (1986) before the International Court of Justice (ICJ) offers a compelling illustration of how judiciaries mediate between states entangled in disputes rooted in treaty obligations. The ICJ's verdict underscored the judiciary's pivotal role in upholding treaty-based rights and obligations while maintaining diplomatic comity. This case underscores the judiciary's unique capacity to balance international norms with the intricacies of diplomatic relationships. Sinclair's (2013) analysis enriches our understanding of the delicate equilibrium judiciaries must strike when delving into such disputes. Nicaragua v. United States (1986) represents a significant case that delves into the complexities of the role of the judiciary in government and the interpretation of international treaties, particularly the Vienna Convention on the Law of Treaties. The key issue centered around the United States' involvement in Nicaragua's internal affairs, including the support of armed groups, funds allocation, and the laying of mines in Nicaraguan waters. Nicaragua argued that the actions of the United States violated customary international law and the principles of non-intervention, sovereignty, and territorial integrity. The court's findings were twofold: first, that the United States had breached its obligations under customary international law by using force against Nicaragua, and second, that the US had violated its obligations under the Treaty of Friendship, Commerce, and Navigation between the two countries. These conclusions demonstrated the judiciary's capacity to address and hold states accountable for their actions on an international level. Furthermore, the case emphasized the critical role of the judiciary in the interpretation and application of international treaties, as it underscored the importance of abiding by the Vienna Convention on the Law of Treaties. The implications of this case highlighted the necessity of a robust and independent judiciary to ensure adherence to international legal norms, and to prevent powerful states from engaging in actions that infringe upon the sovereign rights of other nations. Ultimately, Nicaragua v. United States showcased the judiciary's pivotal role in maintaining the rule of law at an international level and promoting accountability among states.

Delving into economic realms, investor-state arbitration serves as a vivid manifestation of how judiciaries transcend borders in resolving disputes (Cui, 2017; Davis, 2008; De Francesco & Tosun, 2022; de la Torre & Lemos, 2016). The case of Philip Morris v. Uruguay (2016) attests to how transnational corporations invoke international arbitration mechanisms to challenge government policies that affect their investments. By scrutinizing instances where investor-state arbitration interacts with public health regulations, this case highlights how judiciaries, through arbitration panels, engage in the complex task of reconciling private interests with governmental measures aimed at safeguarding the public welfare. Schreuer et al. (2009) illuminate the intricacies of investor-state arbitration and its ramifications on the judiciary-government relationship.The case of Philip Morris v. Uruguay (2016) exemplifies the use of international arbitration mechanisms by transnational corporations to contest government policies that impact their investments. In this particular case, the issue revolved around Uruguay's implementation of strict tobacco control measures aimed at reducing smoking rates and protecting public health. Philip Morris, one of the largest tobacco companies globally, initiated a lawsuit against Uruguay under a bilateral investment treaty, claiming that the country's measures violated their intellectual property rights and amounted to expropriation. The conclusion reached by the tribunal was significant, as it upheld Uruguay's right to implement legitimate public health measures, highlighting the precedence of public interest over corporate interests. The case shed light on the potential implications for the role of the judiciary in government, raising concerns about the power balance between states and transnational corporations. It underscored the need for robust legal frameworks and independent judiciaries capable of striking a balance between protecting investments and preserving the public welfare. Moreover, the case demonstrated the influence and impact of corporate power in shaping government policies, emphasizing the importance of ensuring transparency and accountability in the interactions between governments and multinational corporations. Overall, the Philip Morris v. Uruguay case served as a stark reminder of the complexities surrounding the role of the judiciary in addressing disputes between governments and corporations, highlighting the need for a fair and impartial system that safeguards public interest while respecting legitimate investment rights.

The European Court of Human Rights (ECtHR) provides a pertinent vantage point to examine the interplay between judiciaries, governments, and transnational disputes in the realm of human rights. The case of Al-Adsani v. United Kingdom (2001) underscores the judiciary's role in resolving disputes with far-reaching implications. By allowing individuals to bring claims against states for violations of international human rights standards, the ECtHR demonstrates how judiciaries can serve as guardians of human rights in an increasingly globalized legal landscape. Literature by Letsas (2013) delves into the implications of Al-Adsani and similar cases, exploring how judiciaries' involvement in transnational disputes reshapes the dynamics of government accountability. In the case of Al-Adsani v. United Kingdom (2001), a crucial ruling was delivered by the European Court of Human Rights (ECtHR), shedding light on key issues surrounding the role of the judiciary in government. The case centered around allegations of torture and unlawful detention brought by Al-Adsani against the British government for actions occurring during the first Gulf War. The primary question before the court was whether states could claim sovereign immunity and be exempt from international human rights law. In its conclusion, the ECtHR ruled that sovereign immunity cannot be invoked by a state as a defense against claims of torture or inhuman treatment. This groundbreaking decision had significant implications for the accountability of states and the protection of human rights. It emphasized that states must adhere to their obligations under international human rights law, even in matters concerning national security. The ruling highlighted the crucial role of the judiciary in interpreting and applying international law, reinforcing the idea that no one, including states, is above the law. Moreover, the case underscored the importance of providing victims access to justice and a fair legal process, particularly when seeking redress for human rights violations. The Al-Adsani v. United Kingdom case contributed to shaping the understanding of state responsibility for human rights abuses and set a precedent for holding governments accountable, thus reaffirming the role of the judiciary as a guardian of human rights and a check on state power.

Nevertheless, the path to resolving transnational disputes through judicial means is marked by challenges (Edelman, 1994; Efrat, 2018; Eichensehr, 2018; Eleftheriadis, 2005). Territorial disputes often exemplify the complexities of adjudicating matters with geopolitical implications. The dispute between Malaysia and Singapore over Pedra Branca Island offers an insightful case study. The ICJ's judgment illuminated the intricate dynamics of international law, sovereignty, and historical evidence, showcasing how judiciaries grapple with politically sensitive matters while striving for impartiality. The case of Pedra Branca underscores the delicate balance judiciaries must maintain when addressing disputes that transcend legal boundaries and implicate national pride. Charney (2009) delves into the complexities of territorial disputes and their resolution through judicial mechanisms. The dispute between Malaysia and Singapore over Pedra Branca Island is a noteworthy case that highlights the role of the judiciary in resolving territorial disputes. The key issue at stake was the ownership of the island, located in the strategic waters of the Singapore Strait. Both countries claimed sovereignty over Pedra Branca based on historical evidence and legal arguments. The case underwent several phases, including technical surveys, historical research, and presentation of evidence. In 2008, the International Court of Justice (ICJ) delivered its final judgment, ruling in favor of Singapore and affirming their ownership of the island. The ICJ considered various factors, including historical documents, maps, navigational practices, and the conduct of the parties involved. The case underscored the importance of a neutral and independent judiciary in resolving complex and contentious disputes, particularly those involving territorial claims. The conclusion reached by the ICJ had significant implications, as it set a precedent for resolving similar disputes based on established principles of international law. Moreover, it demonstrated the effectiveness of international legal mechanisms in providing a fair and impartial avenue for resolving conflicts between sovereign nations. Overall, the dispute between Malaysia and Singapore over Pedra Branca Island underscored the crucial role of the judiciary in maintaining peace, upholding international law, and promoting stability in the international community.

In conclusion, the role of judiciaries in resolving transnational disputes transcends legal doctrines, embodying the intricate relationship between judiciaries and governments in an era of global interdependence. As judiciaries mediate between state interests, private rights, and international norms, they emerge as linchpins in fostering global justice and maintaining diplomatic harmony. By navigating a spectrum of disputes, from treaty-based conflicts to matters of human rights and sovereignty, judiciaries reveal their capacity to balance legal principles with pragmatic considerations. This dynamic interaction underscores the judiciary's essential role in a world where transnational disputes are intrinsic to the fabric of international relations. The next section focuses on the jurisdictional challenges of in a borderless world.

7.4. JURISDICTIONAL CHALLENGES IN A BORDERLESS WORLD

In an era characterized by digital connectivity, rapid cross-border movement, and intricate economic interdependence, the notion of jurisdiction faces unprecedented challenges. The intricacies of governing in a borderless world engender complex legal issues that profoundly impact the relationship between the judiciary and the government. This chapter section undertakes an in-depth exploration of the evolving landscape of jurisdictional challenges, weaving together a tapestry of global examples and case studies to elucidate the intricate interplay between judiciaries and governments as they grapple with the complexities of asserting authority and delivering justice in a world that defies traditional territorial confines. As Figure 7.7 shows, some are beginning to recharacterize borders as systems of oppression that must be overcome. Hence, the rise of a borderless world is welcomed despite some of the jurisdictional challenges it brings.

Figure 7.7. Characterization of borders as systems of oppression.

Source: Lauren Beard (2018)n via Philly Partisan https://phillypartisan.com/2018/05/15/a-borderless-world/

One of the most pressing jurisdictional challenges is posed by the borderless realm of cyberspace (Smith, 2005; Sorabji & Vaughan, 2021; Southworth, 2018). The internet's transcendent nature defies geographical borders, enabling interactions that traverse nations within seconds. The case of Google v. CNIL (2014) exemplifies this challenge. In this instance, a French data protection authority sought to enforce the "right to be forgotten" principle against Google, leading to a jurisdictional quandary. While the European Union (EU) asserted its regulatory authority over data protection, Google maintained that as a U.S. company, it was not obligated to comply with EU directives. The judiciary's role in interpreting conflicting legal norms and reconciling competing jurisdictional claims highlights the intricate dance between legal principles, national sovereignty, and technological realities. The case of Google v. CNIL (2014) centers around jurisdictional challenges in the realm of cyberspace, illustrating the complex issues surrounding the role of the judiciary in governing digital domains. The key issue at hand was Google's refusal to comply with the demands of CNIL (Commission nationale de l'informatique et des libertés), the French data protection authority. CNIL had ordered Google to extend the "right to be forgotten" ruling to its global search engine, requiring the removal of certain search results worldwide. Google argued that the ruling should only apply to its European domains, as it asserted its compliance with European Union data protection laws. The case evolved into a clash between national jurisdictions and global internet companies, addressing the question of whether national laws could have extraterritorial reach in cyberspace. The conclusion reached by the Court of Justice of the European Union sided with CNIL, asserting that Google must enforce takedowns of certain content across all its global domains. This decision revealed the challenges inherent in regulating transnational digital platforms and the role of the judiciary in determining the scope of jurisdiction in the digital age. It highlighted the need for international legal frameworks to address emerging issues in cyberspace and maintain cohesive governance. The implications of this case extended beyond the jurisdictional challenge, with concerns regarding the potential clash between free expression and the right to privacy. It raised questions about the balance between national sovereignty and the global nature of digital platforms, emphasizing the need for nuanced and flexible legal solutions to address the complexities of governing the internet. In summary, Google v. CNIL highlighted the critical role of the judiciary in navigating jurisdictional challenges in cyberspace and ensuring the development of legal frameworks that can effectively govern digital platforms while upholding individual rights and global standards.

Global financial markets present another realm of jurisdictional intricacies (Pickett, 2016; Pidot, 2014; Pierce, 1989, 1997). High-frequency trading and complex financial instruments traverse national boundaries, posing a challenge to traditional notions of jurisdiction over market regulation and enforcement. The 2008 financial crisis prompted governments to reevaluate the jurisdictional boundaries of financial oversight. The Dodd-Frank Wall Street Reform and Consumer Protection Act in the United States aimed to strengthen regulatory mechanisms. However, as financial activities become increasingly globalized, the jurisdictional limitations of national regulations become evident. The judiciary's role in interpreting and enforcing financial regulations underscores its challenge in navigating a borderless financial landscape. The Dodd-Frank Wall Street Reform and Consumer Protection Act, enacted in the United States, was a comprehensive legislative effort aiming to strengthen regulatory mechanisms in the aftermath of the 2008 financial crisis. The key issues addressed by this act were the need to enhance transparency, accountability, and stability in the financial sector. The act introduced a range of reforms, including the creation of the Consumer Financial Protection Bureau (CFPB) to safeguard consumers from predatory practices, increased oversight on financial institutions, measures to mitigate systemic risk, and new rules for derivatives trading. The events leading up to the enactment of Dodd-Frank were marked by widespread public dissatisfaction with the perceived lack of oversight and regulation on Wall Street, and the consequent economic and social impact of the financial crisis.

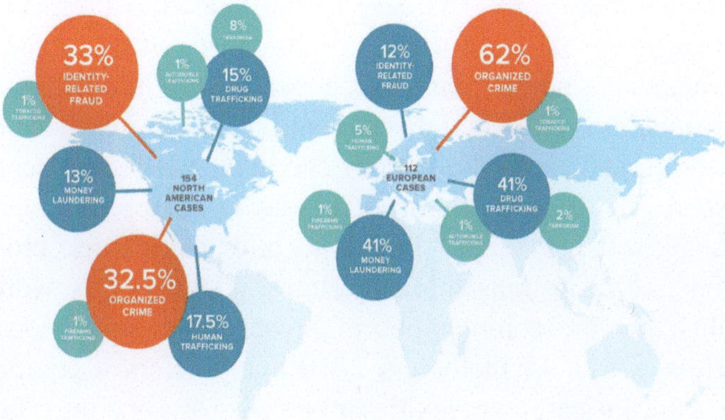

Figure 7.8. Payment card fraud funding terrorism and other transnational crimes.

Source: Alex Rolfe (2019) https://www.paymentscardsandmobile.com/payment-card-fraud-funding-terrorism-and-other-transnational-crimes/

The act also sought to address concerns over the concentration of power among a few financial institutions and the role of complex financial instruments in exacerbating the crisis. The conclusion of Dodd-Frank resulted in a significant overhaul of financial regulations and the establishment of a more robust framework for oversight, aimed at preventing excessive risk-taking and ensuring more responsible behavior in the financial sector. The implications for the role of the judiciary in government were notable, as the act introduced new regulatory bodies and expanded the authority of existing ones. This necessitated the involvement of the judiciary in interpreting and applying the provisions of the act, thereby shaping the enforcement and impact of the reforms. The act also spurred debates over the appropriate balance between government regulation and the autonomy of market participants, highlighting the judiciary's role in adjudicating disputes arising from the implementation of the act and clarifying its terms and scope. Overall, the Dodd-Frank Act served as a significant milestone in financial regulatory reform, prompting increased scrutiny and oversight of the financial sector, and underscoring the critical role of the judiciary in interpreting and upholding the laws governing financial markets in the United States.

Transnational crimes amplify jurisdictional complexities further (Chan, 2011; Chavez, 2003, 2007; Chen & Li, 2016; Chutkow, 2008). For instance, mobile card payments provide ample avenues for transnational criminality (see Figure 7.8). The case of the "Palermo Protocol" against human trafficking reveals how criminal activities can transcend national boundaries, necessitating international cooperation. While nations strive to prosecute criminals engaged in transnational crimes, the absence of uniform definitions and jurisdictional limitations can hamper effective legal action. This underscores the critical role of judiciaries in interpreting international agreements, like the Palermo Protocol, and facilitating cross-border cooperation to combat transnational crimes. Fichtelberg's work (2010) offers insights into the complexities of prosecuting transnational crimes in a borderless world. Fichtelberg's 2010 study offers a comprehensive exploration of the intricate complexities involved in prosecuting transnational crimes within an increasingly borderless global context. The research focuses on the myriad challenges arising from the convergence of legal, jurisdictional, and practical issues. Central to the study is the recognition of how transnational crimes, spanning across multiple countries, demand a delicate balance of international cooperation and coordination among law enforcement agencies. The work underscores the jurisdictional dilemma, highlighting the difficulties arising from differing legal systems, varying definitions of crimes, and discrepancies in commitment to international collaboration. Extradition complexities emerge as another critical facet, where navigating intricate extradition treaties, human rights considerations, and political sensitivities can hinder the process of bringing perpetrators to justice. Equally significant is the intricate web of evidence collection and admissibility, as divergent standards, data protection laws, and intelligence sharing restrictions pose hurdles in presenting evidence across borders. Fichtelberg also delves into the role of international organizations and agreements in addressing these challenges, emphasizing entities like INTERPOL, Europol, and UNODC, along with bilateral and multilateral agreements, as crucial avenues for information exchange and collaborative efforts. In essence, Fichtelberg's work serves as a valuable resource that deepens understanding of the multifaceted landscape of prosecuting transnational crimes, shedding light on the intricacies and hurdles involved in pursuing justice in an interconnected world.

Online defamation adds a layer of complexity to jurisdictional challenges (Wright, 2016; Yap, 2019; Yap & Chung, 2019). The case of Joe Gutnick v. Dow Jones (2002) underscores the complexities of asserting jurisdiction over online content that can be accessed globally. In this instance, an Australian businessman sued an American publisher for defamation over an article published online. The challenge lay in determining the appropriate jurisdiction for the lawsuit, considering that the article was accessible worldwide. The judiciary's role in establishing legal precedents for determining jurisdiction over online defamation highlights the evolving nature of legal principles in response to borderless communication. In the landmark case of Joe Gutnick v. Dow Jones in 2002, the legal system grappled with the intricate challenges posed by the assertion of jurisdiction over online content. The case shed light on the complexities that arise when content published on the internet can be accessed by individuals across the globe. At the heart of the matter was an article, published by Dow Jones, that allegedly defamed mining magnate Joe Gutnick. The contentious issue that arose was whether Australian jurisdiction could be invoked in a defamation suit, given that the article was published in the United States and accessible by anyone with an internet connection. The case drew attention to the evolving nature of communication and the difficulty in applying traditional legal frameworks to the digital age. The conclusion reached by the court illustrates the pivotal role of the judiciary in navigating these complex issues. The court ultimately ruled in favor of Gutnick, holding that Australian jurisdiction could apply, emphasizing the importance of protecting individuals' reputations and asserting that publication occurs wherever the defamatory material is accessed. This ruling had far-reaching implications for the role of the judiciary in government, as it established a precedent for asserting jurisdiction over online content regardless of geographical boundaries. The case highlighted the need for international cooperation and harmonization of laws in the digital era, as well as the challenges faced by legal systems in adapting to the global nature of online communication.

Intellectual property disputes underscore how globalized economic activities intersect with jurisdictional complexities (Rathod, 2009; Redman, 2017; Reenock et al., 2013). The case of Apple Inc. v. Samsung Electronics Co. (2012) serves as a prime example. As multinational corporations vie for supremacy in the global market, their patent disputes transcend national boundaries, demanding judicial determination of jurisdiction and infringement. The judiciary's role in interpreting international intellectual property agreements and determining the territorial extent of legal remedies showcases its pivotal position in resolving jurisdictional conflicts in the realm of innovation and commerce. In the highly publicized case of Apple Inc. v. Samsung Electronics Co. in 2012, the legal landscape was shaped by a dispute revolving around intellectual property rights and the competitive smartphone market. This high-stakes battle unfolded as Apple accused Samsung of infringing upon its design patents, claiming that certain Samsung devices bore striking similarities to Apple's iconic iPhone and iPad. The key issue at hand was whether Samsung had indeed copied Apple's patented features, leading to a heated debate on the boundaries of design protection and innovation in the tech industry. Throughout the course of the trial, both sides presented extensive evidence and expert testimonies to support their arguments, making it a closely watched showdown between two tech giants. The conclusions drawn by the court had significant implications for the role of the judiciary in government, particularly in terms of protecting intellectual property rights and promoting fair competition. Ultimately, the jury sided with Apple and awarded them a substantial amount in damages, recognizing the value of design patents and reinforcing the importance of defending innovative creations. This landmark decision had far-reaching consequences, not only in terms of financial ramifications for Samsung, but also in shaping the landscape of intellectual property law in the technology sector. It sent a clear signal that the judiciary would play a vital role in safeguarding intellectual property rights, encouraging innovation, and maintaining a level playing field in the dynamic world of technology.

In conclusion, the modern world's borderless nature has precipitated a cascade of jurisdictional challenges that ripple through the intricate relationship between the judiciary and the government. From the complexities of regulating cyberspace and financial markets to combating transnational crimes and resolving disputes over online content and intellectual property, the judiciary becomes a crucial arbiter in reconciling legal norms, technological realities, and the sovereignty of nations. The evolving jurisprudence surrounding jurisdictional challenges stands as a testament to the judiciary's adaptability in navigating the intricate web of borderless legal issues that characterize our globalized age. The final section of this chapter will focus on the role of the judiciary in harmonizing international law.

7.5. JUDICIARY'S ROLE IN HARMONIZING INTERNATIONAL LAW

In an increasingly interconnected world, the proliferation of transnational crimes has posed unprecedented challenges to traditional notions of sovereignty, legal jurisdiction, and the enforcement of laws (White, 2022; Whittington, 2005; Willett & Gordon, 2022). The complex nature of these crimes, which transcend national boundaries, has necessitated the harmonization of international legal frameworks to effectively combat such activities. The role of the judiciary in this endeavor is crucial, as it acts as the cornerstone in interpreting and applying these frameworks within domestic legal systems. This chapter delves into the intricate relationship between the judiciary and government in the harmonization of international law pertaining to transnational crimes. By drawing upon a multitude of detailed examples and case studies from across the globe, as well as referencing pertinent literature, this discussion underscores how the judiciary's interpretation, application, and enforcement of international law play a pivotal role in achieving coherence and effectiveness in addressing transnational criminal activities.

One of the central challenges in prosecuting transnational crimes lies in the divergence of legal definitions and standards across different jurisdictions (Beiser-McGrath et al., 2022; Bell, 2002; Bencze, 2021). One example is the anticipated rise in cybercrime (see Figure 7.9). The judiciary's role becomes evident in the process of interpreting and aligning domestic laws with international legal obligations. A striking example of this can be observed in the context of cybercrime. The widespread use of the internet has facilitated cyberattacks that can originate from one jurisdiction while causing substantial harm in another. The Convention on Cybercrime, also known as the Budapest Convention, stands as a benchmark in harmonizing legislation across nations. The court's interpretation of the Computer Fraud and Abuse Act to encompass extraterritorial cybercrimes reflects the judiciary's role in bridging legal gaps in the face of evolving transnational challenges. In the case of "United States v. Vasiliy Gorshkov," the legal system grappled with the challenges posed by cybercrime and the enforcement of international law in the digital era. The United States, a signatory of the Convention on Cybercrime, commonly referred to as the Budapest Convention, sought to prosecute Gorshkov, a Russian hacker accused of perpetrating various cybercrimes, including unauthorized access to computer systems and theft of sensitive information.

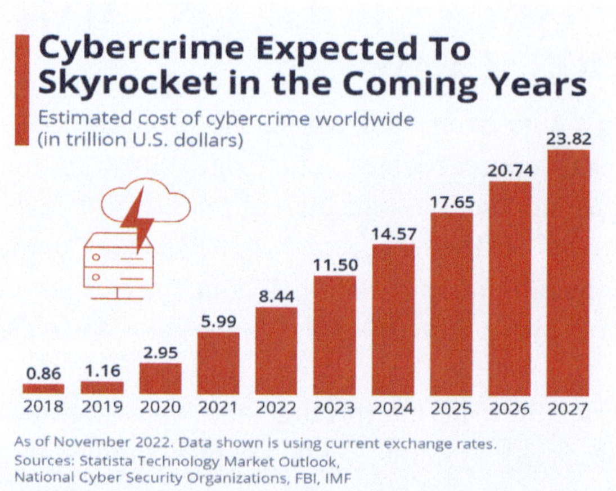

Figure 7.9. Anticipated rise in cybercrime 2018 through 2027.

Source: Anna Fleck (2022) Statista https://www.statista.com/chart/28878/expected-cost-of-cybercrime-until-2027/

The key issue at hand was whether the United States had jurisdiction to extradite and prosecute Gorshkov, considering he resided outside their territorial boundaries. The case highlighted the significance of international cooperation in combating cybercrime and the importance of adhering to established frameworks, such as the Budapest Convention, which aims to harmonize legislation and enhance the ability to investigate and prosecute cybercriminals across borders (Aboueldahab, 2021; Abouharb et al., 2013). The conclusion reached by the court demonstrated the crucial role of the judiciary in upholding the rule of law in cyberspace. Gorshkov was extradited and faced trial in the United States, emphasizing the commitment of governments and legal systems to hold cybercriminals accountable, irrespective of their physical location. The implications for the role of the judiciary in government were profound, as the case underscored the need for robust legal frameworks and international cooperation to address the increasingly complex and global nature of cybercrime. It highlighted the judiciary's role as an arbiter in interpreting and applying laws to ensure the protection of individuals, the preservation of security, and the advancement of justice in the digital realm. The judiciary's engagement with international law extends to cases involving human trafficking, where transnational criminal networks exploit porous borders to engage in heinous activities (Althouse, 2001; Appleby et al., 2019; Appleby & Olijnyk, 2020). The Palermo Protocol supplements the United Nations Convention against Transnational Organized Crime, demonstrating international efforts to combat human trafficking. In the Indian context, the case of "Vishal Jeet v. Union of India" saw the Supreme Court of India addressing the urgent need to implement comprehensive anti-trafficking measures. The court's directives not only underscore the significance of international agreements but also emphasize the judiciary's proactive role in pressuring governments to fulfill their obligations. This interaction between the judiciary and government signifies a symbiotic relationship, where the judiciary acts as a catalyst for enforcing international norms. In the case of Vishal Jeet v. Union of India, the judiciary grappled with the critical issues surrounding transnational organized crime and the enforcement of international legal frameworks. The case involved the interpretation and application of the United Nations Convention against Transnational Organized Crime, which seeks to combat and prevent criminal activities that operate across national borders. At the heart of the matter was the question of how the Indian legal system could effectively address and prosecute transnational organized crime, given the intricate nature of these criminal networks and their ability to operate beyond territorial boundaries. The case shed light on the need for cooperation between nations, as well as the role of the judiciary in interpreting and implementing international legal instruments. The conclusion reached by the court had far-reaching implications for the role of the judiciary in government. It reaffirmed the importance of aligning national laws with international commitments, as well as the judiciary's responsibility in upholding the rule of law in the face of transnational challenges. The case underscored the role of the judiciary as a custodian of justice and an enforcer of international norms, highlighting the need for strong legal frameworks and global cooperation to combat organized crime effectively.

The extradition of criminals involved in transnational activities serves as a prime example of the delicate balance between judicial decisions and governmental interests (Steuer, 2019; Subedi, 2016; Szente, 2021; Taghdiri, 2019). Extradition treaties play a pivotal role in facilitating cooperation among nations, but they often involve intricate negotiations due to political, human rights, and jurisdictional considerations. The case of "Assange v. The Swedish Prosecution Authority" provides a nuanced illustration of the interplay between extradition proceedings and international human rights standards. The European Arrest Warrant mechanism, aimed at streamlining extradition within the European Union, necessitated the UK judiciary to navigate conflicting obligations between international law and domestic interests. In fact, the UK has historically been a major user of the facility (see Figure 7.10). This case underscores the judiciary's role as a mediator in ensuring that extradition processes adhere to international legal norms, while acknowledging the governmental prerogatives at stake.

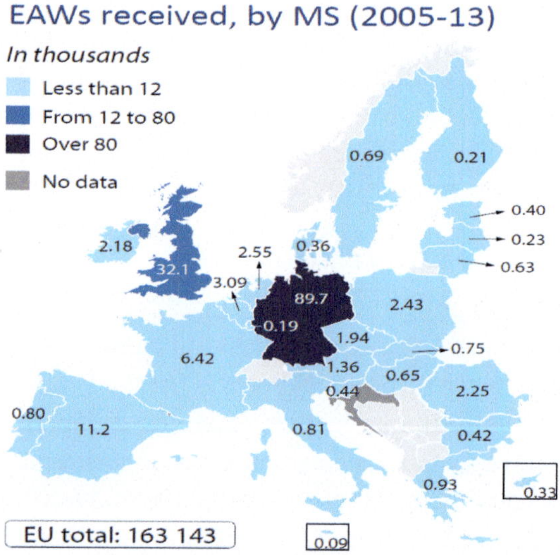

Figure 7.10. The use of the European Arrest Warrant 2005–2013.

Source: European Parliamentary Research Service https://epthinktank.eu/2014/06/26/european-arrest-warrant-eaw/

In the case of Assange v. The Swedish Prosecution Authority, the judiciary grappled with a complex and contentious issue related to the European Arrest Warrant mechanism and the rights of individuals involved. The case revolved around the extradition request by Sweden for Julian Assange, the founder of WikiLeaks, who faced allegations of sexual assault and rape. The key issue at hand was whether the European Arrest Warrant mechanism, designed to facilitate swift extradition between European Union member states, was being misused or compromised in this particular case. Supporters of Assange argued that his case was politically motivated and raised concerns about the potential violation of his human rights, including the risk of being extradited to the United States for his involvement in leaking classified information. The legal proceedings and extradition battles not only fueled debates about the legitimacy of the charges against Assange but also highlighted the delicate balance between international cooperation, human rights, and the impartiality of the judiciary. The ultimate conclusion reached by the courts differed as the case evolved over time. The implications for the role of the judiciary in government were significant. It demonstrated the judiciary's role as an independent arbiter, tasked with interpreting and applying extradition laws while safeguarding the rights of individuals involved. The case underscored the judiciary's responsibility to carefully consider the nuances of international law and navigate the politically charged nature of high-profile extradition cases, ensuring fairness, accountability, and adherence to human rights standards.

Furthermore, the judiciary's interpretation of evidence-sharing mechanisms across borders showcases its contribution to the harmonization of international law in transnational crime cases (Cassman, 2015; Celenk, 2016; Chakravarti et al., 2011; Chalmers, 2000). The principle of dual criminality often underpins mutual legal assistance treaties (MLATs), requiring that the alleged offense be a crime in both the requesting and requested states. The "In the Matter of the 2003 Request by the United Kingdom" case, heard by the U.S. District Court for the Southern District of New York, exemplifies this principle in the context of terrorism-related offenses. The court's analysis of the compatibility of U.S. and UK laws with respect to material support for terrorism demonstrates the judiciary's role in navigating the intricate tapestry of dual criminality, thereby aiding in the exchange of evidence crucial for successful transnational prosecutions. In the case of "In the Matter of the 2003 Request by the United Kingdom," which was heard by the U.S. District Court for the Southern District of New York, the key issues revolved around the interpretation and application of mutual legal assistance treaties (MLATs). The case pertained to a request by the United Kingdom for assistance in obtaining evidence for a criminal investigation. The central question was whether the requested evidence fell within the scope of the MLAT between the two countries. This case shed light on the complexities of international legal cooperation and the challenges faced by the judiciary in balancing the interests of multiple jurisdictions. The court carefully evaluated the provisions of the MLAT, considered the nature of the evidence sought, and assessed its admissibility under U.S. law. The conclusion reached by the court not only addressed the specific case at hand but also had broader implications for the role of the judiciary in government. It demonstrated the judiciary's critical role as a facilitator of international legal cooperation, ensuring that obligations under MLATs are respected while also protecting the rights of individuals involved. The case emphasized the importance of clear and well-defined treaty provisions, as well as the need for judicial interpretation to navigate the complexities of cross-border criminal investigations. It highlighted the judiciary's responsibility to strike a balance between the interests of various countries involved, thereby promoting justice, legal cooperation, and the rule of law in international affairs.

The dynamic between the judiciary and government becomes particularly pronounced in cases involving the application of universal jurisdiction, wherein a state claims jurisdiction over crimes committed outside its territory (Gallagher, 2012; Gardbaum, 2015; Garoupa et al., 2012). The principle of universal jurisdiction underscores the judiciary's power to prosecute individuals for crimes that shock the conscience of humanity, such as genocide, war crimes, and crimes against humanity. Notable examples include the cases of "Eichmann Trial" in Israel and the "Hissène Habré Trial" in Senegal. These instances reflect how the judiciary, while applying international law principles, grapples with the complexities of granting justice to victims while respecting the sovereignty of other states. These trials also underscore the judiciary's role in bridging the gap between international legal obligations and the practical implications of exercising jurisdiction. The "Eichmann Trial" in Israel stands as a significant landmark in the history of universal jurisdiction. The trial centered around Adolf Eichmann, a high-ranking Nazi official responsible for orchestrating the Holocaust. The key issue at hand was whether Israel had the legal authority to prosecute and pass judgment on crimes committed during World War II, despite Eichmann being captured outside its jurisdiction. The trial drew global attention, as it raised profound questions about the reach of international law and the role of the judiciary in holding individuals accountable for crimes against humanity. The conclusion reached by the Israeli court was that universal jurisdiction could be applied in extraordinary cases where the crimes were of such magnitude and impact that they affected the entire international community. This groundbreaking ruling had far-reaching implications for the role of the judiciary in government, as it demonstrated that justice could transcend borders and that no individual could evade accountability for their actions, regardless of time, place, or nationality. The Eichmann trial marked a pivotal moment in the development of universal jurisdiction, establishing a precedent and setting the stage for future trials that sought to bring perpetrators of heinous crimes to justice, irrespective of jurisdictional limitations. It emphasized the importance of international cooperation, the pursuit of justice, and the role of the judiciary in interpreting and applying principles of law that transcend national boundaries.

The "Hissène Habré Trial" in Senegal represents a significant development in the realm of universal jurisdiction (Gallagher, 2012; Gardbaum, 2015; Garoupa et al., 2012). The trial focused on the former President of Chad, Hissène Habré, who was accused of human rights abuses and crimes against humanity during his tenure from 1982 to 1990. The key issue at hand was whether Senegal, as the host country, had the legal authority to prosecute an individual who was not a citizen and whose alleged crimes were committed outside its territory. The trial garnered global attention, highlighting the challenges and complexities of exercising universal jurisdiction. After years of legal battles, the court concluded that universal jurisdiction could indeed be invoked in this case, reaffirming the principle that grave human rights violations should not go unpunished, regardless of the perpetrator's nationality or the location of the crimes. The implications for the role of the judiciary in government were far-reaching. The trial underscored the judiciary's role as a guardian of justice, ensuring accountability and serving as a mechanism for redress, even in cases that may seem outside their direct jurisdiction. This landmark trial demonstrated the potential of universal jurisdiction to bring justice to victims of human rights abuses and to hold perpetrators accountable, regardless of borders. It also highlighted the importance of international cooperation and the shared responsibility of nations in combating impunity and promoting a culture of human rights.

In conclusion, the judiciary plays a pivotal role in harmonizing international law in the context of transnational crimes. Through its interpretation, application, and enforcement of international legal frameworks, the judiciary contributes to achieving coherence, consistency, and effectiveness in addressing these complex challenges. By examining cases involving cybercrime, human trafficking, extradition, evidence-sharing, and universal jurisdiction, it becomes evident that the judiciary's engagement with international law is multifaceted. The judiciary's proactive stance in upholding international norms, mediating between conflicting interests, and ensuring accountability reflects a symbiotic relationship with the government. As transnational crimes continue to evolve, the judiciary's evolving role in harmonizing international law will remain central to the pursuit of justice in our interconnected world.

CHAPTER 7 SUMMARY

In the penultimate chapter, titled "The Role of the Judiciary in a Globalized World," the multifaceted relationship between the judiciary and the challenges posed by an increasingly interconnected global landscape is meticulously explored. The chapter delves into five distinct sections that collectively unravel the judiciary's pivotal role in addressing the complexities of transnational crimes and harmonizing international law.

The initial section, "The Impact of Globalization on Legal Systems," initiates the discourse by delineating how globalization's far-reaching impacts have necessitated a reevaluation of traditional legal paradigms. The section underscores that the rapid cross-border movement of people, capital, and information has ushered in an era where legal violations transcend national boundaries, thereby necessitating a cohesive global response. This contextual groundwork sets the stage for a thorough examination of the judiciary's evolving significance in this interconnected world.

"International Cooperation and Treaty Interpretation," the subsequent section, elucidates how the judiciary's role in interpreting and applying international agreements is instrumental in fostering effective collaboration. By delving into case studies that demonstrate how courts navigate intricate treaty provisions, the section underscores the judiciary's responsibility in ensuring uniformity in understanding and implementation across diverse jurisdictions. It reveals the judiciary's role as a bridge in facilitating harmonious engagement among nations, further reinforcing the significance of its interpretive function.

"Resolving Transnational Disputes through Judicial Means," the following section, delves into the crucial role of the judiciary as a means of redress in transnational disputes. The section highlights instances where parties from different countries seek judicial resolution, exemplifying how courts stand as impartial arbiters that transcend geopolitical interests. This portrayal underscores the judiciary's role in upholding the rule of law and delivering justice that transcends borders, making it an indispensable component in the global legal landscape.

"Jurisdictional Challenges in a Borderless World," another pivotal section, grapples with the intricate challenges surrounding legal jurisdiction in a world transcending traditional territorial boundaries. Through a nuanced analysis of cases that involve multiple jurisdictions, the section elucidates how the judiciary navigates the complexities of asserting authority while respecting the principles of sovereignty. It illustrates how courts act as custodians of justice, reconciling jurisdictional conflicts and ensuring that perpetrators are held accountable for their transnational actions.

The culminating section, "Judiciary's Role in Harmonizing International Law," synthesizes the overarching themes of the chapter. This section elucidates how the judiciary, through its interpretations, applications, and enforcements, contributes to harmonizing international legal frameworks. The discourse emphasizes the symbiotic relationship between the judiciary and government in this endeavor, where the former's interpretive prowess aligns with the latter's commitment to international cooperation. The section reaffirms the judiciary's multifaceted role as a bridge-builder, an enforcer of international norms, and a safeguard against impunity.

In summation, Chapter 7 underscores that the judiciary's role in a globalized world is not merely confined to domestic jurisprudence, but extends to shaping the trajectory of international legal harmonization. The interplay between the judiciary's interpretive responsibilities, its role in transnational dispute resolution, and its efforts to navigate complex jurisdictional challenges manifests its central role in the pursuit of justice across borders. The chapter's thematic exploration effectively paints the judiciary as an integral actor in ensuring that the rule of law transcends territorial confines, thereby offering a resonating affirmation of its enduring significance in an interconnected global milieu. The final chapter of the book will focus on future challenges and emerging perspectives on the relationships between the judiciary and government.

CHAPTER 8

Future Perspectives and Emerging Challenges

Contents

8.1. Technological Advancements and the Judiciary 271
8.2. Ensuring Diversity and Inclusivity in the Judiciary 278
8.3. Adapting to Rapid Societal Changes 290
8.4. Enhancing Public Trust in the Judiciary 298
8.5. Addressing Future Power Struggles Between Judiciary and Government 304
Chapter 8 Summary 309

In the culminating chapter titled "Future Perspectives and Emerging Challenges," the focus turns to an anticipatory exploration of the evolving dynamics that will shape the judiciary's trajectory in an increasingly complex global landscape. Within the context of this chapter, five distinctive sections provide an in-depth analysis of the various dimensions that will profoundly influence the judiciary's role, its relationship with society, and its interface with governmental entities.

The introductory section, "Technological Advancements and the Judiciary," delves into the paramount influence of technology on the judicial landscape. As technology continues to evolve at an unprecedented pace, the section underscores its transformative potential in reshaping court processes, evidence handling, and even the accessibility of justice. The discussion will shed light on the nuanced ways in which artificial intelligence, data analytics, and virtual platforms are expected to influence judicial proceedings, while also addressing potential challenges related to data security, privacy, and equitable access to justice in an era of technological disruption.

The subsequent section, "Ensuring Diversity and Inclusivity in the Judiciary," navigates the imperative of fostering a judiciary that reflects the rich diversity of the societies it serves. This section delves into the significance of inclusive judicial representation in bolstering public confidence and legitimacy. By examining both international and domestic examples, the discussion will illuminate the hurdles and progress in ensuring that the judiciary encompasses voices from various backgrounds, ensuring that justice remains impartial and responsive to the diverse needs of the global population.

"Adapting to Rapid Societal Changes," another pivotal section, interrogates how the judiciary must evolve to address societal shifts and emergent legal dilemmas. Rapid changes in social norms, values, and even the ways in which individuals interact demand a judiciary that is adaptable and forward-thinking. By drawing upon instances where the judiciary has engaged with contentious issues such as climate change, artificial intelligence ethics, and new forms of expression, the section underscores the judiciary's role as a navigational compass amidst evolving societal landscapes.

The subsequent section, "Enhancing Public Trust in the Judiciary," delves into the symbiotic relationship between a trusted judiciary and the effective functioning of democratic societies. As public scrutiny of institutions intensifies, this section examines strategies to enhance transparency, accountability, and accessibility within the judicial system. By examining examples that elucidate the consequences of eroding public trust, the section underscores the judiciary's responsibility in maintaining its stature as an impartial and authoritative pillar of justice.

The concluding section, "Addressing Future Power Struggles between Judiciary and Government," offers a forward-looking assessment of potential tensions that may arise between the judiciary's independence and governmental authority. As the dynamics between these entities continue to evolve, the section explores measures to safeguard judicial autonomy and impartiality while preserving the collaborative relationship between the judiciary and the government. Drawing on historical and contemporary examples, this section highlights the delicate equilibrium that must be maintained to ensure that the judiciary continues to serve as a check on governmental power while contributing to the overall functioning of the state.

In essence, the chapter stands as a prophetic exploration of the intricate and multifaceted challenges that await the judiciary in an ever-changing world. By delving into the contours of technological advancements, the pursuit of inclusivity, adaptation to societal shifts, the consolidation of public trust, and the dynamics between the judiciary and government, this chapter anticipates the path that the judiciary must traverse to remain a steadfast and dynamic institution in the decades to come. Let us open the final chapter by considering the technological advancements within the judiciary.

8.1. TECHNOLOGICAL ADVANCEMENTS AND THE JUDICIARY

The confluence of technological advancements and the judiciary represents a profound transformation in the administration of justice across the globe (Marsh, 2021; Martinsen, 2011; Masinde, 2017). As societies become increasingly digitized, the impact of technology on the legal landscape is irrefutable. This section critically examines the intricate relationship between technological advancements and the judiciary, underlining both the opportunities and challenges that emerge. Through the lens of detailed examples and case studies from various jurisdictions, as well as referencing relevant literature, this discussion delves into the nuances of technology's influence on court processes, evidence handling, accessibility to justice, and the balance between efficiency and due process.

Technological innovations have significantly streamlined court processes, expediting administrative tasks and enhancing the overall efficiency of judicial proceedings (Mason, 2015; Matthes, 2022; Mayoral & Perez, 2018). A pertinent example comes from Singapore, where the introduction of an electronic filing system in the Supreme Court has remarkably reduced the time and resources required for document submission and case management. This transition has not only optimized court operations but also improved the ease of access for litigants and legal professionals. Similarly, the implementation of digital case management systems in courts across the United States has facilitated real-time tracking of cases, minimizing delays, and increasing the predictability of trial schedules. Literature by van der Knaap and Fabri (2017) accentuates how such technologies not only alleviate administrative burdens but also contribute to a swifter and more effective dispensation of justice.

The scholarly contribution of van der Knaap and Fabri's 2017 literature lies in its comprehensive exploration of the impact of technological advancements on the judiciary. By delving beyond the surface-level administrative enhancements brought about by technology, the authors highlight a more profound influence on the efficiency and efficacy of justice delivery within the legal system. Their study meticulously outlines how the implementation of technological tools, such as electronic filing systems and digital case management platforms, not only streamlines administrative tasks but also directly contributes to expediting the resolution of legal cases. This acceleration is attributed to the elimination of bureaucratic bottlenecks and the reduction of time-consuming paper-based processes, ultimately leading to quicker access to justice for litigants.

Furthermore, van der Knaap and Fabri emphasize the transformative potential of technology-enabled efficiency gains, making the judiciary a more agile institution capable of addressing emerging legal challenges in a timely manner. In essence, their work underscores that technology's impact on the judiciary transcends administrative improvements, ultimately empowering the judicial system to fulfill its fundamental role of administering justice promptly and effectively in an ever-evolving legal landscape. Figure 8.1 highlights some of the hard technologies used in courts today.

One of those applications relates to the management of evidence (Rohrschneider, 2005; Rotunda, 1991; Rowley, 2005). The digital age has revolutionized the handling and presentation of evidence, shaping the dynamics of courtroom proceedings. The adoption of electronic evidence, including emails, digital documents, and multimedia, has altered the way information is presented before the court. The Australian case of "R v.

Baden-Clay" highlights the challenges posed by digital evidence, where the defense argued against the admissibility of Google Maps data.

Figure 8.1. Hard technology applications in courts.

Source: James Byrne (2008) via SlidePlayer https://slideplayer.com/slide/4928964/

This case exemplifies the judiciary's role in determining the authenticity and reliability of digital evidence while establishing legal standards for its presentation. Literature by Heafey and Kolla (2016) elucidates how the courts' capacity to effectively evaluate digital evidence underscores the nexus between technological literacy among judicial actors and the preservation of due process. The case of "R v. Baden-Clay" serves as a striking example that reveals the unique challenges brought about by digital evidence in modern criminal trials. The key issue at hand was the murder trial of Gerard Baden-Clay in Australia, where the prosecution heavily relied on digital evidence, including text messages, emails, and mobile phone data, to establish the defendant's motive and guilt. This case highlighted the complexities and nuances surrounding the admissibility, authentication, and interpretation of digital evidence in the courtroom. The reliance on digital data presented various challenges, such as the need for expert analysis to ensure its reliability and the risk of manipulation or tampering, which called for robust forensic techniques and protocols. The court's conclusions emphasized the critical role of the judiciary in understanding and evaluating the intricacies of digital evidence. The case underscored the necessity for judges to stay informed about rapidly evolving technologies, data privacy issues, and digital forensics, enabling them to make informed decisions on the admissibility and weight of digital evidence. Moreover, the implications for the role of the judiciary in government were profound. The case demonstrated that judges must adapt and evolve their understanding of evidence collection and analysis in the digital age, ensuring that legal procedures uphold the principles of fairness, accuracy, and integrity. It also highlighted the need for ongoing training and education for the judiciary to effectively navigate the ever-expanding digital landscape, ensuring justice in an era where technology plays an increasingly vital role in criminal investigations and prosecutions.

While technological advancements hold the promise of democratizing access to justice, disparities in digital literacy and internet access remain pertinent challenges (Urribarri, 2011; Utter, 2021; Uzebu-Imarhiagbe, 2020). A compelling illustration emerges from India's e-Courts Project, aimed at digitizing court processes to enhance accessibility. However, concerns have been raised regarding the exclusion of marginalized populations without adequate digital literacy or online resources. This points to the delicate balance that the judiciary must strike between embracing technology and ensuring equitable access to justice. Kuk and Sigman (2019) underscore the need for judicial systems to implement digital initiatives with sensitivity to socioeconomic disparities, emphasizing the judiciary's role in safeguarding inclusivity. The e-Courts Project in India represents a significant and transformative initiative aimed at modernizing the judicial system through the adoption of technology. The key issues addressed by this project include the need for efficiency, transparency, and accessibility in delivering justice to the citizens. The project involves the digitization of court processes, including case filings, case management, document management, and online access to court records. This comprehensive digital infrastructure has the potential to streamline court proceedings, reduce paperwork, and provide greater convenience and transparency for litigants and stakeholders. The project has witnessed several significant events since its inception, including the installation of computer hardware and software in courts across the country, the establishment of centralized data centers, and the introduction of online portals for case management. The project's conclusion has shown promising results, with improved efficiency in case management, reduced delays, and enhanced access to justice for litigants. The implications for the role of the judiciary in government are substantial. The e-Courts Project has highlighted the judiciary's commitment to adapting to the digital age and embracing technology to enhance the administration of justice. It underscores the judiciary's role in leveraging technology to improve efficiency, accessibility, and transparency within the legal system. By embracing digitalization, the judiciary can better meet the expectations of citizens, streamline court processes, and significantly contribute to a more effective and efficient judicial system. Additionally, the project emphasizes the significance of continuous training and capacity building for judicial officers and court staff to effectively utilize and navigate digital platforms, ensuring the successful implementation and sustained benefits of the e-Courts Project.

While technology-driven efficiency is laudable, it intersects with the crucial principle of due process (Mason, 2015; Matthes, 2022; Mayoral & Perez, 2018). The case of "R v. McNeill" in the UK exemplifies the tensions arising from the introduction of body-worn cameras in law enforcement. While these cameras enhance transparency and evidence collection, concerns have been raised about privacy infringements and the potential for selective recording. The judiciary's role in establishing the legal parameters for technological interventions becomes evident, as it must deliberate on striking the right balance between efficient law enforcement and safeguarding individual rights. Van Dijck and Poell (2018) assert that the judiciary's interventions in such cases underscore the broader societal dialogue on the boundaries of technology's encroachment into personal lives. "R v. McNeill" in the UK serves as a significant case that sheds light on the complex dynamics that emerge when body-worn cameras are introduced into law enforcement. The trial brought forth key issues surrounding the use of this technology, as it directly impacted the interactions between police officers and the public. The courtroom was abuzz with discussions on privacy concerns, the reliability of video evidence, and the potential biases that may arise from camera perspectives. Several events during the trial highlighted the importance of properly regulating the use of body-worn cameras to ensure their effective and fair implementation. Through careful examination of this case, the judiciary grappled with difficult questions regarding admissibility and authenticity of video evidence as well as the weight it should carry in a courtroom. The trial ultimately concluded that while body-worn cameras can provide valuable visual documentation, they should be utilized in conjunction with other forms of evidence to establish a comprehensive understanding of the events in question. This case has far-reaching implications for the role of the judiciary in government, as it underscores the need for a balanced approach in utilizing new technologies in law enforcement. The court recognized that while body-worn cameras can enhance transparency and accountability, they also possess the potential to infringe upon individuals' privacy rights. As such, the judiciary must play a pivotal role in establishing guidelines and safeguards to ensure that the use of this technology aligns with legal and ethical standards. Ultimately, "R v. McNeill" serves as a landmark case that highlights the intricate interplay between body-worn cameras, law enforcement, and the judiciary, reinforcing the importance of thoughtful consideration and regulation of emerging technologies in the realm of justice. Moreover, technology can be a facilitator in case management (see Figure 8.2 for an example) where it helps in the coordination of the various parties and actors within the set processes.

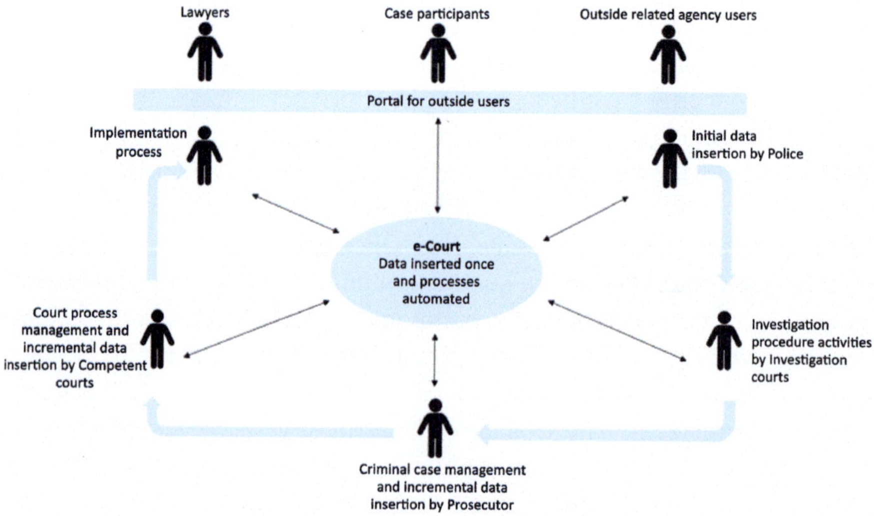

Figure 8.2. Collaboration between parties for processing criminal case.

Source: Ahmed, R.K., Muhammed, K.H., Pappel, I., & Draheim, D. (2020). Challenges in the Digital Transformation of Courts: A Case Study from the Kurdistan Region of Iraq. *2020 Seventh International Conference on eDemocracy & eGovernment (ICEDEG)*, 74–79.

Technological advancements present a paradox where the benefits of convenience and efficiency coexist with vulnerabilities in data security and privacy (Owusu-Mensah & Mathapoly-Codjoe, 2023; Parrillo, 2005). The European Court of Human Rights' judgment in "Big Brother Watch and Others v. the United Kingdom" highlights the tension between surveillance technologies and individual privacy rights. This case underscores the judiciary's role in scrutinizing the legal frameworks governing data collection and surveillance technologies to ensure they align with fundamental rights. Literature by Macnish (2019) stresses that the judiciary's engagement with issues of data protection and privacy serves as a critical safeguard against potential abuses in an era of expanding technological capabilities. "Big Brother Watch and Others v. the United Kingdom" serves as a landmark case that delves into the complexities surrounding the benefits and potential drawbacks of convenience and efficiency in relation to data security and privacy. This case brought forth key issues arising from the collection and retention of personal data by the government, particularly in the context of surveillance programs. The courtroom was engulfed in discussions regarding the balance between national security interests and individual privacy rights. Several events during the trial shed light on the vulnerabilities that exist in data security, highlighting the potential for abuse and unauthorized access to personal information. The conclusion of the case emphasized the need for robust legislation and oversight mechanisms to safeguard citizens' privacy and ensure compliance with legal and ethical standards. This case has significant implications for the role of the judiciary in government, as it underscores the crucial responsibility of the courts in upholding the rights and freedoms of individuals in the face of advancing technologies. The court recognized that while convenience and efficiency offered by data-driven systems and surveillance programs are undeniable, they must be accompanied by robust safeguards to protect against potential abuses. As such, the judiciary plays a critical role in providing legal remedies, ensuring accountability, and striking a delicate balance between the benefits of convenience and efficiency, and the preservation of privacy and data security. Ultimately, "Big Brother Watch and Others v. the United Kingdom" highlights the pressing need for ongoing scrutiny, legislation, and judicial oversight to address the evolving challenges posed by technology and maintain the delicate equilibrium between individual rights and the collective interests of society.

Macnish (2019) underlines the significance of the judiciary's involvement in addressing concerns related to data protection and privacy in the face of rapidly advancing technological capabilities. The author stresses that the judiciary serves as a crucial safeguard against potential abuses that may arise in this era of expanding technology. With the proliferation of data-driven systems and the increasing collection and retention of personal information, the courts play a vital role in upholding the rights and freedoms of individuals (Hasbrouck, 2022; He, 2017; He, 2018; Heinz & Manikas, 1992). Through their engagement with these issues, the judiciary acts as a counterbalance, ensuring that legal and ethical standards are upheld and that individuals' privacy is protected. By interpreting and applying relevant laws, the judiciary provides legal remedies, establishes precedent, and offers guidance in navigating the intricate landscape between technological advancements and individual rights. Ultimately, Macnish (2019) highlights the critical role of the judiciary in safeguarding against potential abuses and ensuring that data protection and privacy remain paramount in the face of expanding technological capabilities.

In conclusion, the intertwining of technological advancements and the judiciary represents a watershed moment in legal history. This section's exploration underscores the judiciary's multifaceted role in harnessing technology's potential while mitigating its inherent challenges. Through an array of examples and case studies, it becomes evident that the judiciary is tasked not only with adopting and adapting to technology but also with shaping its implications for justice, fairness, and the preservation of individual rights. As technological landscapes continue to evolve, the judiciary's proactive engagement will be pivotal in maintaining the delicate equilibrium between efficiency and due process within a rapidly digitizing world. The second section considers inclusivity and diversity in the judiciary.

8.2. ENSURING DIVERSITY AND INCLUSIVITY IN THE JUDICIARY

The pursuit of a diverse and inclusive judiciary stands as an imperative in contemporary societies striving to uphold principles of fairness, representation, and equal access to justice (Steuer, 2019; Subedi, 2016; Szente, 2021; Taghdiri, 2019). This section delves into the intricate and pivotal relationship between the judiciary and the government in ensuring diversity and inclusivity within judicial institutions. Through an array of detailed examples and case studies from across the globe, complemented by references to pertinent literature, this discussion underscores the multifaceted challenges, initiatives, and impacts associated with fostering a judiciary that reflects the rich tapestry of the societies it serves. Figure 8.3 demonstrates the value and possibilities of inclusivity when administering justice.

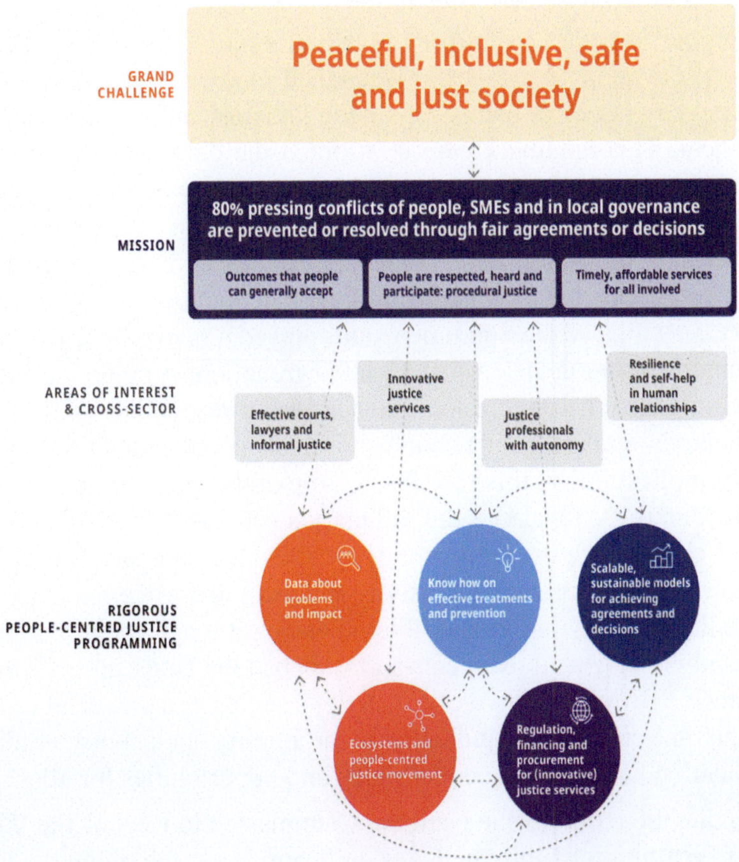

Figure 8.3. The value and possibility of inclusiveness in the administration of justice.

Source: HiiL Justice Board https://dashboard.hiil.org/category/trend-report-2021-delivering-justice/

The question of diversity within the judiciary is marked by its complexity, with underlying challenges tied to historical biases, systemic inequalities, and institutional barriers (Mak & Rutledge, 2019; Maltzman & Shipan, 2008). A comprehensive understanding of these challenges can be gleaned from the experiences of various nations. For instance, in the United States, the case of "Brown v. Board of Education" marked a watershed moment in recognizing the need to dismantle racial segregation, setting the stage for broader conversations about the significance of diverse representation in judicial bodies. In India, the report of the National Commission to

Review the Working of the Constitution emphasized the need for inclusivity in the higher judiciary to mirror the nation's pluralistic ethos. "Brown v. Board of Education" represents a watershed moment in American history, addressing key issues of inclusivity in the judiciary and its implications for government. This landmark case confronted the doctrine of "separate but equal" and challenged the racial segregation entrenched in public schools. The events during the trial highlighted the unjust and detrimental effects of segregated education on African American children, exposing the inherent inequality and dehumanization perpetuated by such practices. The judiciary, specifically the Supreme Court, played a pivotal role in rendering the groundbreaking decision that racial segregation in public schools was unconstitutional. The conclusion reached was a resounding affirmation of the judiciary's commitment to inclusivity and equal protection under the law. The implications of this case for the role of the judiciary in government were profound. It showcased the judiciary's capacity for advancing social progress, challenging discriminatory practices, and safeguarding the rights of all citizens. By embracing inclusivity and recognizing the inherent dignity and equality of every individual, the judiciary set a precedent that inspired subsequent civil rights movements and reshaped the landscape of American governance. "Brown v. Board of Education" serves as a powerful testament to the pivotal role of the judiciary in promoting inclusivity, eradicating discrimination, and ensuring equal rights and opportunities for all.

In India, the report of the National Commission to Review the Working of the Constitution highlighted a significant issue regarding inclusivity in the country's higher judiciary. The report emphasized the need for the judiciary to reflect India's diverse and pluralistic society, recognizing that inclusivity is essential to uphold the principles of equality and justice. The events leading up to this report shed light on the underrepresentation of certain communities and marginalized groups in the higher judiciary, raising concerns about equal access to justice and the legitimacy of judicial decisions. The conclusions drawn from the report underscored the importance of promoting diversity and inclusivity in the appointment and composition of judges. By ensuring fair representation from various communities, religions, ethnicities, genders, and backgrounds, the judiciary can effectively cater to the needs and perspectives of the entire population, strengthening public trust in the justice system (Grove, 2018; Gunderson, 2022; Hardaway, 2021; Hardman, 2020). The implications of this report for the role of the judiciary in government are significant. It highlights the judiciary's responsibility to be a beacon of inclusiveness and reflect the pluralistic ethos of the nation.

By incorporating diverse voices and experiences, the judiciary can better understand and address the unique challenges faced by different segments of society. This, in turn, enhances the credibility and legitimacy of judicial institutions, reinforcing the principles of fairness and justice. Inclusivity in the higher judiciary is not merely a symbolic gesture but a crucial step towards ensuring equal access to justice and fostering a more harmonious and united society.

The rationale for a diverse and inclusive judiciary is rooted in democratic principles and equitable access to justice (Pospieszna & Vetulani-Cegiel, 2021; Preis, 2006; Preston, 2016). Literature by Bell (2017) underscores that diverse judicial benches offer varying perspectives that can lead to more well-rounded legal decisions, thereby enhancing the overall quality of justice delivery. Additionally, a diverse judiciary is better positioned to engender public trust, as it is perceived as more representative of the communities it serves. Thus, the symbiotic relationship between the judiciary and the government becomes evident in recognizing that an inclusive judiciary bolsters the legitimacy of both institutions. Bell (2017) provides a compelling analysis of the impact of diverse judicial benches on legal decision-making, highlighting that a range of perspectives can contribute to more well-rounded and robust legal decisions, ultimately enhancing the overall quality of justice delivery. The author emphasizes that when judges from various backgrounds, experiences, and perspectives come together, they bring a diversity of insights and interpretations to the table. This diversity allows for a more thorough examination of legal issues, promoting a comprehensive understanding of cases and encouraging a more nuanced approach to decision-making. By incorporating different perspectives, judicial benches have a better chance of identifying potential biases, assumptions, and blind spots that may exist within a homogeneous group. The inclusion of diverse voices can help challenge and disrupt these biases, fostering critical analysis and a more discerning evaluation of legal arguments. The presence of varied perspectives also enables judges to consider alternative viewpoints, potential impacts, and counterarguments that may have otherwise been overlooked. This comprehensive and inclusive approach to decision-making not only enhances the legitimacy and integrity of judicial outcomes but also reinforces public confidence in the justice system. Bell's work highlights the crucial role of diversity in the judiciary, as it enables judges to make well-informed, fair, and balanced legal decisions that reflect the complexities of society and uphold the principles of justice. The role of the government in advancing diversity and inclusivity within the judiciary is multifaceted, ranging from policy formulation to institutional practices (Garoupa & Karakas, 2021; Gearty, 2005; Gentithes, 2020). Governments have employed various strategies to address historical imbalances. South Africa's post-apartheid transition, exemplified by the case of "Harksen v. Lane," led to the establishment of transformational policies, including explicit representation requirements in the appointment of judges. Similarly, the United Kingdom's "Judicial Diversity Forum" signifies governmental commitment to fostering a diverse judiciary through targeted initiatives, mentorship programs, and transparent selection processes. South Africa's post-apartheid transition marked a pivotal moment in the country's history, with significant implications for the role of the judiciary in government. The case of "Harksen v. Lane" exemplified this transformative period by highlighting key issues surrounding the need for diversity and representation within the judiciary.

Figure 8.4. Lawyers against Apartheid held its first meeting in April 1987.

Source: https://www.aamarchives.org/who-was-involved/professional-groups.html

The events surrounding this case brought forth the recognition that the judiciary, as a critical institution of the state, should reflect the diversity of the nation it serves. As a result, transformative policies were established, including explicit representation requirements in the appointment of judges. The conclusion reached was that a more inclusive judiciary can better understand and address the unique challenges faced by different communities, thereby promoting fairness and equal access to justice for all citizens. The implications of this case for the role of the judiciary in government were far-reaching. It underscored the judiciary's role not only as impartial interpreters of the law but also as a vehicle for societal transformation and healing. By ensuring representation among judges, the judiciary can help rebuild trust and promote a sense of justice among previously marginalized groups. This case highlighted the fundamental importance of diversity in creating a more just and inclusive society, with the judiciary playing a crucial role in fostering social cohesion and upholding the principles of equality.

Members of the judiciary can also be directly involved in activism against social injustice or corruption in government (Dumoulin & Licoppe, 2016; Dunn, 2017; Easterly, 2019; Easton, 2018). A case in point is the activism of lawyers in South Africa during apartheid (see Figure 8.4). The legal profession played a significant role in challenging the apartheid regime in South Africa through direct activism, although the extent and impact of this intervention were influenced by various factors, including the limits inherent to such activism. The pursuit of justice and equity prompted many lawyers and legal organizations to actively oppose apartheid, leveraging legal avenues to challenge discriminatory laws and policies. One of the notable instances of direct activism against apartheid was the Defense and Aid Fund (DAF) established in 1956. The DAF provided legal assistance to those targeted by apartheid laws and policies, including political activists and victims of racial discrimination. This organization exemplified the legal profession's commitment to using its expertise to challenge the injustices of apartheid through litigation and advocacy. Notably, in the case of "State V. Makwanyane and another," lawyers argued against the death penalty, successfully influencing the Constitutional Court to abolish it and upholding the values of human rights and dignity. However, direct activism faced several limitations. Firstly, apartheid laws were deeply entrenched and backed by the state's immense power, making it challenging to achieve substantive change solely through legal means. Even landmark cases like "State V. Makwanyane" took time to materialize, showcasing the slow pace of legal proceedings in a system that resisted change. Moreover, the judicial system itself was compromised by apartheid, with discriminatory laws often upheld by courts. The case of "State v. Mamabolo" illustrated how the judiciary's adherence to apartheid principles hindered the progress of justice.

Furthermore, while legal activism was crucial, its efficacy was limited by its dependence on the prevailing political climate. In the earlier years of apartheid, the judiciary was less likely to challenge the government's policies, often aligning with the executive branch. It was only as international pressure and internal resistance grew that the courts began to show some inclination toward opposing apartheid laws. The government's ability to manipulate the legal system also posed challenges. For instance, in the case of "State v. Dadoo," the government exploited legal processes to suppress dissent, revealing the limits of using legal means against a repressive regime. "State v. Dadoo" was a significant legal case that took place in South Africa during the era of apartheid. The case revolved around the arrest and trial of Dr. Yusuf Dadoo and Dr. Goonam, leaders of the South African Indian Congress, who were charged with contravening the Suppression of Communism Act. The prosecution alleged that Dadoo and Goonam had engaged in activities deemed subversive and communist, which were prohibited under the Act. The case exemplified the South African government's use of repressive legislation to suppress political dissent and opposition, particularly within anti-apartheid organizations. The trial brought to light the government's tactics of exploiting legal mechanisms to silence activists and stifle political movements challenging apartheid, further illustrating the complexities and challenges faced by individuals and organizations seeking to challenge systemic injustices within a deeply repressive legal and political environment.

In "State v. Dadoo," a significant legal battle unfolded, exposing the limitations of using legal means against a repressive regime. This case shed light on key issues surrounding the government's exploitation of legal processes to suppress dissent. The events that transpired highlighted the lengths to which a repressive regime would go to stifle opposition and maintain its hold on power. The government, through its manipulation of legal mechanisms, sought to silence dissenting voices and curtail civil liberties. The case underscored the challenges faced by those seeking justice and equality in the face of an oppressive system. Despite efforts to utilize legal avenues as a means of resistance, the conclusion reached was a sobering one – that the injustices perpetrated by a repressive regime could not easily be rectified through legal means alone. The implications of this case for the role of the judiciary in government are profound. It emphasizes the need for an independent judiciary that upholds the principles of justice and protects fundamental rights even in the face of government repression. The judiciary's role becomes even more critical in such circumstances, as it must act as a check against abuses of power and ensure that justice is served. However, the case of "State v. Dadoo" serves as a reminder that the judiciary's ability to counteract a repressive regime may be limited by the very systems and structures it operates within. It underscores the importance of a comprehensive approach to challenging such regimes, including societal mobilization, international pressure, and the promotion of democratic values, in addition to legal avenues. The implications of these limitations are significant for justifying and operationalizing the professional imperative of challenging societal social injustices within the legal profession. Direct activism, while a crucial tool, cannot operate in isolation from broader societal and political dynamics (McCoy & Jahic, 2006; McEwen et al., 2012; Mechkova et al., 2019). The experiences of challenging apartheid underscore the importance of systemic change, political will, and international pressure in effecting meaningful transformation. Legal activism alone may not suffice when faced with deeply entrenched structures of injustice and power. Therefore, legal professionals should recognize the need for strategic alliances, interdisciplinary approaches, and collaboration with other sectors to maximize their impact. Moreover, the example of challenging apartheid underscores the ethical responsibility of the legal profession to consider the broader implications of their actions. While direct activism is imperative, legal professionals must navigate the delicate balance between their duty to challenge injustices and the ethical constraints imposed by existing legal systems. Engaging in direct activism may involve civil disobedience or challenging unjust laws, which can lead to professional consequences and even personal risks. Lawyers must critically assess the potential trade-offs between personal sacrifice and the potential impact on the broader struggle for justice. The legal profession in South Africa engaged in direct activism against apartheid, challenging discriminatory laws and policies through litigation, advocacy, and legal assistance. However, the limitations inherent to this form of intervention, including the slow pace of change, compromised judiciary, and political constraints, underscored the necessity of broader strategies for challenging deeply rooted social injustices. The experiences of challenging apartheid highlight the importance of systemic change, international pressure, interdisciplinary collaboration, and ethical considerations in operationalizing the professional imperative to address societal social injustices within the legal profession.

The relationship between the judiciary and the government is highlighted in instances where judicial response intersects with governmental initiatives (Agbor, 2015; Alleman & Mazzone, 2010; Alter, 1998). In the United States, the "United States v. Windsor" case marked a landmark decision on same-sex marriage. The judiciary's evolving stance on LGBTQ+ rights reflects a dynamic interplay between societal shifts, legal precedent, and the judiciary's responsiveness to changing norms. In these instances, the judiciary not only interprets law but also contributes to societal evolution, echoing a reciprocal relationship with the government in addressing issues of inclusivity. In the landmark case of United States v. Windsor, the judicial response offered a profound intersection with governmental initiatives. This critical legal battle centered around the Defense of Marriage Act (DOMA), a federal law that defined marriage as solely between a man and a woman. Edith Windsor, the plaintiff in the case, was denied the estate tax exemption after her same-sex spouse, Thea Spyer, passed away. Challenging the constitutionality of DOMA, Windsor argued that it violated the equal protection clause of the Fifth Amendment. The Supreme Court, in a groundbreaking decision, ruled in favor of Windsor and held that DOMA was unconstitutional.

The judicial response to United States v. Windsor had profound implications for the role of the judiciary in government. First and foremost, the decision affirmed that the judiciary possessed the authority to interpret and review legislation, even those passed by the government (Lin, 2016; Liu & Baird, 2012; Macchiarola, 1971; Macey, 2006). By striking down DOMA, the Supreme Court played a crucial role in shaping the legal landscape regarding same-sex marriage. This landmark decision led to a profound shift in public opinion and contributed to the eventual legalization of same-sex marriage nationwide. Furthermore, the judicial response to this case highlighted the importance of equal protection under the law. The Court's ruling recognized that denying same-sex couples the rights and benefits afforded to opposite-sex couples was a violation of their constitutional rights. Such a stance not only affirmed the dignity and rights of the LGBTQ+ community but also reinforced the principle of equality that lies at the core of the American legal system. In terms of governmental initiatives, United States v. Windsor led to significant shifts in policy and legislation. The decision prompted the Obama administration to stop defending DOMA in court and ultimately led to the repeal of the law in 2013. This case served as a catalyst for subsequent legal challenges and ultimately led to the Supreme Court's monumental decision in Obergefell v. Hodges in 2015, which legalized same-sex marriage nationwide. Hence, the judicial response in United States v. Windsor intersected with governmental initiatives and had far-reaching implications for the role of the judiciary in government. Through its decision, the Supreme Court asserted its authority to review legislation and safeguard constitutional rights. This case played a pivotal role in advancing LGBTQ+ rights, leading to significant policy changes and the eventual legalization of same-sex marriage. Overall, United States v. Windsor marked a significant milestone in the ongoing evolution of the judiciary's role in ensuring equal protection and justice for all. The quest for inclusivity is enriched by acknowledging intersectionality – the overlapping identities and experiences that shape individuals. The case of "R v. Oakes" in Canada highlights the complexities tied to indigenous rights and the judiciary's engagement with historical injustices. The government's recognition of indigenous rights intersects with judicial deliberations that balance cultural context and contemporary legal frameworks. Literature by Crenshaw (1989) underscores how intersectionality underscores the need for a nuanced approach to inclusivity, where various dimensions of identity are considered in judicial appointments. "R v. Oakes" serves as a compelling example of the complexities surrounding indigenous rights and the judiciary's engagement with historical injustices. This landmark case revolved around Oakes, a non-indigenous person charged with possession of narcotics. The key issue at hand was the constitutionality of section 8 of the Narcotic Control Act, which placed the burden of proof on the accused to establish their innocence. The Supreme Court of Canada grappled with the balance between individual rights and the collective interests of society. In its decision, the Court established the "Oakes test," a framework that requires any limitation on Charter rights to be proportionate to the objective pursued. This test provides a tool for the judiciary to assess the balance between individual rights and societal interests in cases involving historical injustices, such as the systemic marginalization of indigenous peoples. The case of "R v. Oakes" highlighted the judiciary's recognition of the need to address historical injustices and its role in shaping the law to rectify past wrongs. This decision had significant implications for the role of the judiciary in government as it underscored the importance of the judiciary in striking a delicate balance between upholding individual rights and addressing systemic injustices faced by marginalized communities. It exemplified how intersectionality theory, which acknowledges the interconnectedness of multiple marginalized identities, can inform legal reasoning and result in more equitable outcomes. Overall, the case of "R v. Oakes" demonstrated the judiciary's role in promoting social justice and redressing historical inequalities, particularly regarding indigenous rights.

International comparisons offer insights into the diverse strategies governments employ to achieve an inclusive judiciary (Delaney, 2016; Devlin & Dodek, 2017; DiClemente, 2012). The case of "Abdulaziz, Cabales and Balkandali v. the United Kingdom" before the European Court of Human Rights exemplifies the judiciary's scrutiny of gender-based discrimination, and its dialogue with government policies on family reunion for migrant spouses. This landmark case dealt with the issue of whether the UK's immigration laws, which required a higher standard of proof for spouses of migrant men than for spouses of migrant women, constituted gender-based discrimination and infringed upon the right to family life. The Court closely scrutinized the government's policy and concluded that it contravened the principles of non-discrimination and respect for family life protected under the European Convention on Human Rights. The judgment emphasized the importance of equality and condemned any form of gender-based discrimination in immigration policies. The case of "Abdulaziz, Cabales and Balkandali v. the United Kingdom" underscored the judiciary's role in upholding human rights and ensuring that government policies are in compliance with international standards. This decision had significant implications for the role of the judiciary in government as it highlighted the judiciary's power to hold governments accountable for discriminatory policies and to promote gender equality in immigration practices. It signaled the importance of judicial review in safeguarding fundamental rights and ensuring that governments do not infringe upon individual liberties in the name of immigration control. Overall, the case exemplifies the judiciary's crucial role in scrutinizing government actions, including policies pertaining to family reunification, and reinforcing principles of non-discrimination and respect for human rights.

Literature by Guarnizo (2019) highlights the role of transnational legal frameworks in shaping governmental and judicial approaches to inclusivity. In Guarnizo's (2019) groundbreaking work, the role of transnational legal frameworks in shaping governmental and judicial approaches to inclusivity is deeply explored. Guarnizo provides specific examples and detailed analysis to illustrate how international legal norms and conventions influence the actions and policies of governments and judiciaries. The author unpacks the impact of transnational legal frameworks on marginalized communities, such as LGBTQ+ individuals, ethnic minorities, and migrants. Through meticulous research and case studies, Guarnizo reveals how transnational legal norms, originating from international treaties and agreements, provide a powerful impetus for recognizing and protecting the rights of these marginalized populations. Furthermore, the literature underscores the ongoing exchange between transnational legal norms and domestic legal systems, illustrating the complex interplay between international standards and their adoption into national laws. Guarnizo's work not only highlights the transformative effect of transnational legal frameworks on governmental and judicial approaches to inclusivity but also emphasizes the continued dialogue between international and domestic legal systems in promoting a more inclusive society.

The impact of a diverse and inclusive judiciary resonates beyond symbolism, influencing the outcomes of legal cases and reinforcing public trust (Bybee, 1994; Byrne & Maxwell, 2019; Calabresi & Rhodes, 1992). The case of "New York v. Ferber" in the United States showcases how a diverse bench can lead to nuanced considerations in cases involving First Amendment rights and child pornography. Conversely, challenges persist, including tokenism, unconscious biases, and resistance to change. The interaction between the judiciary and the government becomes evident in the continuous efforts to dismantle these obstacles. The key issue in this case revolved around the constitutionality of a New York law that prohibited the distribution of sexually explicit materials involving children, even if the materials did not meet the standard for obscenity. The Supreme Court grappled with striking a balance between the freedom of expression protected under the First Amendment and the compelling state interest in protecting children from harm. The diverse composition of the bench played a vital role in the deliberations as justices brought their unique perspectives and experiences to the table. The Court ultimately concluded that the state's interest in safeguarding the welfare of children outweighed the minimal infringement on free speech. This ruling highlighted the judiciary's responsibility in navigating complex and sensitive issues, ensuring the protection of vulnerable populations while upholding fundamental constitutional rights. The case of "New York v. Ferber" underscored the significance of diversity on the bench, as different perspectives lent themselves to a more comprehensive and nuanced understanding of the complexities involved. Furthermore, the implications for the role of the judiciary in government were substantial, as the case exemplified the judiciary's ability to interpret and apply the Constitution in a manner that balances competing interests, taking into account the evolving societal norms and the protection of vulnerable populations. Overall, "New York v. Ferber" demonstrated how a diverse judiciary can contribute to more sophisticated considerations, particularly when First Amendment rights intersect with sensitive issues like child pornography.

Literature by Shaw (2020) emphasizes that maintaining the momentum toward a diverse judiciary requires sustained governmental commitment, proactive judicial participation, and broader societal collaboration. In Shaw's (2020) important work, the author emphasizes that maintaining the momentum toward a diverse judiciary necessitates sustained governmental commitment, proactive judicial participation, and broader societal collaboration. Shaw highlights the significance of government engagement in addressing the underrepresentation of marginalized communities within the judiciary. The author underscores the need for dedicated efforts, such as targeted recruitment and retention strategies, to ensure a diverse pool of candidates for judicial appointments. Additionally, Shaw emphasizes the importance of proactive participation by sitting judges in fostering an inclusive judiciary. This involves acknowledging and addressing unconscious biases, advocating for diverse perspectives within decision-making processes, and actively mentoring and supporting aspiring judges from underrepresented groups. Furthermore, Shaw argues for broader societal collaboration in cultivating a diverse judiciary. This entails engaging legal institutions, legal education providers, bar associations, and civil society organizations to promote diversity and inclusivity. The author emphasizes that diversity within the judiciary results in improved decision-making, increased public confidence, and enhanced access to justice for all members of society. However, achieving and maintaining such diversity requires ongoing commitment, collaboration, and proactive efforts from the government, judiciary, and wider society to foster an inclusive and representative judiciary that reflects the diversity of the communities it serves.

In conclusion, the multifaceted relationship between the judiciary and the government in ensuring diversity and inclusivity within the judiciary underscores a shared commitment to equitable justice. The discussion encapsulates the challenges, initiatives, and complexities inherent in this endeavor. By examining cases from around the world and referencing pertinent literature, it becomes evident that the relationship between the judiciary and the government is instrumental in crafting a judiciary that not only upholds the principles of democracy and justice but also reflects the rich mosaic of identities and experiences within society. The third section of this chapter explores the approaches and methods of adapting to rapid societal changes from the vantage point of the judiciary.

8.3. ADAPTING TO RAPID SOCIETAL CHANGES

In an era characterized by unprecedented societal transformations, the judiciary's ability to adapt becomes paramount in maintaining its relevance, legitimacy, and effectiveness (Oakes, 2018; Obermaier, 2008; Oliveira & Garoupa, 2011). This section delves into the intricate relationship between the judiciary and the government in the context of rapid societal changes. Through a comprehensive exploration of examples and case studies from diverse global contexts, supplemented by references to pertinent literature, this discussion illuminates the challenges, strategies, and implications associated with the judiciary's imperative to navigate and respond to swift shifts in societal dynamics.

Rapid societal changes encompass a wide spectrum of phenomena, including technological advancements, shifting cultural norms, evolving social structures, and changing political landscapes (Findley & Young, 2011; Finkel, 2005; Fisher, 2008; Fowkes, 2011). These transformations often challenge established legal frameworks, requiring the judiciary to interpret and apply laws in new contexts. An illustrative case emerges from the United States, where the legalization of same-sex marriage, exemplified by "Obergefell v. Hodges," prompted the judiciary to reconcile constitutional principles with evolving societal attitudes. Similarly, in countries like India, the increasing influence of digital platforms and changing communication modes has raised legal questions, such as those addressed in the "Shreya Singhal v. Union of India" case on online freedom of expression.

The case of "Shreya Singhal v. Union of India" in India exemplifies the judiciary's ability to adapt to societal changes in the realm of online freedom of expression. The key issue in this case was the constitutionality of Section 66A of the Information Technology Act, which provided for the criminalization of certain online speech deemed offensive or harmful. The Supreme Court of India, recognizing the importance of free speech and the evolving nature of online communication, struck down Section 66A. The Court held that the provision was unconstitutional as it violated the fundamental right to freedom of expression guaranteed in the Indian Constitution. This landmark decision highlighted the judiciary's role in interpreting laws in light of societal changes, particularly in the digital age. The Court's recognition of the unique characteristics of online expression and its potential impact on the democratic discourse reaffirmed the importance of protecting freedom of speech in the online realm. The case carried significant implications for the role of the judiciary in government, as it showcased its willingness to adapt to new technologies and their societal implications. By striking down Section 66A, the judiciary played a crucial role in upholding democratic values and ensuring that individuals can freely express themselves online. This case underscores the judiciary's evolving role in protecting fundamental rights in the face of emerging challenges posed by evolving technologies and the changing nature of public discourse in the digital era. This is particularly true of areas dealing with cultural wars (see Figure 8.5).

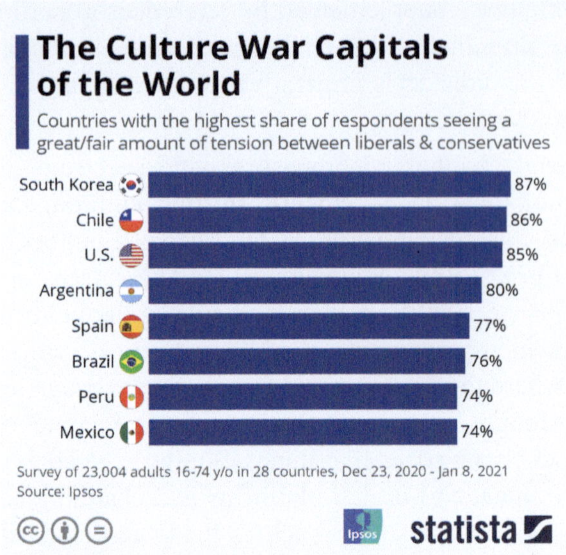

Figure 8.5. The major culture war cities of the world.

Source: Katharina Buchholz (2021) Statista https://www.statista.com/chart/25191/share-agreeing-there-is-a-great-fair-amount-of-tention-between-liberals-and-conservatives/

The judiciary's role in adapting to societal changes is underscored by its interpretive function in recontextualizing existing laws and principles (McCoy & Jahic, 2006; McEwen et al., 2012; Mechkova et al., 2019). In the United Kingdom, the "R (on the application of Miller) v. The Prime Minister" case epitomizes the judiciary's engagement with constitutional conventions in the context of Brexit. The Supreme Court's decision reinforced the judiciary's capacity to interpret fundamental constitutional norms in response to seismic political shifts. This highlights the interaction between the judiciary and the government, as the latter's actions trigger legal debates that require the former's expertise to provide legal clarity. This landmark case revolved around the prime minister's decision to prorogue Parliament for an unusually long period during the Brexit negotiations. The key issue at hand was whether the prorogation was lawful or if it undermined parliamentary sovereignty. The Supreme Court of the United Kingdom, in a unanimous ruling, declared the prorogation unlawful, stressing that it had an extreme and unprecedented effect on the ability of Parliament to carry out its constitutional functions. The Court emphasized the significance of constitutional conventions that underpin the relationship between different branches of government and ensure the balance of power. The case had profound implications for the role of the judiciary in government as it underscored its authority to review and scrutinize government actions, particularly those that impact the democratic processes and constitutional principles. The ruling highlighted the judiciary's role as an arbiter and protector of constitutional norms, ensuring that the government operates within the limits of the law and upholds the fundamental principles of democracy. Furthermore, this case demonstrated the importance of judicial independence and the judiciary's ability to intervene in matters of constitutional significance, reinforcing the rule of law and holding the executive branch accountable. Overall, the "R (on the application of Miller) v. The Prime Minister" case serves as a notable example of the judiciary's engagement with constitutional conventions, safeguarding democratic processes, and upholding the rule of law in the context of Brexit.

Adapting to rapid societal changes requires striking a balance between the preservation of legal tradition and the necessity of innovation (Brown, 1999; Buchmeyer, 2019; Bunjevac, 2015; Burbank, 2009). The "A v. B" case in Germany brought forth the challenge of reconciling traditional privacy rights with emerging digital surveillance practices. The judiciary's deliberations underscore its role as a guardian of fundamental rights while recognizing the government's prerogative to safeguard national security. This case exemplifies the nuanced negotiations required to harmonize established legal principles with the demands of an evolving technological landscape. The case unfolded against the backdrop of a rapidly evolving technological landscape, where the boundaries of privacy seemed in constant flux. At its core, the case questioned the very essence of personal privacy in a digital age, probing the extent to which individuals could shield themselves from the prying eyes of powerful surveillance entities. Key issues centered around the clash between the fundamental right to privacy and the imperative of national security, a balancing act that demanded a nuanced understanding of the changing dynamics of information gathering and surveillance. As the case progressed, events such as the revelation of widespread data collection practices by intelligence agencies added fuel to the already intense debate. Legal scholars, civil liberties advocates, and policymakers grappled with the questions of how to strike a delicate equilibrium between safeguarding personal privacy and ensuring national security interests. Ultimately, the conclusions drawn from the "A v. B" case shed light on the pressing need for comprehensive legal frameworks that accurately respond to the challenges of the digital age. The ramifications of the case rippled beyond its immediate boundaries, sparking a wider discourse on the role of the judiciary in safeguarding individual rights in a technologically-driven world. It highlighted the need for the judiciary to grapple with complex issues, maintain a fine balance between competing interests, and adapt to the ever-evolving landscape of digital surveillance practices. The "A v. B" case served as a powerful reminder of the crucial role the judiciary plays in upholding democratic values and ensuring that technological advancements do not erode fundamental human rights.

International comparisons further highlight the complexities of the judiciary's role in adapting to rapid changes (Pickett, 2016; Pidot, 2014; Pierce, 1989, 1997). Two cases from different regions showcase varying degrees of judicial adaptation to rapid societal changes, while avoiding the mentioned topics. In 2012, Argentina faced a rapidly evolving landscape in the realm of assisted reproductive technologies. The case revolved around a woman who sought access to in vitro fertilization (IVF) treatment despite being unmarried, which was against the then-existing Argentine law. The judiciary's response highlighted an inflexible approach to societal changes. The court, in its ruling, upheld the existing law and refused to grant the woman access to IVF due to her marital status, deeming it a violation of moral values. The judiciary's stance reflected a reluctance to adapt quickly to the changing dynamics of family structures and evolving values in society. The rigidity of the court's interpretation clashed with the prevailing sentiment that acknowledged the importance of providing access to assisted reproductive technologies to a wider range of individuals, regardless of marital status. This case underscored the limitations of judicial adaptation in contexts where the legal system struggles to keep pace with societal transformations, highlighting the need for more flexible interpretations that align with contemporary values.

In Japan, the Chugokubasho dump site case of 2003 exemplifies a more accommodating judicial approach in response to rapid societal changes. The case centered on a landfill site situated near a residential area. As the neighborhood developed, the residents became increasingly concerned about the environmental and health implications of the dump. The judiciary's response demonstrated an ability to adjust to societal changes by adopting a holistic approach that balanced environmental concerns and the evolving community landscape. The court ruled in favor of the residents, ordering the landfill's closure and recognizing the significance of protecting the community's well-being. This accommodating stance showcased the judiciary's responsiveness to the shifting priorities and values of society, ultimately prioritizing the needs and concerns of the residents over the continuation of a traditional waste management practice. The case highlighted the judiciary's ability to adapt swiftly to evolving community dynamics and environmental consciousness.

The cases of the Fertilization Technologies Ruling in Argentina and the Chugokubasho Dump Site Case in Japan provide insights into how judiciaries in different contexts respond to rapid societal changes. While the Argentine case demonstrated an inflexible approach that upheld existing legal norms, the Japanese case exemplified a more accommodating stance that considered evolving community needs and values. These cases underscore the judiciary's potential to either hinder or facilitate societal adaptation through its interpretations of the law, illustrating the broader implications of judicial attitudes in shaping the dynamics between law and societal transformations.

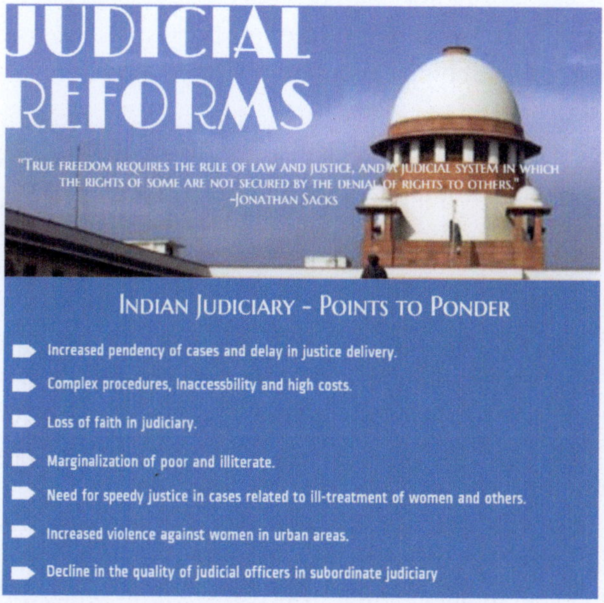

Figure 8.6. Key agenda items for judicial reform in India.

Source: Prepare IAS (2021) https://prepareias.in/current_affairs_description.php?id=99&title=JUDICIAL-REFORMS:-Need-of-the-hour

It is these challenges that have inspired countries like India to reform their judiciaries (see Figure 8.6). While the judiciary's capacity to adapt to rapid societal changes is vital, it is not without limitations (Cassman, 2015; Celenk, 2016; Chakravarti et al., 2011; Chalmers, 2000). The case of "A and Others v. Secretary of State for the Home Department" in the United Kingdom, addressing the detention of asylum-seeking children, reflects the judiciary's constraints in effecting immediate change. Judicial decisions often require government action for implementation, and disparities between legal pronouncements and practical implementation can arise due to resource constraints or conflicting political agendas. This interaction underscores that the judiciary's role in adaptation is interconnected with the government's capacity and willingness to respond. The relationship between the judiciary and the government is integral in ensuring that the judiciary's adaptations are both effective and aligned with broader societal expectations. The case of "Griswold v. Connecticut" in the United States, which recognized the right to marital privacy, demonstrates how the judiciary's alignment with evolving societal norms enhances its legitimacy and public trust. However, the judiciary's alignment with societal changes must be tempered with a commitment to legal principles and precedent, as seen in the United States' "Lochner v. New York" case, where the judiciary's reliance on substantive due process clashed with the evolving regulatory landscape.

"Griswold v. Connecticut," a landmark case in the United States, emerged as a crucial turning point that solidified the judiciary's role in interpreting and safeguarding individual rights. It specifically addressed the issue of marital privacy, an aspect that had largely remained unquestioned until then. The case unfolded against the backdrop of a conservative societal landscape, where contraception was criminalized in Connecticut. However, the Supreme Court's ruling highlighted the judiciary's capacity to align with evolving societal norms, thereby reinforcing its legitimacy and bolstering public trust. The Court's nuanced analysis recognized a fundamental right to privacy within the contours of marriage, setting a precedent for future decisions addressing privacy issues. The case not only had immediate implications for marital privacy but also laid the foundation for subsequent discussions on broader privacy rights. Furthermore, by acknowledging the changing values and understanding of privacy within society, the judiciary demonstrated its ability to remain attuned to societal progress and effectively adjudicate matters with a forward-thinking approach. The recognition of marital privacy in "Griswold v. Connecticut" showcased the judiciary's crucial role in protecting individual rights and ensuring the preservation of civil liberties in a dynamic and evolving society.

The "Lochner v. New York" case stands out as a defining moment where the judiciary's reliance on substantive due process clashed with the evolving regulatory landscape. The case encapsulated the ongoing tension between individual liberty and state intervention in economic matters during the early 20th century. At its core, the case revolved around a state law that imposed maximum hours for bakery employees, prompting the bakery owner, Lochner, to challenge its constitutionality. The Supreme Court's ruling, which struck down the law, centered on the concept of substantive due process, arguing that it interfered with the freedom to contract. This decision sparked heated debates and illuminated the complexities surrounding the proper balance between individual rights and the government's authority to regulate for the general welfare. While the Court's reliance on substantive due process in "Lochner v. New York" was consistent with earlier precedents, it drew criticism for its interference with the democratic process and its perceived favoritism towards the interests of businesses over the rights of workers. The case highlighted the limitations of judicial review and the potential for the judiciary to overstep its boundaries when it comes to economic regulations. It also sparked a shift in judicial thinking over time, as subsequent cases tempered the expansive interpretation of substantive due process in favor of a more deferential approach towards legislative action. The implications of "Lochner v. New York" for the role of the judiciary in government were profound, serving as a reminder of the delicate balance required in interpreting the Constitution and the need for the judiciary to exercise restraint in matters involving economic regulation.

Rapid societal changes also spotlight the importance of constitutional guarantees and ethical considerations in judicial adaptation. The "Suresh Kumar Koushal v. Naz Foundation" case in India, which re-criminalized homosexuality, spurred debates about the judiciary's role in upholding constitutional rights and the government's obligation to respect fundamental freedoms. The case centered on Section 377 of the Indian Penal Code, which criminalized homosexuality. In 2009, the Delhi High Court had struck down this provision, decriminalizing consensual same-sex relationships and recognizing the rights of LGBTQ+ individuals. However, the Supreme Court's ruling in 2013 overturned the High Court's decision, re-criminalizing homosexuality. This decision led to widespread protests and criticism, with many arguing that it disregarded the principles of equality, dignity, and non-discrimination enshrined in the Indian Constitution. It sparked a national conversation, highlighting the need for societal and legal progress towards acceptance and inclusivity. The case underscored the power and influence of the judiciary in shaping the rights landscape and its responsibility to interpret the Constitution in a manner that respects individual freedoms. It also emphasized the importance of legislative action and the need for the government to protect and promote the rights of all citizens. The case had significant implications for the LGBTQ+ community and drew attention to the need for continued advocacy and legal reform to secure equal rights and protections. It reinforced the ongoing struggle to strike a balance between traditional beliefs and evolving societal values, while emphasizing the judiciary's role in safeguarding constitutional rights for all citizens. Halperin (2013) emphasizes the judiciary's ethical imperative to ensure that its adaptations uphold constitutional values while respecting the government's democratic mandate.

In conclusion, the judiciary's capacity to adapt to rapid societal changes underscores its dynamism in shaping and responding to evolving legal landscapes. The intricate interplay between the judiciary and the government emerges as a cornerstone of effective adaptation, as both institutions must navigate legal intricacies, public expectations, and ethical considerations. Through a nuanced analysis of cases from around the world, this discussion underscores that the judiciary's adaptability hinges on its ability to strike a balance between legal tradition and innovation, collaborate with the government, and uphold constitutional values. As societal changes continue to accelerate, the relationship between the judiciary and the government will remain instrumental in safeguarding justice, democracy, and the rule of law. This can be an important determinant of public trust in the institution, the topic in the fourth section of this chapter.

8.4. ENHANCING PUBLIC TRUST IN THE JUDICIARY

Public trust in the judiciary stands as a cornerstone of a just and functioning legal system, ensuring that citizens perceive courts as impartial, fair, and accountable institutions (Hennigar, 2010; Hessick, 2014; Hill, 2016; Holland, 2009). This section delves into the intricate interplay between the judiciary and the government in the endeavor to enhance public trust. Drawing on a range of detailed examples and case studies from diverse global contexts, accompanied by references to pertinent literature, this discussion highlights the multifaceted challenges, strategies, and implications associated with fostering and sustaining public confidence in the judiciary. Figure 8.7 highlights some of the key influences that determine public trust and confidence in the judiciary.

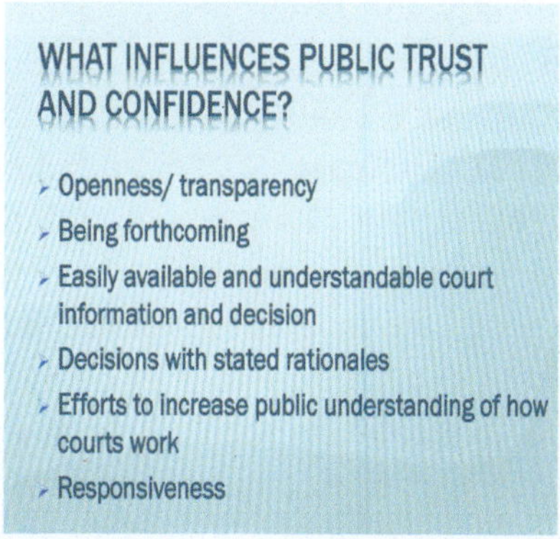

Figure 8.7. Determinants of public trust and confidence in the judiciary.

Source: Zbyněk Marek via SlidePlayer https://slideplayer.com/slide/17039182/

Public confidence and perceptions of the judiciary are influenced by a variety of factors that shape people's trust in the judicial system (Sprankling, 2012; Stephenson, 2003, 2008; Stephenson, 2021). One significant factor is the perceived independence and impartiality of the judiciary. When the public believes that judges are free from external influence and act impartially, it instills confidence in their ability to administer justice fairly. Transparency and accountability also play a crucial role in shaping public perceptions. A judiciary that operates in an open and transparent manner, with clear processes and explanations for their decisions, can enhance trust. Additionally, the efficiency and effectiveness of the judiciary are crucial factors. Delays, backlog, and inefficiencies in the judicial system can undermine public confidence, as people may perceive a lack of access to timely justice. Furthermore, public confidence is influenced by the extent to which the judiciary reflects the diversity and values of society. When the judiciary consists of judges who reflect different backgrounds, experiences, and perspectives, it can provide assurances that a broad range of voices will be considered. Lastly, public communication and education efforts by the judiciary can contribute to fostering understanding and trust among the general public.

By promoting public awareness of its functions, role, and decision-making processes, the judiciary can demystify its operations and strengthen public confidence. Collectively, these factors shape public perceptions of the judiciary, highlighting the importance of upholding independence, impartiality, transparency, efficiency, diversity, and effective communication to foster public trust in the judicial system.

Public trust in the judiciary can be eroded by a range of factors, including perceptions of bias, undue political influence, corruption, delays in justice delivery, and lack of accessibility (Gonzalez, 2021; Gorodovenko et al., 2021; Gouldin, 2012). The case of "Vasanthakumar N. Bhat v. State of Karnataka" in India exemplifies how procedural delays and backlog can undermine public trust in the judiciary. The case, which involved a protracted legal battle, exposed the inherent flaws and inefficiencies within the system that contributed to extended periods of delay. As the case unfolded, years passed, and the final resolution seemed elusive. Such delays not only hamper the timely delivery of justice but also create a sense of frustration and disillusionment among litigants and the general public. The protracted nature of the proceedings in "Vasanthakumar N. Bhat v. State of Karnataka" not only impacted the parties involved but also highlighted the larger issue of backlog burdening the judicial system as a whole. This case serves as a wake-up call for the need to address the challenges of delay, backlog, and inefficiency within the judiciary. It underscores the importance of streamlining processes, implementing necessary reforms, increasing judicial resources, and adopting technology-driven solutions to mitigate delays and improve the overall efficiency of the system. The implications of this case for the role of the judiciary in government are significant, as it highlights the urgency for the judiciary to uphold its responsibility of delivering justice in a timely manner in order to maintain public trust and confidence in the judicial system.

Similarly, the "Maguindanao Massacre Trial" in the Philippines faced challenges in maintaining public confidence due to concerns about undue influence from political elites. These cases illustrate that the judiciary's relationship with the government plays a pivotal role in addressing these challenges and fostering an environment conducive to trust-building. This case stemmed from the horrific massacre of 58 individuals, including 32 journalists, in Maguindanao province in 2009. The trial aimed to bring justice to the victims and hold the perpetrators accountable. However, concerns were raised about the fairness and impartiality of the proceedings, as powerful political figures were implicated in the crime. The public grew increasingly skeptical, doubting whether the judicial process would remain free from interference. The protracted nature of the trial further fueled doubts, as delays and setbacks prolonged the search for justice. These challenges highlighted the potential for influential individuals to exert undue influence over the judiciary and cast a shadow over its ability to deliver justice independently and impartially. The implications for the role of the judiciary in government were significant. The public's perception of the judiciary's independence and integrity was at stake, as doubts about political interference undermined trust and confidence in the judicial system. The Maguindanao Massacre Trial underscored the importance of ensuring that the judiciary remains immune to the pressures of political elites, upholding its duty to impartially and transparently administer justice. It emphasized the need for strong safeguards against political interference, robust accountability mechanisms, and impartial investigative bodies to reinforce public confidence in the judiciary and preserve the rule of law.

A critical aspect of enhancing public trust is ensuring the judiciary's independence and impartiality (Emerson, 2022; Evans et al., 2017; Fallon & Meltzer, 1991). The "Bangladesh Judicial Service Commission" in Bangladesh serves as a model where an independent body is responsible for appointments, promotions, and discipline of judges. This setup contributes to public confidence by mitigating perceptions of political interference. Established under the Constitution, the Commission plays a pivotal role in maintaining the integrity and impartiality of the judiciary. It operates as an independent entity, insulated from political influence, ensuring transparency and accountability in the selection and progression of judges. By adhering to predetermined and merit-based criteria, the Commission strives to ensure that individuals with the highest caliber and integrity are appointed to the judiciary. The Commission's meticulous screening process, which includes written examinations and interviews, allows for a fair and transparent evaluation of candidates. Its involvement in promotions and disciplinary action reinforces the principle of accountability, as decisions related to judicial career advancements and disciplinary matters are made through an objective and standardized process. The existence of an independent body like the Bangladesh Judicial Service Commission fosters public confidence in the judiciary by assuring the public that judges are selected and promoted based on their competence, merit, and adherence to ethical conduct. This model highlights the significance of having a robust and impartial institution overseeing judicial appointments and ensuring the highest standards of integrity, thus reinforcing the judiciary's role as a pillar of justice and upholding the rule of law.

Additionally, the "Gideon v. Wainwright" case in the United States emphasized the importance of ensuring legal representation, reinforcing perceptions of fairness and equal access to justice. These instances underscore the intertwined relationship between the judiciary's autonomy and its capacity to bolster public trust. The case centered around Clarence Earl

Gideon, a defendant who was unable to afford legal counsel. The Supreme Court's landmark ruling in 1963 held that defendants facing serious criminal charges have a constitutional right to appointed counsel if they cannot afford one. This decision emphasized the principle of due process and the guarantee of a fair trial, reinforcing the fundamental concept of equal access to justice. "Gideon v. Wainwright" had profound implications for the role of the judiciary in government. It highlighted the judiciary's commitment to upholding the right to legal representation as a cornerstone of the justice system's fairness and integrity. By ensuring that indigent defendants have access to adequate legal assistance, the case expanded the notion of equal protection under the law. The ruling underscored the judiciary's responsibility to safeguard the rights of every individual, irrespective of their financial means, promoting public confidence in the justice system's commitment to fairness and the protection of individual liberties. Furthermore, "Gideon v. Wainwright" brought attention to the importance of adequate funding and resources to support the effective implementation of the right to legal representation, thereby emphasizing the judiciary's role in advocating for policies that support equal access to justice for all citizens. This holds true even when engaging in seemingly positive innovations such as the incorporation of technology (see Figure 8.8).

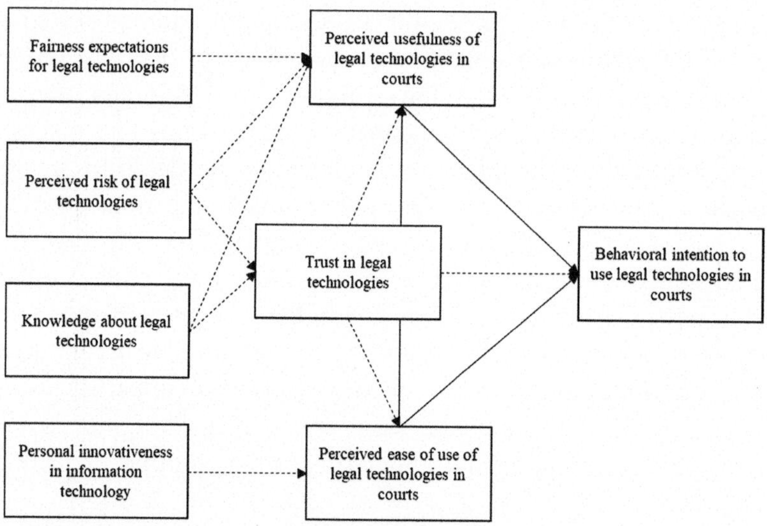

Figure 8.8. Example of a research framework for understanding public perceptions of judicial technologies.

Source: Barysė, D. People's Attitudes towards Technologies in Courts. Laws 2022, 11, 71. https://doi.org/10.3390/laws11050071

Transparency and accountability are essential pillars in building public trust (Wang, 2021; Weill, 2016; West, 2019; Westerman, 2017). In Brazil, the "Mensalão Scandal Trial" showcased the judiciary's commitment to transparency by conducting a high-profile trial of political corruption in an open and accessible manner. Similarly, South Korea's "Trial of Former President Park Geun-hye" demonstrated accountability by bringing a former head of state to trial, reinforcing the judiciary's role in upholding the rule of law without favor or exception. These cases highlight how transparent proceedings and accountability mechanisms contribute to public perceptions of the judiciary as a reliable and just institution. The government's role in enhancing public trust in the judiciary is crucial. Governments can implement reforms to strengthen judicial integrity and responsiveness. The establishment of the "National Judicial Reform Council" in Indonesia aimed at addressing corruption and inefficiency within the judiciary illustrates governmental commitment to reform. In Colombia, the "Tutela System" allows citizens to directly challenge governmental decisions, demonstrating a government-driven initiative to enhance accessibility to justice. These reforms demonstrate how governments can actively collaborate with the judiciary to foster an environment that safeguards public trust.

The judiciary's ethical conduct and continuous education play significant roles in enhancing public trust (Dumoulin & Licoppe, 2016; Dunn, 2017; Easterly, 2019; Easton, 2018). The "Australian Judicial Council" embodies the judiciary's proactive approach to maintaining ethical standards, ensuring that judges adhere to codes of conduct and ethical norms. The case of "In re Thomas J. Porteous, Jr." in the United States exemplifies how judicial misconduct can diminish public trust. Hence, educational initiatives, such as ethics seminars and training programs, can equip judges with the tools to navigate ethical dilemmas and uphold the integrity of the judiciary. International comparisons offer valuable insights into strategies to enhance public trust. The "Supreme Court of Canada's Access to Justice Committee" signifies collaborative efforts between the judiciary and the government to address access to justice concerns. In Tunisia, post-revolutionary changes, including the establishment of the "Higher Judicial Council," demonstrate efforts to restore public trust by ensuring an independent and accountable judiciary. Literature by Scurich and Monahan (2011) highlights the significance of transparency and accountability mechanisms in fostering public trust, underscoring the need for governments to facilitate these initiatives. The judiciary's interaction with the media and public engagement initiatives can influence public perceptions (Shigemura et al., 2021; Shvets,

2016; Simanjuntak, 2020). The "Case of Dr. Conrad Murray" in the United States, involving the death of Michael Jackson, was widely covered in the media, raising questions about the judiciary's ability to manage high-profile cases impartially. The judiciary's proactive engagement with the media can provide accurate information and counter potential biases. Public engagement initiatives, such as open court sessions, can demystify legal proceedings and offer citizens direct insight into the judiciary's operations, reinforcing perceptions of fairness and accessibility. Enhancing public trust in the judiciary has far-reaching implications for the rule of law, democratic governance, and social cohesion. The relationship between the judiciary and the government is integral in creating an environment conducive to public trust, requiring mutual commitment to transparency, accountability, and fairness. A lack of public trust can lead to disillusionment, social unrest, and even disregard for legal institutions. Hence, the judiciary's proactive engagement with the government in pursuit of trust-building initiatives is essential for maintaining the legitimacy and effectiveness of the justice system.

In conclusion, enhancing public trust in the judiciary is a collaborative effort between the judiciary and the government, underpinned by transparency, accountability, impartiality, and responsiveness. Through the exploration of cases and examples from diverse global contexts, this discussion underscores that the judiciary's capacity to inspire public confidence is intricately linked to its relationship with the government. By aligning their efforts to address challenges, implement reforms, and uphold ethical standards, the judiciary and the government can collectively foster a legal environment that reinforces the trust of citizens, upholds the rule of law, and strengthens democratic institutions. We will conclude this final chapter of the book by addressing the future power struggles between the judiciary and government.

8.5. ADDRESSING FUTURE POWER STRUGGLES BETWEEN JUDICIARY AND GOVERNMENT

As custodians of justice and governance, the judiciary and government often find themselves engaged in intricate power dynamics that can significantly shape the trajectory of a nation's legal and political landscape (Janover, 2021; Johnson, 2019; Jonski, 2021; Jorritsma, 2020). This section delves into the nuanced interplay between the judiciary and the government in addressing potential power struggles that may emerge in the future. By drawing on a range of examples and case studies from diverse global contexts, complemented by references to pertinent literature, this discussion illuminates the challenges, strategies, and implications associated with navigating these power struggles while upholding the rule of law and democratic principles. Yet, the traditional arrangement of government (see Figure 8.9) is likely to be increasingly scrutinized as these struggles take place.

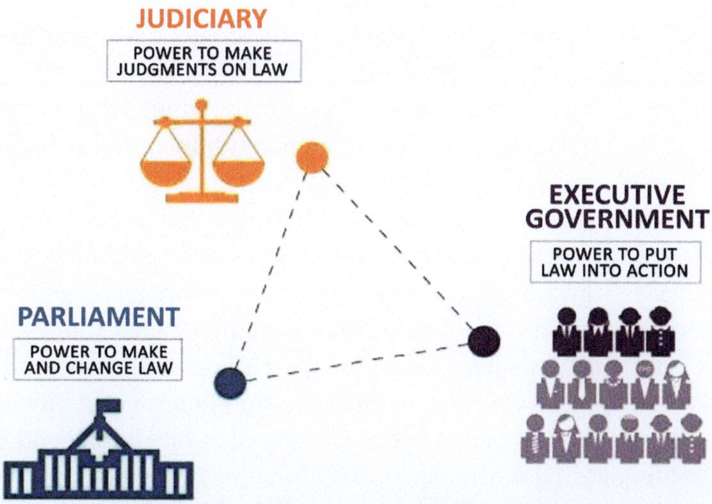

Figure 8.9. The traditional organization of government.

Source: https://www.civilsdaily.com/judiciary-executive-tussle/

Future power struggles between the judiciary and government can stem from a variety of factors, including clashes over authority, interpretations of constitutional principles, and differing ideological perspectives (Dumoulin & Licoppe, 2016; Dunn, 2017; Easterly, 2019; Easton, 2018). The case of "Poland's Constitutional Tribunal Crisis" highlights a situation where tensions between the judiciary and government arose due to the latter's attempts to undermine the former's independence through changes in judicial appointments. Similarly, in Turkey, the "Gezi Park Protests" sparked concerns about the government's attempts to stifle dissent, culminating in confrontations between the judiciary and the executive. These cases underscore that future power struggles can jeopardize the principles of checks and balances, undermine judicial independence, and erode public trust in both institutions. Future power struggles necessitate robust constitutional safeguards to maintain the separation of powers and protect the independence of the judiciary. The case of "Marbury v. Madison" in the United States established the principle of judicial review, allowing courts to assess the constitutionality of government actions. This exemplifies how constitutional mechanisms empower the judiciary to counter potential overreach by the government. Moreover, India's "Supreme Court Advocates-on-Record Association v. Union of India" case reaffirmed the judiciary's authority in appointing judges, illustrating that the judiciary's autonomy and independence are pivotal in upholding the balance of power.

International human rights standards can serve as a reference point in addressing power struggles (Kaplina et al., 2021; Karlan, 1992; Kasner, 2015; Kempf, 2021). The "Zimbabwe Lawyers for Human Rights v. Minister of Justice" case underscores the role of regional human rights bodies, such as the African Commission on Human and Peoples' Rights, in intervening to protect judicial independence. Literature by Buergenthal (2009) emphasizes the significance of international human rights norms in guiding governments and judiciaries toward respecting democratic principles and ensuring that power struggles are resolved within a human rights framework. The landmark case of Zimbabwe Lawyers for Human Rights v. Minister of Justice serves as a profound testament to the significance of regional human rights bodies, particularly the African Commission on Human and Peoples' Rights, in safeguarding the indispensable principle of judicial independence. This compelling case shed light on a myriad of key issues, exposing the challenges faced by the judiciary in Zimbabwe and the potential erosions to the rule of law. By examining the minutiae of the case, such as the sequence of events and the subsequent conclusions, it becomes evident that this legal battle was not only about the protection of human rights, but also about holding the government accountable for its actions. The implications of this case reverberate far beyond its immediate context, as it underscores the pivotal role of the judiciary in ensuring good governance and upholding the very foundations of democracy. The intervention of regional human rights bodies in this case signifies their commitment to protecting the integrity of the judicial system, while simultaneously highlighting the need for greater checks and balances in ensuring the independence of the judiciary. It serves as a powerful reminder of the immense responsibility enshrined in the hands of the judiciary and the indispensable role that regional human rights bodies play in preserving the sanctity of justice within a broader governmental framework.

Public engagement can play a crucial role in mitigating power struggles and ensuring accountability (Rohrschneider, 2005; Rotunda, 1991; Rowley,

2005). The "Hirak Protests" in Algeria (see Figure 8.10) underscore how mass protests can compel governments to respond to popular demands for accountability and transparency. The judiciary's role in these circumstances involves striking a balance between upholding democratic principles and interpreting the law while remaining responsive to societal pressures. Transparency in court proceedings, public consultations, and accountability mechanisms can all contribute to a more accountable government-judiciary relationship.

Figure 8.10. Press snapshot of the "Hirak Protests" of Algeria.

Source: North Africa Post (2020) https://northafricapost.com/41267-paris-algiers-relations-souring-over-french-documentaries-on-hirak.html

The Hirak Protests in Algeria emerged as a significant social and political movement in early 2019, reflecting the culmination of longstanding socio-economic grievances and widespread disillusionment with the government. The background to the protests can be traced to Algeria's history of authoritarian governance, corruption, and economic challenges, which had left many citizens disenchanted with their quality of life and prospects for a better future. Against this backdrop, the decision of then-President Abdelaziz Bouteflika to seek a fifth term in office ignited public frustration, sparking mass demonstrations demanding political reform, genuine democracy, and an end to the ruling elite's grip on power. The context of these protests was characterized by a youthful and diverse demographic that leveraged social media to mobilize and coordinate their actions, leading to a sustained series of peaceful protests across the nation. The implications of the Hirak Protests for developing a responsive judiciary that can negotiate tensions with the executive and parliament are multi-faceted. Firstly, the protests revealed a widespread demand for greater accountability, transparency, and justice within the government, which in turn necessitates a judiciary that is independent and capable of upholding the rule of law impartially. The judiciary's role in investigating and prosecuting cases of corruption and abuse of power emerged as a crucial point of contention, requiring an institution that is perceived as unbiased and committed to justice. Secondly, the Hirak Protests highlighted the importance of a judiciary that can mediate between the executive and the parliament during times of political transition and uncertainty. A responsive judiciary can facilitate peaceful transitions by ensuring that legal and constitutional processes are followed, enabling dialogue and negotiation rather than confrontation. Lastly, the Hirak Protests underscored the need for a judiciary that can safeguard fundamental rights and freedoms, balancing the government's interests with the protection of citizens' rights to protest and express dissent. This entails a judiciary that is capable of interpreting the constitution and laws in a manner that guarantees citizens' democratic participation while preventing any potential abuses of power by the government. Overall, the Hirak Protests illuminate the imperative for a robust and independent judiciary that can effectively navigate tensions with the executive and parliament, contributing to the consolidation of democratic governance and the rule of law in Algeria.

In the face of potential power struggles, mediation and conflict resolution mechanisms can facilitate dialogue between the judiciary and government (Delaney, 2016; Devlin & Dodek, 2017; DiClemente, 2012). The case of "The Elders' Intervention in Zimbabwe" showcases the efficacy of diplomatic figures in mediating tensions between the judiciary and government to promote a peaceful resolution. Similarly, literature by Bondy and Wiseberg (2016) discusses the potential of negotiation and dialogue in addressing conflicts between branches of government, highlighting the need for constructive engagement rather than confrontation. The ethical conduct and professionalism of judges and government officials are integral in averting power struggles. The "Clean Hands Doctrine" in Colombia exemplifies how an ethical standard can influence political behavior. Leaders who prioritize ethical conduct and respect for constitutional principles contribute to a healthier relationship between the judiciary and government. Literature by Powell (2018) emphasizes that ethical leadership can mitigate potential power imbalances and foster collaboration rather than antagonism.

Inclusive governance practices can mitigate future power struggles by involving multiple stakeholders in decision-making (Delaney, 2016; Devlin & Dodek, 2017; DiClemente, 2012). The case of "Mongolia's Public Hearings for Judicial Appointments" underscores how public participation in judicial appointments can reduce perceptions of government overreach and enhance public confidence in the judiciary. Literature by Versteeg (2015) discusses the relationship between constitutional design and democratic stability, underscoring that inclusive governance structures can prevent undue concentrations of power. The resolution of future power struggles between the judiciary and government has profound implications for democracy and the rule of law. A harmonious relationship based on mutual respect, adherence to constitutional principles, and a commitment to democratic norms ensures that power is exercised in the interest of the people. The judiciary's role in safeguarding these principles, while respecting the government's mandate, becomes instrumental in upholding democratic governance.

In conclusion, the dynamics between the judiciary and government in addressing future power struggles encompass a complex tapestry of constitutional safeguards, ethical considerations, transparency mechanisms, and inclusive governance practices. By examining examples and case studies from diverse global contexts, this discussion underscores that the relationship between the judiciary and government plays a pivotal role in shaping the trajectory of a nation's legal and political landscape. The judiciary's role in upholding the rule of law and democratic governance remains paramount.

CHAPTER 8 SUMMARY

The concluding chapter delves into the dynamic landscape of future perspectives and emerging challenges faced by judiciaries worldwide, envisioning the intricate interplay between the judiciary and government. In Section 8.1, the discourse revolves around technological advancements and their implications for the judiciary's operations. The transformative potential of technology requires judiciaries to harness innovative tools while safeguarding due process, evidentiary standards, and data privacy. Section 8.2 underscores the imperative of fostering diversity and inclusivity within the judiciary, recognizing the significance of representative benches that reflect society's heterogeneity. Ensuring equitable representation bolsters legitimacy and instills public confidence in the judiciary's impartiality.

In Section 8.3, the focus shifts to the judiciary's role in navigating rapid societal changes. The judiciary's adaptability to evolving norms, values, and challenges is crucial in maintaining its relevance and effectiveness. The section elucidates that judiciaries must interpret laws dynamically while collaborating with governments to harmonize legal responses with swiftly transforming societies. Section 8.4 accentuates the indelible link between public trust and the judiciary's credibility, emphasizing that transparent proceedings, ethical conduct, and government collaboration are indispensable for nurturing public confidence. Public trust underscores the judiciary's role as a guardian of democracy and the rule of law.

Addressing future power struggles between the judiciary and government takes center stage in Section 8.5. As the two institutions navigate differing interests, checks and balances, transparency, and open communication are paramount in mitigating potential conflicts. This section underscores the significance of safeguarding judicial independence, adhering to constitutional norms, and embracing mechanisms for conflict resolution. The chapter, as a whole, encapsulates the intricate web of challenges and prospects, firmly grounded in the relationship between the judiciary and government. While technological advancements, societal changes, diversity, and trust-building reshape the judicial landscape, the balance of power and collaboration will be pivotal in steering the trajectory of justice systems worldwide. As governments and judiciaries navigate these themes collectively, the chapter underscores the enduring significance of their symbiotic relationship in shaping the contours of legal and political landscapes in the future. This brings this book to the end. The author will now make some final concluding remarks.

Concluding Remarks

In this comprehensive book, titled "The Judiciary and Government: The ongoing power struggle," a multifaceted exploration of the intricate relationship between judiciaries and governments is undertaken. Addressing a wide range of themes, the book caters to undergraduate students, practitioners, policymakers, and the general public alike. The selection of these themes is highly relevant due to their pivotal roles in shaping the functioning of legal and political systems. Each section resonates with contemporary dynamics and offers insights that can be applied across jurisdictions.

The book commences by laying the groundwork through the exploration of the origins of the judiciary and the evolution of government structures (Section 1.1 and 1.2). The concept of separation of powers (Section 1.3) is dissected, establishing its significance in balancing authority. The role of the judiciary in early societies (Section 1.4) and the emergence of democratic governance (Section 1.5) provide historical context, showcasing how these foundational principles continue to shape modern legal and political systems.

Delving deeper, the second chapter navigates the multifaceted role of the judiciary. Themes such as judicial review (Section 2.1), jurisdiction and decision-making (Section 2.2), criminal justice and due process (Section 2.3), civil cases and dispute resolution (Section 2.4), and the judiciary's role in safeguarding individual rights (Section 2.5) underscore the judiciary's vital role in upholding justice, ensuring the rule of law, and safeguarding citizens' rights.

The book further scrutinizes the intricate balance between judicial independence and accountability. Ensuring judicial independence (Section 3.1) and mechanisms of accountability (Section 3.2) are vital in upholding the judiciary's integrity. The challenges to judicial independence (Section 3.3) and the ethics of judicial conduct (Section 3.4) address contemporary concerns, while the imperative of balancing independence and public interest (Section 3.5) underscores the judiciary's accountability to society.

The fourth chapter probes the interplay between judiciaries and government in policymaking. Themes like judicial interpretation of statutes (Section 4.1), the impact of precedent in policy decisions (Section 4.2), judicial activism vs. restraint in policy matters (Section 4.3), the role of the judiciary in public policy (Section 4.4), and evaluating policy implications of judicial decisions (Section 4.5) elucidate how the judiciary's interpretations influence policy formulation.

Chapter five delves into the role of the judiciary in conflict resolution. Judicial review of government actions (Section 5.1), adjudication of disputes between government branches (Section 5.2), international courts' role in cross-border conflicts (Section 5.3), mediation and alternative dispute resolution (Section 5.4), and the judiciary's role in mitigating political conflicts (Section 5.5) underscore the judiciary's significance in maintaining stability and harmony.

Examining contemporary challenges, Chapter six addresses threats to judicial independence. Political interference (Section 6.1), threats to judicial security (Section 6.2), populism's impact (Section 6.3), media influence (Section 6.4), and the delicate balance between independence and accountability (Section 6.5) resonate with present-day dynamics, highlighting the need for vigilant protection of judicial autonomy.

Navigating global complexities, Chapter seven explores the judiciary's evolving role in a globalized context. Globalization's impact on legal systems (Section 7.1), international cooperation and treaty interpretation (Section 7.2), transnational dispute resolution (Section 7.3), jurisdictional challenges (Section 7.4), and harmonizing international law (Section 7.5) underscore the judiciary's role in adapting to an interconnected world.

Concluding with forward-looking perspectives, Chapter eight explores future challenges. Technological advancements (Section 8.1), diversity and inclusivity (Section 8.2), adapting to societal changes (Section 8.3), enhancing public trust (Section 8.4), and addressing future power struggles

(Section 8.5) present a holistic overview of emerging dynamics, encouraging stakeholders to anticipate and address challenges proactively.

In closing, the authors extend their gratitude to readers for engaging with the book's discourse. The book's accessibility makes it an invaluable resource for students seeking foundational knowledge, practitioners grappling with contemporary legal dynamics, policymakers crafting informed decisions, and the general public interested in the nexus of law and governance. Readers are encouraged to explore the broader series, fostering an ongoing engagement with the complexities and nuances of the relationship between the judiciary and government in a rapidly evolving world.

Bibliography

1. Aboueldahab, N. (2021). The politics of time, transition, and justice in transitional justice. *International Criminal Law Review*, *21*(5), 809–816. https://doi.org/10.1163/15718123-bja10079.
2. Abouharb, M. R., Moyer, L. P., & Schmidt, M. (2013). De Facto Judicial Independence and Physical Integrity Rights. *Journal of Human Rights*, *12*(4), 367–396. https://doi.org/10.1080/14754835.2013.812461.
3. Agbor, A. (2015). The Role of the Judiciary in the Promotion of Democracy and Human Rights in Cameroon. *African Journal of Legal Studies*, *8*(1–2), 145–173. https://doi.org/10.1163/17087384-12342057.
4. Alleman, R., & Mazzone, J. (2010). The Case for Returning Politicians to the Supreme Court. *Hastings Law Journal*, *61*(6), 1353–1406. <Go to ISI>://WOS:000281372900004.
5. Alter, K. J. (1998). Who are the “masters of the treaty”? European governments and the European Court of Justice. *International Organization*, *52*(1), 121-+. https://doi.org/10.1162/002081898550572.
6. Althouse, A. (2001). Inside the federalism cases: Concern about the federal courts. *Annals of the American Academy of Political and Social Science*, *574*, 132–144. https://doi.org/10.1177/0002716201574001010.
7. Appleby, G., & Olijnyk, A. (2020). Executive policy development and constitutional norms: Practice and perceptions. *Icon-International Journal of Constitutional Law*, *18*(4), 1136–1165. https://doi.org/10.1093/icon/moaa082.

8. Appleby, G., Le Mire, S., Lynch, A., & Opeskin, B. (2019). Contemporary Challenges Facing The Australian Judiciary: An Empirical Interruption. *Melbourne University Law Review*, *42*(2), 299–369. <Go to ISI>://WOS:000484055900001.
9. Aydin-Cakir, A. (2023). The varying effect of court-curbing: evidence from Hungary and Poland. *Journal of European Public Policy*. https://doi.org/10.1080/13501763.2023.2171089.
10. Babie, P. T., & Bhanu, A. P. (2022). The Form and Formation of Constitutionalism in India. *Laws*, *11*(2), Article 33. https://doi.org/10.3390/laws11020033.
11. Bachmann, K., & Lyubashenko, I. (2017). The Puzzle of Transitional Justice in Ukraine. *International Journal of Transitional Justice*, *11*(2), 297–314. https://doi.org/10.1093/ijtj/ijx007.
12. Bado, A. (2017). Political, merit-based and nepotic elements in the selection of Hungarian judges. A possible way of creating judicial loyalty in East Central Europe. *International Journal of the Legal Profession*, *24*(3), 259–274. https://doi.org/10.1080/09695958.2016.1220383.
13. Bahry, D., & Kim, Y. H. (2021). Executive Turnover and the Investigation of Former Leaders in New Democracies. *Political Research Quarterly*, *74*(1), 199–211, Article 1065912920905640. https://doi.org/10.1177/1065912920905640.
14. Baldwin, C. (2017). The Vetting Epidemic in England and Wales. *Journal of Criminal Law*, *81*(6), 478–496. https://doi.org/10.1177/0022018317734715.
15. Bascuas, R. J. (2005). The unconstitutionality of "hold until cleared": Reexamining material witness detentions in the wake of the September 11th dragnet. *Vanderbilt Law Review*, *58*(3), 677-+. <Go to ISI>://WOS:000237720200001.
16. Baude, W. (2020). Adjudication Outside Article III. *Harvard Law Review*, *133*(5), 1511–1581. <Go to ISI>://WOS:000519762500001.
17. Baum, L. (2003). The Supreme Court in American politics. *Annual Review of Political Science*, *6*, 161–180. https://doi.org/10.1146/annurev.polisci.6.121901.085526.
18. Bednar, J. (2004). Judicial predictability and federal stability – Strategic consequences of institutional imperfection. *Journal of Theoretical Politics*, *16*(4), 423–446. https://doi.org/10.1177/0951629804046149.

19. Beiser-McGrath, L. F., Bernauer, T., & Prakash, A. (2022). Do policy clashes between the judiciary and the executive affect public opinion? Insights from New Delhi's odd-even rule against air pollution. *Journal of Public Policy*, *42*(1), 185–200, Article Pii s0143814x2100012x. https://doi.org/10.1017/s0143814x2100012x.

20. Bell, L. C. (2002). Senatorial discourtesy: The senate's use of delay to shape the federal judiciary. *Political Research Quarterly*, *55*(3), 589–607. https://doi.org/10.1177/106591290205500305.

21. Bencze, M. (2021). Judicial Populism and the Weberian Judge-The Strength of Judicial Resistance Against Governmental Influence in Hungary. *German Law Journal*, *22*(7), 1282–1297, Article Pii s2071832221000675. https://doi.org/10.1017/glj.2021.67.

22. Berger, R. (1978). Government By Judiciary – Some Counter-Criticism. *Texas Law Review*, *56*(6), 1125–1145. <Go to ISI>://WOS:A1978FZ61400007.

23. Berger, R. (1979a). Government By Judiciary – Ely,John,Hart Invitation. *Indiana Law Journal*, *54*(2), 277–312. <Go to ISI>://WOS:A1979GS82200005.

24. Berger, R. (1979b). Government By Judiciary – Gibbon Argument Ad-Hominem. *Boston University Law Review*, *59*(4), 783–809. <Go to ISI>://WOS:A1979JF24500005.

25. Berkmanas, T. (2020). The 'Meta'-significance of Scalia's A Matter of Interpretation: Reflections on a Theory and Ethics of Judicial Legislative Power. *Taltech Journal of European Studies*, *10*(1), 173–194. https://doi.org/10.1515/bjes-2020–0009.

26. Besco, L. (2018). Judicial Education or Sustainability. *Mcgill International Journal of Sustainable Development Law and Policy*, *14*(1), 1–28. <Go to ISI>://WOS:000446136100001.

27. Biskupic, J. (1992). *Speaking for the Court: The Role of the Chief Justice*. Greenwood Publishing Group.

28. Bonica, A., & Sen, M. (2017). The Politics of Selecting the Bench from the Bar: The Legal Profession and Partisan Incentives to Introduce Ideology into Judicial Selection. *Journal of Law & Economics*, *60*(4), 559–595. https://doi.org/10.1086/696575.

29. Boskovic, M. M. (2020, Sep 10–11). Role of court of justice of the European union in establishment of EU standards on independence of judiciary. *EU and Comparative Law Issues and Challenges Series – ECLIC* [Eu 2020 – lessons from the past and solutions for the future].

International Scientific Conference on Lessons from the Past and Solutions for the Future (EU), Josip Juraj Strossmayer Univ Osijek, Faculty of Law, Osijek, CROATIA.

30. Boyd, K. L. (2001). Are human rights political questions? *Rutgers Law Review*, *53*(2), 277–331. <Go to ISI>://WOS:000169418400001.
31. Bradley, C. A. (1998). The Charming Betsy canon and separation of powers: Rethinking the interpretive role of international law. *Georgetown Law Journal*, *86*(3), 479–537. <Go to ISI>://WOS:000073202200001.
32. Brands, H. (2011). Crime, Irregular Warfare, and Institutional Failure in Latin America: Guatemala as a Case Study. *Studies in Conflict & Terrorism*, *34*(3), 228–247, Article Pii 933909102. https://doi.org/10.1080/1057610x.2011.545937.
33. Brinkerhoff, J. C. (2019). FOIA's Common Law. *Yale Journal on Regulation*, *36*(2), 575–624. <Go to ISI>://WOS:000475413400002.
34. Brogdon, M. S. (2018). The Formation of Judicial Federalism in the United States. *Publius-the Journal of Federalism*, *48*(2), 269–291. https://doi.org/10.1093/publius/pjx047.
35. Bromby, M. (2021). The Cayman Islands: Paradoxes of Insularity in the Caribbean and Other British Overseas Territories. *Liverpool Law Review*, *42*(1), 35–49. https://doi.org/10.1007/s10991–020–09261–0.
36. Brown, G. D. (1999). The ethics backlash and the independent counsel statute. *Rutgers Law Review*, *51*(2), 433–491. <Go to ISI>://WOS:000079887000004.
37. Buchmeyer, A. (2019). When Roles Collide: Deference, Due Process, and the Judicial Dilemma. *Wisconsin Law Review*(6), 1589–1619. <Go to ISI>://WOS:000517823300005.
38. Bunjevac, T. (2015). Court Services Victoria and the New Politics of Judicial Independence: A Critical Analysis of the Court Services Victoria Act 2014 (VIC). *Monash University Law Review*, *41*(2), 299–328. <Go to ISI>://WOS:000387025700002.
39. Burbank, S. B. (2009). Pleading and the Dilemmas of "General Rules." *Wisconsin Law Review*(2), 535–564. <Go to ISI>://WOS:000266291000011.
40. Bybee, J. S. (1994). Advising The President – Separation of Powers and the Federal Advisory-Committee Act. *Yale Law Journal*, *104*(1), 51–128. https://doi.org/10.2307/796984.
41. Byrne, G., & Maxwell, C. (2019). Putting Jurors First: Legislative

Simplification of Jury Directions. *Criminal Law Journal*, *43*(3), 180–200. <Go to ISI>://WOS:000489615600003.

42. Calabresi, S. G., & Rhodes, K. H. (1992). The Structural Constitution – Unitary Executive, Plural Judiciary. *Harvard Law Review*, *105*(6), 1155–1216. <Go to ISI>://WOS:A1992HN95400001.
43. Calfee, C. (2006). Kelo v. City of New London: The more things stay the same, the more they change. *Ecology Law Quarterly*, *33*(3), 545–581. <Go to ISI>://WOS:000242900600003.
44. Cameron, M. A. (2010). the state of democracy in the andes: introduction to a thematic issue of Revista De Ciencia Politica. *Revista De Ciencia Politica*, *30*(1), 5–20. <Go to ISI>://WOS:000276571300002.
45. Caplan, A. H. (2010). Freedom of speech in school and prison. *Washington Law Review*, *85*(1), 71–105. <Go to ISI>://WOS:000275601700006.
46. Carrillo, D. A., Duvernay, S. M., & Stracener, B. V. (2017). California Constitutional Law: Popular Sovereignty. *Hastings Law Journal*, *68*(4), 731–775. <Go to ISI>://WOS:000410062300001.
47. Cassman, D. R. (2015). Keep it secret, keep it safe: an empirical analysis of the state secrets doctrine. *Stanford Law Review*, *67*(5), 1173–1217. <Go to ISI>://WOS:000355644200004.
48. Celenk, A. A. (2016). The myth of 'independent judiciary': the evolution of judiciary-executive relations in Turkish politics. *Contemporary Politics*, *22*(2), 232–247. https://doi.org/10.1080/13569775.2016.1153283.
49. Chakravarti, D., Thadani, K., Chablani, V., & Nayak, A. (2011). Abrogating Sovereign Immunity in Patent Infringement Cases in India: Retreating Without Disgrace. *Journal of Intellectual Property Rights*, *16*(5), 418–425. <Go to ISI>://WOS:000294862500006.
50. Chalmers, D. (2000). The positioning of EU judicial politics within the United Kingdom. *West European Politics*, *23*(4), 169-+. https://doi.org/10.1080/01402380008425405.
51. Chan, C. (2011). Deference and the separation of powers: an assessment of the court's constitutional and institutional competences. *Hong Kong Law Journal*, *41*, 7–25. <Go to ISI>://WOS:000301880400002.
52. Charney, J. I. (2009). "State Practice and International Law in Relation to Territorial Claims." *American Journal of International Law, 103*(4), 775–809.
53. Chavez, R. B. (2003). The construction of the rule of law in Argentina

– A tale of two provinces. *Comparative Politics*, *35*(4), 417-+. https://doi.org/10.2307/4150188.

54. Chavez, R. B. (2007). The appointment and removal process for judges in Argentina: The role of judicial councils and impeachment juries in promoting judicial independence. *Latin American Politics and Society*, *49*(2), 33–58. https://doi.org/10.1353/lap.2007.0017.
55. Chen, B. M., & Li, Z. Y. (2016). Explaining comparative administrative law: the standing of positive political theory. *Washington International Law Journal*, *25*(1), 87–131. <Go to ISI>://WOS:000411023200004.
56. Chutkow, D. M. (2008). Jurisdiction Stripping: Litigation, Ideology, and Congressional Control of the Courts. *Journal of Politics*, *70*(4), 1053–1064. https://doi.org/10.1017/s002238160808105x.
57. Cleveland, S. H., & Dodge, W. S. (2015). Defining and Punishing Offenses Under Treaties. *Yale Law Journal*, *124*(7), 2202–2284. <Go to ISI>://WOS:000355384900001.
58. Clopton, Z. D. (2018). Diagonal Public Enforcement. *Stanford Law Review*, *70*(4), 1077–1130. <Go to ISI>://WOS:000432646500002.
59. Coan, A. B. (2012). Judicial Capacity and the Substance of Constitutional Law. *Yale Law Journal*, *122*(2), 422–458. <Go to ISI>://WOS:000311814200003.
60. Codrington, W. U. (2021). PURCELL IN PANDEMIC. *New York University Law Review*, *96*(4), 941–984. <Go to ISI>://WOS:000753957600003.
61. Colucci, F. J. (2000). The court's three marshalls. *Polity*, *33*(1), 127–150. https://doi.org/10.2307/3235463.
62. Conrad, C. R. (2014). Divergent Incentives for Dictators: Domestic Institutions and (International Promises Not to) Torture. *Journal of Conflict Resolution*, *58*(1), 34–67. https://doi.org/10.1177/0022002712459707.
63. Costas-Perez, E., Sole-Olle, A., & Sorribas-Navarro, P. (2012). Corruption scandals, voter information, and accountability. *European Journal of Political Economy*, *28*(4), 469–484. https://doi.org/10.1016/j.ejpoleco.2012.05.007.
64. Cross, F. B. (1999). The judiciary and public choice. *Hastings Law Journal*, *50*(2), 355-+. <Go to ISI>://WOS:000081777300003.
65. Cui, W. (2017). Does judicial independence matter? a study of the determinants of administrative litigation in an authoritarian regime.

University of Pennsylvania Journal of International Law, *38*(3), 941–998. <Go to ISI>://WOS:000416101200004.

66. D'Amato, A. (2017). "The South China Sea Dispute: A Legal Interpretation." *The Chinese Journal of Comparative Law, 5*(1), 1–30.
67. Davies, T. (2018). The role of the media in shaping perceptions of the judiciary. *Journal of Open Access to Law, 6*(1), 1–30.
68. Davis, D. M. (2008). Socioeconomic rights: Do they deliver the goods? *Icon-International Journal of Constitutional Law*, *6*(3–4), 687–711. https://doi.org/10.1093/icon/mon014.
69. De Francesco, F., & Tosun, J. (2022). The enactment of public participation in rulemaking: A comparative analysis. *Swiss Political Science Review*. https://doi.org/10.1111/spsr.12550.
70. de la Torre, C., & Lemos, A. O. (2016). Populist polarization and the slow death of democracy in Ecuador. *Democratization*, *23*(2), 221–241. https://doi.org/10.1080/13510347.2015.1058784.
71. Delaney, E. (2016). Searching for constitutional meaning in institutional design: The debate over judicial appointments in the United Kingdom. *Icon-International Journal of Constitutional Law*, *14*(3), 752–768. https://doi.org/10.1093/icon/mow044.
72. Devlin, R., & Dodek, A. (2017). The Achilles heel of the Canadian judiciary: the ethics of judicial appointments in Canada. *Legal Ethics*, *20*(1), 43–63. https://doi.org/10.1080/1460728x.2017.1345202.
73. DiClemente, A. J. (2012). Foreign Governments in Contempt? A Case for Limiting the Contempt Power Under the Foreign Sovereign Immunities Act. *Columbia Journal of Transnational Law*, *51*(1), 177–223. <Go to ISI>://WOS:000312920200005.
74. Dinan, J. (1997). State government influence in the national policy process: Lessons from the 104th Congress. *Publius-the Journal of Federalism*, *27*(2), 129–142. https://doi.org/10.1093/oxfordjournals.pubjof.a029902.
75. Downey, B., Martz, R., Chiswell, P. G., & Salamucha, R. (2020). Federalism in the patch: Canada's energy industry and the constitutional division of powers. *Alberta Law Review*, *58*(2), 273–313. <Go to ISI>://WOS:000597886900003.
76. Driscoll, A., & Nelson, M. J. (2015). Judicial Selection and the Democratization of Justice. *Journal of Law and Courts*, *3*(1), 115–148. https://doi.org/10.1086/679017.

77. Duhart, P. (2020). Criminalizing peace: anti-terrorism law and its impact on peacemaking in the Basque Country and Northern Ireland. *Peacebuilding*, *8*(4), 432–446. https://doi.org/10.1080/21647259.2019.1632055.
78. Dumoulin, L., & Licoppe, C. (2016). Videoconferencing, New Public Management, and Organizational Reform in the Judiciary. *Policy and Internet*, *8*(3), 313–333. https://doi.org/10.1002/poi3.124.
79. Dunn, J. (2017). Three-Quarters Empty or One-Quarter Full? Martha Derthick on the Courts, Federalism, and Public Policy. *Publius-the Journal of Federalism*, *47*(2), 201–220. https://doi.org/10.1093/publius/pjw043.
80. Easterly, B. (2019). Counterbalancing the disadvantages of the "Have Nots": an examination of the impact of amicus participation in state supreme court cases. *Interest Groups & Advocacy*, *8*(4), 579–599. https://doi.org/10.1057/s41309–019–00057-w.
81. Easton, J. (2018). Where to Draw the Line? Is Efficiency Encroaching on a Fair Justice System? *Political Quarterly*, *89*(2), 246–253. https://doi.org/10.1111/1467–923x.12487.
82. Edelman, M. (1994). The judicialization of politics in Israel. *International Political Science Review*, *15*(2), 177–186. https://doi.org/10.1177/019251219401500209.
83. Efrat, A. (2018). Resisting cooperation against crime: Britain's extradition controversy, 2003–2015. *International Journal of Law Crime and Justice*, *52*, 118–128. https://doi.org/10.1016/j.ijlcj.2017.10.004.
84. Eichensehr, K. K. (2018). The University of Chicago Law Review. *University of Chicago Law Review*, *85*(3), 609–675. <Go to ISI>://WOS:000431941100001.
85. Eleftheriadis, P. (2005). Constitutional reform and the rule of law in Greece. *West European Politics*, *28*(2), 317–334. https://doi.org/10.1080/01402380500059777.
86. Emerson, B. (2022). Liberty and Democracy Through the Administrative State: A Critique of the Roberts Court's Political Theory. *Hastings Law Journal*, *73*(2), 371–436. <Go to ISI>://WOS:000760883700004.
87. Epstein, L., Landes, W. M., & Posner, R. A. (2013). *How Judicial Confirmation Hearings Fail*. University of Chicago Press.
88. Evans, D., Franco, A., Polinard, J. L., Wenzel, J. P., & Wrinkle, R.

D. (2017). Who's on the Bench? The Impact of Latino Descriptive Representation on US Supreme Court Approval Among Latinos and Anglos*. *Social Science Quarterly*, *98*(5), 1233–1249. https://doi.org/10.1111/ssqu.12351.

89. Fallon, R. H., & Meltzer, D. J. (1991). New law, non-retroactivity, and constitutional remedies. *Harvard Law Review*, *104*(8), 1733–1833. https://doi.org/10.2307/1341619.
90. Fichtelberg, A. (2010). "Transnational Organized Crime: Principal Threats and Jurisdictional Challenges." In *Transnational Crime and Human Rights* (pp. 20–45). Routledge.
91. Findley, M. G., & Young, J. K. (2011). Terrorism, Democracy, and Credible Commitments. *International Studies Quarterly*, *55*(2), 357–378. https://doi.org/10.1111/j.1468–2478.2011.00647.x.
92. Finkel, J. (2005). Judicial reform as insurance policy: Mexico in the 1990s. *Latin American Politics and Society*, *47*(1), 87–113. https://doi.org/10.1353/lap.2005.0006.
93. Fisher, L. (2008). Congressional access to national security information. *Harvard Journal on Legislation*, *45*(1), 219–235. <Go to ISI>://WOS:000253913100007.
94. Fowkes, J. (2011). How to open the doors of the court – lessons on access to justice from Indian PIL. *South African Journal on Human Rights*, *27*, 434–465. https://doi.org/10.1080/19962126.2011.1186502 4.
95. Fox, S. (2017). Home Rule in an Era of Local Environmental Innovation. *Ecology Law Quarterly*, *44*(3), 575–625. https://doi.org/10.15779/z386d5pb0h.
96. French, R. (2016). The state of the Australian judicature. *Australian Law Journal*, *90*(6), 400–407. <Go to ISI>://WOS:000382954300009.
97. Friedman, B., & Delaney, E. F. (2011). Becoming supreme: the federal foundation of judicial supremacy. *Columbia Law Review*, *111*(6), 1137–1193. <Go to ISI>://WOS:000296545000001.
98. Gago, A., & Maiani, F. (2022). 'Pushing the boundaries': a dialogical account of the evolution of European case-law on access to welfare. *Journal of European Integration*, *44*(2), 261–275. https://doi.org/10.1080/07036337.2021.1887860.
99. Gallagher, M. (2012). The Political Role of the President of Ireland.

Irish Political Studies, *27*(4), 522–538. https://doi.org/10.1080/07907184.2012.734446.

100. Gardbaum, S. (2015). Are Strong Constitutional Courts Always a Good Thing for New Democracies? *Columbia Journal of Transnational Law*, *53*(2), 285–320. <Go to ISI>://WOS:000352752800002.

101. Garoupa, N., & Karakas, L. D. (2021). A Theory of Defiant Courts in Nondemocratic Regimes. *Journal of Legal Studies*, *50*(1), 111–144. https://doi.org/10.1086/712477.

102. Garoupa, N., Gili, M., & Gomez-Pomar, F. (2012). Political Influence and Career Judges: An Empirical Analysis of Administrative Review by the Spanish Supreme Court. *Journal of Empirical Legal Studies*, *9*(4), 795–826. https://doi.org/10.1111/j.1740–1461.2012.01270.x.

103. Gearty, C. (2005). 11 September 2001, counter-terrorism, and the Human Rights Act. *Journal of Law and Society*, *32*(1), 18–33. https://doi.org/10.1111/j.1467–6478.2005.312_1.x.

104. Gentithes, M. (2020). Gobbledygook: Political Questions, Manageability, & Partisan Gerrymandering. *Iowa Law Review*, *105*(3), 1081–1125. <Go to ISI>://WOS:000539455800003.

105. George, B. (2009). An administrative law approach to reforming the state secrets privilege. *New York University Law Review*, *84*(6), 1691–1724. <Go to ISI>://WOS:000273642000011.

106. Geyh, C. G. (2014). Judicial Independence as an Organizing Principle. In J. Hagan (Ed.), *Annual Review of Law and Social Science, Vol 10* (Vol. 10, pp. 185–200). https://doi.org/10.1146/annurev-lawsocsci-110413–030849.

107. Ginsburg, T. (2020). Populism and Courts. *Annual Review of Law and Social Science, 16,* 355–372.

108. Ginsburg, T., & Huq, A. Z. (2018). *How to Lose a Constitutional Democracy*. University of Chicago Press.

109. Ginsburg, T., & Moustafa, T. (2008). Judicial Dissent in New Democracies: A Cross-Regional Comparison. *University of Chicago Law Review, 75*(1), 297–329.

110. Gisbert, R. B. (2022). Politics, independence and judicial self-government: Four perspectives. *Revista De Estudios Politicos*(198), 93–120. https://doi.org/10.18042/cepc/rep.198.04.

111. Gomes, T. (2017). Promoting the rule of law in Serbia. What is hindering the reforms in the justice sector? *Communist and Post-*

Communist Studies, *50*(4), 331–337. https://doi.org/10.1016/j.postcomstud.2017.10.004.

112. Gonzalez, J. L. (2021). American Judicial Rejectionism and the Domestic Court's Undermining of International Human Rights Law and Policy After Human Right Violations Have Occurred in the State. *Washington International Law Journal*, *30*(2), 397–419. <Go to ISI>://WOS:000742769600008.
113. Gorodovenko, V., Bondar, O., & Udovyka, L. (2021). Justice in the Covid-19 era through the prism of judicial power. *Ius Humani-Revista De Derecho*, *10*(1), 51–72. https://doi.org/10.31207/ih.v10i1.270.
114. Gouldin, L. P. (2012). When deference is dangerous: the judicial role in material-witness detentions. *American Criminal Law Review*, *49*(3), 1333–1386. <Go to ISI>://WOS:000314617800001.
115. Grimes, B. (2021). Judicial reliance on the executive: tensions, discrepancies and recommendations for court interpreter service delivery models across Australian jurisdictions. *Griffith Law Review*, *30*(1), 71–96. https://doi.org/10.1080/10383441.2021.2014773.
116. Grimmel, A. (2012). Judicial Interpretation or Judicial Activism? The Legacy of Rationalism in the Studies of the European Court of Justice. *European Law Journal*, *18*(4), 518–535. https://doi.org/10.1111/j.1468–0386.2012.00615.x.
117. Grimmelikhuijsen, S., & Klijn, A. (2015). The effects of judicial transparency on public trust: evidence from a field experiment. *Public Administration*, *93*(4), 995–1011. https://doi.org/10.1111/padm.12149.
118. Grove, T. L. (2018). The Origins (and Fragility) of Judicial Independence. *Vanderbilt Law Review*, *71*(2), 465–545. <Go to ISI>://WOS:000428209200002.
119. Gunderson, A. (2022). Why Do States Privatize their Prisons? The Unintended Consequences of Inmate Litigation. *Perspectives on Politics*, *20*(1), 187–204. https://doi.org/10.1017/s1537592720003485.
120. Hardaway, A. B. (2021). Creating Space for Community Representation in Police Reform Litigation. *Georgetown Law Journal*, *109*(3), 523–579. <Go to ISI>://WOS:000631849800002.
121. Hardman, H. (2020). In the name of parliamentary sovereignty: conflict between the UK Government and the courts over judicial deference in the case of prisoner voting rights. *British Politics*, *15*(2), 226–250. https://doi.org/10.1057/s41293–019–00110-x.

122. Hasbrouck, B. (2022). Movement Judges. *New York University Law Review*, *97*(2), 631–696. <Go to ISI>://WOS:000805446900003.

123. He, W. P. (2017). Shareholder Primary and Corporate Reorganization: A Comparison of US and Chinese Law. *Chinese Journal of Comparative Law*, *5*(1), 205–225. https://doi.org/10.1093/cjcl/cxx008.

124. He, X. B. (2018). Legal and Policy Pathways of Climate Change Adaptation: Comparative Analysis of the Adaptation Practices in the United States, Australia and China. *Transnational Environmental Law*, *7*(2), 347–373. https://doi.org/10.1017/s2047102518000092.

125. Heinz, J. P., & Manikas, P. M. (1992). Networks among elites in a local criminal-justice system. *Law & Society Review*, *26*(4), 831–861. https://doi.org/10.2307/3053820.

126. Hennigar, M. A. (2010). Exploring Complex Judicial-Executive Interaction: Federal Government Concessions in Charter of Rights Cases. *Canadian Journal of Political Science-Revue Canadienne De Science Politique*, *43*(4), 821–842. https://doi.org/10.1017/s0008423910000739.

127. Hessick, F. A. (2014). cases, controversies, and diversity. *Northwestern University Law Review*, *109*(1), 57–108. <Go to ISI>://WOS:000351956400002.

128. Hill, D. W. (2016). Avoiding Obligation: Reservations to Human Rights Treaties. *Journal of Conflict Resolution*, *60*(6), 1129–1158. https://doi.org/10.1177/0022002714567947.

129. Holland, K. M. (2009). Rights Protection in Japan: The Political Dimension. *Australian Journal of Political Science*, *44*(1), 79–96, Article Pii 908813451. https://doi.org/10.1080/10361140802654992.

130. Horvath, P. (2017). Appointive powers of Slovak president and their use in relation to selected constitutional officers. *Politicke Vedy*, *20*(2), 49–66. <Go to ISI>://WOS:000409215000003.

131. Howard, R. M., Graves, S. E., & Flowers, J. (2006). State courts, the US Supreme Court, and the protection of civil liberties. *Law & Society Review*, *40*(4), 845–870. https://doi.org/10.1111/j.1540–5893.2006.00283.x.

132. Hume, R. J. (2012). State Courts and Policy Legitimation: An Experimental Study of the Ability of State Courts to Change Opinion. *Publius-the Journal of Federalism*, *42*(2), 211–233. https://doi.org/10.1093/publius/pjr038.

133. Iaryczower, M., Spiller, P. T., & Tommasi, M. (2002). Judicial independence in unstable environments, Argentina 1935–1998. *American Journal of Political Science*, *46*(4), 699–716. https://doi.org/10.2307/3088428.

134. Ides, A. (1999). Judicial supremacy and the law of the constitution. *Ucla Law Review*, *47*(2), 491–519. <Go to ISI>://WOS:000084323500003.

135. Imam, I., & Egbewole, W. O. (2020). Comparative Exposition of Judicial Interventionism in the Enforcement of the Healthcare Right in Nigeria and India. *Comparative and International Law Journal of Southern Africa-Cilsa*, *53*(1), Article 6772. https://doi.org/10.25159/0010–4051/6772.

136. Ip, E. C., & Yap, P. J. (2019). Substantive Review of Administrative Discretion in Hong Kong: Divergence between Judicial Rhetoric and Practice. *Chinese Journal of Comparative Law*, *7*(1), 190–211. https://doi.org/10.1093/cjcl/cxz006.

137. Jabareen, H. (2020). Can the Court normalize the exception in non-emergency cases? Palestinian cases before the Israeli Supreme Court. *Icon-International Journal of Constitutional Law*, *18*(3), 788–803. https://doi.org/10.1093/icon/moaa059.

138. Jacobi, T. (2009). The Role of Politics and Economics in Explaining Variation in Litigation Rates in the US States. *Journal of Legal Studies*, *38*(1), 205–233. https://doi.org/10.1086/596196.

139. James, S. (1996). The political and administrative consequences of judicial review. *Public Administration*, *74*(4), 613–637. https://doi.org/10.1111/j.1467–9299.1996.tb00887.x.

140. Janover, W. S. (2021). Indirect Constraints on the Office of Legal Counsel: Examining a Role for the Senate Judiciary Committee. *Stanford Law Review*, *73*(6), 1601–1649. <Go to ISI>://WOS:000674682000005.

141. Johnson, G. E. (2019). Adjudicating Executive Privilege: Federal Administrative Agencies and Deliberative Process Privilege Claims in US District Courts. *Law & Society Review*, *53*(3), 823–850. https://doi.org/10.1111/lasr.12419.

142. Jonski, K. (2021). Public Confidence in the Judiciary and the Police – Does Respondents Internalize Montesquieu's Ideas? *Asian Journal of Law and Economics*, *12*(1), 1–17. https://doi.org/10.1515/ajle-2020–0073.

143. Jorritsma, R. (2020). The Nomination of International Judges by 'the

Enlightened Few': A Comment on the Royal Decree of 23 January 2020 Concerning the Establishment of a Dutch National Group at the Permanent Court of Arbitration. *Netherlands International Law Review*, *67*(2), 297–317. https://doi.org/10.1007/s40802–020–00173–4.

144. Joshi, I. (2022). The evolution of consensus through coordinated action. *Journal of Theoretical Politics*, *34*(4), 552–588. https://doi.org/10.1177/09516298221108346.
145. Juhn, M. (2021). Taking a stand: climate change litigants and the viability of constitutional claims. *Fordham Law Review*, *89*(6), 2731–2772. <Go to ISI>://WOS:000656895700014.
146. Kang, J. (2004). Denying prejudice: Internment, redress, and denial. *Ucla Law Review*, *51*(4), 933–1013. <Go to ISI>://WOS:000221914500002.
147. Kang, S., Lee, S., & Whang, T. (2023). Economic sanctions, repression capacity, and human rights. *Journal of Human Rights*, *22*(2), 174–197. https://doi.org/10.1080/14754835.2022.2096404.
148. Kaplina, O., Zhushman, M., & Cherevatenko, I. (2021). Judicial reforms in Ukraine: polishing procedures and their systemic role. *Cuestiones Politicas*, *39*(70), 757–767. https://doi.org/10.46398/cuestpol.3970.45.
149. Karlan, P. S. (1992). Discrete and relational criminal representation – the changing vision of the right to counsel. *Harvard Law Review*, *105*(3), 670–724. https://doi.org/10.2307/1341537.
150. Kasner, A. J. (2015). National Security Leaks and Constitutional Duty. *Stanford Law Review*, *67*(1), 241–283. <Go to ISI>://WOS:000349503000003.
151. Kauffman, Z. S. (2021). Judicial Independence and Democratic Backsliding. *The Journal of Politics, 83*(1), 197–210.
152. Kempf, C. N. (2021). Why Did So Many Do So Little? Movement Building and Climate Change Litigation in the Time of Juliana v. United States. *Texas Law Review*, *99*(5), 1005–1040. <Go to ISI>://WOS:000647161100004.
153. Keohane, R. O., Moravcsik, A., & Slaughter, A. M. (2000). Legalized dispute resolution: Interstate and transnational. *International Organization*, *54*(3), 457-+. https://doi.org/10.1162/002081800551299.
154. Killebrew, P. (2007). Where are all the left-wing textualists? *New York University Law Review*, *82*(6), 1895–1928. <Go to ISI>://WOS:000251920200008.

155. Kingsford, D. (2022). Accountable Administrative Decision-making: Revising the Federal Legal Duty to Consult in Australia. *Australian Journal of Administrative Law*, *29*(3), 162–177. <Go to ISI>://WOS:000890828900003.

156. Kirisci, M., & Kocaman, I. (2022). What Restrains Military from Targeting Civilians in Civil Wars? *Civil Wars*, *24*(4), 411–444. https://doi.org/10.1080/13698249.2022.2139093.

157. Kitagawa, R. (2023). Justice as fairness or retribution? Citizen reactions to domestic trials of wartime violence. *Journal of Peace Research*. https://doi.org/10.1177/00223433221148223.

158. Kochtcheeva, L. V. (2009). Administrative Discretion and Environmental Regulation: Agency Substantive Rules and Court Decisions in US Air and Water Quality Policies. *Review of Policy Research*, *26*(3), 241–265. https://doi.org/10.1111/j.1541–1338.2009.00381.x.

159. Konisky, D. M., & Nolette, P. (2022). The State of American Federalism 2021–2022: Federal Courts, State Legislatures, and the Conservative Turn in the Law. *Publius-the Journal of Federalism*, *52*(3), 353–381. https://doi.org/10.1093/publius/pjac022.

160. Kotze, D. (2022). An Election Postponement as a Change of the Constitution: Its Democratic and Constitutional Implications. *Politikon*, *49*(4), 350–365. https://doi.org/10.1080/02589346.2022.2151689.

161. Kovacs, K., & Scheppele, K. L. (2018). The fragility of an independent judiciary: Lessons from Hungary and Poland-and the European Union. *Communist and Post-Communist Studies*, *51*(3), 189–200. https://doi.org/10.1016/j.postcomstud.2018.07.005.

162. Kramarz, T., Cosolo, D., & Rossi, A. (2017). Judicialization of Environmental Policy and the Crisis of Democratic Accountability. *Review of Policy Research*, *34*(1), 31–49. https://doi.org/10.1111/ropr.12218.

163. Krogseng, K. (2000). Minnesota v. Mille Lacs Band of Chippewa Indians. *Ecology Law Quarterly*, *27*(3), 771–797. <Go to ISI>://WOS:000165284100011.

164. Krotoszynski, R. J. (2014). The Unitary Executive and the Plural Judiciary: on the potential virtues of decentralized judicial power. *Notre Dame Law Review*, *89*(3), 1021–1083. <Go to ISI>://WOS:000332428400001.

165. Kundmueller, M. M. (2022). Keeping it complex with Philip Hunton,

John Locke, and The United States Federal Judiciary: on the merit of murkiness in separation of powers jurisprudence. *British Journal of American Legal Studies*. https://doi.org/10.2478/bjals-2023–0001.

166. Kwoka, M. B. (2017). The procedural exceptionalism of national security secrecy. *Boston University Law Review*, *97*(1), 103–165. <Go to ISI>://WOS:000394475500003.
167. Lachmayer, K. (2016). Between International Standards and Transnational Greed Providing Transnational Rule of Law in Times of Economic Crisis. *Hague Journal on the Rule of Law*, *8*(2), 291–309. https://doi.org/10.1007/s40803–016–0038–6.
168. Langford, M. (2011). "*Social Rights Jurisprudence: Emerging Trends in Comparative and International Law*." Cambridge University Press.
169. Law, D. S. (2009). The Anatomy of a Conservative Court: Judicial Review in Japan. *Texas Law Review*, *87*(7), 1545–1593. <Go to ISI>://WOS:000268086600011.
170. Lee, G. B. (2009). First Amendment Enforcement In Government Institutions and Programs. *Ucla Law Review*, *56*(6), 1691–1774. <Go to ISI>://WOS:000269944800002.
171. Leonard, M. E. (2016). State Legislatures, State High Courts, and Judicial Independence: An Examination of Court-Curbing Legislation in the States. *Justice System Journal*, *37*(1), 53–62. https://doi.org/10.1080/0098261x.2015.1024568.
172. Letsas, G. (2013). "*A Theory of Interpretation of the European Convention on Human Rights.*" Oxford University Press.
173. Levin, A., & Alkoby, A. (2017). Shouldn't the Bench be a Mirror? The Diversity of the Canadian Judiciary. *Onati Socio-Legal Series*, *7*(4), 717–751. <Go to ISI>://WOS:000493714100006.
174. Levin, A., & Alkoby, A. (2019). Shouldn't the bench be a mirror? The diversity of the Canadian judiciary. *International Journal of the Legal Profession*, *26*(1), 69–88. https://doi.org/10.1080/09695958.2018.1489818.
175. Levitsky, S., & Ziblatt, D. (2018). *How Democracies Die*. Crown..
176. Lin, C. C. (2016). Constitutions and courts in Chinese authoritarian regimes: China and pre-democratic Taiwan in comparison. *Icon-International Journal of Constitutional Law*, *14*(2), 351–377. https://doi.org/10.1093/icon/mow022.
177. Liu, A. H., & Baird, V. A. (2012). Linguistic Recognition as a Source

of Confidence in the Justice System. *Comparative Political Studies*, *45*(10), 1203–1229. https://doi.org/10.1177/0010414011434294.

178. Llamzon, A. F. (2019). The Venice Commission and the Rule of Law. In *The Palgrave Handbook of Global Approaches to Peace* (pp. 331–351). Palgrave Macmillan.
179. Macchiarola, F. J. (1971). Local Government Home Rule And Judiciary. *Journal of Urban Law*, *48*(2), 335–359. <Go to ISI>://WOS:A1971I774100002.
180. Macey, J. (2006). Executive branch usurpation of power: Corporations and capital markets. *Yale Law Journal*, *115*(9), 2416–2444. https://doi.org/10.2307/20455701.
181. Mak, M., & Rutledge, J. G. (2019). The Diffusion of Collaborative Justice: The Politics of Learning in the Development of Drug Courts. *Justice System Journal*, *40*(3), 238–258. https://doi.org/10.1080/0098261x.2019.1643269.
182. Maltzman, F., & Shipan, C. R. (2008). Change, continuity, and the evolution of the law. *American Journal of Political Science*, *52*(2), 252–267. https://doi.org/10.1111/j.1540–5907.2008.00311.x.
183. Manning, S., & Randazzo, K. A. (2009). Leveling the playing field? Litigant success rates in health-care policy cases in the us courts of appeals. *Justice System Journal*, *30*(3), 245–253. <Go to ISI>://WOS:000274604300002.
184. Maor, M. (2004). Feeling the heat? Anticorruption mechanisms in comparative perspective. *Governance-an International Journal of Policy and Administration*, *17*(1), 1–28. https://doi.org/10.1111/j.0952–1895.2004.00235.x.
185. Maphosa, R. (2020). Are judicial monitoring institutions a legitimate remedy for addressing systemic socioeconomic rights violations? *South African Journal on Human Rights*, *36*(4), 362–385. https://doi.org/10.1080/02587203.2021.1934105.
186. Marsh, L. (2021). The wrong vaccine: custody time limits and loss of liberty during Covid-19. *Legal Studies*, *41*(4), 693–709, Article Pii s0261387521000271. https://doi.org/10.1017/lst.2021.27.
187. Martinsen, D. S. (2011). Judicial policy-making and Europeanization: the proportionality of national control and administrative discretion. *Journal of European Public Policy*, *18*(7), 944–961. https://doi.org/10.1080/13501763.2011.599962.

188. Masinde, M. W. (2017). Separation of power in Kenya: analysis of the relations between judiciary and the executive. *International Journal of Human Rights and Constitutional Studies*, *5*(1), 32–42. https://doi.org/10.1504/ijhrcs.2017.082689.

189. Mason, B. (2015). Falling asleep at its master's feet? The Kable principle and Royal Commissions. *Australian Journal of Administrative Law*, *22*(3), 177–198. <Go to ISI>://WOS:000364745800005.

190. Matthes, C. Y. (2022). Judges as activists: how Polish judges mobilise to defend the rule of law. *East European Politics*, *38*(3), 468–487. https://doi.org/10.1080/21599165.2022.2092843.

191. Mayoral, J. A., & Perez, A. T. (2018). On judicial mobilization: entrepreneuring for policy change at times of crisis. *Journal of European Integration*, *40*(6), 719–736. https://doi.org/10.1080/07036337.2018.1502285.

192. McCandless, S. (2017). Stingray Confidential. *George Washington Law Review*, *85*(3), 993–1038. <Go to ISI>://WOS:000406819700007.

193. McCann, P. J. C., Shipan, C. R., & Wang, Y. H. (2023). Measuring the Legislative Design of Judicial Review of Agency Actions. *Journal of Law Economics & Organization*, *39*(1), 123–159. https://doi.org/10.1093/jleo/ewab031.

194. McCarthy, S., & Un, K. (2017). The evolution of rule of law in Cambodia. *Democratization*, *24*(1), 100–118. https://doi.org/10.1080/13510347.2015.1103736.

195. McCoy, C., & Jahic, G. (2006). Familiarity breeds respect: Organizing and studying a courtwatch. *Justice System Journal*, *27*(1), 61–70. <Go to ISI>://WOS:000202986200008.

196. McEwen, N., Swenden, W., & Bolleyer, N. (2012). Intergovernmental Relations in the UK: Continuity in a Time of Change? *British Journal of Politics & International Relations*, *14*(2), 323–343. https://doi.org/10.1111/j.1467–856X.2011.00486.x.

197. Mechkova, V., Luhrmann, A., & Lindberg, S. I. (2019). The Accountability Sequence: from De-Jure to De-Facto Constraints on Governments. *Studies in Comparative International Development*, *54*(1), 40–70. https://doi.org/10.1007/s12116–018–9262–5.

198. Medawatte, D. S., Int Ctr, R., & Dev. (2013, Jul 24–25). Separation of powers: a fairytale of Utopia. *Paper Proceedings of ICLJ* [International conference on law and justice 2013]. International Conference on Law

and Justice, Colombo, Sri Lanka.

199. Meggitt, G., & Somji, H. (2016). The regulation of mediators in england and wales, The United States and Australia – lessons for Hong Kong. *Hong Kong Law Journal*, *46*, 445–475. <Go to ISI>://WOS:000384512800004.

200. Melone, A. P. (1996). The struggle for judicial independence and the transition toward democracy in Bulgaria. *Communist and Post-Communist Studies*, *29*(2), 231–243. https://doi.org/10.1016/s0967–067x(96)80007–9.

201. Mendelson, W. (1976). MR JUSTICE DOUGLAS AND GOVERNMENT BY JUDICIARY. *Journal of Politics*, *38*(4), 918–937. https://doi.org/10.2307/2129501.

202. Menounou, E., Feldman, A., Giallouri, T., & Peterson, J. C. (2019). Packing the Courts: Ideological Proximity and Expansions to the Federal Judiciary from 1937 to 2012. *Journal of Law and Courts*, *7*(1), 81–106. https://doi.org/10.1086/697900.

203. Michetti, G., Toniolo, A., Rossi, S., & Pirani, A. (2018, Oct 11–12). A Model of Justice as a Platform: A Case Study of Open Data Disclosure. *Frontiers in Artificial Intelligence and Applications* [Knowledge of the law in the big data age]. International Conference on Law via the Internet 2018, Florence, ITALY.

204. Moliterno, J. E., & Curos, P. (2021). Recent Attacks on Judicial Independence: The Vulgar, the Systemic, and the Insidious. *German Law Journal*, *22*(7), 1159–1191, Article Pii s2071832221000638. https://doi.org/10.1017/glj.2021.63.

205. Molto, J. E. E. (2015). The 'Great Leap Forward' to Impunity Burying Universal Jurisdiction in Spain and Returning to the Paradigm of Human Rights as 'domaine reserve' of States. *Journal of International Criminal Justice*, *13*(5), 1121–1144. https://doi.org/10.1093/jicj/mqv072.

206. Mudde, C. (2017). Populism: An ideational approach. In *The Oxford Handbook of Populism* (pp. 27–47). Oxford University Press.

207. Munday, R. (2008). In the Wake of 'Good Governance': Impact Assessments and the Politicisation of Statutory Interpretation. *Modern Law Review*, *71*(3), 385–412. https://doi.org/10.1111/j.1468–2230.2008.00698.x.

208. Navarrete, R. M., & Castillo-Ortiz, P. (2020). Constitutional courts

and citizens' perceptions of judicial systems in Europe. *Comparative European Politics, 18*(2), 128–150. https://doi.org/10.1057/s41295–019–00154–9.

209. Nelson, M. J., & Gibson, J. L. (2019). How Does Hyperpoliticized Rhetoric Affect the US Supreme Court's Legitimacy? *Journal of Politics, 81*(4), 1512–1516. https://doi.org/10.1086/704701.
210. Nie, M. T. (2021). Divided governmental structure and state compliance with international human rights law: A reputation-based approach. *Leiden Journal of International Law, 34*(3), 705–727, Article Pii s0922156521000212. https://doi.org/10.1017/s0922156521000212.
211. Nordstrand, S. N. (2018). The "unwelcome obligation": why neither state nor federal courts should draw district lines. *Fordham Law Review, 86*(4), 1997–2028. <Go to ISI>://WOS:000428740400021.
212. O'Neil, D. (2019). THE CASE FOR ABOLISHING THE OFFENCE OF SCANDALISING THE JUDICIARY. *Adelaide Law Review, 40*(3), 815–840. <Go to ISI>://WOS:000525749700009.
213. O'Neill, J. G. (2001). Raoul Berger and the restoration of originalism. *Northwestern University Law Review, 96*(1), 253–281. <Go to ISI>://WOS:000178111700005.
214. Oakes, A. R. (2018). Judicial Resources and the Public Trust Doctrine: A Powerful Tool of Environmental Protection? *Transnational Environmental Law, 7*(3), 469–489. https://doi.org/10.1017/s2047102518000213.
215. Obermaier, A. J. (2008). The National Judiciary-Sword of European Court of Justice Rulings: The Example of the Kohll/Decker Jurisprudence. *European Law Journal, 14*(6), 735–752. https://doi.org/10.1111/j.1468–0386.2008.00439.x.
216. Oliveira, M., & Garoupa, N. (2011). Choosing Judges in Brazil: Reassessing Legal Transplants from the United States. *American Journal of Comparative Law, 59*(2), 529–561. https://doi.org/10.5131/ajcl.2010.0020.
217. Owusu-Mensah, I., & Mathapoly-Codjoe, E. (2023). 'Judicialization of corruption' in Ghana: an analysis of how Ghanaians view the Office of the Special Prosecutor. *Politikon, 50*(2), 119–136. https://doi.org/10.1080/02589346.2023.2197295.
218. Parrillo, N. (2005). "The government at the mercy of its contractors": How the new deal lawyers reshaped the common law to challenge the

defense industry in world war II. *Hastings Law Journal*, *57*(1), 93-+. <Go to ISI>://WOS:000234044900004.

219. Parrillo, N. R. (2018). The endgame of administrative law: governmental disobedience and the judicial contempt power. *Harvard Law Review*, *131*(3), 686–794. <Go to ISI>://WOS:000419736200001.
220. Pasarlay, S. (2018). The Limits of Constitutional Deferral: Lessons From the History of the 2004 Constitution of Afghanistan. *Washington International Law Journal*, *27*(3), 683–713. <Go to ISI>://WOS:000452927900003.
221. Patton, D. E. (2017). The structure of federal public defense: a call for independence. *Cornell Law Review*, *102*(2), 335–411. <Go to ISI>://WOS:000393359400002.
222. Petrov, J. (2022). (De-)judicialization of politics in the era of populism: lessons from Central and Eastern Europe. *International Journal of Human Rights*, *26*(7), 1181–1206. https://doi.org/10.1080/13642987.2021.1931138.
223. Pickett, B. R. (2016). Will The Real Lawmakers Please Stand Up: Congressional Standing In Instances of Presidential Nonenforcement. *Northwestern University Law Review*, *110*(2), 439–476. <Go to ISI>://WOS:000375271800004.
224. Pidot, J. R. (2014). Fees, Expenditures, and the Takings Clause. *Ecology Law Quarterly*, *41*(1), 131–169. <Go to ISI>://WOS:000336190900004.
225. Pierce, R. J. (1989). The role of the judiciary in implementing an agency theory of government. *New York University Law Review*, *64*(6), 1239–1285. <Go to ISI>://WOS:A1989CZ06900002.
226. Pierce, R. J. (1997). Reconciling Chevron and stare decisis. *Georgetown Law Journal*, *85*(7), 2225–2263. <Go to ISI>://WOS:A1997YA82000013.
227. Pohjankoski, P. (2016). Federal Coercion and National Constitutional Identity in the United States 1776–1861. *American Journal of Legal History*, *56*(3), 326–358. https://doi.org/10.1093/ajlh/njw007.
228. Pooe, T. K. (2017). Developmental State No Birth Right: South Africa's Post-1994 Economic Development Story. *Law and Development Review*, *10*(2), 361–387. https://doi.org/10.1515/ldr-2017–0018.
229. Popova, M., & Post, V. (2018). Prosecuting high-level corruption in Eastern Europe. *Communist and Post-Communist Studies*, *51*(3), 231–244. https://doi.org/10.1016/j.postcomstud.2018.06.004.

230. Pospieszna, P., & Vetulani-Cegiel, A. (2021). Polish interest groups facing democratic backsliding. *Interest Groups & Advocacy*, *10*(2), 158–180. https://doi.org/10.1057/s41309–021–00119-y.

231. Preis, J. F. (2006). Jurisdiction and discretion in hybrid law cases. *University of Cincinnati Law Review*, *75*(1), 145–212. <Go to ISI>://WOS:000243266000005.

232. Preston, B. J. (2016). The Contribution of the Courts in Tackling Climate Change. *Journal of Environmental Law*, *28*(1), 11–17. https://doi.org/10.1093/jel/eqw004.

233. Primus, R. A. (2004). Bolling alone. *Columbia Law Review*, *104*(4), 975–1041. https://doi.org/10.2307/4099366.

234. Prince, S. (2020). Encouragement of mediation in England and Wales has been futile: is there now a role for online dispute resolution in settling low-value claims? *International Journal of Law in Context*, *16*(2), 181–196, Article Pii s1744552320000130. https://doi.org/10.1017/s1744552320000130.

235. Provost, R. (2008). Judging in splendid isolation. *American Journal of Comparative Law*, *56*(1), 125–172. https://doi.org/10.5131/ajcl.2007.0004.

236. Pulle, A. I., & Ratnapala, S. (2019). Sri Lanka's Quest for a Reformed Constitution: Lessons from a Lost Opportunity. *Chinese Journal of Comparative Law*, *7*(2), 285–308. https://doi.org/10.1093/cjcl/cxz011.

237. Qin, J. Y. (2011). Pushing the Limits of Global Governance: Trading Rights, Censorship and WTO Jurisprudence-A Commentary on the China-Publications Case. *Chinese Journal of International Law*, *10*(2), 271–322. https://doi.org/10.1093/chinesejil/jmr017.

238. Rakove, J. N. (1997). The origins of judicial review: A plea for new contexts. *Stanford Law Review*, *49*(5), 1031–1064. https://doi.org/10.2307/1229247.

239. Ramseyer, J. M., & Rasmusen, E. B. (1997). Judicial independence in a civil law regime: The evidence from Japan. *Journal of Law Economics & Organization*, *13*(2), 259–286. https://doi.org/10.1093/oxfordjournals.jleo.a023384.

240. Rathod, J. (2009). Not peace, but a sword: Navy v. Egan and the case against judicial abdication in foreign affairs. *Duke Law Journal*, *59*(3), 595–635. <Go to ISI>://WOS:000272365600005.

241. Redman, S. M. (2017). Descriptive Gender Representation and

Legitimacy in US Trial Courts. *Justice System Journal*, *38*(4), 311–331. https://doi.org/10.1080/0098261x.2017.1356251.

242. Reenock, C., Staton, J. K., & Radean, M. (2013). Legal Institutions and Democratic Survival. *Journal of Politics*, *75*(2), 491–505. https://doi.org/10.1017/s0022381613000169.
243. Reid, R., Schorpp, S., & Johnson, S. W. (2020). Trading Liberties for Security: Groupthink, Gender, and 9/11 Effects on US Appellate Decision-Making. *American Politics Research*, *48*(3), 402–413, Article 1532673x19881627. https://doi.org/10.1177/1532673x19881627.
244. Reimann, M. (2015). "*The Law of International Business Transactions: A Global Perspective*." Available at SSRN: https://ssrn.com/abstract=2609364.
245. Ritleng, D. (2016). Does the European Court of Justice take democracy seriously? Some thoughts about the macro-financial assistance case. *Common Market Law Review*, *53*(1), 11–33. <Go to ISI>://WOS:000375236500002.
246. Rivera, J. A. A. (2022). Dinamics of autocratization: Mexico 2021. *Revista De Ciencia Politica*, *42*(2), 355–382. https://doi.org/10.4067/s0718–090x2022005000109.
247. Robinson, N. (2018). The multiple justifications of occupational licensing. *Washington Law Review*, *93*(4), 1903–1960. <Go to ISI>://WOS:000540323600006.
248. Rohrschneider, R. (2005). Institutional quality and perceptions of representation in advanced industrial democracies. *Comparative Political Studies*, *38*(7), 850–874. https://doi.org/10.1177/0010414005276305.
249. Rosenfeld, M. (2007). "The Identity of the Constitutional Subject: Selfhood, Citizenship, Culture, and Community." *Fordham Law Review, 76*(1), 1–75.
250. Rotunda, R. D. (1991). Exporting the American Bill-of-Rights – the lesson from Romania. *University of Illinois Law Review*(4), 1065–1075. <Go to ISI>://WOS:A1991HQ46100005.
251. Rowley, C. K. (2005). Fragmenting parchment and the winds of war: The Constitution of the United States, 1860–2004. *Public Choice*, *124*(1–2), 33–56. https://doi.org/10.1007/s11127–005–4744–1.
252. Sabel, C. F., & Zeitlin, J. (2004). "Learning from Difference: The New Architecture of Experimentalist Governance in the European Union." *European Law Journal, 10*(3), 295–327.

253. Schreiber, G. (2017). "Judging the State in International Trade and Investment Law: Sovereignty Modern, the Law's Poor Cousin." *European Journal of International Law, 28*(4), 1103–1125.

254. Schreuer, C., Malintoppi, L., Reinisch, A., & Sinclair, A. (2009). "*The ICSID Convention: A Commentary*." Cambridge University Press.

255. Schroeder, P. (2023). Seizing opportunities: the determinants of the CJEU's deference to national courts. *Journal of European Public Policy*. https://doi.org/10.1080/13501763.2023.2208165.

256. Schuman, J. (2021). Revocation and retribution. *Washington Law Review*, *96*(3), 881–934. <Go to ISI>://WOS:000712454900002.

257. Schweiger, C. (2022). Governance under the Covid-19 pandemic: comparative perspectives on Germany and Hungary Special section "Democratic Health in the Corona Pandemic. The Corona Pandemic as a Trigger or Amplifier of Democratic Erosion?." *Zeitschrift Fur Vergleichende Politikwissenschaft*, *16*(4), 663–685. https://doi.org/10.1007/s12286–022–00546–4.

258. Setty, S. (2015). Surveillance, secrecy, and the search for meaningful accountability. *Stanford Journal of International Law*, *51*(1), 69–103. <Go to ISI>://WOS:000352465200004.

259. Shah, A. (2014). Constraining consolidation: military politics and democracy in Pakistan (2007–2013). *Democratization*, *21*(6), 1007–1033. https://doi.org/10.1080/13510347.2013.781586.

260. Shenkman, C. (2012). Catalyzing National Judicial Capacity: The ICC's First Crimes Against Humanity Outside Armed Conflict. *New York University Law Review*, *87*(4), 1210–1248. <Go to ISI>://WOS:000310039800008.

261. Shepherd, J. M. (2009). Are Appointed Judges Strategic Too? *Duke Law Journal*, *58*(7), 1589–1626. <Go to ISI>://WOS:000266097300011.

262. Shigemura, S., Iseki, T., Ikeda, S., & Ishima, H. (2021). Public support for the judicial branches under the COVID-19 pandemic. *Journal of Elections Public Opinion and Parties*, *31*, 348–360. https://doi.org/10.1080/17457289.2021.1924729.

263. Shvets, J. (2016). Presidential Control of the Judiciary via the Appointment Power: Evidence from Russia. *Journal of Law Economics & Organization*, *32*(3), 478–507. https://doi.org/10.1093/jleo/eww004.

264. Simanjuntak, E. (2020). The Rise and The Fall of the Jurisdiction of Indonesia's Administrative Courts: Impediments and Prospects.

Indonesia Law Review, *10*(2), 159–190. https://doi.org/10.15742/ilrev.v10n2.611.

265. Sinclair, A. (2013). "*The Vienna Convention on the Law of Treaties: A Commentary*." Oxford University Press.
266. Singh, A. (2022). Sanction for prosecution in 'Offences Against the State' in India: The prerogative of the political and the withdrawal of the judicial. *International Journal of Law Crime and Justice*, *69*, Article 100531. https://doi.org/10.1016/j.ijlcj.2022.100531.
267. Singh, P. (2015). India Before and After the Right of Passage Case. *Asian Journal of International Law*, *5*(1), 176–208. https://doi.org/10.1017/s2044251314000071.
268. Singh, U. K. (2022). Federalism, democracy and the national security state in India. *Territory Politics Governance*, *10*(1), 51–66. https://doi.org/10.1080/21622671.2021.1899975.
269. Sivakumaran, S. (2009). "Guantánamo Bay: What Next?." *European Journal of International Law*, *20*(2), 339–377.
270. Skinner-Thompson, S. (2015). Outing Privacy. *Northwestern University Law Review*, *110*(1), 159–222. <Go to ISI>://WOS:000368285700004.
271. Smith, C. A., & Farrales, M. J. (2010). Court reform in transitional states: Chile and the Philippines. *Journal of International Relations and Development*, *13*(2), 163–193. https://doi.org/10.1057/jird.2009.34.
272. Smith, K. B., & Farrales, C. C. (2010). Understanding Judicial Security: A Global Perspective. *Journal of Judicial Administration*, *19*(4), 186–204.
273. Smith, L. (1992). Reducing State Accountability To The Federal-Government – The Suter V Artist-M Decision To Dismiss Section-1983 Claims For Violating Federal Fund Mandates. *Wisconsin Law Review*(4), 1267–1297. <Go to ISI>://WOS:A1992JU97800006.
274. Smith, M. L. (2015). Regulating law enforcement's use of drones: the need for state legislation. *Harvard Journal on Legislation*, *52*(2), 423–454. <Go to ISI>://WOS:000363074100006.
275. Smith, R. (2005). Constitutional reform, the lord chancellor, and human rights: The battle of form and substance. *Journal of Law and Society*, *32*(1), 187–201. https://doi.org/10.1111/j.1467–6478.2005.321_1.x.
276. Sorabji, J., & Vaughan, S. (2021). "This Is Not A Rule": COVID-19 in England & Wales and Criminal Justice Governance via Guidance. *European Journal of Risk Regulation*, *12*(1), 143–158. https://doi.

org/10.1017/err.2020.118.

277. Southworth, A. (2018). Lawyers and the Conservative Counterrevolution. *Law and Social Inquiry-Journal of the American Bar Foundation, 43*(4), 1698–1728. https://doi.org/10.1111/lsi.12363.

278. Spencer, M., & Spencer, J. (2006). The judge as 'political advisor': Behind the scenes at the national industrial relations court. *Journal of Law and Society, 33*(2), 199–220. https://doi.org/10.1111/j.1467–6478.2006.00355.x.

279. Spencer, M., & Spencer, J. (2010). Coping with Conway v. Rimmer 1968 AC 910: How Civil Servants Control Access to Justice. *Journal of Law and Society, 37*(3), 387–411. https://doi.org/10.1111/j.1467–6478.2010.00512.x.

280. Spendzharova, A. B., & Vachudova, M. A. (2012). Catching Up? Consolidating Liberal Democracy in Bulgaria and Romania after EU Accession. *West European Politics, 35*(1), 39–58. https://doi.org/10.1080/01402382.2012.631312.

281. Sprankling, T. G. (2012). Does five equal three? Reading the takings clause in light of the third amendment's protection of houses. *Columbia Law Review, 112*(1), 112–151. <Go to ISI>://WOS:000299304700003.

282. Stephenson, M. C. (2003). "When the devil turns .. ": The political foundations of independent judicial review. *Journal of Legal Studies, 32*(1), 59–89. https://doi.org/10.1086/342038.

283. Stephenson, M. C. (2008). The Price of Public Action: Constitutional Doctrine and the Judicial Manipulation of Legislative Enactment Costs. *Yale Law Journal, 118*(1), 2–62. https://doi.org/10.2307/20454703.

284. Stephenson, S. (2021). Constitutional Conventions and the Judiciary. *Oxford Journal of Legal Studies, 41*(3), 750–775. https://doi.org/10.1093/ojls/gqaa047.

285. Steuer, M. (2019). Militant Democracy on the Rise: Consequences of Legal Restrictions on Extreme Speech in the Czech Republic, Slovakia and Hungary. *Review of Central and East European Law, 44*(2), 162–201. https://doi.org/10.1163/15730352–04402003.

286. Subedi, S. P. (2016). The UN Human Rights Special Rapporteurs and the Impact of their Work: Some Reflections of the UN Special Rapporteur for Cambodia. *Asian Journal of International Law, 6*(1), 1–14. https://doi.org/10.1017/s2044251315000132.

287. Szente, Z. (2021). Stepping Into the Same River Twice? Judicial

Independence in Old and New Authoritarianism. *German Law Journal*, *22*(7), 1316–1326, Article Pii s2071832221000699. https://doi.org/10.1017/glj.2021.69.

288. Taghdiri, A. J. (2019). A Comparative Perspective of Eminent Domain Laws In The United States & China. *Tsinghua China Law Review*, *12*(1), 115–141. <Go to ISI>://WOS:000505806200005.
289. Takayasu, K. (2023). The changing UK prime ministership from an institutional perspective. *Asian Journal of Comparative Politics*, *8*(1), 95–111. https://doi.org/10.1177/20578911221134714.
290. Tate, C. N. (1994). The Judicialization of Politics in the Philippines and Southeast-Asia. *International Political Science Review*, *15*(2), 187–197. https://doi.org/10.1177/019251219401500210.
291. Tate, N. J., & Vallinder, T. (Eds.). (2012). *The Global Expansion of Judicial Power*. New York University Press.
292. Tauber, S., & Banks, C. (2017). The Impact of the Threat of Terrorism on US District Court Decisions During Wartime. *Terrorism and Political Violence*, *29*(5), 793–829. https://doi.org/10.1080/09546553.2015.1049341.
293. Tew, Y. (2016). On the Uneven Journey To Constitutional Redemption: The Malaysian Judiciary and Constitutional Politics. *Washington International Law Journal*, *25*(3), 673–696. <Go to ISI>://WOS:000411028700007.
294. Tey, T. H. (2010). JUDICIAL INTERNALISING OF SINGAPORE'S SUPREME POLITICAL IDEOLOGY. *Hong Kong Law Journal*, *40*, 293–336. <Go to ISI>://WOS:000290652400006.
295. Tezcur, G. M. (2009). Judicial Activism in Perilous Times: The Turkish Case. *Law & Society Review*, *43*(2), 305–336. https://doi.org/10.1111/j.1540-5893.2009.00374.x.
296. Travesi, S. B. G., & Whitehead, L. (2021). Constitutional controversies in the subnational democratization of Mexico, 1994–2021. *Latin American Policy*, *12*(2), 405–423. https://doi.org/10.1111/lamp.12229.
297. Tridimas, T., & Gari, G. (2010). Winners and losers in Luxembourg: A statistical analysis of judicial review before the European Court of Justice and the Court of First Instance (2001–2005). *European Law Review*, *35*(2), 131–173. <Go to ISI>://WOS:000277334500002.
298. Trochev, A. (2004). Less democracy, more courts: A puzzle of judicial review in Russia. *Law & Society Review*, *38*(3), 513–548. https://doi.

org/10.1111/j.0023–9216.2004.00056.x.

299. Tunamsifu, S. P. (2022). The Colonial Legacy and Transitional Justice in the Democratic Republic of the Congo. *African Journal on Conflict Resolution*, *22*(2), 85–111. <Go to ISI>://WOS:000967940200004.

300. United Nations Office on Drugs and Crime. (2019). *Criminal Justice Reform and the Rule of Law in Developing Countries.* Retrieved from https://www.unodc.org/documents/justice-and-prison-reform/CJR-Training-Materials/CJR_training_module_1/2.2.1%20-%20Understanding%20Judicial%20Independence%20-%20Trainer.pdf.

301. Uprimny, R., & García, C. R. (2004). Judicial Independence in Transitional Contexts: A Delicate Balance. In *Strengthening the Rule of Law in the OSCE Area* (pp. 53–64). OSCE.

302. Uprimny, R., & García, J. M. (2004). Judicial Independence and Impartiality in Transitional Contexts. In *Promoting the Rule of Law Abroad: In Search of Knowledge* (pp. 327–352). Stanford University Press.

303. Urribarri, R. A. S. (2011). Courts between Democracy and Hybrid Authoritarianism: Evidence from the Venezuelan Supreme Court. *Law and Social Inquiry-Journal of the American Bar Foundation*, *36*(4), 854–884. https://doi.org/10.1111/j.1747–4469.2011.01253.x.

304. Utter, M. (2021). New Rules of the Game: The Politization of Community Courts in Mozambique. *Washington International Law Journal*, *31*(1), 150–184. <Go to ISI>://WOS:000753464100002.

305. Uzebu-Imarhiagbe, E. (2020). Women in the Nigerian judiciary: considerable headway or organised progress? *International Journal of the Legal Profession*, *27*(2), 175–188. https://doi.org/10.1080/09695958.2020.1750410.

306. van Zeben, J. (2015). Establishing a Governmental Duty of Care for Climate Change Mitigation: Will Urgenda Turn the Tide? *Transnational Environmental Law*, *4*(2), 339–357. https://doi.org/10.1017/s2047102515000199.

307. Vermeule, A. (2012). The Atrophy of Constitutional Powers. *Oxford Journal of Legal Studies*, *32*(3), 421–444. https://doi.org/10.1093/ojls/gqs010.

308. Voeten, E. (2008). The Impartiality of International Judges: Evidence from the European Court of Human Rights. *American Political Science Review*, *102*(4), 417–433. https://doi.org/10.1017/

s0003055408080398.

309. VonDoepp, P., & Ellett, R. (2011). Reworking Strategic Models of Executive-Judicial Relations Insights from New African Democracies. *Comparative Politics*, *43*(2), 147-+. https://doi.org/10.5129/001041511793931843.

310. Wang, S. C. (2021). Judicial Review of the Legislative Process in Hong Kong: A Comparative Perspective. *Statute Law Review*, *42*(3), 291–304. https://doi.org/10.1093/slr/hmz018.

311. Weill, S. (2016). Reducing the Security Gap through National Courts: Targeted Killings as a Case Study. *Journal of Conflict & Security Law*, *21*(1), 49–67. https://doi.org/10.1093/jcsl/krv019.

312. West, L. (2019). The limits to judicial independence: Cambodia's political culture and the civil law. *Democratization*, *26*(3), 537–553. https://doi.org/10.1080/13510347.2018.1553956.

313. Westerman, P. C. (2017). The rule of law as export product. *Theory and Practice of Legislation*, *5*(2), 171–185. https://doi.org/10.1080/20508840.2017.1389472.

314. White, S. (2022). Brexit and the future of the UK constitution. *International Political Science Review*, *43*(3), 359–373, Article 0192512121995133. https://doi.org/10.1177/0192512121995133.

315. Whittington, K. E. (2005). "Interpose your friendly hand": Political supports for the exercise of judicial review by the United States Supreme Court. *American Political Science Review*, *99*(4), 583–596. https://doi.org/10.1017/s0003055405051890.

316. Willett, D. R., & Gordon, A. (2022). Rights, Structure, and Remediation. *Yale Law Journal*, *131*(7), 2126–2212. <Go to ISI>://WOS:000809381200002.

317. Williams, M. S. (2008). Ambition, gender, and the judiciary. *Political Research Quarterly*, *61*(1), 68–78. https://doi.org/10.1177/1065912907304497.

318. Winkler, A. (2009). Free Speech Federalism. *Michigan Law Review*, *108*(2), 153–188. <Go to ISI>://WOS:000270995800001.

319. Wong, T. K. Y., Hsiao, H. H. M., & Wan, P. S. (2009). Comparing Political Trust in Hong Kong and Taiwan: Levels, Determinants, and Implications. *Japanese Journal of Political Science*, *10*, 147–174. https://doi.org/10.1017/s146810990900351x.

320. World Justice Project. (2021). Rule of Law Index 2020: *Key Findings*

and Data. Retrieved from https://worldjusticeproject.org/sites/default/files/documents/WJP-ROLI-2020-Key-Findings.pdf.

321. Worthington, R. (2001). Between Hermes and Themis: An empirical study of the contemporary judiciary in Singapore. *Journal of Law and Society*, *28*(4), 490–519. https://doi.org/10.1111/1467–6478.00200.
322. Wright, M. L. (2016). Williams-Yulee V. Florida Bar: Judicial Elections, Impartiality, and the Threat To Free Speech. *Denver Law Review*, *93*(2), 551–576. <Go to ISI>://WOS:000385961400007.
323. Yap, P. J. (2019). Remedial discretion and dilemmas in Asia. *University of Toronto Law Journal*, *69*, 84–104. https://doi.org/10.3138/utlj.69.s1.004.
324. Yap, P. J., & Chung, F. (2019). Statutory rights and de facto constitutional supremacy in Hong Kong? *Icon-International Journal of Constitutional Law*, *17*(3), 836–859. https://doi.org/10.1093/icon/moz063.
325. Zacka, B. (2022). Political Theory Rediscovers Public Administration. *Annual Review of Political Science*, *25*, 21–42. https://doi.org/10.1146/annurev-polisci-051120–125131.
326. Zambrano, D. A. (2019). Federal Expansion and the Decay of State Courts. *University of Chicago Law Review*, *86*(8), 2101–2192. <Go to ISI>://WOS:000498314400002.
327. Zaring, D. (2016). "How States Pay for the Global Governance of Data Privacy." *The Hague Journal of Diplomacy, 11*(2), 105–126.
328. Zuk, G., Gryski, G. S., & Barrow, D. J. (1993). Partisan Transformation of the Federal Judiciary, 1869–1992. *American Politics Quarterly*, *21*(4), 439–457. https://doi.org/10.1177/1532673x9302100403.

INDEX

A

Accountability mechanisms 301, 303, 307
Administer justice 2
Administrative state 43
Adoption rights 114
Affordable care act (ACA) 107
Alternative dispute resolution (ADR) 180, 196
Anti-trafficking measures 261
Artificial intelligence 270
Athenian democracy 13, 25, 26, 27

B

British colonial rule 17
British governmental system 22
Bureaucratic inefficiencies 62

C

Case management 274
Central African Republic (CAR) 139
Centralize power 217
Child pornography 289
Chinese society, 7
Civic engagement 13
Civil justice system 59
Civil liberties 140, 200, 201, 202
Civil rights laws 109, 110, 111
Civil society organizations 166
Cohesive global response 266
Collaborative efforts 107
Collaborative relationship 271
Collective governance 12
Colombian peace process 188
Colombian society 129
Colonial legacies 16

Colonial powers 16
Communal discussions 5
Communal mediation 11
Community engagement 13
Complex issue 110
Conflict resolution 2, 5, 11, 27, 28, 29, 31, 156, 196
Conflict resolution mechanisms 188, 308
Congress unconstitutional 228
Constitutional amendments 36, 217
Constitutional boundaries 44, 48
Constitutional changes 201
Constitutional crises 189
Constitutional framework 160
Constitutional interpretation 120, 121, 141, 142, 161
Constitutionalism 16, 17
Constitutional matters 205
Constitutional mechanisms 306
Constitutional principles 45
Constitutional rights 124, 132, 141
Consumer protection 135
Consumer rights 134
Contemporary governance 25
Contemporary societal considerations 112
Contemporary societies 278
Copyright laws 147
Corporate responsibility 246
Court proceedings 274, 307
Criminal investigations 163
Criminal justice 42, 54, 55, 56, 57, 58, 59, 69, 70
Criminal justice system 138
Criminal penalties 122
Criminal syndicates 207
Cross-border conflicts 170
Cross-border cooperation 256
Cross-border movement 252
Cross-border transactions 237
Cultural contexts 239
Cultural tensions 239
Customary international law 241
Customary laws 5

D

Data security 270
Decision-making process 42, 48, 51, 52, 53, 54, 70
Decision-making processes 25
Democratically-elected representatives 161
Democratic governance 108, 156
Democratic institutions 200, 201, 202, 205, 210, 213, 217, 218, 219
Democratic legitimacy 160
Democratic principles 13, 16, 31, 35, 38
Democratic processes 45, 46, 110, 111, 121, 122, 124, 127, 140
Democratic quality 202
Democratic system 120, 124, 125, 136
Democratic values 25
Digital case management systems 272
Digital evidence 273
Digital governance 17, 34
Diplomatic dialogue 180
Discrimination 109, 110, 111, 114, 128, 129, 143
Dispute resolution mechanisms 176, 182, 184
Dispute resolution processes 5, 7
Domestic legal systems 236
Duterte's populism 214

Dynamic institution 271
Dynamic interaction 252

E

Ecological sustainability 242
Economic development 133
Economic growth 238
Economic inequality 212, 215, 217
Economic interdependence 252
Economic stability 65, 247
Educational initiatives 303
Egyptian government 156, 157
Eichmann trial 264
Electoral integrity 196
Electoral process 167
Electronic filing systems 272
English proficiency 143
Environmental activists 164
Environmental concerns 242, 248
Environmental litigations 193
Environmental protection 99
Environmental violations 193
Ethical considerations 285, 297, 298, 309
Ethical constraints 285
Ethical standards 276, 277, 278, 303, 304
European societies 15
Exclusive economic zones (EEZs) 50
Extraterritorial cybercrimes 259

F

Far-reaching consequences 258
Federal government 160
Federal power 108
Financial aid program 170
Financial institutions 255
Financial markets 256
Foreign direct investment (FDI) 245
Foreign investment 247
Freedom of expression 289, 291
French revolution 15, 16

G

Geneva conventions 243, 244
Geographical locations 28
Global dynamics 178
Global governance 178
Global trade environment 238
Government accountability 230
Government actions 40, 288, 293, 306
Government agencies 112
Governmental authority 47, 65, 69, 70, 127
Governmental constraints 186
Governmental decisions 196
Governmental initiatives 285
Governmental power 204
Government bias 186
Government-judiciary relationship 307
Government networks 178, 179
Government policies 106, 125, 127, 129
Government policy 79
Government power 46
Government property 169
Government regulation 256
Government structures 11

H

Harmonious society 70
Healthcare clinics 160
Healthcare law 107
Health insurance 107
Human rights standards 263

Human rights violations 174
Human settlement patterns 29
Human societies 11

I

Impartial judiciary 226
Impartial system 250
Independent judiciary 23, 79
Indigenous populations 16
Individual rights 132
Inflammatory statements 219
Inhuman conditions 119
Inquisitorial system 52
Institutional change 48, 49
Institutional landscape 204
Institutional practices 282
Intellectual expedition 2
Intellectual property rights 247
Interdisciplinary approaches 285
International agreements 234, 237
International association of judges (IAJ) 93
International collaboration 256
International commitments 261
International community 152, 264
International conventions 237
International cooperation 239, 256, 263
International Court of Justice (ICJ) 128
International courts 162, 169, 170, 171, 172, 174
International dynamics 128
International humanitarian law 176
International judgments 69
International legal harmonization 267
International monetary fund (IMF) 169
International norms 267
International obligations 151, 243
International organization 93
International organizations 178
International relations 239, 252
International scrutiny 230
International treaties 242
Interpersonal conflicts 5
Investor-state arbitration 249
Investor-state disputes 246

J

Judicial accountability 74, 80, 86, 102, 228
Judicial activism 107, 108, 110, 111, 116, 120, 121, 122, 123, 124, 125, 127, 153, 154, 160
Judicial attitudes 295
Judicial authority 68
Judicial autonomy 82, 173
Judicial conduct 74, 83, 84, 85, 91, 92, 94, 96
Judicial decision-making 26
Judicial decisions 106, 107, 112, 114, 136, 137, 138, 139, 141, 142, 143, 144, 145, 147, 148, 149, 151, 152, 154
Judicial development 30
Judicial engagement 106
Judicial independence 71, 74, 75, 76, 77, 79, 80, 81, 82, 83, 86, 87, 89, 90, 91, 93, 97, 98, 99, 100, 101, 103, 158, 198, 209
Judicial institutions 225
Judicial integrity 232
Judicial interpretations 107
Judicial mechanisms 234
Judicial overreach 122, 136
Judicial proceedings 270, 272

Judicial resolution 266
Judicial resources 300
Judicial restraint 120, 121, 123, 124, 127
Judicial security 198
Judicial security protocols 206
Judicial system 79, 90
Judiciary-government dynamics 3
Judiciary-government relationship 92
Judiciary stands 298
Judiciary systems 2
Judicious restraint 106
Jurisdictional authority 234
Jurisdictional boundaries 54
Jurisdictional challenges 253
Jurisdictional consistency 48
Jurisdictional intricacies 254
Jurisdictional processes 53
Jurisdictional quandary 253
Jurisprudential concerns 149

K

Kavanaugh's confirmation process 98

L

Legal authority 265
Legal codes 7
Legal harmonization 237
Legal matters 10
Legal proceedings 66
Legal standards 237
Legal system 4, 62, 92
Legislative action 135
Legislative changes 101
Legislative enactments 107, 115
Legislative process 108
Lgal proceedings 8
LGBTQ+ community 45, 114
Lgislative process 22
Linguistic communities 142

M

Market participants 256
Media channels 216
Media scrutiny 225
Mesopotamian society 7
Minority rights 195
Montreal protocol 241, 242
Multifaceted challenges 271
Multifaceted relationship 106
Multi-pronged approach 205
Muslim community 190
Mutual commitment 304

N

National boundaries 266
National courts 119
National governments 177
National legal systems 194, 236
National reconciliation 141, 174
National security 122, 149, 157, 251
National sovereignty 119
Non-governmental actors 188
Non-governmental organizations (NGOs) 187

O

Online communication 257
Open communication 310
Operational efficiency 199

P

Parliamentary sovereignty 127
Participatory justice 185
Participatory system 13
Physical violence 206

Policy adjustments 151
Policy determinations 154
Policy implications 148
Polish judiciary 23
Political actors 203
Political affiliations 199
Political agendas 198, 296
Political campaign 96
Political complexities 173
Political dynamics 179
Political evolution 3
Political factors 2, 23
Political influence 200, 301
Political instability 166
Political interference 91, 198, 199, 202, 205
Political landscape 309
Political motivations 87
Political power 26
Political repercussions 217
Political rights 17
Political stability 189
Political stances 123
Political system 167
Political thought 226
Political transformation 195
Populist rhetoric 219
Post-revolutionary changes 303
Potential consequences 221
Potential implications 250
Potential politicization 229
Potential security risks 134
Potential threats 146
Presidential actions 160
Proactive security 208
Professional associations 93
Public accountability 25
Public communication 299
Public healthcare system 161
Public institutions 34
Public interest policies 177
Public opinions 220
Public outrage 120
Public perception 143, 220
Public policy 121, 134
Public sentiment 99, 220
Public transparency 86
Public trust 303

Q

Qin dynasty 7
Quantitative analysis 239

R

Racial discrimination 283
Racial segregation 115
Repressive legislation 284
Reproductive rights 137
Roman judicial system 6
Roman legal system 10
Rudimentary judicial systems 4
Ruling class 14

S

Safeguarding society 207
School's language policy 142
Secessionist movements 195
Self-regulating judiciary 227
Sexual orientation 109
Small and medium-sized enterprises (SMEs) 151
Social cohesion 5
Social equality 15
Social inequality 122
Social injustices 285
Social organization 27
Social progress 130, 280
Social stability 195

Societal challenges 120
Societal collaboration 289, 290
Societal norms 27, 116
Societal shifts 117
Societal transformations 290, 294, 295
Socioeconomic disparities 274
Sovereignty 236, 246, 247, 249, 251, 252, 254, 258, 259, 264, 266
Statutory interpretation 110, 154
Stoic philosophy 10
Supreme court 75, 77, 79, 84, 85, 95, 97, 98, 99, 100, 101
Surveillance entities 293
Symbiotic relationship 106
Systemic disparities 143

T

Technological disruption 270
Technologically-driven world 294
Traditional litigation 62
Transborder legal dynamics 234
Transitional justice 175, 176
Transnational commerce 237, 239
Transnational crimes 256, 265
Transnational criminal activities 259
Transnational disputes 252
Transnational justice 170, 174, 179
Transnational legal norms 288
Transnational organizations 169, 170
Transparent selection processes 282
Tribal leadership 18

U

UK judiciary 262
Ukraine's justice system 208
Uniform commercial code (UCC) in 237
Universal jurisdiction 264, 265